Shadows of Empire

The Indian nobility of the Andes – many descended from the Inca rulers and other preconquest lords – occupied a crucial economic and political position in late colonial Andean society, a position widely accepted as legitimate until the Tupac Amaru rebellion. *Shadows of Empire* traces the history of this late colonial elite and examines the preconquest and colonial foundations of their privilege and authority. It brings to light the organization and the ideology of the Indian nobility in the bishopric of Cusco in the decades before the rebellion and uses this nobility as a lens through which to study the internal organization and tensions of late colonial Indian communities. The work further analyzes the collapse of this Indian elite, repudiated by both the Indian commons and the crown in the last years of Spanish rule and marginalized in the emergence of the creole-dominated republican order after 1825.

David T. Garrett is Associate Professor of History at Reed College. Specializing in the Andes, he researches the social and intellectual history of Spanish colonialism. He is the author of articles in the journals *Revista Andina* and *Hispanic American Historical Review*.

CAMBRIDGE LATIN AMERICAN STUDIES

General Editor
Herbert S. Klein
Gouverneur Morris Professor of History, Columbia University
Director of the Center of Latin American Studies, Stanford University

90
Shadows of Empire
The Indian Nobility of Cusco, 1750–1825

Other Books in the Series

(Continued after index)

Shadows of Empire

The Indian Nobility of Cusco, 1750–1825

DAVID T. GARRETT

Reed College

CAMBRIDGE
UNIVERSITY PRESS

CAMBRIDGE UNIVERSITY PRESS
Cambridge, New York, Melbourne, Madrid, Cape Town,
Singapore, São Paulo, Delhi, Mexico City

Cambridge University Press
The Edinburgh Building, Cambridge CB2 8RU, UK

Published in the United States of America by Cambridge University Press, New York

www.cambridge.org
Information on this title: www.cambridge.org/9781107405479

First published 2005
Reprinted 2008
First paperback edition 2011

A catalogue record for this publication is available from the British Library

Library of Congress Cataloguing in Publication Data

Garrett, David T.
Shadows of empire : the Indian nobility of Cusco, 1750–1825 / David T. Garrett.
p. cm. – (Cambridge Latin American studies ; 90)
Includes bibliographical references and index.
ISBN 0-521-84634-X (hardback)
1. Incas – Peru – Cuzco – Kings and rulers – Genealogy. 2. Incas – Peru – Cuzco – Politics
and government. 3. Incas – Peru – Cuzco. 4. Nobility – Peru – Cuzco – History.
5. Aristocracy (Social class) – Peru – Cuzco – History. 6. Caciques (Indian leaders) –
Peru – Cuzco – History. 7. Spain – Colonies – America. 8. Cuzco (Peru) – History.
9. Peru – History – 1548–1820. I. Title. II. Series.
F3429.1.C9G37   2005
985´37.00498323 – dc22   2005000259

ISBN 978-0-521-84634-9 Hardback
ISBN 978-1-107-40547-9 Paperback

To My Parents,
Ann and Bill Garrett

And in memory of
Mario Marcone Flores

Contents

List of Illustrations

Charts

Tables

Maps

Acknowledgments

In more than a decade of graduate school, archival research, and writing I have accumulated many debts and bonds that I happily and gratefully acknowledge. Columbia University, the Social Science Research Council, the Tinker Foundation, Reed College, and the Levine Fund have kindly provided the financial support without which this project would have been impossible. Of at least equal importance has been the generosity, in time, knowledge, and help, of archivists across Peru, Bolivia, Argentina, and Spain. I am most obliged to those at the Archivo Regional del Cusco under the leadership of Dr. Jorge Polo y la Borda, and later Dr. Manuel Jesús Aparicio Vega and Roberto Cáceres Olivera; this project was inconceivable without the unstinting help of the ARC's dedicated staff. I have also benefited from the dedication and professionalism of those at the Archivo Arzobispal del Cusco, the Archivo Departmental de Puno, the Archivo de Límites at Peru's Ministerio de Relaciones Exteriores, Peru's Archivo General de la Nación and Biblioteca Nacional, the Archivo Nacional de Bolivia and the Archivo de La Paz, the Archivo General de la Nación in Buenos Aires, and the Archivo General de la Indias and the Archivo General de Simancas in Spain.

This book began as a dissertation, and I was fortunate in the committee that advised, reviewed, and greatly improved it. At all stages this project has benefited from the support, insight, and criticism of Herb Klein. Sinclair Thomson has been so generous as to labor through various versions of the work from dissertation to manuscript and to offer invaluable commentary. At the earlier stage Pablo Piccato and Martha Howell read through multiple drafts and were crucial in giving form to a sprawling project. Terence D'Altroy's thoughtful criticism has helped a late colonial historian to grapple with the dazzlingly complex topic of the Incas before and immediately after the Spanish conquest. A few other debts require special mention. This project would have been impossible without the skills and unflagging help of Donato Amado Gonzales and Margareth Najarro in Cusco, from whom I learned a great deal about both archival research and the history of Cusco.

At the final stage, Kenneth Andrien's comments on the manuscript were of great help in clarifying and elaborating tricky sections of the work.

More broadly, this work (and I) have benefited greatly from comments from, conversations with, and the camaraderie of many other Andeanists, including Scarlett O'Phelan Godoy, Donato Amado, Jean-Jacques Decoster, Ramón Mujica, Luis Miguel Glave, Sabine MacCormack, Chuck Walker, Ward Stavig, Kathryn Burns, Carolyn Dean, Catherine Julien, Beth Penry, Tom Abercrombie, Ken Mills, Karen Spalding, Roberto Choque Canqui, Sergio Serulnikov, Mercedes del Rio, and Ana María Presta. And many of my thanks must go to friends and colleagues from Columbia, Reed, and elsewhere whose expertise is not colonial Peru, but who in countless conversations and in comments on my work have brought new perspectives and made demands for rigor and clarification which account for much that is strongest in the work. Foremost, among many, are Ritu Birla, Julie Schonfeld, Natasha Gray, Joshua Rosenthal, Mario Marcone, David Mandell, Alex Hrycak, and Laura Lucas.

My deepest debts remain to my own family, for whose constant support I am extremely grateful. I have also had the great good fortune of being taken into the family of my late friend and colleague Mario Marcone in Lima, and I cannot imagine the past decade without the friendship of the Marcone Flores. It is in acknowledgment of these debts that I dedicate this work to my parents and to the memory of Mario Marcone Flores.

Portions of Chapter 6 appeared in modified form in *Hispanic American Historical Review* 84:4 (November 2004) and I thank Duke University Press for permission to include them here.

Pueblos Mentioned in Text

Pueblo	Province	Pueblo	Province
Abancay	*Abancay*	Colquemarca	*Chumbivilcas*
Accha	*Paruro*	Colquepata	*Paucartambo*
Achaya	*Azángaro*	Conima	*Huancané*
Acomayo	*Quispicanchis*	Copacabana	*Omasuyos*
Acora	*Chucuito*	Coporaque	*Tinta*
Acos	*Quispicanchis*	Corca	*Paruro*
Andaguaylillas	*Quispicanchis*	Cotabambas	*Cotabambas*
Anta	*Abancay*	Coya	*Calca y Lares*
Asillo	*Azángaro*	Crusero	*Caravaya*
Ayavire	*Lampa*	Cupi	*Lampa*
Azángaro	*Azángaro*	Curaguasi	*Abancay*
Belén	*Cercado*	Guaquirca	*Aymaraes*
Cacha	*Tinta*	Guanoquite	*Paruro*
Calapuja	*Lampa*	Guarocondo	*Abancay*
Calca	*Calca y Lares*	Guasac	*Paucartambo*
Caminaca	*Azángaro*	Guayllabamba	*Urubamba*
Capacmarca	*Chumbivilcas*	Hatuncolla	*Lampa*
Carabuco	*Omasuyos*	Hospital	*Cercado*
Catca	*Paucartambo*	Huancané	*Huancané*
Cathedral	*Cercado*	Ilave	*Chucuito*
Cavana	*Lampa*	Jesús de Machaca	*Pacajes*
Cavanilla	*Lampa*	Juli	*Chucuito*
Caycay	*Paucartambo*	Juliaca	*Lampa*
Chinchaypucyo	*Abancay*	Laja	*Omasuyos*
Chinchero	*Calca y Lares*	Lamay	*Calca y Lares*
Chucuito	*Chucuito*	Lampa	*Lampa*
Coasa	*Caravaya*	Layo	*Tinta*
Cotaguasi	*Chumbivilcas*	Livitaca	*Chumbivilcas*
Colcha	*Paruro*	Macarí	*Lampa*

Pueblo	Province	Pueblo	Province
Mamara	*Cotabambas*	San Taraco	*Azángaro*
Maras	*Urubamba*	Sandia	*Caravaya*
Maranganí	*Tinta*	Sangarará	*Quispicanchis*
Moho	*Huancané*	Santa Ana	*Cercado*
Mollepata	*Abancay*	Santa Rosa	*Lampa*
Muñani	*Azángaro*	Santiago	*Cercado*
Nicacio	*Lampa*	Santo Tomás	*Chumbivilcas*
Ñuñoa	*Lampa*	Sicuani	*Tinta*
Ollantaytambo	*Urubamba*	Sorata	*Larecaja*
Omacha	*Paruro*	Soraya	*Aymaraes*
Oropesa	*Quispicanchis*	Taray	*Calca y Lares*
Pacarectambo	*Paruro*	Tiquillaca	*Huancané*
Paruro	*Paruro*	Tungasuca	*Tinta*
Paucartambo	*Paucartambo*	Umachire	*Lampa*
Pisac	*Calca y Lares*	Urcos	*Quispicanchis*
Pomata	*Chucuito*	Urubamba	*Urubamba*
Pucará	*Lampa*	Usicayos	*Caravaya*
Pucarani	*Omasuyos*	Velille	*Chumbivilcas*
Pucyura	*Abancay*	Vilcabamba	*Urubamba*
Pusi	*Azángaro*	Vilquechico	*Huancané*
Quiquijana	*Quispicanchis*	Yanaoca	*Tinta*
Sabaino	*Aymaraes*	Yauri	*Tinta*
Saman	*Azángaro*	Yaurisque	*Paruro*
San Blas	*Cercado*	Yucay	*Urubamba*
San Cristóbal	*Cercado*	Yunguyo	*Chucuito*
San Gerónimo	*Cercado*	Zepita	*Chucuito*
San Salvador	*Calca y Lares*	Zurite	*Abancay*
San Sebastián	*Cercado*		

Pueblos on Maps, by Province

Cusco Cercado
San Gerónimo
San Sebastián

Paruro
Colcha
Corca
Guanoquite
Omacha
Paruro
Yaurisque

Abancay
Abancay
Anta
Chinchero
Curaguasi
Guarocondo
Pucyura
Zurite

Urubamba
Guayllabamba
Maras
Ollantaytambo
Urubamba
Yucay

Paucartambo
Caycay
Colquepata
Guasac
Paucartambo

Quispicanchis
Accha
Andaguaylillas
Acomayo
Acos
Oropesa
Quiquijana
Sangarará
Urcos

Aymaraes
Guaquirca
Soraya

Cotabambas
Cotabambas
Mamara

Chumbivilcas
Colquemarca
Livitaca
Santo Tomás
Velille

Azángaro
Achaya
Asillo
Azángaro
Caminaca
Pusi
Saman
San Taraco

Huancané
Conima
Huancané
Moho
Tiquillaca
Vilquechico

Chucuito
Acora
Chucuito
Ilave
Juli
Pomata
Yunguyo
Zepita

Calca y Lares	*Tinta*	*Lampa*
Calca	Cacha	Ayavire
Coya	Layo	Calapuja
Lamay	Coporaque	Cavana
Pisac	Layo	Cavanilla
Taray	Sicuani	Cupi
	Tinta	Juliaca
	Tungasuca	Lampa
	Yanaoca	Macarí
	Yauri	Nicacio
		Ñuñoa
		Pucará
		Santa Rosa
		Umachire
		Caravaya
		Coasa
		Crusero
		Usicayos

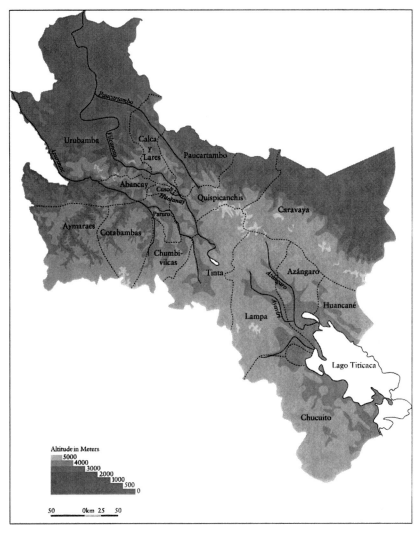

Map 1. Area of Study, Topography and Political Boundaries

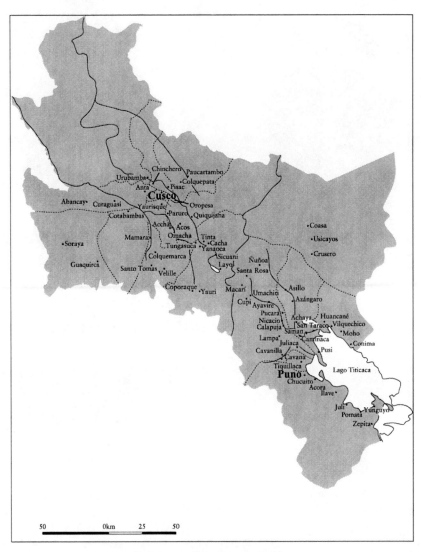

Map 2. Area of Study, Major Pueblos

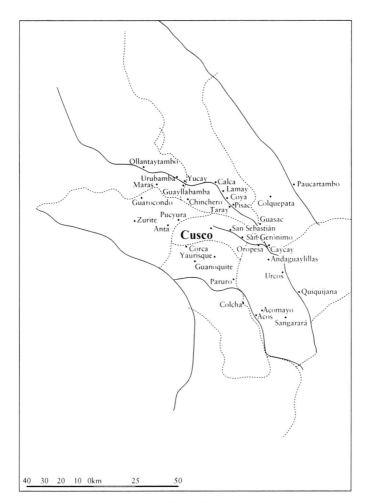

Map 3. Pueblos in Cusco Area

Introduction

On June 8, 1824, when Lima had fallen to Bolívar, Peru's viceroy had retreated to Cusco, and Spanish rule in the Andes had less than a year to go, Cusco's Inca nobility petitioned the viceregal court that on ". . . the eve and day of the glorious apostle Lord Santiago the functions of the Royal Standard be celebrated [by] . . . one of the Indian nobles of the eight parishes of this capital, named by the 24 electors of the [Inca] *cabildo*; being the said functions, the most vivid demonstration of our fidelity, gratitude, and jubilee, that are performed according to the example of our ancestors."[1] A reminder of the existence, nearly three centuries after the conquest of the Inca empire in the 1530s, of an indigenous Andean nobility, the request wonderfully captures the complexity of colonial Andean society. The descendants of the Inca royalty whose vast empire had been seized by the Spanish did not simply swear allegiance to Ferdinand VII as the viceroyalty collapsed, but insisted on their right to do so. With them, the highland Indian nobility generally repudiated the creole-dominated drive for independence, just as in the 1780s their fathers and grandfathers had rallied to the defense of the crown against the massive indigenous uprisings of Tupac Amaru and the Cataris. While there is a superficial irony in the transformation, over three centuries, of the descendants of the Inca royalty and other preconquest elites into "Indian nobles and faithful vassals of His Majesty," their defense of the colonial order underscores how these Indian nobles were, simultaneously, an artifact of preconquest civilization and the continuously evolving creation of Spanish colonialism.[2] This duality emerges clearly in their petition, where – in a practice with centuries of precedence – the nineteenth-century Incas called on the Spanish crown to preserve their peculiar privileges.

A study of Cusco's Indian nobility and its role in colonial society from the middle of the eighteenth century through the rebellions of the 1780s

---

1 ARC, INT, Vir., Leg. 159 (1823–24).

2 An expression frequently used in petitions by Indian nobles; see, for example, the cacicazgo claim by Don Fernando Tapara of Ñuñoa (ARC, RA, Adm, Leg. 167 (1808–9)).

to the moment of the Incas' petition in support of a collapsing empire, this work both uses that group as a lens through which to analyze late colonial society more generally, and argues that the Indian elite was an essential, and accepted, part of that society until the crises of the late eighteenth century. From its inception, the structure of Spanish rule – dividing Andean society into two ethnic "republics" of Indians and Spaniards, with their own laws, hierarchies, and relation to the crown – had depended on a symbiotic, if often contentious, alliance between the crown and an indigenous elite.[3] Both to show its own obedience to natural law and to limit the control of private Spaniards over the indigenous Andean population, under Philip II the crown established a system of colonial governance that placed the rule of (and collection of tribute from) individual Indian communities under the control of an Indian nobility, a privileged stratum through which the crown would lead the people of the Andes from pagan barbarity to Christian civilization. While over two centuries there was considerable social movement within indigenous society, the basic contours of this colonial order remained unchanged until the late 1700s.

As a result, the Indian elite occupied a liminal position in the colonial order, on the frontier between the two republics. Their privilege and authority derived simultaneously from their rootedness in the Indian republic and from their obligation to bring indigenous society into conformity with Spanish ideals. Whether the Incas of Cusco or the great Aymara lords of the Titicaca basin, Indian elites grounded their hereditary precedence in ancestors dating to the "time of the gentility," yet they relied for its perpetuation on the legal structure and economic organization of the viceroyalty of Peru. But although situated on this colonial frontier, the Indian nobility was marginal to neither the Indian nor the Spanish republic. The pinnacle of indigenous society, Indian nobles dominated ceremonial, political, and economic life in their communities, and in many instances – above all, the Inca nobility around Cusco – were aggressive performers of a self-conscious, indigenous identity. They were also by far the most hispanicized segment of indigenous society, often literate and fluent in Spanish, the owners of private property, and active participants in the market economy and

---

3 Legally, the Indian republic included all those of purely indigenous ancestry; the Spanish republic included all others. Properly, mestizos were people of mixed Spanish and Indian ancestry. In fact, many Indian nobles counted Spaniards among their ancestors, and a number of Cusco's leading Spanish families had Inca blood. These people were rarely called mestizos. Rather, the term referred to those at the bottom of the república de españoles – the illiterate laboring classes of urban Cusco, or the rural poor who settled in Indian pueblos; it is in this sense that I have used the word. The other major division within Cusco's Spanish republic was between creoles (people of European ancestry born in the Americas) and *peninsulares* – those born in Iberia. In this work, "Spanish" and "Spaniard" refer to all non-Indians; mestizo, creole, and peninsular are used to distinguish among the component parts of the Spanish republic.

ceremonial life of creole Peru. Indeed, given the dual nature of the colonial order, their very liminality placed them at the center of colonial society, with strong ties of kinship and material interest to both their communities and highland Spaniards. If the actions and position of the Indian nobility appear contradictory, it is simply because they were the fullest embodiment of the contradictions of colonial rule in the Andes, with its simultaneous efforts to conjoin and to keep separate Spanish and Indian. As a result, the Indian nobility was inextricably enmeshed within the colonial order, and did not survive the collapse of the viceroyalty: if in 1750 "indio noble" was a basic category of highland society, by 1850 it was an oxymoron. For independence replaced the ideal of a society divided into two republics, each with its hierarchies, with that of a unitary society stratified by ethnicity, one with no space for Indian privilege.

Peru's colonial Indian nobility began to attract academic attention in the 1940s, with Ella Temple Dunbar's articles on colonial Inca lineages.[4] Growing interest in the Great Rebellion (1780–3) further fed interest in the Indian elite, as John Rowe sought in them an anticolonial protonationalism culminating in Tupac Amaru.[5] However, Andean historiography greatly lagged behind Mesoamerican in the study of colonial, indigenous society, which – both because of the influence of Charles Gibson's pioneering works of the 1950s and because of the survival of substantial archives in indigenous languages – has focused on ethnohistory and the transformation of societies during the colonial era.[6] In contrast, only in the past three

---

4 Ella Temple Dunbar, "Don Carlos Inca," *Revista Histórica {Lima}* 17 (1948): 135–79; "Un linaje incaico durante la dominación española: Los Sahuaraura," *Revista Histórica {Lima}* 18 (1949): 45–77.

5 John H. Rowe, "El movimiento nacional Inca del siglo XVIII," *Revista Universitaria {Cusco}* 7 (1954): 17–47; *Quechua Nationalism in the Eighteenth Century* (Berkeley: University of California Press, 1959); and "Colonial Portraits of Inca Nobles," in *The Civilization of Ancient America. Selected Papers of the XXIX International Congress of Americanists*, ed. Sol Tax (Chicago: University of Chicago Press, 1951), pp. 258–68.

6 For Gibson's impact on the field, James Lockhart, *Nahuas and Spaniards: Postconquest Central Mexican History and Philology* (Stanford: Stanford University Press, 1991), pp. 161–82. Charles Gibson, *Tlaxcala in the Sixteenth Century* (New Haven: Yale University Press, 1952); "The Aztec Aristocracy in Colonial Mexico," in *Comparative Studies in Society and History*, Vol. 2 (1959), pp. 169–96; and *The Aztecs under Spanish Rule: A History of the Indians of the Valley of Mexico, 1519–1810* (Stanford: Stanford University Press, 1964). James Lockhart, *Nahuas and Spaniards; The Nahuas after the Conquest: A Social and Cultural History of the Indians of Central Mexico, Sixteenth through Eighteenth Centuries* (Stanford: Stanford University Press, 1992); William B. Taylor, *Landlord and Peasant in Colonial Oaxaca* (Stanford: Stanford University Press, 1972) and *Drinking, Homicide and Rebellion in Colonial Mexican Villages* (Stanford: Stanford University Press, 1979); Enrique Florescano, *Memory, Myth and Time in Mexico: From the Aztecs to Independence*, translated by Albert G. and Kathryn Bork (Austin: University of Texas Press, 1994); Serge Gruzinski, *The Conquest of Mexico: The Incorporation of Indian Societies into the Western World, 16th–18th Centuries*, translated by Eileen Corrigan (Cambridge: Polity Press, 1993); Robert S. Haskett, *Indigenous Rulers: An Ethnohistory of Town Government in Colonial Cuernavaca* (Albuquerque: University of New Mexico Press, 1991); Kevin Terraciano, *The Mixtecs of Colonial Oaxaca: Ñudzahui*

decades has a large canon addressing colonial indigenous societies in the
Andes developed; and in lieu of the emphasis on negotiation and evolution
in the Mesoamerican literature, the Andean historiography first focused on
the destructive and dislocative effects of Spanish rule – or, as Steve Stern
put it, "how conquest transformed vigorous native peoples of the Andean
sierra into an inferior caste of 'Indians' subordinated to Spanish coloniz-
ers and Europe's creation of a world market."[7] These studies have generally
focused on the economic exploitation and political marginalization of native
Andeans, and on indigenous resistance to the imposition, or emergence, of
the colonial order.

With their materialist concerns, many of these works devoted considerable attention to the cacique (or *curaca*), a cross between local lord, tax

History, Sixteenth through Eighteenth Centuries (Stanford: Stanford University Press, 2001); Nancy M.
Farriss, *Maya Society under Colonial Rule: The Collective Enterprise of Survival* (Princeton: Princeton Uni-
versity Press, 1984); Robert W. Patch, *Maya and Spaniard in Yucatan, 1648–1812* (Stanford: Stanford
University Press, 1994); Matthew Restall, *The Maya World: Yucatec Culture and Society, 1550–1850*
(Stanford: Stanford University Press, 1997).

7 Steve J. Stern, *Peru's Indian Peoples and the Challenge of Spanish Conquest: Huamanga to 1640* (Madison:
University of Wisconsin Press, 1982), p. xv. Karen Spalding, *Huarochirí: An Andean Society under
Inca and Spanish Rule* (Stanford: Stanford University Press, 1984); Nathan Wachtel, *The Vision of
the Vanquished: The Spanish Conquest of Peru through Indian Eyes, 1530–1570*, translated by Ben and
Siân Reynolds (New York: Harper and Row, 1977); Nicolás Sánchez-Albornoz, *Indios y tributos en
el Alto Perú* (Lima: Instituto de Estudios Peruanos, 1978); Manuel Burga, *De la encomienda a la
hacienda capitalista: el valle del Jequetepeque del siglo XVI al XX* (Lima: Instituto de Estudios Peruanos,
1976); Franklin Pease, *Curacas, reciprocidad y riqueza* (Lima: Pontificia Universidad Católica del Perú,
1992); Luis Miguel Glave and Isabel Remy, *Estructura agraria y vida rural en una región Andina:
Ollantaytambo entre los siglos XVI y XIX* (Cusco: Centro Bartolomé de Las Casas, 1983); Luis Miguel
Glave, *Trajinantes: Caminos indígenas en la sociedad colonial, siglos XVI y XVII* (Lima: Instituto de
Apoyo Agrario, 1989) and *Vida, símbolos y batallas: Creación y recreación de la comunidad indígena. Cusco,
siglos XVI–XX* (Lima: Fondo de Cultura Económica, 1993); Brooke Larson, *Cochabamba, 1550–1900:
Colonialism and Agrarian Transformation in Bolivia*, 2nd ed. (Durham: Duke University Press, 1998);
Thierry Saignes, *Caciques, Tribute and Migration in the Southern Andes: Indian Society and the Seventeenth
Century Colonial Order* (London: University of London, 1985); Roberto Choque Canqui, *Sociedad y
economía colonial en el sur andino* (La Paz: Hisbol, 1993); Roger Rasnake, *Domination and Cultural
Resistance: Authority and Power among an Andean People* (Durham: Duke University Press, 1988); Ann
Wightman, *Indigenous Migration and Social Change: The Forasteros of Cuzco, 1520–1720* (Durham: Duke
University Press, 1990); Karen Vieira Powers, *Andean Journeys: Migration, Ethnogenesis and the State in
Colonial Quito* (Albuquerque: University of New Mexico Press, 1995); Carlos Sempat Assadourian,
El sistema de la economía colonial: el mercado interior, regiones, y espacio económico (Mexico: Nueva Imagen,
1983) and *Transiciones hacia el Sistema Colonial Andino* (Lima: Instituto de Estudios Peruanos, 1994);
Steve J. Stern, ed., *Resistance, Rebellion, and Consciousness in the Andean Peasant World, 18th to 20th
Centuries* (Madison: University of Wisconsin Press, 1987); Irene Silverblatt, *Moon, Sun, and Witches:
Gender Ideologies and Class in Inca and Colonial Peru* (Princeton: Princeton University Press, 1987);
Ward Stavig, *The World of Túpac Amaru: Conflict, Community, and Identity in Colonial Peru* (Lincoln:
University of Nebraska Press, 1999); Kenneth Andrien, *Andean Worlds: Indigenous History, Culture,
and Consciousness under Spanish Rule, 1532–1825* (Albuquerque: University of New Mexico Press,
2001).

collector, and justice of the peace who personified the point of contact between the Indian community and the Spanish colonial order, and organized the flow of tribute into the royal coffers and the market economy of Spanish Peru.[8] In this paradigm, indigenous elites generally occupy one of two roles: that of resister and defender, or that of collaborator.[9] For some, the novel forms of property and new material logics of class imposed by the Spanish transformed the caciques and "indios ricos" of colonial Peru into (incipient) agrarian capitalists, necessarily in conflict with the communities whose land and labor they expropriated.[10] Others have stressed the disruption of cacical succession provoked by demographic collapse, the colonial economy, the intervention of Spanish officials, and the imposition of Spanish ideals of succession.[11] Coupled with the colonial cacique's economic activities as a violation of the Andean moral economy is the colonial cacique as a usurper of traditional Andean political authority. Implicit in these analyses is an assumption of the "illegitimacy" of colonial innovation in the material and social relations of Andean society, as the history of colonial indigenous societies becomes the erosion of the authentically Andean and its replacement by the colonial.

This meta-narrative has created challenges largely absent in the Mesoamerican literature, with its greater interest in the transformation of indigenous society than in the collapse of preconquest organization. Most important is that of late colonial Andean society: under the Bourbons as well as the Habsburgs, overwhelmingly the indigenous peoples of the Andes lived in self-governing pueblos, under the rule of the Indian nobility. Certainly these communities differed profoundly from their preconquest forebears, but they remained "Andean," and "Indian." Two trends in recent historiography have addressed this question, in somewhat different ways.

---

8 Karen Spalding, "Social Climbers: Changing Patterns of Mobility among the Indians of Colonial Peru," *Hispanic American Historical Review* 50:4 (November 1970): 645–64; "Kurakas and Commerce: A Chapter in the Evolution of Andean Society," *Hispanic American Historical Review* 54:4 (November 1973): 581–99; and *Huarochirí*, pp. 209–38; Pease, *Curacas*; Saignes, *Caciques*; Stern, *Peru's Indian Peoples*, pp. 158–83; Larson, *Cochabamba*, pp. 159–70; Glave, *Trajinantes*, pp. 279–304; Jean Piel, *Capitalismo agrario en el Perú* (Lima/Salta: IFEA/Universidad Nacional de Salta, 1995), pp. 186–92, 207–13; Powers, *Andean Journeys*, pp. 133–68; Silverblatt, *Moon*, pp. 148–58; Carlos J. Díaz Rementería, *El cacique en el virreinato del Perú: estudio histórico-jurídico* (Sevilla: Publicaciones de la Universidad de Sevilla, 1977).

9 For curacas as defenders of their communities, Pease, *Curacas*; although Wachtel argues that they oversaw the transformation of Andean reciprocity into a system of Spanish extraction. *Vision*, pp. 130–1.

10 Sánchez-Albornoz, *Indios y tributos*, pp. 99–107; Stern, *Peru's Indian Peoples*, pp. 158–83; Spalding, "Social Climbers," and "Kurakas and Commerce"; Larson, *Cochabamba*, pp. 159–70; Piel, *Capitalismo agrario*, pp. 186–92, 207–13.

11 Powers, *Andean Journeys*, pp. 133–68; Silverblatt, *Moon*, pp. 148–58; Díaz Rementería, *El cacique*, pp. 111–24.

Glave and others have focused on the histories of particular communities and societies over the *longue durée*, using a paradigm of evolution and
re-creation rather than one of loss to explore the colonial (and postcolonial)
histories of native Andeans.[12] Similarly, recent studies of colonial Andean
religion and culture have emphasized the complexity of the beliefs, iden-
tities, and relations constructed by Peru's indigenous people during the
colonial period.[13] Others have turned to the eighteenth century, and in
focusing on the structures, contradictions, and political beliefs of late colonial indigenous societies in the area of the Great Rebellion have revealed
their complex politics.[14] Here, too, the narrative has been of collapse, but
of the larger colonial order, with a resulting restructuring, and democra-
tization, of authority within indigenous communities. These studies have
focused primarily on the popular classes, and the Indian nobility appear
only as individuals, or, insofar as they form a group, as the object of class
antagonism in the highly stratified societies of Upper Peru.[15]

    This book continues both of these projects by examining in detail the
organization of Cusco's mid-eighteenth-century Indian nobility and their
role in society, and locating this group temporally in two stages of Spanish
Andean colonialism: the consolidation of the "mature" order of the early
Bourbons and the collapse of the entire colonial order from 1780 to 1825. In

12 Glave, *Vida, símbolos*, also *Trajinantes*; Choque Canqui, *Sociedad*; Rasnake, *Domination*; Thomas Aber-
    crombie, *Pathways of Memory and Power: Ethnography and History among an Andean People* (Madison:
    University of Wisconsin Press, 1998); Nathan Wachtel, *Le Retour des Ancêtres: Les Indiens Urus de
    Bolivie XXeme–XVIeme siècle: Essai d'Histoire Régressive* (Paris: Gallimard, 1990).
13 Kenneth Mills, *Idolatry and Its Enemies: Colonial Andean Religion and Extirpation, 1640–1750*
    (Princeton: Princeton University Press, 1997); Carolyn Dean, *Inka Bodies and the Body of Christ:
    Corpus Christi in Colonial Cuzco, Peru* (Durham: Duke University Press, 1999); Manuel Burga,
    Nacimiento de una utopía: muerte y resurrección de los incas (Lima: Instituto de Apoyo Agrario, 1988).
14 Sinclair Thomson, *We Alone Will Rule: Native Andean Politics in the Age of Insurgency* (Madison: Univer-
    sity of Wisconsin Press, 2002); Sergio Serulnikov, *Subverting Colonial Authority: Challenges to Spanish
    Rule in Eighteenth-Century Southern Andes* (Durham: Duke University Press, 2003); "Customs and
    Rules: Bourbon Rationalizing Projects and Social Conflicts in Northern Potosí during the 1770s,"
    Colonial Latin American Review 8:2 (December 1999): 245–74 and "Disputed Images of Colonialism:
    Spanish Rule and Indian Subversion in Northern Potosí, 1777–1780," *Hispanic American Historical
    Review* 76:2 (May 1996): 189–226; S. Elizabeth Penry, "Transformations in Indigenous Authority
    and Identity in Resettlement Towns of Colonial Charcas (Alto Perú)" (Ph.D. diss., University of
    Miami, 1996); Stavig, *The World of Túpac Amaru*; Choque Canqui, *Sociedad*; Glave, *Vida, símbolos*,
    pp. 93–178.
15 A striking and important exception has been O'Phelan Godoy's work on the upper ranks of the
    Indian nobility in Cusco around the time of the Rebellion, which has analyzed the changing relations
    of this indigenous elite to the crown under the Bourbon Reforms. *La Gran Rebelión en los Andes:
    De Túpac Amaru a Túpac Catari* (Cusco: Centro Bartolomé de Las Casas, 1995), pp. 47–68; *Kurakas
    sin sucesiones: Del cacique al alcalde de indios, Perú y Bolivia 1750–1835* (Cusco: Centro Bartolomé de
    Las Casas, 1997); and "Repensando el Movimiento Nacional Inca del siglo XVIII," in *El Perú en el
    siglo XVIII: la era borbónica*, ed. Scarlett O'Phelan Godoy (Lima: Pontificia Universidad Católica del
    Perú, 1999), pp. 263–78.

doing so, the work has three major foci: the history of the Indian nobility's legal and economic space within the colonial order; the organization of Cusco's Indian nobility and their role in society in the mid-1700s; and the collapse of the colonial order, and with it of this indigenous elite, from 1780 to 1825.

Central to this work is the argument that the defining relations and institutions of mid-eighteenth-century Andean society were primarily products of the sixteenth-century Toledan reforms, which in turn co-opted and transformed significant aspects of the Inca order. Chapter 1 concentrates on the 1500s and the material, political, and ideological factors that created a space for an Indian elite within the emergent colonial order. Although these parameters left enormous room for negotiation and localized contestation, the general rejection of the basic elements of Spanish hegemony was almost unheard of for two centuries. The imposition of this colonial order, and the collapse of the indigenous population, did, however, effect profound changes in Andean society over the long seventeenth century, and these are discussed in Chapter 2. In particular, it examines the impacts of population decline, migration, and the imposition of monogamy and reformulation of kinship and community bonds on the indigenous elite, and the impact of the expansion of the Spanish population, rural Spanish landholding, and the market economy on Andean society generally. While these changes could have disastrous effects on particular families, groups, and communities, they did not fundamentally alter the legal ordering established in the sixteenth century.

The remainder of the book focuses on the Indian nobility from 1750 to 1825. In concentrating on the late colonial period in Cusco and the Titicaca basin, I have attempted to negotiate two, often competing, goals. The first has been to examine the organization of the indigenous nobility and its role in mid-eighteenth-century Andean society. Certainly that society was marked by contradictions and tensions, but it also shared widely held understandings of its proper order and functioning. If, in hindsight, the fitful collapse, from 1780 to 1825, of the colonial order established in the sixteenth century appears inevitable, in 1750 it did not. I have sought to balance a reading of mid-eighteenth-century society that exposes the internal contradictions leading to its collapse with one that examines the *habitus* of the late colonial Indian nobility and emphasizes the mechanisms by which they reproduced their authority.[16]

The central portion of the book thus provides a longitudinal study of the Indian nobility in mid-eighteenth-century Cusco, one that pays particular attention to regional variation within the bishopric (and northern

---

16 For *habitus*, Pierre Bourdieu, *Outline of a Theory of Practice*, translated by Richard Nice (Cambridge: Cambridge University Press, 1977).

La Paz), particularly between the Inca nobility of Cusco and the Aymara cacical elite of the Titicaca basin. Chapter 3 assesses the extent to which hereditary, provincial elites existed within the Indian republic, and, where they existed, examines their histories and their strategies for reproducing their authority. Chapter 4 is a study of the role of indigenous elites in the material economy of the Indian pueblo, concentrating on the structural role of the cacique in the pueblo economy, the importance of private property in eighteenth-century indigenous communities, and the household and familial economies of the upper ranks of the indigenous elite. Chapter 5 turns to the politics of the Indian republic. It first analyzes competition for and conflict surrounding cacicazgos to identify multiple, interrelated *loci* of social conflict in the late colonial pueblo, and then explores various mechanisms by which individuals and families sought to legitimate their possession of the office. Thus, Part II as a whole examines the Indian nobility of mid-eighteenth-century Peru by exploring the interrelated dynamics of hereditary status and family organization, material relations, and the political and performative aspects of indigenous authority.

The final section turns to the breakdown of the Andean colonial order in the face of rebellion, the crown's repudiation of the Indian nobility, the expansion of creole authority in the countryside, the collapse of the Spanish empire, and, finally, the formal abandonment of the two-republic system at independence. Using the Indian elite as a vantage point allows an examination that exposes the interaction of various processes that led to the restructuring of Andean politics and society at all levels. In examining the Great Rebellion(s) of 1780–3, Chapter 6 illuminates the central role of the loyalist Indian nobility, both highlighting the complex relations of class and ethnicity in the Indian republic and excavating the political ideology and strategies of the loyalist elite. Chapter 7 then turns to the royal response to the rebellion, and argues that while the rebellion greatly weakened the Indian nobility – particularly in the Titicaca basin – the collapse of this indigenous elite was ultimately the product of the crown's redefinition of the relations between the two ethnic republics in a way that eliminated the legal protections of Indian privilege. Here I seek to explain the collapse of a powerful Indian elite committed to the corporate order of colonial society in the decades preceding independence, thereby clearing the way for the creole imposition of the problematic liberalism of postcolonial Peru.

As a social history of a large group, this book relies overwhelmingly on archival sources. Indeed, the Indian nobility is the one stratum of indigenous society in colonial Peru for whom substantial archival evidence survives, both because they were the members of indigenous society with the resources to leave their mark in the written record and because they were the Indians to which literate, Spanish Peru paid most attention. Almost all the information is filtered through the notary's lens, and the rare documents actually written by Indian nobles were carefully crafted to appeal to crown officials; I have attempted to be attentive to the challenges that reading such documents present. But wills and other notarized documents; genealogies and proofs of nobility; lawsuits – between rival cacical claimants, between caciques and their communities, between the Inca nobility and colonial officials; petitions to the crown, all allow the study of genealogy, kinship, domestic economy, self-presentation, and ideology among the Indian nobility – and, through them, allow us to peer a bit deeper into the world of the colonial pueblo.

The area under study in this work is best described as either the bishopric of Cusco or the intendancies of Cusco and Puno (established in 1784).[17] Or, using the divisions of Inca rule, the area covered consists of the Inca heartland within a fifty-mile radius of Cusco, along with the northern portion of the Inca quadrant of Collasuyo (extending southeast from Cusco into northern Argentina) and the eastern section of Condesuyo (stretching southwest toward Arequipa and the Pacific). A third of these roughly 75,000 square miles are tropical jungle, outside the regional political economy until the twentieth century. Half the remaining area is above 12,000 feet, and a considerable portion above 15,000, effectively uninhabitable. The population ranged from perhaps a million under the Incas to scarcely one hundred fifty thousand in the late 1600s and more than a quarter of a million a century later.

The area divides into several distinct regions, ecologically, culturally, and economically. The city of Cusco and its immediate hinterland are located in an area of rugged, temperate highland valleys at an altitude between 7,000 and 14,000 feet. Most communities are located in the *quechua* and *suni*:

---

17 I have also drawn on evidence from communities around Titicaca in the bishopric of La Paz. The bishopric of Cusco's provinces were Cusco Cercado, Abancay, Marquesado of Oropesa [Urubamba], Calca y Lares, Paucartambo, Quispicanchis, Chilques y Masques [Paruro], Chumbivilcas, Canas y Canchis [Tinta], Cotabambas, and Aymaraes, all subject to the Audiencia of Lima; and Lampa, Azángaro, and Caravaya, subject to the Audiencia of Charcas. The intendancy of Cusco included those provinces in the bishopric of Cusco subject to the Audiencia of Lima; the intendancy of Puno included those subject to the Audiencia of Charcas, plus the two northwestern provinces of the bishopric of La Paz [Paucarcolla (or Huancané) and Chucuito]. At the provincial level, jurisdictional boundaries within the area were stable throughout the seventeenth and eighteenth centuries, although the names of some provinces did change. In the late eighteenth century, Chilques y Masques became Paruro and Canas y Canchis became Tinta. In the middle of the century, the province of the Marquesado of Oropesa was combined with that of Vilcabamba, and the pueblo of Ollantaytambo was moved from Calca y Lares to this new province, renamed Urubamba. In Chapters 1 and 2, dealing with the sixteenth and seventeenth centuries, I have used the earlier terms; for the sake of convenience and consistency in the remainder of the work I have used the later names, even though the transition was occurring during the period under study. "Cusco" in this study refers to both the city of Cusco (and its Cercado) and the bishopric. Where context has not made clear which is meant, I have attempted to do so explicitly.

these are agricultural societies, whose foundation was corn, with potato cultivation and llama herding on the higher slopes; the Spanish added wheat, sheep, and cattle.[18] Historically Quechua-speaking, this area was the heartland of the Incas; the region was also the site of intensive Spanish colonization and settlement. The city of Cusco was a center of Spanish population and authority in the highlands and the largest city between Potosí and Lima; as a result, urban society and the urban economy were extremely important to the colonial Inca nobility.

To the south and west, the upper reaches of the Vilcanota and Apurímac valleys were home to hundreds of communities with roots in the preconquest Aymara societies of Condesuyo and Collasuyo.[19] At altitudes of 10,000–14,000 feet, these communities' material foundation was the potato and Andean camelids and, after the conquest, sheep. Just as the Pumanota–Chimboya mountain ridge divides the Titicaca and Amazonian watersheds, so the societies along it divided the Incas of Cusco from the societies of the Titicaca basin. Historically Aymara, but linguistically Quechua-speaking by the eighteenth century, the pueblos of Chumbivilcas, Tinta, and northern Lampa had a colonial history quite different from that of the Inca pueblos to the north. Subject to the mining *mitas* of Potosí and Cailloma, the Indian communities of this region bore particularly heavy colonial burdens and were subject to high rates of migration and dislocation; they also saw relatively little Spanish settlement and landowning. These *puna* communities also differed considerably from those further south where, in the Titicaca basin, larger Aymara societies continued to hold sway. Also subject to heavy mita burdens, these societies were historically more hierarchical and politically organized than those to the north – perhaps because they were more agricultural, depending for their subsistence on the fertile farmland of the lake's floodplain and tributary valleys. Their agricultural lands; their position at a critical juncture in the colonial economy, where the roads from Cusco and Arequipa join to head to Upper Peru; and the crown's early policy, to protect the mita, of discouraging Spanish settlement here combined to make the communities unusually rich and well-defended from Spanish

18 The standard work of Peruvian geography, Javier Pulgar Vidal's *Geografía del Perú: las ocho regiones naturales del Perú* (Lima: Textos Universitarios, 1972) divides the republic of Peru into eight ecological zones: *chala* (coast), *quechua* (temperate highland valleys), *suni* (arable highlands, above the quechua), *puna* (highland pasture above 13,000 feet), *janca* (rocky mountain peaks, glaciers, etc.), *yunga* (semitropical lowland valleys), *selva alta* and *selva baja* (upper and lower jungle). For a useful, briefer discussion, Terence N. D'Altroy, *Provincial Power in the Inka Empire* (Washington, D.C.: Smithsonian Institution Press, 1992), pp. 26–35.

19 The region had other ethnolinguistic groups – for example, the Uros and the Putina – but since the colonial period, Spanish, Quechua, and Aymara have expanded dramatically at the expense of others. For the linguistic and geographical evolution of Quechua, see Bruce Mannheim, *The Language of the Inka since the European Invasion* (Austin: University of Texas Press, 1991).

settlement, allowing a high level of stratification to continue from the pre-conquest era to the end of the colonial period. United by Spanish rule, these regions nonetheless had distinct colonial histories.

A few general comments about nomenclature and orthography are also in order. First, I have generally opted for the term "Indian" rather than "indigenous" because the latter was a postindependence innovation; the legal category by which people of the "república de indios" were identified (and, in the albeit filtered accounts of the notary, identified themselves) was "indio" or "india." I have also preferred Indian to Inca or Inka as a broad category for reasons that will, I hope, become obvious throughout the work: I have reserved "Inca" to refer to those claiming descent from the preconquest royalty of Cusco, a group that represented only a small minority of both Cusco's Indian population and the Indian nobility of the bishopric generally. Finally, I have chosen "Inca" over the increasingly common "Inka" because of the latter's conscious effort to distance the indigenous from the Spanish. A central argument of this work is that the Indian elite of late colonial Peru was simultaneously indigenous and a product of Spanish rule, and I believe "Inca" better captures this claim. I have chosen "Inca" because of its widespread contemporary use; I should note "Ynga" and "Ynca" would have been the common, late colonial spellings.

The use of family names in colonial Indian society was not standardized according to European practice. Among the Indian elite, by the eighteenth century sons generally took the surname of their fathers; daughters might take that of either their mother or their father. Like the Spanish elite, the Indian elite piled on names to indicate impressive genealogies; as a result, the same individual might appear with four or five surname variants in different documents, a variety which in some cases I have maintained to highlight self-presentation. The orthography of Quechua and Aymara was also not standardized in the colonial era. I have standardized the spelling of *ayllus'* and individuals' names throughout for ease of reference. For pueblos, provinces, rivers, and so forth I have generally used current spellings. For the names of the Inca monarchs and their *panacas*, I have followed Inca Garcilaso. As people's names almost never include stress accents in the archival records consulted, I have not included them here.

PART I

Indian Elites and the Colonial Order

I

Spanish Conquest and the
Habsburg Reforms

The dynamics of late colonial society determined the contours of the social space that Bourbon Cusco's Indian elites occupied, but the boundaries of that space were created in the 1500s through the interaction of three fundamental principles of Spanish rule in the Andes. First, the Habsburgs were committed to a legal and cultural boundary between Spanish and Indian Peru, the latter to be composed of self-governing rural communities, ideally off-limits to Spanish settlement. Second, under Philip II the monarchy aggressively pursued the integration of the Andes into the royal economy as a centralized, tributary colony, establishing the fundamental characteristic of the colonial highlands' political economy. Finally, the Habsburgs and their officials believed strongly in the existence of innate nobility, and that preconquest elites formed a natural nobility whose authority and privileges should enjoy recognition by the crown.

The reformist bureaucrats of the 1500s did not confront a *tabula rasa* in the Andes: the region was home to one of the great empires of the Americas, ruled by the Incas of Cusco.[1] In the century before Pizarro's arrival in Peru they had conquered much of the Andes to forge an empire millions strong. In doing so they had confronted challenges similar to those that the Spanish would face, most importantly how to construct an imperial superstructure that drew labor and produce from the societies of the Andes to the service of empire. The political and economic relationship that supported this superstructure was tribute, and to organize its flow the Incas created a variegated Andean elite, composed of the Incas of Cusco and the ruling groups of subject societies. Spanish conquest and centuries of colonial rule removed the control of imperial, even regional, polities and economies from Indian hands, and in this the subject Indian elite of colonial Cusco differed enormously from their imperial forebears. However, the Inca legacy continued to shape colonial Cusco for two reasons. First, the

---

1 Unless otherwise indicated, in this work I have used the term "Inca" in its narrow sense, to refer to the ethnic group (and later noble caste) around Cusco; the difficulties of determining who around Cusco was "Inca" in the 1700s are discussed in Chapter 3.

sixteenth-century reforms were a direct response to Inca rule, and incorporated aspects into the organization of colonial society. Second, because Cusco was the Inca heartland, the imperial history was also the local history. Precisely because the complex hierarchies of Inca rule were organized around Cusco's ethnic Incas, the legacy of Inca imperialism remained especially pronounced in the bishopric.

The Legacy of Inca Rule

After the fall of Cusco in the 1530s, Inca history was related to the *conquistadores* as the evolution of a maximal *ayllu* into an imperial power.[2] According to legend, the Incas were founded by Manco Capac, his brothers, and his sister-wives, who migrated thirty miles from Pacarectambo to the Huatanay valley.[3] The area was already populated by other ayllus, whom the Incas displaced from present-day Cusco.[4] This was the beginning of Ayllu Chima, who traced their descent from Manco Capac and had ancestral precedence, although not political dominion, over the other Inca ayllus. The reconstruction, from early Spanish accounts, of how the Incas organized and divided themselves remains a topic of much debate.[5] But

2 The basic unit of Andean society, the ayllu is a grouping of people, generally bound by claims of common ancestry. Colonial ayllus were essentially hamlets or neighborhoods; larger ethnic ayllus (termed "maximal ayllus" by Platt, and composed of many smaller, local ayllus) were the regional forms of association in the preconquest Andes. Moietal division of larger groups was also common and repeated the basic logic of ayllu organization. Tristan Platt, "Mirrors and Maize: The Concept of *Yanantin* among the Macha of Bolivia" in *Anthropological History of Andean Polities*, ed. John V. Murra et al. (Cambridge: Cambridge University Press, 1986), pp. 228–59. For the colonial *ayllu*, Spalding, *Huarochirí*; Wachtel, *Le Retour des Ancêtres*. Glave, *Vida, símbolos y batallas*; Thierry Saignes, "Ayllus, mercado y coacción colonial: el reto de las migraciones internas en Charcas (siglo XVII)" in *La participación indígena en los mercados surandinos: estrategias y reproducción social, siglos XVI a XX*, ed. Olivia Harris et al. (La Paz: CERES, 1987), pp. 111–58; Herbert S. Klein, *Haciendas and Ayllus: Rural Society in the Bolivian Andes in the Eighteenth and Nineteenth Centuries* (Stanford: Stanford University Press, 1993).

3 Juan de Betanzos, *Narrative of the Incas* [155?], trans. by Roland Hamilton and Dana Buchman (Austin: University of Texas Press, 1996), pp. 13–14. For a more imperial account, Inca Garcilaso de la Vega, *Royal Commentaries of the Incas and General History of Peru*, trans. by Harold V. Livermore (Austin: University of Texas Press, 1994), pp. 40–9.

4 Betanzos, *Narrative*, pp. 19–20, and Inca Garcilaso, *Royal Commentaries*, pp. 43–5, for differing accounts.

5 For historical readings, Catherine J. Julien, *Reading Inca History* (Iowa City: University of Iowa Press, 2000); John H. Rowe, "Inca Culture at the Time of the Spanish Conquest," in *The Handbook of South American Indians*, ed. Julian Steward, vol. II (Washington, DC: U.S. Government Printing Office, 1946), pp. 185–330; and María Rostworowski de Diez Canseco, *History of the Inca Realm*, trans. by Harry B. Iceland (Cambridge: Cambridge University Press, 1999); versus R. Tom Zuidema, *The Ceque System of Cusco: The Social Organization of the Capital of the Inca* (Leyden: E. J. Brill, 1964); Pierre Duviols, "La dinastía de los Incas: Monarquía o diarquía?" *Journal de la Société des Américanistes* 66 (1979): 67–83.

Table 1.1. *Inca Sovereigns*

Inca Ruler	Reign – 1[a]	Reign – 2[b]	Panaca/Ayllu[c]
Manco Capac	Mythical	To 1107	Chima
Sinchi Roca	Mythical	To 1136	Rauraua
Lloque Yupanqui	Mythical	To 1171	Hahuanina
Capac Yupanqui	Mythical	To 1211[d]	Apu Mayta
Mayta Capac	Unknown	To 1252[d]	Usca Mayta
Inca Roca	Unknown	To 1303	Vicaquirau
Yahuar Huacac	Unknown	To 1323[e]	Ailli [Aucaylli]
Viracocha	To 1438	To 1373	Çocço [Sucso]
Inca Pachacutec	1438–71	To 1423	Inca [joint]
Inca Yupanqui		To 1453	Inca [joint]
Tupac Inca Yupanqui	1471–93	To 1483	Capac
Huayna Capac	1493–1528	To 1523	Tumipampa
Huascar	1528–32	To 1528[e]	Huascar
Atahuallpa	1532–3	To 1533	

[a] Years of Reign – 1 are from Susan A. Niles, *Callachaca: Style and Status in an Inca Community* (Iowa City: University of Iowa Press, 1987), p. 7, using modifications to John Rowe's chronology in *An Introduction to the Archaeology of Cuzco* (Cambridge, MA: Peabody Museum, 1944).

[b] Years of Reign – 2 are from Hipólito Unanue, *Guía política, eclesiástica, y militar del virreinato del Perú* [1793], ed. José Durand (Lima: COFIDE, 1985), p. x.

[c] The order and panaca names are from Inca Garcilaso, *Royal Commentaries*, p. 626; this was the order used by the eighteenth-century Inca Cabildo.

[d] Unanue switches the order of Mayta Capac and Capac Yupanqui.

[e] Overthrow, not death.

all accounts link a dozen or so ayllus (generally referred to as *panacas*) as "descendants" of Manco Capac and his offspring, with each new "monarch" establishing his own panaca (Table 1.1). This organization was recorded by sixteenth-century Spanish observers in terms of unified kingship and dynastic succession, and then definitively transformed into a four-century dynasty of twelve rulers by Inca Garcilaso de la Vega in the early 1600s. While over the past decades scholars have agreed that Viracocha, Pachacutec, Tupac Yupanqui, and Huayna Capac were historical rulers, accounts of earlier Inca history are generally viewed as largely mythic. In contrast, the eighteenth-century inhabitants of Cusco – Indian and Spanish – accepted Inca Garcilaso's account and viewed their political history in Spanish monarchic terms.

In any event, by the early 1400s, these panacas that descended from Manco Capac (later referred to as the "Incas by blood") had come to dominate dozens of other ayllus within fifty miles of Cusco (collectively, the "Incas by privilege") through intermarriage, alliances, and warfare. Inca Garcilaso described this confederation and its members through the use of earplugs.

While the leaders of the Incas by blood wore enormous gold earplugs, for other groups " . . . [t]here was a limitation as to the size of the hole . . . and they were to wear different objects as ear-plugs according to their various names and provinces. . . . "[6] The superiority and dominion of the Incas by blood within their Huatanay heartland were performed each year during Capac Raymi, the "rich" or "principal" festival, when all but the Incas by blood were ritually driven from Cusco, forbidden to return until the completion of the holiday.[7]

The imperial expansion of the fifteenth and early sixteenth centuries extended the rule of Cusco throughout the Andes and the coastal valleys, over a population of perhaps ten million.[8] From countless subject societies the Incas received tribute, largely demanded and understood in terms of labor.[9] Tributary societies provided the Incas with their porters and soldiers, and the people who built and maintained Inca settlements and the extraordinary imperial road system. The Andean masses worked the lands of the Incas, scattered throughout the empire; they supplied the hundreds of thousands of llamas essential to Inca military campaigns; and they produced the wool and cloth that were the staple products of the Andes. The organization of exchange and the nature of political authority in the Inca Andes have long been the subject of academic interest.[10] Such scholarship has exposed the complexity of the imperial Inca economy, but it has underscored its reliance on exchange through tribute and reciprocal gifting.

The Incas sought to centralize their rule, directing the wealth of the empire to themselves and to Cusco – as the number of imperial projects around the city testifies.[11] But there were insurmountable barriers to the penetration of Inca authority and culture deep into all of their subject societies: the ruggedness of the terrain, the absence of draft animals, and the illiteracy of Andean civilization, all hindered the Incas' efforts to fashion a world with Cusco at its center. Moreover, the process by which the Incas extended their control had its own complex history, and the extent to which Inca rule provoked the reorganization of their subject societies varied enormously.[12] Whole communities were moved across the empire to form frontier colonies (and shatter rival confederations), and thousands

---

6 Brian S. Bauer, *The Development of the Inca State* (Austin: University of Texas Press, 1992), pp. 29–30, pp. 18–35 for Incas by privilege.

7 Bernabé Cobo, *Inca Religion and Customs* [1653], trans. by Roland Hamilton (Austin: University of Texas Press, 1990), pp. 126–34.

8 Terence N. D'Altroy, *The Incas* (Oxford: Blackwell, 2002) and Rostworowski, *History*.

9 John V. Murra, *The Economic Organization of the Inka State* (Greenwich, CT: JAI Press, 1980), pp. 89–119.

10 D'Altroy, *The Incas*, pp. 204, 249–62 for a synthesis of the sizable literature.

11 John Hyslop, *Inka Settlement Planning* (Austin: University of Texas Press, 1990), pp. 29–68.

12 D'Altroy, *Provincial Power*, pp. 16–17, and *The Incas*, pp. 231–62.

of tributaries were resettled near Cusco to provide labor for the imperial elite.[13] Other ethnic ayllus remained intact, but were transformed into tributary societies. At the same time, with the Incas constituting just a small percentage of the empire's population, for many communities the Inca presence remained removed from daily life, acknowledged seasonally or yearly by dispatching tribute to the Incas' provincial centers.

To maintain authority over this far-flung empire the Incas relied on force, but they also ushered in a *pax incaica*, facilitating exchange and spurring population growth, and across the Andes they promoted a worldview that placed Cusco at the center and the Incas above other peoples.[14] The Incas often let stand the rulers of societies that accepted their suzerainty, incorporating them into the imperial elite by receiving their daughters as tribute, often redistributing them, and Inca nobles, as spouses to other non-Inca elites.[15] The result was the creation of hybrid Inca lineages within the ruling groups of subject societies, along with secondary hybrid lineages within the panacas of the Incas by blood. Materially, Inca imperialism relied on the flow of labor and goods to Cusco and to its expansionist enterprise; politically, it required a return flow of Inca royalty to create these new provincial elites and forge them into a vast kin empire, presided over by the Cusqueño ruler.

All sixteenth-century accounts stress the polygamy of the Inca elite, which expanded with the empire in the fifteenth century.[16] An Inca ruler's offspring formed their own royal kinship group, or panaca, controlling lands and tributary labor and venerating the mummy of the late ruler.[17] One son became the next ruler and established his own panaca; the need to provide for the ever-expanding panaca network thus fueled imperial expansion.[18] Marriage between the panacas, as well as with other groups in the empire, reinforced the ties of the ruling panaca to its Inca kin and the dominant groups throughout the Andes. This organization created its own internal conflicts. At the height of imperial ascendancy in the late fifteenth century, Pachacutec and Tupac Yupanqui closed the imperial elite by privileging

---

13 Franklin Pease, "The Formation of Tawantinsuyu: Mechanisms of Colonization and Relationship with Ethnic Groups" in *The Inca and Aztec States, 1400–1800: Anthropology and History*, ed. George A. Collier et al. (New York: Academic Press, 1982), pp. 173–98; Nathan Wachtel, "The *Mitimas* of the Cochabamba Valley: The Colonization Policy of Huayna Capac," in ibid., pp. 199–235; John H. Rowe, "What Kind of a Settlement Was Inca Cusco?" *Ñawpa Pacha* 5 (Berkeley, 1967): 59–76.

14 D'Altroy, *The Incas*, pp. 141–76.

15 Pilar Alberti Manzanares, "La influencia económica y política de las acllacuna en el incanato" *Revista de Indias* 45:176 (1985): 557–85; Pease, *Curacas*, pp. 17–31 and 110–21; Silverblatt, *Moon*, pp. 80–108.

16 Bernabé Cobo, *History of the Inca Empire* [1653], trans. by Roland Hamilton (Austin: University of Texas Press, 1979), p. 122; also Betanzos, *Narrative*, pp. 17–22.

17 Such was the practice under the imperial Incas; how the earlier panacas formed is not clear. Julien, *Reading Inca History*, p. 38; Rowe, "Inca Culture," p. 202.

18 D'Altroy, *The Incas*, pp. 86–108.

"capac" children, those descended from Manco Capac through both maternal and paternal lines.[19] While this excluded from imperial succession those
born to the Inca ruler and non-capac women, it permitted considerable competition and politicking among the Inca panacas as to which woman's son
would succeed. Tupac Yupanqui married his full sister, thereby avoiding this
problem; but Huayna Capac and his principal (sister)wife had no children.[20]
As a result, after Huayna Capac's death in the late 1520s a fratricidal civil war
broke out between two sons, Atahuallpa and Huascar, whose mothers came
from different panacas.[21] In 1532 Atahuallpa's troops destroyed Huascar's
near Cusco; Huascar was captured and the panacas that had sided with
him were slaughtered. Strikingly, this was not the history as it was known
in eighteenth-century Cusco; instead, following Inca Garcilaso's account,
Atahuallpa was understood as the "bastard" son of Huayna Capac and a
Quiteña princess (and thus not qualified to rule), who had waged war on
the Cusqueño royalty.[22] This colonial Cusqueño understanding of Incaness
stressed geography (the supremacy of Cusco) over inter-panaca politics.[23]

There could have been no more advantageous moment for foreign
invaders to arrive on Peru's shores. But if the Inca empire teetered on collapse as the Spanish alit at Tumbes, in the preceding century it had reworked
the Andes in ways that determined the evolution of colonial society. At the
local and provincial levels, Inca rule had contributed to greater social stratification, but it also maintained the basic ayllu structure of society. The Incas
had already forged an empire of ayllus, and the Spanish would continue.
The Spanish also inherited a tradition of imperial, tributary rule extremely
well established in the Andes, which they adopted, and adapted, to the
benefit of the crown and Spanish colonists. Finally, the Spanish would celebrate, indeed elevate, the role of the Incas as the "civilizers" of the Andes,
making claims of Inca ancestry symbolically potent in colonial society, and
contributing to the emergence of an anticolonial Inca utopianism.[24]

19 Julien, *Reading Inca History*, pp. 22–48 for marriage, lineage, and "capac" status; for arguments of
   sex-specific reckonings of Inca lineage, Floyd G. Lounsbury, "Some Aspects of the Inka Kinship
   System," in *Anthropological History of Andean Polities*, ed. John V. Murra et al. (Cambridge: Cambridge
   University Press, 1986) pp. 137–48.
20 Cobo, *History*, p. 121; Julien, *Reading Inca History*, pp. 39, 263–4.
21 According to Betanzos, Atahuallpa was a great-grandson of Pachacutec, and fully part of the Inca
   royalty (*Narrative*, p. 178). Rostworowski, *History*, pp. 110–25; Julien, *Reading Inca History*, p. 39;
   D'Altroy, *The Incas*, pp. 76–83.
22 Inca Garcilaso de la Vega, *Royal Commentaries*, pp. 608–24.
23 *Colección Documental del Bicentenario de la Revolución Emancipadora de Túpac Amaru*, ed. Luis Durand
   Flórez (Lima: Comisión Nacional del Bicentenario de la Rebelión Emancipadora de Túpac Amaru,
   1980) [hereafter CDBR], II, 243, for an eighteenth-century Inca noble's version (based on the
   Garcilaso account) of the Atahuallpa–Huayna Capac conflict.
24 Alberto Flores Galindo, *Buscando un Inca: identidad y utopía en los Andes*, 3rd edn (Lima: Editorial
   Horizonte, 1988); Burga, *Nacimiento*.

Spanish Conquest

The civil war was a catastrophe for Cusco, but it was the arrival of Francisco Pizarro and his cohort immediately following that brought catastrophe to the Andes. Encountering an empire riven by civil war, the Spanish soon shattered the Incas' imperial networks and plunged the Andes into anarchy. In 1532, they met Atahuallpa at Cajamarca, where they seized and held him for ransom; from captivity, Atahuallpa ordered the execution of Huascar. The ransom paid, the Spanish garroted Atahuallpa, leaving the Inca empire leaderless, and they encountered little opposition on their march to Cusco. Manco Inca (another of Huayna Capac's sons) then assumed the throne, although more in name than in fact, reigning as a puppet prince.[25] After a year, supported by a faction of Cusco's Incas, he orchestrated a siege of the city that dragged on for months, until Spanish and Indian reinforcements arrived from throughout Peru to battle Manco's forces – a reminder that, in 1536, many Andeans inclined toward the Spanish rather than the Incas.[26] Non-Inca groups in Cusco – especially the Chachapoya and Cañari – joined the Spanish, not Manco Inca; the Cañari *curaca*, Don Francisco Chilche, remained an implacable foe of the city's Inca royalty for the next decades.[27] These forces broke the siege and expelled Manco and his allies, who retreated to the remote site of Vilcabamba and established a new royal court.

The court at Vilcabamba prolonged the existence of an independent Inca entity for almost forty years. In 1545 Spaniards who had sought refuge there assassinated Manco Inca; his son Sayri Tupac succeeded him, married a granddaughter of Huascar, and reigned for thirteen years until he was induced to abandon Vilcabamba by royal deputies.[28] The Inca and his wife were baptized and retired to Yucay, an Inca community along the Vilcanota, twenty miles from Cusco; Sayri Tupac died there in 1560.[29] His half brother, Tito Cusi Yupanqui, refused to acknowledge Spanish sovereignty and ruled for ten years, dying shortly after he and his son converted to Christianity and began negotiations to acknowledge the Castilian crown. Tupac Amaru,

---

25 Since his mother was not part of the dynastic elite, Manco Inca's claim was weaker than those of Huascar and Atahuallpa, though not by Spanish succession practice. Julien, *Reading Inca History*, pp. 42–4.

26 Horacio H. Urteaga, *Relación del sitio del Cusco y principio de las guerras civiles del Perú hasta la muerte de Diego de Almagro, 1535–9* (Lima: Librería Gil, 1934); Burga, *Nacimiento*, p. 98; Stern, *Peru's Indian Peoples*, pp. 27–50.

27 Carolyn Dean, "Ethnic Conflict and Corpus Christi in Colonial Cuzco," *Colonial Latin American Review* 2:1–2 (1993): 93–120.

28 Luís A. Pardo, *El imperio de Vilcabamba: el reinado de los cuatro últimos Incas* (Cusco: Editorial Garcilaso, 1972).

29 Sayri Tupac received *encomiendas* worth roughly 15,000 pesos a year, which passed to his daughter, Ñusta Beatriz. José de la Puente Brunke, *Encomienda y encomenderos en el Perú: estudio social y político de una institución colonial* (Seville: Diputación Provincial, 1992), pp. 345, 350, 358–9, 373, 382.

Manco's youngest son, then assumed the Vilcabamba throne and ruled until 1572, when the viceroy Francisco de Toledo opted for war, and Tupac Amaru was captured and taken to Cusco. There, following his baptism, he was publicly executed.[30]

The execution of Tupac Amaru marked the end of the Vilcabamba Incas as anything but a politically potent memory. But despite its pretensions, Manco's house was never of more than regional importance. The retreat to the jungle had not resolved the two crises facing Inca imperial rule after Atahuallpa: the component parts of the empire had broken free of Cusco's grip and had no desire to return, and the various Inca lineages and panacas were divided among themselves. The consequences of the former were clear at the siege of Cusco, as provincial lords replaced their forced fealty to the Incas with a no less forced, but no less solid, fealty to the Spanish. Nathan Wachtel has coined the term "destructuration" to describe the collapse of Andean institutions and customs in the chaotic years of the sixteenth century, and it describes particularly well the fate of Inca rule.[31] The empire unraveled into the *señorios* and ethnic confederations that had been its raw material; these became the building blocks of the Spanish viceroyalty.[32] In many, ruling lineages of mixed Inca, local, and occasionally Spanish ancestry maintained authority, leaving much of Peru's colonial Indian elite somehow "Inca."[33] But these local lords no longer sent tribute to Cusco. Manco's court had an unequaled provenance, but the empire to which he laid claim no longer existed.

Nor did he enjoy the united support of Cusco's Incas. Many among the panacas did not rally behind their Vilcabamba cousins.[34] Instead, the surviving descendants of Manco Capac negotiated their own courses in the radically changed world of Andean politics. Paullu, another son of Huayna Capac, allied himself with the Spanish and founded a dynasty that rivaled Manco Inca's.[35] Paullu had children with various wives, but he and his principal wife, Mama Ussica, were baptized in 1543, as Cristobal and Catalina. Their son and heir, Carlos Inca, was educated with the sons of conquistadores, and married the daughter of Extremeño *hidalgos*.[36] Paullu

30 Pardo, *El imperio*, pp. 122–3.

31 Wachtel, *Vision*, pp. 85–139.

32 For Condesuyo, Catherine J. Julien, *Condesuyo: The Political Division of Territory under Inca and Spanish Rule* (Bonn: Seminar für Völkerkunde, Universität Bonn, 1991).

33 Rostworowski, *Señorios indígenas*, pp. 77–80; and Rafael Varón Gabai, *Curacas y encomenderos: acomodamiento nativo en Huaraz, siglos XVI y XVII* (Lima: P. L. Villanueva, 1980), p. 45.

34 Charles Gibson, *The Inca Concept of Sovereignty and the Spanish Administration in Peru* (Austin: University of Texas Press, 1948), pp. 71–87.

35 Although Paullu's mother was not Inca; Julien, *Reading Inca History*, 43–5. For Cristobal Paullu Ynga's line, Temple Dunbar, "Don Carlos Inca."

36 Ibid., p. 155.

and Carlos held court in the compound of Colcampata; the area became Cusco's San Cristóbal parish, its church erected by Paullu in honor of his patron.[37] The crown granted Paullu *encomiendas* yielding 9,000 pesos a year in the 1560s, which passed to Carlos on his father's death.[38] The only other Inca to enjoy such a pension was Sayri Tupac, and following his death, Colcampata became the center of what remained of Cusco's panacas.

Those panacas were powerful in their own right, and their members sought to preserve or improve their positions by allying with the Spanish. Among Huayna Capac's close cousins, leading men of Capac panaca supported the conquistadores against the pretensions of Vilcabamba.[39] They were joined by nobles of other panacas, as well as by Incas by privilege and provincial, hybrid dynasties.[40] More than a century later Don Juan Guachaca, from the province of Aymaraes, proudly noted in his proof of nobility that his forebear, the cacique Don Francisco Supayque Caqui, "was one of the first that gave obedience to His Majesty in the conquest of this kingdom."[41] This varied indigenous elite was no longer politically united behind the Inca ruler. Imperial Inca rule never recovered from Atahuallpa and Huascar's war, and after the 1530s the Incas – both the imperial networks and the ethnic confederation of Cusco – ceased to constitute a unified group or locus of power in the Andes. The result was the collapse of the Incas' tributary system, as Indian lords and Spanish warriors sought to create their own fiefdoms and the former Inca realms slid into decades of anarchic decentralization.

The Spaniards were themselves riven by faction. Open warfare broke out between the Pizarro brothers and Diego Almagro in 1538; Almagro was killed, but in 1541 Francisco Pizarro was assassinated by an *almagrista*. Now under Gonzalo, the Pizarro forces won the renewed fighting. At this point, the crown tried to assert its dominion by restricting the privileges of its American vassals, provoking them into a rebellion (led by Gonzalo) against the first viceroy, who died in battle in 1546. The president of the newly founded Audiencia of Lima then waged war against Pizarro, defeating him in 1548 and beheading him the next day in Lima's main plaza. The second viceroy's arrival in 1550 brought little respite, as he died (unusually, of

---

37 Ibid., pp. 143–53; Víctor Angles Vargas, *Historia del Cusco (Cusco Colonial)* (Lima: Industrial Gráfica, 1975), II, 510–15.

38 Puente Brunke, *Encomienda*, pp. 358, 364, 371, 381.

39 Francisco de Xérez, *Verdadera relación de la conquista del Perú* [153?] (Madrid: Historia 16, 1985), p. 142 and n218 (by Concepción Bravo Guerreira, ed.); AGN, DI, Exp. 413 (1785).

40 Steve J. Stern, "The Rise and Fall of Indian–White Alliances: A Regional View of 'Conquest' History," *Hispanic American Historical Review* 61:3 (August 1981): 461–72; Spalding, *Huarochirí*, pp. 116–23; Varón Gabai, *Curacas y Encomenderos*, pp. 44–94; Rostworowski, *Señoríos indígenas*, p. 51.

41 The 1786 *probanza* of Don Pedro Nolasco Aronis; ARC, INT, RH, Leg. 203 (1796). Also ARC, INT, RH, Leg. 173 (1785), for the Guamantica nobility claim.

natural causes) soon after. The last *encomendero* rebellion, led by Francisco Hernández Girón, broke out in 1553; it was suppressed and Girón's head followed Gonzalo Pizarro's onto a pole in the middle of Lima.[42]

Fueling both the conquistadores' internecine violence and their rebellions against the crown was the loot of conquest, in particular, the labor and tribute of the people of the Andes. In the 1530s and 1540s, the Spanish victors fought over the grants of Indian communities made by the crown and its officers as a reward to deserving individuals. Literally the "entrusting" of a group of Indians (from an ayllu to a province) to an individual who became responsible for their Christianization, an encomienda brought with it the right to "customary" tribute.[43] Highland Peru had hundreds of encomiendas, but there were not enough to satisfy all aspirants, provoking conflict among the Spanish within a decade. While the conquistadores fought among themselves to win the rewards of the encomienda system, by the 1540s that system was the subject of widespread attack in Spain and America. The population of Spanish America plummeted in the sixteenth century. If modern historians place most of the blame on disease, contemporaries attributed it to the abusive rule of both encomenderos and native elites. From 1540 on, criticism by priests and bureaucrats helped propel the crown to reorganize the encomienda by limiting grants to two generations.[44] The Habsburgs' determination in the face of powerful resistance also owed much to their opposition to the emergence of hereditary, feudal lords in their rich American possessions. The conflict would determine whether Peru would be integrated into the Castilian realms as a series of private fiefdoms or as a single administrative entity run by a crown-appointed bureaucratic elite.[45] It was a battle between conquistadores seeking to reproduce the seigniorial authority awarded to the heroes of the *reconquista* and Europe's first great state-building monarchy. The Habsburgs triumphed. Considerable wrangling followed the tumults of the 1550s, but by the

---

42 Diego de Esquivel y Navia, *Noticias cronológicas de la gran ciudad del Cusco*, ed. Félix Denegri Luna (Lima: Banco Wiese, 1980), I, 175.

43 For the Peruvian *encomienda*, Puente Bunke, *Encomienda*; also, Spalding, *Huarochirí*, pp. 124–64; Silvio Zavala, *El servicio personal de los indios en el Perú, extractos del siglo xvi* (Mexico: Colegio de México, 1978), I, 3–61; James Lockhart, *Spanish Peru, 1532–60: A Colonial Society* (Madison: University of Wisconsin Press, 1968), pp. 11–33; and Burga, *De la encomienda*, pp. 83–102.

44 Especially Bartolomé de Las Casas' *Brevísima relación de la destrucción de las Indias* (Madrid: Sarpe, 1985); for Peru, Fray Bartolomé de la Vega, "Memorial al Real Consejo de Indias sobre los agravios que reciben los Indios del Perú," in *Nueva colección de documentos inéditos para la historia de España y sus Indios*, ed. Francisco de Zabálburu (Madrid, 1890–8), VI, 106–31.

45 Guillermo Lohmann Villena, *Las ideas jurídico-políticas en la rebelión de Gonzalo Pizarro: La tramoya doctrinal del levantamiento contra las Leyes Nuevas en el Perú* (Valladolid: Casa-Museo del Colón y Seminario Americanista, Universidad de Valladolid, 1977), pp. 40–63; Burga, *Nacimiento*, pp. 94–5.

1570s the crown had limited the duration of encomiendas.[46] Some were renewed, but as grants lapsed the crown took over the religious instruction, and the tribute, of Indian communities. By 1640 the number of encomiendas within the jurisdiction of Cusco had fallen from a high of nearly 200 to just 104; in 1720 there were a scant 44.[47]

The Political Economy of the Indian Republic

The defeat of the encomendero rebellions allowed the crown to assert its authority over the Andes. In the second half of the century royal officials (particularly under Viceroy Toledo) aggressively reworked basic structures of Inca imperialism, and of Andean civilization more generally, both to create a colonial, indigenous society and to define its relation to the crown. Despite massive structural transformations in the seventeenth century and a new series of reforms under the Bourbons in the eighteenth century, the foundations of this order would perdure until the early nineteenth century. The physical "reduction" of much of the native population into pueblos, and the erection of a *república de indios* as their legal space, defined the political and administrative structures of indigenous society for the remainder of the colonial period (and beyond).[48] Overwhelmingly, Peru's indigenous peoples were vassals of the crown, and royal policy tried to limit the jurisdiction and authority of private Spaniards over them. Indian commoners instead came under the rule of royal governors, parish priests, and Indian lords, and they performed their vassalage to the Castilian king through the payment of tribute.

In return, native Andeans were entitled to royal protection, which in the Andes extended to their souls as well as their lives. Habsburg reformers found strong evidence of Andean barbarity in the idolatry, sacrifice, and polygamy at the heart of Andean life, and in the perceived despotism of Andean social organization. Charles I and Philip II took seriously their obligation to save the souls of their Indian vassals and move them from barbarity to civility. At the same time, in the preceding decades, Spanish legists had developed strong defenses of the political and cultural

---

46 Spalding, *Huarochirí*, pp. 142–58; and Marvin Goldwert, "La lucha por la perpetuidad de las encomiendas en el Perú virreinal (1550–1600)," *Revista Histórica* 22 (Lima, 1955–6): 350–60, and ibid., 23 (Lima, 1957–8): 207–20.

47 Puente Brunke, *Encomienda*, pp. 95–105, 141, 247–74, 305. The average Cusco *encomienda* paid about 300 pesos annually in the late 1600s. Donald Gibbs, *Cuzco, 1680–1710: An Andean City Seen through Its Economic Activities* (Ph.D. diss., University of Texas, Austin, 1979), pp. 158–61.

48 Throughout this work, I use "pueblo" to mean "pueblo de indios," or "reducción": the villages or towns founded as part of the Toledan reductions that became the basic unit of indigenous society, at least as it appears in the archival record.

autonomy of subject societies.[49] Insofar as they did not violate natural law, the laws of indigenous American societies remained valid and the refusal to recognize them constituted tyranny. In particular this posed few problems, as Spaniards happily viewed Andean customs and laws they deemed problematic as counter to natural law. However, the juridical debates on imperialism had produced a general understanding of "just" colonial rule, which included a political and economic space inhabited by native Andeans and characterized by relative local autonomy.

That space was the *república de indios,* enshrined by legislation in the late 1500s. The Indian republic was a legal, not geographical, space: bilateral Indian parentage placed one under its laws and privileges, and Spaniards and Indians living next to each other were in their respective *res publicae.* Nonetheless, central to the division of Peru into two ethnic republics was an attempt to segregate the two physically. In the late sixteenth century thousands of *pueblos de indios*, modeled on the Castilian municipality, were created by the "reduction," or resettlement, of ayllus into larger communities.[50] Their stated goal was "... so that the Indians be instructed in the sainted Catholic faith and evangelical law and forgetting the errors of their ancient rites and ceremonies live in good order and polity ... [they] be reduced to pueblos and that they not live divided and separated by mountains and valleys, depriving themselves of all spiritual and temporal benefice."[51] These Indian pueblos were an enormous innovation in the organization of Andean societies, imposing on them Castilian institutions of government and religion. The extent to which the reductions met their goals of creating viable Indian municipalities, introducing orthodox Catholicism, and improving royal administration has been the subject of considerable inquiry.[52] But the Toledan reforms did make the Indian pueblo a legal reality in the Andes, and as such it had great impact on the Indian republic.

The Indian pueblo was defined as exclusively Indian. Priests, of course, were at its heart (or at least of the parish, which often had several pueblos), and were active in local politics. But laws forbade mestizos, mulattos, and private Spaniards from settling in Indian communities.[53] Certainly these laws went unenforced. Spanish merchants, landowners, and miners

49 María Lourdes Redondo Redondo, *Utopia vitoriana y realidad indiana* (Madrid: Fundación Universitaria Española, 1992), pp. 135–55; Anthony Pagden, *The Fall of Natural Man: The American Indian and the Origins of Comparative Ethnology* (Cambridge: Cambridge University Press, 1986), pp. 119–45.

50 Alejandro Malaga Medina, "Las reducciones en el Perú (1532–1600)," *Historia y Cultura* 8 (Lima, 1974): 141–72.

51 *Recopilación de Leyes de los Reynos de las Indias, mandadas imprimir y publicar por la magestad católica del Rey Don Carlos II* (Madrid: Ibarra, 1791), Vol. II, Book VI, Title III, Law 1.

52 Spalding, *Huarochirí*, pp. 178–81, 214–6; Wightman, *Indigenous Migration*, pp. 9–44; Choque Canqui, *Sociedad*, pp. 53–86; Glave, *Vida, símbolos*, pp. 50–6.

53 *Recopilación*, Book VI, Title III, Laws 21–5.

settled around the town plazas, while impoverished mestizos rented bits of the Indian commons, and their role in the pueblo was an endless source of conflict. But even in the eighteenth century most pueblos remained overwhelmingly Indian; more importantly, these laws produced an ideal of ethnic political division and local Indian autonomy that defined colonial Andean society.

The embodiment of this autonomy, and of the municipality, was to be the *cabildo* (or town council), while one or two *alcaldes* and two to four *regidores*, elected annually, were, rather sweepingly, responsible for "the government of the pueblos."[54] Information from eighteenth-century court cases makes it clear that the actual organization of pueblo government often bore faint resemblance to this idealized form.[55] However, the fact that the Indian pueblo was self-governing within a limited jurisdiction was an unchallenged principle of Spanish colonial rule. Materially, the most important aspect of this rule was the division of the pueblo's common land among its members, and these pueblos (and their ayllus) controlled most of the land in the Indian republic.[56] Thus, from its foundation the Indian pueblo was central to the legal and social definition of Peru's Indians as individuals and households. As such, it formed a principal arena for conflict, competition, and organization within Indian Peru.

In undertaking the "reduction" policy, Spanish reformers viewed themselves as acting on a blank slate: introducing the true faith to those who had lived in invincible ignorance and reducing them to "live politically."[57] In fact, the people of the Andes had lived politically for millenia, and the Indian pueblo was imposed on the varied and layered forms of ayllu association.[58] All sixteenth-century commentators on Andean society realized the centrality of the ayllu in the Andes. Their commitment to respecting Andean custom insofar as it followed natural law prevented any frontal assault on this building block of Andean society. Numerous aspects of the ayllu did meet with condemnation: the polygamy of ayllu leaders and the veneration of mummified ancestors and indigenous deities.[59] The assault on these central practices of ayllu life transformed the ayllu, reworking its internal relationships of kinship and marriage, so that the colonial ayllu differed

54 *Recopilación*, Book VI, Title III, Law 16; for pueblo government, Tomás de Ballesteros, *Tomo primero de las ordenanzas del Perú* (Lima: Francisco Sobrino y Bados, 1752), Book II, Title II; Spalding, *Huarochirí*, pp. 216–20.

55 Lockhart found that the *alcalde* and *regidor* were far more important in central Mexican communities than was the *cabildo*; Lockhart, *The Nahuas*, pp. 35–43. The rarity of mentions of *cabildos*, and the frequency of *alcaldes*, suggest a similar pattern in southern Peru.

56 Ballesteros, *Ordenanzas*, Book II, Titles VII and IX; *Recopilación*, Book VI, Title III, Law 8.

57 For vincible and invincible ignorance, Pagden, *Fall*, p. 38.

58 Tristan Platt, "Mirrors and Maize: The concept of *Yanantin* among the Macha of Bolivia" in *Anthropological History of Andean Polities*, pp. 228–59, for the layered forms of the ayllu.

59 Spalding, *Huarochirí*, p. 214.

considerably from its preconquest forebear. However, as a corporation the ayllu retained its importance, incorporated into, rather than displaced by, the pueblo.[60]

Most pueblos were composed of several ayllus, each a distinct neighborhood or hamlet with its own corporate identity and lands.[61] However, ayllu organization was not the object of specific legislation, allowing great variety. The thousands of ayllus ranged in size from two or three compounds to communities of several hundred people with complex internal hierarchies.[62] Moreover, rights of possession were largely customary. Ayllus were small enough to be wiped out in an epidemic, emptied by emigration, or absorbed by a larger, neighboring ayllu; in such cases the lands could be absorbed by other ayllus, or declared vacant and sold by the crown. But from its creation the Andean *pueblo de indios* was understood as a collection of ayllus. The extent to which the pueblo subsumed the ayllu varied. In the Titicaca basin, the moiety often became the highest unit of indigenous political organization, reproducing the duality of many Andean societies within the context of the pueblo. Around Cusco, most ayllus had their own caciques, in some cases coming under the authority of the pueblo's *cacique principal*, while in others there was no overarching pueblo authority. Nor was the relationship between a pueblo's ayllus fixed, instead forming a structural point of tension. Indeed, these relations were often the objects of royal justice, as ayllus – and their elites – took intrapueblo grievances to the courts. Whether conducted in front of a royal judge or during pueblo celebrations, the negotiations and conflicts between pueblos' constituent ayllus formed a central part of the political histories of the bishopric's Indian republic.

Officially, these were the only political histories of the colonial Indian republic. For as Toledo sought to urbanize the scattered Indian populations of the Andes through the reductions, he also waged an aggressive campaign against the larger polities (the "maximal ayllus") that had bound discrete ayllu settlements together. Preconquest provincial polities were understood simply as administrative units of the Inca empire, and viceregal governors carved new provinces from their territories. The crown recognized no Indian political unit above the pueblo: larger forms of association and administration fell within Spanish, not Indian, Peru.

The Incas of Cusco suffered enormously from this official destructuration. The chaos of the 1530s stripped them of their empire, but the Incas

---

60 Toledo made clear that alcaldes and regidores should be chosen from the constituent ayllus, and that no one ayllu should dominate the cabildo. Ballesteros, *Ordenanzas*, Book II, Title II, Law 8.

61 *Recopilación*, Book VI, Title III, Law 9; although Toledo decreed that lands could be removed: Ballesteros, *Ordenanzas*, Book II, Title II, Law 37.

62 *Cuzco 1689, Documentos: Economía y sociedad en el sur andino*, ed. Horacio Villanueva Urteaga (Cusco: Centro Bartolomé de Las Casas, 1982); Table 2.2 for sources for eighteenth-century ayllus.

remained the dominant indigenous group around Cusco. The rift between Manco's line and Paullu's further divided them, but the Incas' survival as a complex kin-based polity continued into the 1570s. The 1571 festivities for the baptism of Melchor Carlos Ynga – a grandson of Paullu who described himself as "the last legitimate descendant, recognized as such, of the emperor Huayna Capac" – show the extent of Inca authority.[63] One Spanish soldier described the communities whose nobles had come to venerate the royal heir: ". . . all of the Yngas of the parishes of Cusco, Pacarectambo, Araypalpa, Colcha, Cucharipampa, Pampacuchu, Pacopata, Accha, Pilpinto, Pocoray, Huaihuacunca, Parcoos, Juquissana, Urcos, Andaguaylillas, Oropesa, San Gerónimo, San Sebastián, Anta, Pucyura, Conchacalla, Xaquissahuana, Marco, Equeque, Zurite, Limatambo, Maras, Tambo, Urubamba, Yucay, Chinchero, Urcos, Palpa, Pisac, and San Salvador, all of which are pueblos that the Incas inhabit. . . ."[64] It is a respectable list, but just the principal settlements within thirty or forty miles of Cusco – more a city-state than an empire. And Paullu and Carlos's attempts to claim dynastic rule over even that small area soon met with defeat.

When Toledo arrived in Cusco in 1571, the city's encomenderos and Inca nobility received him in splendor.[65] Paullu and Carlos Ynga had sworn fealty to Charles and Philip; Paullu had named his son after their Castilian lord. Toledo's arrival must have brought hopes that he would recognize this line of Huayna Capac's descendants over their troublesome kin in Vilcabamba. Instead, when the viceroy launched the military campaign against Vilcabamba he accused Carlos Ynga's circle of *lese majesté* for styling themselves "*señores de la tierra*," and (improbably) of allying with Vilcabamba.[66] Toledo ordered the exile of Paullu's line to Mexico and the forfeiture of their encomiendas, and the exile of other Inca notables to Arequipa. These provisions were overturned; Toledo was reprimanded for ignoring the royal *fuero* of the Paullu Yngas, and part of Paullu's encomienda was returned to Carlos.[67]

Nonetheless, the upheaval of the 1570s ended any possibility that the Spanish crown might recognize its Inca vassals as the lords of Indian Cusco. The rejection of Inca pretensions was reinforced by the removal from Cusco of those with the clearest claim to the throne. Sayri Tupac's daughter, Ñusta Beatriz, was married to Martín García Loyola (corregidor of Cusco and a nephew of St. Ignatius); after their deaths their daughter, Lorenza Ñusta de

63 Temple Dunbar, "Don Carlos Inca," p. 162. In fact, Melchor's claim was much more problematic; Julien, *Reading Inca History*, pp. 42–7.
64 Ocampo Conejero, quoted in Temple Dunbar "Don Carlos Inca," p. 163.
65 Angles Vargas, *Historia*, I, 44–57.
66 Temple Dunbar "Don Carlos Inca," p. 170–7.
67 Pardo, *El imperio*, pp. 137–8.

Loyola, was ordered to Spain by the king and married to Juan de Borja, further binding the Jesuits and the Incas.[68] The scion of Paullu's line, Melchor Carlos Ynga, was sent to Spain in 1601, where he took up residence at the court in Valladolid; he died in Seville in the next decade.[69] Hundreds of Inca royals and nobles remained in Cusco, but without the focal point of a recognized successor. As a result the Incas were reworked into a regional noble caste that dominated the Indian pueblos in the area of the Inca heartland, but among whom there was no clear hierarchy or authority binding these communities into a larger, recognized polity.

This disintegration of the Incas' dominion had its parallel throughout the highlands. To the south in the Titicaca basin, the Aymara señorios became colonial provinces ruled by Spanish governors and composed of anywhere from a half-dozen to twenty Indian parishes. The long-distance colonies that the most powerful of these señorios had held gradually acquired independence and became parts of localized, autonomous pueblos.[70] Within the señorios, individual pueblos were no longer formally bound into larger political confederations recognized as the constituent parts of the empire. To be sure, the reductions and the refusal to recognize larger Indian polities did not end extralocal bonds within Indian society. Larger ethnic groups successfully reproduced themselves; the lack of recognition did not constitute open opposition.[71] But the reproduction of complex ethnic polities grew increasingly exceptional as the pueblo became the new maximal political unit of Indian society, and all government beyond it lay in the Spanish republic.[72] The pueblo thus defined the basic political relations of indigenous society under Spanish rule.

The reductions were but one part of the reforms of the late sixteenth century. The Habsburgs were committed to Christianizing the Andes and introducing their version of civilization, but they never proposed to do so at a loss. Castile's Andean realms turned a spectacular profit for their peninsular sovereigns: from the mid-1500s, the mines of Upper Peru produced a flood of silver, much of which found its way to royal coffers.[73] This production, and much of the crown's income from the Andes, depended on

---

68 Angles Vargas, *Historia*, I, 397. For Beatriz's will, ARC, BE, III, 145–54.

69 ARC, BE, III, 587–622.

70 Larson, *Cochabamba*, pp. 40–3.

71 For indigenous societies (or ethnic, "maximal" ayllus) beyond the pueblo, Glave, *Vida, símbolos* for Canas y Canchis; Rasnake, *Domination*, for the Yura of Potosí; Wachtel, *Le Retour*, for the Uru.

72 For the pueblo and identity, Penry, "Transformations," esp. pp. 311–58.

73 John J. TePaske and Herbert S. Klein, *The Royal Treasuries of the Spanish Empire in America*, I [Peru] and II [Upper Peru] (Durham: Duke University Press, 1982). For Potosí, Peter Bakewell, *Miners of the Red Mountain: Indian Labor in Potosí, 1545–1650* (Albuquerque: University of New Mexico

a reworked version of the Inca tributary economy. Tribute – in the form of a semiannual head tax, labor corvees, and the forced purchase of goods at inflated prices – would define the rural Andean economy until independence. The flow of money, labor, and goods from largely self-sufficient Indian societies supported the vast, thinly spread networks of bureaucracy and trade holding together Spanish Peru, and provided a sizable surplus for the peninsula.

Sixteenth-century legists stressed the tradition of tributary rule in the Inca empire and argued that the reforms made by Philip II redressed injustices in tribute collection, without violating the legitimate customs of indigenous society.[74] In particular, many of Toledo's advisors viewed the control of Andean lords, or curacas, over local and regional economies as tyrannical; many understood Andean society as having no concept of private property, with demands made arbitrarily of tributaries. Therefore, while tribute was maintained as the foundation of the Andean economy, ideally it was calculated on a per capita basis, with each adult male Indian tributary (under the age of fifty) owing defined amounts of cash and labor. For two and a half centuries, a great majority of adult Indian men in the Andes owed a handful of pesos to the crown twice a year. The per capita assessment for *originarios* (married men living in their native communities with access to communal land) varied by community, although it became increasingly standardized (at roughly eight pesos annually in the bishopric of Cusco) in the eighteenth century.[75] Ideally, this came to about one month's wages for unskilled labor.[76] *Forasteros*, who had left their native communities and had no set rights to communal land in their adopted ones, paid a lower tribute, creating incentives for internal migration that had an enormous impact on Andean society in the seventeenth century.[77]

Press, 1984); Jeffrey A. Cole, *The Potosí Mita: Compulsory Indian Labor in the Andes* (Stanford: Stanford University Press, 1985); and Enrique Tandeter, *Coacción y Mercado: La minería de la plata en el Potosí colonial, 1692–1826* (Cusco: Centro Bartolomé de Las Casas, 1992).

74 For example, Juan de Matienzo, *El gobierno del Perú* [1567], ed. with prologue by Guillermo Lohmann Villena (Lima-Paris, 1967), pp. 11–12.

75 Stern, *Peru's Indian Peoples*, pp. 81–2. In Chucuito province in the 1760s, Aymara *originarios* were universally assessed at 8 pesos, and *forasteros* at 5 pesos. However, the tribute of the Urus varied by pueblo, from .75 to 5.5 pesos. AGI, Charcas, Exp. 591. For eighteenth-century La Paz, Klein, *Haciendas*, pp. 62–74.

76 Unskilled urban laborers earned 2.5 reales a day in the late 1700s. ARC, INT, RH: Legs. 175 (1786), 190 (1790), and 206 (1798), for municipal construction accounts.

77 The category of "forastero" was further divided as colonial society and law grew more complex, but in the eighteenth century the parallel categories ("indios con tierras" and "indios sin tierras") restored the basic dichotomy. In the seventeenth century most forasteros owed tribute to the caciques of their native communities; later, they were matriculated in their communities of residence. Wightman, *Indigenous Migration*, pp. 82–8, 128–32; Sánchez-Albornoz, *Indios*, pp. 51–60; Klein, *Haciendas*, pp. 10–13.

Male Andean commoners also owed Spanish society another form of tribute: labor. *Mitas* – corvees modeled on Inca labor tribute – had been instituted in the 1530s across Peru to provide labor for cities and Spanish landowners, to staff the mails and maintain roads.[78] The mita was obligatory labor, but it was not unpaid. In an economy where markets and wage labor were recent transplants, the mitas funneled labor from self-sufficient ayllus to the creole economy of workhouses and haciendas, whose products allowed Spaniards to enter the viceroyalty's larger market economy. Mitas were essential to many parts of the Andean economy well into the seventeenth century, although they declined in importance by the eighteenth century.[79] The economic and social effects of these local mitas varied enormously by region. In the coca-growing regions of Paucartambo, the mitas to semitropical plantations were the bane of the highland pueblos on the mountain ridge above.[80] In contrast, in the temperate agricultural regions closer to Cusco, mitas were local phenomena, one of many means to bring agricultural labor from Indian villages to Spanish properties. They could arouse considerable opposition, but they also brought in cash needed to pay tribute.[81] The relation was well described in a 1689 report by the priest of Sangarará: "[t]o pay their tribute they leave to rent themselves to the haciendas, or to the city, or to the mines, and they pay them for a month of their work seven and a half pesos, which comes to two reales a day."[82] The underlying logic of the Spanish mita resembled the Inca: Indian commoners provided labor to imperial authorities and the ethnic elite. The Spanish crown simply monetized that relation, stimulating the market economy of creole Peru so that Indian tribute could be paid in silver and shipped across the Atlantic.

This stood in stark contrast to the highland provinces to the south and the west, where the mining mitas of Potosí and Huancavelica drew tributaries to work, in a seven-year rotation, in the silver and mercury mines. The scope of these mitas caused havoc along the altiplano: Potosí was to have 14,000 mitayos at any time, reduced to 4,000 after 1691.[83] Ayllus from as far as

---

78 Zavala, *El Servicio Personal*; Spalding, *Huarochirí*, pp. 164–91; Cole, *The Potosí Mita*; Bakewell, *Miners*, pp. 54–9, 81–118.

79 For the decline of the Quiteña *mita*, Powers, *Andean Journeys*, pp. 46–7, 103. Other local *mitas* remained heavy burdens; Spalding, *Huarochirí*, p. 185.

80 *Cuzco 1689*, p. 286.

81 ARC, COR, Prov., Civ., Leg. 74 (1772–5); and BNP, Man., C-2738 (1775) for complaints against Don Bernardo Gongora. Also, complaints against the Marquis of Valleumbroso; Stavig, *The World of Túpac Amaru*, p. 147.

82 *Cuzco 1689*, p. 168. Also ARC, INT, Gob., Leg. 131 (1785), for the dispute between a hacendado and the cacique of Lamay over payment for a labor corvee; and the will of Don Gregorio Mamani, ARC, NOT, Acuña, Leg. 10, 401 ff., December 6, 1774.

83 Bakewell, *Miners*, pp. 81–137; Cole, *The Potosí Mita* (pp. 73–6 for the size of seventeenth-century mita drafts); Tandeter, *Coacción*.

Quispicanchis – 500 miles distant – sent contingents. Here the mita became a central organizing relation of colonial society: Aymara societies effectively became tributaries of Potosí's mining elite.[84] But their unique economic position sheltered them from Spanish settlement and the emergence of a local Spanish economy, forces that would have a great impact on Cusco and its agricultural hinterland. Around Titicaca and on the Altiplano, the mita and high tribute rates required centralized authority and command of the local economy, leaving these communities deeply stratified and creating an exceptionally rich and powerful indigenous elite.

Mita-driven production at Potosí allowed the monetization of tribute (indeed, of the Andean economy), although the point at which tribute was converted from labor or goods to specie varied enormously and was often far above the level of the tributary household.[85] Although the personalization of tribute set up a legal ideal that served as a valuable weapon when communities (or Spanish officials) moved against caciques in the courts, in practice tribute remained a communal obligation.[86] The centrality of the ayllu in the Andean economy and the absence of strong rural markets meant that tribute moved from Indian society to the crown at the level of the ayllu or pueblo; the involvement of imperial officials in tribute collection stopped at the communal level. Tribute collectors were personally responsible for tribute, and they assessed their communities based on the total owed, not the ideal amount each individual should pay. Harvests of communal lands were set aside for tribute. Caciques collected wages for agricultural corvees directly from *hacendados* and used them for tribute; they marketed local production in distant cities. As it had been under the Incas, it was the lords of communities, rather than the tributaries in them, who ultimately paid tribute to imperial officials.

The Toledan reorganization of the tributary economy defined the basic flows of wealth in the colonial Andes. The Inca tributary system had channeled wealth and labor from subject societies to the Incas, and above all to Cusco. This changed in the sixteenth century. The Andes as a whole were invariably net contributors to the Spanish empire, above all through the royal fifth (the crown's share of all silver mined) and Indian tribute: over the centuries, tens of millions of pesos flowed from the highlands to Lima and on to Spain.[87] The burdens were not evenly distributed. A secondary tributary

---

84 Particularly through the *entero de plata* – cash payment to avoid mita service. Cole, *The Potosí Mita*, pp. 36–44, 125–6.

85 See Chapter 4, pp. 116–123, for the cacique's role between local production and the market. Spalding argues that in Huarochirí this was the province of Spaniards; *Huarochirí*, p. 162. For the mix of tribute in cash, goods, and labor in Huamanga, Stern, *Peru's Indian Peoples*, pp. 81–9.

86 Lawsuits against caciques invariably accused them of demanding tribute from men over fifty and adolescents (both technically exempt). See the case against Don Blas Quispe Uscamayta and Don Manuel Corimanya of Pucyura, ARC, INT, RH, Leg. 211 (1801), pp. 31–7.

87 Klein and TePaske, *The Royal Treasuries*, I and II.

flow occurred within the Andes, from the area of the mining mitas to Potosí. Finally, the tributary system funneled wealth and labor from Indian society to Spanish – not only at the imperial and regional levels, but also locally, as Spanish landowners, merchants, and officials benefited at the expense of the Indian population. The cumulative effect of all of these was to impoverish Indian society.

The Toledan tributary system also undermined the ideal of corporate governance in the pueblo. The organization of mitas and the collection of tribute presupposed officials at the village level. And because demands were made of households and communities with limited access to markets and wages, Spanish rule required a class of intermediaries between village and viceregal economies. In the chaotic days of the conquest the encomienda had awarded this crucial position to individual Spaniards. The conquistadores' civil wars made clear the need to establish royal authority and suppress private jurisdictions, but it is striking that the crown opposed the formation of a Spanish bureaucracy to organize the local material economy, in marked contrast to its creation of a Spanish ecclesiastical bureaucracy that controlled the spiritual economy. Instead, for two centuries after Toledo, Spanish officials held that the juncture between local and regional economies and the basic administration of the Indian village was the province of Indian society – in particular, the space of a reconstituted Indian elite.

Caciques and the Indian Nobility

Despite the "two republic" legal organization of the Spanish Andes, there was never any question of Spanish superiority, and as a whole the indigenous population was reduced to subaltern status. But both the organization of Spanish rule and the ideology of those who undertook the "reform" of Andean society required an elite stratum in the Indian republic, whose material and legal position set them apart and placed them at a critical juncture between Spanish and Indian Peru. Although somewhat fluid in its constitution, this Indian nobility comprised families who exercised authority and preserved wealth across generations – in some cases, from before the Spanish conquest to independence. Indian nobles owed their privileges to two tenets of Spanish rule: the Habsburg insistence that local rule of Indian pueblos remain in Indian hands, and the equally strong belief that societies were inherently hierarchical and naturally stratified into nobles and commoners. The intersection of these two commitments led to the placement of tribute collection with the cacique, rather than the Indian alcalde. A hispanicized Carib word, "cacique" referred to local Indian lords throughout Spanish America; in the Andes, the office was institutionalized through royal decrees in the sixteenth and early seventeenth centuries, but it had clear roots in the preconquest *curacazgo*, or ayllu lordship. Indeed, sixteenth- and seventeenth-century writers were as likely to use "curaca" as "cacique," but the latter term was standard by the time of the Bourbons.[88] Although common, the term was ill-defined in the colonial period, and remains so to this day, for two reasons – one a product of colonial law, the other of the complexity and variety of social organization in the Indian republic.

The colonial Andean cacique occupied a position of considerable authority in Indian society, but the nature of and limits to this authority were unclear. The two dozen laws dealing with caciques in the *Recopilación de leyes de las Indias* range from the sweepingly general to the very specific and do not in themselves constitute a definition of the cacique's powers or duties.[89] Indeed, the most important role of the cacique – that of tribute collector – scarcely appears in Title VII of Book VI (*On Caciques*): only that Spanish officials are to limit excessive tribute collection by caciques. The importance of the Title lies instead in its clear recognition of caciques and its efforts to establish the parameters of the cacique's role in his community. The Title forbade that caciques seize the lands occupied by their tributaries and ordered that caciques pay wages for work by tributaries on the cacique's private lands. The laws also placed the cacique outside of local justice, ordering that their complaints, as well as disputes over succession, be heard by royal courts, not provincial governors. As a whole, the Title recognized the existence of Indian lords and ordered that they not be abused by Spanish officials and not abuse their own tributaries.

Toledo further elaborated specifics of the *cacicazgo* in the 1570s, when he made clear his unease with this indigenous elite.[90] Caciques were to collect tribute, but only to place it in strong boxes, "without that it enter into [the cacique's] power."[91] The decrees emphasized the limits on caciques' authority over the pueblo economy and sought to ban any assessments of tributaries by caciques beyond royal tribute; they also stressed the cacique's responsibility for the Christianization, good conduct, and industriousness of his tributaries. Caciques could enforce corporal justice, above all in order to obtain tribute payment; they also had certain privileges for themselves and their eldest sons – principally the exemption from tribute and personal service.

Strikingly, at no point in the *Recopilación de las leyes* nor in the *Ordenanzas del Perú* is the relationship between caciques and alcaldes spelled out,

---

88 For reasons of consistency, I have used "cacique" throughout this book, unless quoting or referring to an instance in which "curaca" was used.

89 *Recopilación*, Book VI, Title 7; Díaz Rementería, *El cacique*, pp. 59–96; Spalding, *Huarochirí*, pp. 275–92.

90 Ballesteros, *Ordenanzas*, Book II, Title 6. Díaz Rementería, *El cacique*, pp. 59–65; and Spalding, *Huarochirí*, pp. 217–26.

91 Ballesteros, *Ordenanzas*, Book II, Title 6, Law 1.

beyond Toledo's insistence "that for the stated offices of alcalde, regidor, and the rest, . . . caciques not be chosen."[92] Implicit in the cacical legislation was the assumption that the Andes contained a hereditary ruling class, who had collected tribute under the Incas. But the organization of the Indian pueblo put forward in the *reducciones* called for local self-rule, respect for private property and personal freedom, and cabildo control over communal land. If enforced, these would undermine the cacique's ability to collect tribute, which often required resorting to legally questionable actions: seizing tributaries' property, jailing those who failed to pay, appropriating communal land and its harvests to cover the shortfall. On the other hand, a successful cacique acquired considerable control over the communal economy, undermining the authority and autonomy of other pueblo officials. The contradiction of the simultaneous establishment of both self-government and seigniorial rule created a central dynamics in the communal histories of Peru's Indian pueblos.

Just as colonial legislation left the extent of cacical authority ill-defined in theory, in practice the term "cacique" was applied to a wide array of offices. If caciques were "local" lords, what constituted the "locality" was by no means set. "Cacique" was a catchall title, referring to Indian officials who collected tribute from and presided over some basic social unit. Any term that includes both the college-educated hereditary ruler of a thousand-strong pueblo and the illiterate tribute collector of an ayllu with forty inhabitants seeks to impose uniformity on a wide array of offices, individuals, and communities. Indeed, the tension between the Andean ayllu and the Spanish pueblo is clear in the organization of the cacical class. Some ayllus had their own caciques; other caciques collected tribute from and presided over entire pueblos. Other pueblos had not only several ayllu caciques but also a "cacique principal," who took precedence and was the dominant force in the community's economy and political life. And some pueblos had independent ayllu or moiety caciques and no dominant governor. The complexity of social organization in the Indian republic – with thousands of ayllus existing in interrelations of dependence and autonomy – produced an equally complex cacical elite.

That there were "caciques principales" as well as "caciques" shows how aware people were of the complex relations within the *república de indios*. Many adjectives modify "cacique" in colonial documents, seeking to clarify and limit cacical authority, the cacique's position in local hierarchies, and claims to office.[93] A "cacique principal" might be described as a "cacique gobernador," suggesting both preeminence and authority that extended

---

92 Ibid., Book II, Title 1, Laws 5 and 6.
93 For *cacicazgo* nomenclature in seventeenth-century Cusco, Nada B. Hughes, "Poder y abuso: el cacicazgo de Lamay, siglo XVII," *Revista del Archivo Departmental del Cusco*, 14 (November, 1999): 61–2.

beyond the economic sphere of tribute collection. Conversely, others are referred to as "cacique cobrador," stressing the duties of tribute collection and implying a more limited role in communal governance. In the eighteenth century, still other terms – "segunda," "recaudador," and "curaca" – described officials who collected tribute from lesser ayllus, generally in situations where a "cacique principal" or "gobernador" presided over the larger community. Finally, caciques were variously described as proprietary, interim, or, by opponents, as "intruso." The first referred to those with hereditary claim to the office – the true aristocracy of the Indian republic. Interim caciques, in contrast, were appointed by the corregidor and, in theory, had no proprietary claim. In practice, the boundary between proprietary and interim cacicazgos could be a generation or simply a decade: a "cacique interino" of one document might present himself years later as "cacique proprietario" – while opponents might describe him as an intruder, someone whom the corregidor had appointed improperly.[94]

The fluidity and variety of cacical terminology expose the ambiguity of and the competition for authority in the colonial pueblo, as families and individuals sought to solidify control over the cacicazgo, while opponents described the community's ruler as a mere tribute collector, or an intruder. At the same time, the need to modify the term "cacique" in an effort to clarify claims to the office and limit its authority also indicates the near-universal acceptance of the cacique as an integral part of Indian society. The vagueness of the laws on these matters meant that there was an enormous variety between communities, so that beyond the most general sketches, the actual workings of cacical power and communal politics must be studied at the local level. However, the general recognition by the crown, that tribute collection at the local level was in the hands of caciques, constituted a bulwark of colonial Peru's Indian elites.

Equally important to Indian elites was the Spanish understanding that social status was ideally hereditary. Two deep-rooted beliefs about the nature of society and just rule enabled preconquest elites, and colonial newcomers, to reproduce their authority across generations, while tying them to the crown as the defender of their privileges: natural lordship (*señorio natural*) and nobility by birth (*hidalguía*). The first, with origins in medieval Castile, held that the rights of vassal lords could not be abrogated, except through their tyrannical actions or betrayal of the king.[95] Justifying the dispossession of the Incas' empire was not difficult, as Manco Inca at first accepted and

---

94 Don Eugenio Sinanyuca became "cacique interino" of Coporaque in 1768; his will refers to him as the "cacique proprietario." ARC, NOT, Vargas, Leg. 236, 357 ff., November 27, 1804.

95 Robert S. Chamberlain, "The Concept of the *Señor Natural* as Revealed by Castilian Law and Administrative Documents," *Hispanic American Historical Review* 19 (1939): 129–37; Díaz Rementería, *El cacique*, pp. 53–7.

then rejected Spanish sovereignty. But in the 1530s many Andean lords had joined the Spanish against the Incas, and much of Cusco's Inca royalty also swore fealty to Charles I after Manco's uprising. Just rule required that the Castilian king recognize the privileges and powers of these loyal vassals and their descendants.

Not all of the crown's officials felt obliged to respect the privileges of royalist Andean lords. Toledo moved against both the Vilcabamba Incas and their royalist cousins; Sarmiento provided a legal basis for this by arguing that curacas had been appointed by the Incas: as the officers of a tyrannical (and later rebel) government, they had no legitimate claim to their positions.[96] This view was transmitted to the crown, which from the late 1580s to 1614 demanded further information and ordered that "customary practice" be maintained.[97] Philip III finally set policy on July 19, 1614, decreeing that "since the provinces of Peru were discovered it has been ... the custom among the Indian caciques that the sons succeed the fathers in the cacicazgos, and my will is that the said custom be conserved and guarded."[98] In fact, it was not clear that such succession was the norm: an earlier decree had mentioned that cacicazgos "are inherited by succession from fathers to sons, brothers, and nearest relatives."[99] The decree of 1614 sought to hispanicize cacical succession. Although the passage of office from father to son did not become universal, its recognition as customary practice helped to cement cacical families' claims of hereditary authority. As Don Marcos Chillitupa Pumaguallpa averred in an early nineteenth-century dispute over the cacicazgos of Oropesa, "the rights of the *cacicazgos* by blood have the force and entail of the *mayorazgo*."[100] And in recognizing the existence of hereditary cacicazgos, the decree rejected Toledo's efforts to place cacical appointments under the absolute discretion of royal officials.

The cacicazgo was thus defended by two distinct colonial logics: that of tributary rule, according to which the cacique was a local official responsible for tribute collection, and that of natural lordship, in which preconquest ruling lineages had hereditary claim to various cacicazgos. The result was considerable confusion about the nature and strength of claims to individual cacicazgos. Whether new families who arose as old cacical dynasties died out had hereditary claims, and whether the corregidor could remove hereditary

96 Murra, *Economic Organization*, p. 43, n57.

97 Díaz Rementería, *El cacique*, pp. 111–24, 215–18.

98 Ibid., p. 218.

99 February 22, 1602; in Díaz Rementería, *El cacique*, p. 218. Alejandro Diez, *Pueblos y cacicazgos de Piura, siglos XVI y XVII* (Piura: Biblioteca Regional, 1988), pp. 45–6; and Silverblatt, *Moon*, pp. 150–3, for the impact on female succession.

100 Nuria Sala i Vila, *Y se armó el tole tole: tributo indígena y movimientos sociales en el virreinato del Perú, 1784–1814* (Huamanga: Instituto de estudios regionales José María Arguedas, 1996), p. 101.

caciques who failed in tribute collection – such was the stuff of colonial lawsuits. Given the paucity of legal records in Indian communities, it was often very difficult to establish the origins of various claims to cacicazgos. Nonetheless, the principal of hereditary cacical authority was acknowledged in the abstract (if not always the particular) until the 1780s.

The crown showed an equally strong commitment to hidalguía. To the middling and upper ranks of sixteenth-century Spanish society, it was beyond question that societies were stratified along natural lines of nobility, and that nobility was both hereditary and fairly widespread. Spain was among the most densely noble lands in Europe. In the 1590s, one in ten Castilians was legally noble; by 1700, the proportion was one in eight Spaniards.[101] These nobles were not evenly distributed: Old Castile accounted for much of Spain's nobility, and two of three Castilian nobles lived in Burgos or León. Their nobility was not based on wealth, nor on feudal privilege. Rather, it sprang from the imputation of superiority given the descendants of the Old Christians of northwestern Iberia who had never converted to Islam, and from concessions made by state-building Castilian monarchs to buy their loyalties.[102]

The social landscape of colonial Peru showed the marks of similar forces. The Spanish never questioned that so complex a society as the Inca empire contained an innately noble group. From there, the just rule of the Habsburgs dictated that the Inca elite enjoy the privileges of nobility under their new monarchs. Not until the end of the eighteenth century did the crown back away from this commitment, so that for two centuries Spanish rule created a space within Indian communities for a hereditary nobility. "Created" is perhaps the wrong word: many Andean societies had their own entrenched hierarchies, and that society stratified naturally was as self-evident in the Andes (particularly to dominant groups) as it was in Spain. In the early 1600s, Guaman Poma attributed nobility to "the Christian law that God put in the world"; nearly two centuries later the cacique of Cusco's Ayllus Ayarmaca and Pumamarca claimed that "this entire community enjoys the privileges of nobility, by nature."[103] Spanish rule in the sixteenth century sought to co-opt the existing Andean elites, transforming them into a subject nobility that would serve as the crown's privileged ally in Indian society.

While Indian nobility was clearly recognized by the crown, the details and privileges of that nobility remained vague. Exemption from tribute and

101 M. L. Bush, *Rich Noble, Poor Noble* (Manchester: Manchester University Press, 1983), pp. 7–13.
102 Ibid., p. 12–13.
103 Felipe Guaman Poma de Ayala, *El primer nueva corónica y buen gobierno* [161?], ed. John V. Murra and Rolena Adorno (Mexico D. F.: Siglo XXI, 1988), II, 719. "Don Rafael Amau . . . ," ARC, INT, RH, Leg. 181 (1786–7), 1.

personal service were its main hallmarks, although in communities subject to the mining mita the latter was more important.[104] Indian nobles also had the right to seek justice in royal courts (rather than at the hands of the corregidor) – an expensive privilege to invoke, but one that afforded the upper reaches of the Indian elite some protection from provincial officials.[105] With these modest privileges and the social superiority they imputed, Peru's Indian nobility bore more than a passing resemblance to Castilian hidalgos; indeed, it was common for the eighteenth-century Indian noble to refer to himself as a "cavallero hidalgo."[106] However, unlike the privileges of the cacique established by various royal decrees and recorded in the *Recopilaciones* of the colonial legal canon, those of nobility operated more commonly through custom. In this regard, Cusco was unique in Peru: in the 1540s Charles I had granted patents of nobility to a number of Cusco's Inca elite who had accepted Spanish rule. In addition to spelling out exemption from tribute and personal service, these patents also accorded their recipients coats of arms – that granted to several men from the Sucso panaca was exceptionally rich in the signs of Inca authority, consisting of " . . . a sun of gold with a colored *mascapaycha* at its head in a red field, and at the sides two black vultures carrying a *mascapaycha* in their beaks. And in the other part fringes of blood and in the middle of them a crowned gold lion with a *chambi* in its hands."[107] This official recognition of royal Inca ancestry by the Spanish crown formed the ideological and legal foundation of Inca privilege until 1825.

Such explicit concessions of nobility were not unique to Cusco, although the former imperial capital certainly received far more than its share.[108] Patented nobles enjoyed a unique degree of protection for their privileges. The bundles of paper (stamped with magnificent royal seals) that attested to their status were prized heirlooms, carefully tended over generations as invaluable safeguards against Spanish officials' efforts to reduce their possessors to tributary status. In 1562, just seventeen years after Charles I had awarded them patents, a group of Inca nobles appealed to the Audiencia of Charcas when the encomendero Martin de Olmos attempted to charge them tribute.[109] A decade later, Toledo reduced the illegitimate offspring

---

104　RREE, PRA, Exp. 482; and ANB, EC, 1762–18.

105　See the February 1780 letter by Don Toribio Tamboguacso explicitly reminding Cusco's *cabildo* that it had no jurisdiction over the Inca nobility; ARC, CAB, Ped., Leg. 114 (1773–86).

106　Don Agustin Alferez Poma Orcosupa insisted on his rights "de todos los señorios y privilegios como cavallero hidalgo." AGN, DI, Exp. 413 (1785).

107　ARC, COR, Civ., Leg. 49, Exp. 1122 (1768).

108　In 1746, the Audiencia of Lima observed that descendants of *indios principales* who helped Pizarro in the conquest, and the originarios of Huánuco (who had sided with the viceroy against Girón) were also noble. In the Cusipaucar y Leon *probanza*; ARC, INT, Gob., Leg. 145 (1792–3).

109　In the Puma Ynga nobility proof; ARC, INT, RH, Leg. 202 (1796).

of Paullu Ynga (who had received a similar grant from Charles that they "enjoy the honors, graces, and favors, freedoms, and immunities that those who are of legitimate matrimony enjoy") to tributary status.[110] In both cases, the Inca nobles won reinstatement of their privileges.

This recognition of Inca privilege left Cusco with an Indian nobility unique in the Andes in its size and history. But those with royal concessions did not constitute all of colonial Peru's Indian nobles. The basic privileges of Indian nobility were also enjoyed by caciques and their eldest sons, and the distinction between blood nobility and the nobility of cacical office was fluid. As Guaman Poma described it, "... the emperor Don Carlos made restitution to all the lord caciques and principals and to the ladies, daughters, and sons, their descendants, that they be called lord and principal Don Fulano and Doña Fulana and that they be exempted from tribute and personal services ... and similarly the principal ladies and their children and grandchildren."[111] In fact, the concessions of nobility were not nearly this sweeping, but his remarks illustrate the extent to which Andean notions of nobility had been reconceived in terms of the legal privileges of royally conceded patents.

Nobility brought a degree of royal protection for one's social position within the Indian republic. In 1762 Don Lucas Mango Turpa, an illegitimate son of the cacical family of Azángaro Urinsaya, complained to the Audiencia of Charcas that the cacique of Azángaro Anansaya was requiring him to serve as his assistant, despite "various Royal Decrees that neither the Corregidores nor the Governors and Caciques employ [Indians] of noble blood in servile occupations of less estimation than merited by their quality, on account of the distinction that exists in all pueblos, towns, cities, and places between the nobles and the plebeians."[112] The fiscal of the audiencia concurred, declaring that if Lucas were in fact a Mango Turpa, he was noble, and therefore "a principal Indian, and in consequence exempt from the obligation to [perform] base services in conformity with the [royal] ordinance which so orders."[113]

But within pueblos the determination of noble status was often ill-defined. Written records were poorly kept (note the audiencia judge's qualification, that *if* Lucas were a Mango Turpa, he would be noble); and just as families might move from interim to proprietary possession of a cacicazgo over a few generations, so too might they acquire the reputation, and therefore the privileges, of hereditary nobility. Households that had performed onerous burdens (for instance, serving as mita captain in Potosí)

---

110 Temple Dunbar, "Un linaje incaico," p. 47.
111 *El primer nueva corónica*, II, 719.
112 ANB, EC, 1762–18, 1r.
113 Ibid., 3v.

might be exempted from "base" service to the community in gratitude. Or caciques might not collect tribute from their younger sons or brothers, creating de facto Indian nobilities in communities without explicit royal concessions. More broadly, among the scores, or hundreds, of households in larger ayllus and pueblos were those who dominated local government, who were responsible for tribute collection, and generally formed the local elite. Referred to in documents as "principales," such notables often enjoyed the honorific "Don," a verbal – and written – indicator of their status, and of the deference they expected and generally received.[114] In some cases, these local elites were the descendants of preconquest elites – among them, the Inca nobility of Cusco and the cacical dynasties of the Titicaca basin. Others were noble in the eyes of their communities; whether this translated into legal nobility depended on the attitude of the crown and of its provincial officials. Whatever their standing in the eyes of crown officials, these were the de facto local Indian elites.

It is impossible to say what proportion of the viceroyalty's population was recognized as legally noble or enjoyed "principal" status. The latter existed in any sizable community; of the former, it is only clear that they were an important presence in some places and that they were not evenly distributed throughout the Andes. In Huarochirí and the adjacent *repartimiento* of Chaclla, one in thirty and one in twenty households, respectively, were listed as noble in a 1751 census; in 1785, almost one in ten of Cusco's 2,800 adult male Indians had noble status.[115] Nor were they uniformly distributed within these communities: in Chaclla, all of the nobles lived in six ayllus, out of dozens. In Cusco, 220 of the Indian noblemen lived in two of the city's nine parishes – San Sebastián and San Gerónimo, which together were home to 815 adult male Indians. All of these 220 were from five Inca ayllus – the panacas of Sucso, Aucaylli, and Chima, and the Ayllus Sahuaraura and Pumamarca. As Spalding notes, it is often more accurate to speak of noble ayllus than of individuals or households.[116]

Cusco's Inca parishes had such large noble populations because of Charles I's patents. The origins of Chaclla and Huarochirí's eighteenth-century nobles are not clear. This confusion was the norm; Cusco and its Inca nobility were the exception. Like colonial Peru's cacical class, its Indian nobility

---

114 By the eighteenth century, the use of "Don" was widespread in Spanish Peru. Within Indian society, the attribution was made more sparingly, to caciques, Indian nobles, alcaldes of large pueblos, and those who were held in high regard in the surrounding area. Because the use of "Don" was regulated by custom, its attribution by a notary or witness and its assumption by individuals give insight into stratification within Indian society. For the first mention of an individual I have included the title when it appears; I have often refrained from repeating it. For the use of honorifics and social distinctions among the colonial Nahuas, Lockhart, *The Nahuas*, pp. 130–40.

115 Spalding, *Huarochirí*, pp. 235–6; ARC, INT, RH, Leg. 173 (1785).

116 Spalding, *Huarochirí*, p. 236.

was the product of both Inca-era stratification and the ideals and demands of Spanish rule. Demographic, social, and economic forces all reworked Andean society during the long seventeenth century between the Toledan and the Bourbon reforms. However, throughout those changes one constant was the belief, in Indian as well as Spanish Peru, that hierarchies of birth – based in theory on preconquest nobility and also, in practice, on authority within the community and its recognition by Spanish officials – were a natural part of society. This belief would constitute a central defense of Indian elites in their efforts to monopolize the positions of power and privilege afforded by the organization of colonial society.

The late-sixteenth-century reform of Andean society defined the basic organization of Indian Peru for the next two centuries. The core economic relationship between the crown and its Indian vassals remained one of tribute, in practice (if not theory) assessed at the level of the ayllu or pueblo, placing power in the hands of those who controlled its local collection. Politically, the relationship between the state and the Indian republic also took place at the level of the local community. Royal concerns about the power of Peru's Spanish population, and a concern for "just rule" as understood by sixteenth-century Spanish officials, led to a commitment to the Indian pueblo as a largely self-governing entity. This legal division of colonial society into two republics created a large sphere of daily life in Indian communities in which Spanish participation was discouraged, and in many areas officially forbidden. Thus, while the Toledan reforms greatly reworked indigenous societies, in their daily life and their economic organization, the pueblos remained under Indian, not Spanish, authority.

The combination of the colonial tributary order and the commitment to pueblo autonomy made Indian elites necessary to Spanish fiscal and political administration. At the same time, a hierarchical social ideology in which hereditary nobility played a central role defended the authority of those who already held power. These aspects of colonial rule in the Peruvian highlands created a space for a hereditary indigenous elite. At the same time, these ideals and policies were neither consistent nor coherent. Whether priority was given to effective tribute collection, the equitable government of the pueblo, or the defense of hereditary privilege might give precedence to competing claimants for the offices of the Indian elite. Not all caciques were hereditary nobles; nor were all hereditary nobles caciques. Similarly, while in some communities caciques had extensive political and economic authority, in others the cacique was little more than a tax collector. Nor did the relations and balances of power within particular communities remain static over two centuries. Rather, while the social space of the Indian elite remained largely unchanged for almost two centuries, the determination of who occupied that space, and possessed its privileges, was constantly challenged and changed.[117] But these changes and challenges occurred within the parameters of the colonial order outlined in this chapter. Membership in, and the privileges and powers of, the Indian elite were repeatedly contested, but the existence of such an elite was upheld by the economic and political organization of colonial society and the ideals that underlay it. Not until the final decades of Spanish rule would these basic tenets of Habsburg colonialism be discarded.

117 For social mobility and Indian elites in the Habsburg era, Spalding, "Social Climbers"; Stern, *Peru's Indian Peoples*, pp. 158–83.

2

The Long Seventeenth Century

The social space and privileges conceded to Peru's Indian elites in the later sixteenth century remained intact for almost two centuries. However, indigenous societies underwent enormous changes in the Andes' "long seventeenth century" between the Toledan and Bourbon reforms, or the epidemics of the 1580s and that of 1720.[1] As a result, the Indian elites of Bourbon Cusco were a creation not only of preconquest stratification and attempts by sixteenth-century officials to reform indigenous society, but also of the complex colonial society that emerged in the next century. Driving these changes were the histories of Peru's two ethnic republics: demographic, economic, and cultural collapse and contraction in the Indian, expansion in the Spanish. Catastrophic population decline, coupled with the heavy demands of the crown, provoked widespread migration, the destruction of many communities and the creation of others. Because the Indian elites of the colonial Andes were generally defined locally, and their authority and wealth stemmed from their position within their *ayllus* and pueblos, the dynamics of community collapse and formation affected them not as a legal estate, but as families and lineages whose privileged position was as precarious as the survival of their communities. In addition, the mass death destroyed the tributary labor on which the high civilization of the Incas had depended, and the religious practices, arts, and organization of the sixteenth-century Andes suffered terribly over the next century, as indigenous societies were now too small to maintain them. Preconquest civilization also suffered from the imposition of many aspects of Spanish civilization – Christianity, monogamy, Spanish literacy, courts of law – both through aggressive, sporadic campaigns and a gradual, and more

---

1 For indigenous societies in the seventeenth-century Andes, Spalding, *Huarochirí*; Andrien, *Andean Worlds*; Powers, *Andean Journeys*; Stern, *Peru's Indian Peoples*; Burga, *Nacimiento*; Glave, *Trajinantes* and *Vida, símbolos*; Wightman, *Indigenous Migration*; Glave and Remy, *Estructura agraria*; Wachtel, *Retour*; Larson, *Cochabamba*; Saignes, *Caciques*; Sánchez-Albornoz, *Indios*. For the colonial economy and society generally, Kenneth Andrien, *Crisis and Decline: The Viceroyalty of Peru in the Seventeenth Century* (Albuquerque: University of New Mexico Press, 1985); John Phelan, *The Kingdom of Quito in the Seventeenth Century* (Madison: University of Wisconsin Press, 1967); Cole, *The Potosí Mita*.

profound, permeation. As a result, while eighteenth-century Inca nobles considered themselves the direct descendants of Huayna Capac, Viracocha, and other Inca royals, in their dress, self-identification, group organization, and occupation they bore almost no resemblance. Instead, in many ways by the mid-1700s indigenous elites had come to resemble their peers in the Spanish Andean society that had emerged over the preceding two centuries.

The "Spanish republic" enjoyed a dual dynamism in those centuries. First, fueled by silver production in Alto Peru, the alienation of land from Indian communities, and Indian labor corvees and other preferences claimed by Peru's conquerors, the economy of Peru's Spanish republic grew dramatically in the seventeenth century. Although partly dependent on Indian tribute, the Spanish republic operated through and stimulated the growth of a complex market economy. This created new networks of exchange and possibilities for the sale of goods and labor. Second, the population of *peninsulares*, creoles, and mestizos grew throughout the colonial period. Its growth did not precisely parallel the decline of the Indian republic: in the 1600s the Spanish population increased relatively slowly, reaching just 5 percent of the bishopric of Cusco's total by 1700. The eighteenth century then witnessed the rapid growth of the bishopric's non-Indian population, which by the 1790s made up nearly 30 percent of its inhabitants. This growth placed enormous strain on the colonial order organized in the sixteenth century and contributed to its collapse in the decades following the Tupac Amaru Rebellion.

Demographic Collapse and the Indian Republic

The catastrophic decline of the indigenous population is without question the dominant feature of sixteenth- and seventeenth-century Andean history: Peru's population plummeted as diseases that had long been scourges of the Old World hit the virgin societies of America with ferocity. N. D. Cook estimates that from 1525 to 1570 the population of present-day Peru fell by five-sixths – roughly, from ten million to one and a third. In 1620, Peru's Indian population stood at scarcely 600,000.[2] Behind the catastrophic decline lay huge regional differences. The death toll was greatest by far in tropical and coastal regions, although the highland Indian population fared well only in the most relative terms. By 1620 the population of highland southern Peru (Cusco, Arequipa, and Puno) was one-sixth its level under Huayna Capac – 350,000 in place of two million. The nadir came a century later, and not until the middle of the eighteenth century

2 Noble David Cook, *Demographic Collapse: Indian Peru, 1520–1620* (Cambridge: Cambridge University Press, 1981), p. 52; also Sánchez-Albornoz, *Indios*, pp. 19–34.

did Peru's indigenous population begin a sustainable recovery; not until the twentieth would it reach the level of 1500.[3]

Such a decline, of course, affected the elites of the Indian republic. Most obviously, they too died in the savage epidemics that swept the Andes. The last of the great colonial pandemics, in 1720, wiped out all the ayllu caciques and many of their families in Quiquijana.[4] The election book of Cusco's Inca *cabildo* gives a measure of the impact on the Indian nobility. In June 1721, the corregidor had to appoint sixteen new electors, "because the rest are dead, and no more than eight have remained when there ought to be 24, . . . [the rest] having died in the general epidemic."[5] Seven of the dead left sons, two more were succeeded by close relatives, and other Inca nobles filled the remaining seats. The cabildo continued on, and given the endogamy of the Inca nobility, those who replaced the dead were relatives in some degree. But that a single plague could kill two in three men in the small group who formed the city's Inca elite – and that half of these left no sons – exposes the precariousness of intergenerational survival.

Communities as well as families faced great challenges in reproducing themselves across the generations. Epidemics were a factor, but royal policy (or, rather, neglect) greatly exacerbated the challenges confronting ayllus and even pueblos. Royal officials repeatedly refused to recalculate *mita* and tribute burdens as communities' populations plummeted.[6] One response – indeed a defining aspect of seventeenth-century Andean society – was migration, which has rightly received considerable attention from historians.[7] Migrants exploited the differential tribute burdens of *originarios* and *forasteros*: by abandoning their pueblos tributaries could escape the mita and reduce their tribute; in return they lost access to communal lands. The number of migrants, above all from provinces subject to the mining mitas, shows that many found the advantages of migration to outweigh this cost: in 1689, 93 of the bishopric of Cusco's 134 parishes reported forastero populations, with some pueblos composed almost entirely of migrants.[8]

These migrations reworked the organization and distribution of highland society. Several broad patterns stand out. First, people left old, heavily

3 Cook, *Demographic Collapse*, pp. 59–74, 96, 114; Wightman, *Indigenous Migration*, pp. 42–7.
4 Ward Stavig, "Ethnic Conflict, Moral Economy, and Population in Rural Cuzco on the Eve of the Thupa Amaro II Rebellion," *Hispanic American Historical Review* 68:4 (November 1988): 757.
5 June 5, 1721. ARC, COR, Civ., Leg. 29, Exp. 620, 1r.
6 Wightman, *Indigenous Migration*, pp. 129–31; Cole, *The Potosí Mita*, pp. 72–9.
7 Sánchez-Albornoz, *Indios*; Powers, *Andean Journeys*; Wightman, *Indigenous Migration*; Saignes, *Caciques*; and Ann Zulawski, "Migration and Labor in Seventeenth Century Alto Peru" (Ph.D. diss., Columbia University, 1985).
8 Wightman, *Indigenous Migration*, p. 201. The following discussion of migration is based on *Cuzco 1689* and Wightman's analysis in *Indigenous Migration*.

burdened communities.[9] Second, they moved to areas of economic activity
and onto Spanish properties. In the bishopric of Cusco this shifted population away from high pueblos of the southern provinces (subject to the
mita), toward the plantations and haciendas of Abancay, Paucartambo, and
the temperate valleys closer to the city (and to the city itself).[10] Third, many
people moved just a short distance, settling in Indian pueblos with similar
climate, economy, and language, trading the burdens of the originario for
the secondary status of the forastero.[11] The closely linked histories of Ñuñoa
and its annex pueblo of Santa Rosa illustrate all these interrelated dynamics.
Located at 13,000 feet along the ridge dividing the Titicaca and Vilcanota
watersheds, Ñuñoa was an important town in the sixteenth century.[12] In
the 1600s, this left it with staggering burdens: a Potosí mita obligation of
ninety workers and an annual tribute of 2,907 pesos from its two moieties.[13]
By 1690 there were just twenty originarios in Urinsaya and a pathetic eight
in Anansaya. Almost all the pueblo's 400 Indians were forasteros who had
settled on its empty lands. The priest lamented that "it is impossible to
comprehend the tribulations [the originarios] undergo, and those to which
they subject the forasteros, who live on their lands, so that they can pay so
great an amount."[14] In contrast, Ñuñoa's annex of Santa Rosa was thriving.
Just ten miles away, Santa Rosa sat at the head of the Ayavire river alongside
the royal road from Cusco to Potosí. It was a young town, founded in the
early 1670s "with Indians who wandered as vagrants"; by 1689 its population of 550 had surpassed that of Ñuñoa.[15] The priest did not indicate
the tribute or mita levels of Santa Rosa, but its rapid growth suggests that
while the slowness of royal officials to revise the burdens hurt established
towns, it spurred the expansion of new communities.

The effects of these migrations on Indian elites were as varied as, and
intimately linked to, those on their communities.[16] Successful pueblos,
and even the remains of ethnic, maximal ayllus, used forastero colonies

---

9 Major sixteenth-century pueblos had declined greatly by 1689: Ñuñoa, Hatuncolla, Tintay, Matara
   (*Cuzco 1689*, pp. 61, 347, 392–3).
10 In Abancay, Paucartambo, Quispicanchis, and Chilques y Masques, 10–40% of Indians lived on
   Spanish properties. *Cuzco 1689*, passim; and Wightman, *Indigenous Migration*, pp. 45–73 and 196–
   223.
11 See the very detailed reports on Livitaca, Sabaina, and Guaquirca; *Cuzco 1689*, pp. 319–35, 370–423.
12 Ñuñoa was one of three northern Titicaca towns depicted on Diego Mendez's 1574 map, "Peruviae
   Aurifere Regionis Typus"; *Atlas histórico, geográfico, y de paisajes peruanos* (Lima: Instituto Nacional
   de Planificación, 1970), pp. 67–8. In 1689 the parish priest commented on its former grandeur;
   Cuzco 1689, p. 81.
13 Cole, *The Potosí Mita*, p. 75; *Cuzco 1689*, p. 81.
14 Ibid.
15 In the Guampoco claim to the *cacicazgo*, ARC, RA, Ord., Leg. 8 (1791) [3]; *Cuzco 1689*, p. 82.
16 Powers, *Andean Journeys*, pp. 133–67, for Quito; Saignes, *Caciques*, pp. 4–10, for La Paz.

and migration between pueblos to reproduce themselves.[17] In 1689 the priests' reports from the main pueblos of Collana Aymara, Sabaina and Guaquirca, show how such colonies allowed communities to distribute themselves across the colonial economy.[18] Guaquirca's priest reported 759 people under his charge and listed 82 tributaries from the pueblo and its annex of Matara who were "absent in distinct parts" – more than 10 percent of the population. Those absent – in Cusco (where the pueblo owned a compound), on lands owned by the community in another province, on Spanish haciendas, at the mines of Cailloma – remained part of Guaquirca. They had not escaped their obligations to Guaquirca: according to the priest, "the caciques themselves go and send their officers to collect their tributes."[19] And the strong community of Collana Aymara had an equally strong ruling dynasty. The interrelated cacical families of Guaquirca and Sabaina, the Ayquipa Arcos Guachaca and the Aronis, descended from the sixteenth-century lord, Francisco Supayque Caque, who had early allied with the Spanish.[20] In 1689 their domain had over a thousand people. The pueblos' success in adapting to the colonial order brought success to the ruling families, who by the eighteenth century had channeled wealth into a sugar plantation in the Apurímac valley.[21] The caciques also controlled communal assets: the pueblos' land, holdings in Cusco and other parishes, and investments.[22] With factors in Cusco, private lands, hereditary claims to office, and a centuries-old *señorio* under their rule, the Guachaca had the resources to keep track of tributaries who left their pueblos, and court cases show that they traced down tributaries who fled.[23] So powerful a cacical family could counteract the centrifugal forces at work in the seventeenth-century Andes.

Many, however, could not. The heavy tribute and mita burdens faced by communities with declining populations weighed especially hard on caciques, who were ultimately responsible to the corregidor for these obligations. As a result, caciques no longer able, or willing, to guarantee these payments resigned their offices throughout the colonial period; and in some instances it was difficult to find Indian nobles willing to take the office.[24] Such was the case in Ñuñoa. As an old and important pueblo, Ñuñoa

---

17 Glave argues that in Canas y Canchis, interpueblo migration allowed maximal ayllus to reproduce themselves across the province. Glave, *Vida, símbolos*, p. 84.
18 *Cuzco 1689*, pp. 370–92 and 392–423, respectively.
19 Ibid., p. 418.
20 Information in Don Juan Guachaca's 1663 *probanza de nobleza*, in the late eighteenth-century Aroni *probanza*; ARC, INT, RH, Leg. 203 (1796).
21 Ibid., for the purchase of a sugar hacienda in the eighteenth century.
22 ARC, COR, Civ., Leg. 39, Exp. 832.
23 Wightman, *Indigenous Migration*, p. 132, 280 n14.
24 For particularly grisly testimony to this problem, *Cuzco 1689*, p. 226.

would have had cacical dynasties. However, by 1689 they appear to have vanished; as the priest put it, "there is no Indian who wants to be *curaca*, on account of the enormous difficulty that they encounter in complying with one or other obligation, and the Corregidores and [their] lieutenants name by force the Indian who has the greatest ability to be curaca of these ayllus, even if they are not originarios of the pueblo."[25]

The fact that corregidores installed immigrants as caciques of Ñuñoa shows how the different logics supporting the position of the cacical elite could come into conflict. Here, fulfillment of the cacique's fiscal duties outweighed any commitment to protecting the hereditary rights of cacical families, or even originario control of the pueblo. While according to the priest no one in Ñuñoa wanted to be a cacique, even where there were claimants a corregidor might depose them in favor of his own allies.[26] For while the crown had officially adopted the position that *cacicazgos* could be, and generally were, held hereditarily by families, many corregidores took the (self-serving) view of Toledo, that caciques were local officials of the crown who could be deposed by their superiors. Heavy mita and tribute burdens combined with hostile corregidores toppled many caciques, either leaving a vacuum or creating an opportunity for caciques linked to the province's Spanish governor.

The dire report of the parish priest in 1689 notwithstanding, Ñuñoa survived as a pueblo (and does to this day). Whether the Ñuñoa of 1690, with 75 percent of its population made up of immigrants, can be considered the same community as that founded in the sixteenth century is debatable.[27] But with their churches, salaried priests, and recognition as both administrative units and corporate entities, pueblos were protected from the mobility of seventeenth-century Andean life and few were abandoned. The other basic association of Andean society – the ayllu – was less favored by colonial legislation, and proved far more susceptible to the dislocations of the seventeenth century.[28] The priest of Capacmarca captured this process as it occurred. In listing the ayllus in his parish, he put Ayllu Cancaguana, then noted "in which are included Ayllus Arequea and Pisuro, and because these ayllus have already been consumed by the mita of Huancavelica I mention those who have remained."[29]

25 Ibid., p. 81.
26 Spalding, "Social Climbers"; Stern, *Peru's Indian Peoples*, pp. 133–4; Powers, *Andean Journeys*, pp. 134–41; Alfredo Moreno Cebrián, *El Corregidor de Indios y la Economía Peruana del siglo XVIII: Los Repartos Forzosos de Mercancias* (Madrid: Instituto G. Fernández de Oviedo, 1977), pp. 231–42; Sánchez-Albornoz, *Indios*, pp. 95–9; Saignes, *Caciques*, pp. 21–8.
27 Also Chupa, composed entirely of immigrants by 1689; *Cuzco 1689*, p. 117.
28 For example, compare the detailed account of Omacha's ayllus in 1689 with the 1792 tribute rolls. Ibid., pp. 450–62; ARC, INT, RH, Leg. 198 (1793–4).
29 *Cuzco 1689*, p. 303.

Ayllus bore the brunt of the demographic tragedy and seventeenth-century migrations, and certainly their collapse affected local elites. Here, however, so little evidence has been left in the archival record that only the most tentative observations are possible. Once again, the diligent priest of Guaquirca comes to our aid. Guaquirca's annex of Matara had once been the principal seat of Aymaraes, and in the late sixteenth century had had twenty-two ayllus, most of which bore the name of their curacas; in 1689 it had just two ayllus.[30] Some with the family names appear as *principales* and ayllu caciques in Sabaina and Guaquirca in 1689, but how those elites reconstituted themselves as their larger communities imploded, and the kin groupings of perhaps one hundred people of whom they were head disappeared, is lost to us. But overall it is safe to say that the dislocations of the seventeenth century threw into flux the internal hierarchies of many pueblos and their constituent ayllus.

The dislocations did not, however, destroy the Indian elite as a stratum of society. The organization of colonial rule required caciques and other Indian officials: where old noble families collapsed, new ones rose to take their place. By the mid-eighteenth century, only near Cusco and in the large pueblos around Titicaca did most caciques root their claims in descent from preconquest elites; however, throughout the bishopric many claimed hereditary possession, on the basis of descent from colonial era caciques. In some cases such families held office from the time of Toledo to the end of the eighteenth century, a reminder of the complexity of "legitimate" hereditary rule in colonial, indigenous communities. Indeed, Santa Rosa raises the intriguing issue of new Indian pueblos formed in the sixteenth and seventeenth centuries: these created a need for new local elites. In 1689 Santa Rosa was less than two decades old; obviously it had no established hereditary dynasty. It did, however, have a cacique, Don Francisco Guampoco, described in eighteenth-century documents as the "founder of this pueblo." The family maintained control of the pueblo for the next century; indeed, Francisco's grandson, Don Martin Guampoco, "obtained the cacicazgo in propriety ... having paid for the construction of the church and endowed it with a capital of 1000 sheep for wax and wine."[31] Precisely who conceded the family a proprietary right to the cacicazgo is unclear, but for five generations men of the Guampoco family served as caciques of Santa Rosa. And in neighboring Ñuñoa, by the eighteenth century the Tapara had established a strong (if not undisputed) hereditary claim to the cacicazgo of Urinsaya that lasted generations; tellingly, this old, established

---

30 For example, the Ayllus Don Juan Aycho, Don Francisco Aroni, Don Pedro Aymarasto, Don Baltazar Guacraguachaca. Ibid., p. 393.
31 In the Guampoco cacicazgo claim. ARC, RA, Ord., Leg. 8 (1791) [3].

ruling family had difficulty tracing itself back much farther than the late seventeenth century.[32]

Other cacical dynasties survived the length of Spanish rule. Around Cusco, descendants of the Inca emperors ruled rural villages up to the Tupac Amaru rebellion; in the Titicaca basin descendants of Aymara kings were collecting tribute and organizing labor corvees on the eve of independence. The reorganization of Indian society in the seventeenth century manifested itself locally, along a continuum. At one extreme were Guaquirca and Sabaino, sufficiently large and cohesive to maintain complex internal hierarchies and to send out their own colonies to adapt to the demands of colonialism. At the other were pueblos and ayllus that dissolved and formed in response to the strains of death, tribute, and migration. In between were communities that succeeded in reproducing themselves across generations, but whose internal organization and hierarchies changed dramatically over the century. In other towns – both new ones, like Santa Rosa, and established communities whose elites collapsed under the burdens of colonialism – new families established hereditary control over pueblos. Still other communities were marked by the absence of cacical dynasties, and were ruled by interim caciques, often occupying the post for only brief periods. This variety was evident in all parts of the bishopric, because to some extent all communities were subject to the same larger forces. At the same time, different provinces had distinct histories, and so too did their cacical families. The following chapter will explore those differences in detail while examining the organization and authority of the eighteenth-century Indian nobility.

Continuity and Change among the Indigenous Elite: The Incas of Cusco

These demographic and political changes were but part of the transformation of Andean society in the seventeenth century, and of its elites. Spanish policy did not entail a frontal assault on all aspects of Andean culture: indeed, a performance of "Incaness" was central to Cusco's Inca nobility's privileged colonial position. But over generations indigenous culture, and particularly that of the Indian elite, changed. Most important was religion, one area where the Spanish were set on eradication and conversion. That ideal was never met, but parish priests, pueblo churches, anti-idolatry campaigns, confession manuals, a pantheon of saints, all entered into and transformed religion in the Andes.[33] Indian elites were a particular focus of

---

32 For the family's claim to the cacicazgo, ARC, RA, Adm., Leg. 167 (1808–9).

33 Pablo José de Arriaga, *The Extirpation of Idolatry in Peru* [1621], trans. by L. Clark Keating (Lexington: University of Kentucky Press, 1968); Pierre Duviols, *La destrucción de las religiones andinas (conquista*

this conversionary zeal, and with them a real attempt was made at indoctrination in orthodox dogma. In 1621 the Jesuits founded the College of San Borja in Cusco to educate the sons of caciques in the bishoprics of Cusco, Huamanga, and Arequipa in "Christian doctrine, reading, writing, counting, and music."[34] Certainly the upper reaches of the colonial Indian elite – Inca nobles and prominent caciques – thus had a different understanding of, and relation to, Christianity than did their tributaries. Whether this created a religious or cultural divide is difficult to assess; rather, it is impossible to draw generalizations. Cacical piety could be coupled with a benign, and willful, ignorance of "idolatrous" practices in their communities, or even participation in them.[35] Or caciques could team with priests in campaigns against unacceptable practices in local religion, or accuse priests of lack of zeal. These were the issues of local politics in the colonial Andes.[36] Overall, though, Catholicism exemplifies the cultural transformation of the indigenous elite, and the extent to which it distanced them from their communities. In dress, language (as Indian nobles were far more competent in Spanish than were the masses), houses (with local prominents roofing theirs in tiles, tributaries in thatch), and so on, the Indian nobility was decidedly more "hispanicized" than the commons.

Materially, too, Spanish ideals of private property served to divide indigenous elites from their communities. Overwhelmingly the land possessed by Indians in the colonial Andes continued to belong to ayllus or pueblos. However, the collapse of the indigenous population left these communities, in the opinion of a cash-strapped crown, with surfeit lands; these reverted to the crown and were sold to individuals, in *composición*.[37] This produced a transfer of lands to the Spanish republic, but caciques and Indian nobles

y colonia), trans. by Albor Maruenda (Mexico: Universidad Nacional Autónoma de México, 1977); Sabine MacCormack, *Religion in the Andes: Vision and Imagination in Early Colonial Peru* (Princeton: Princeton University Press, 1991); Mills, *Idolatry*; Carlos Alberto Romero, "Idolatrías de los indios Huachos y Yauyos," *Revista Histórica* [Lima] 6:2 (1981): 180–97; Salomon's essay in *The Huarochirí Manuscript: A Testament of Ancient and Colonial Andean Religion*, trans. by Frank Salomon and George L. Urioste (Austin: University of Texas Press, 1991); Andrien, *Andean Worlds*, pp. 153–91.

34 According to the notary Pedro Joseph de Gamarra in 1766; "Indios de sangre real," *Revista del Archivo Histórico del Cusco* 1:1 (1950): 207. For San Borja, Angles Vargas, *Historia del Cusco*, II, 657–60; Monique Alaperrine-Bouyer, "Saber y poder: la cuestión de la educación de las elites indígenas," in *Incas e indios cristianos: elites indígenas e identidades cristianas en los Andes coloniales*, ed. Jean-Jacques Decoster (Cusco: Centro Bartolomé de las Casas, 2002), pp. 154–63.

35 Karen Spalding, "La otra cara de la reciprocidad," in ibid., pp. 61–78; also *Huarochirí*, pp. 227–8; Frank Salomon, "Ancestor Cults and Resistance to the State in Arequipa, ca. 1748–1754" in *Resistance, Rebellion, and Consciousness in the Andean Peasant World, 18th to 20th Centuries*, ed. Steve Stern (Madison: University of Wisconsin Press, 1987), pp. 148–65.

36 Penry, "Transformations," pp. 188–269, for Chayanta.

37 For the impact of composiciones, Keith Davies' study of seventeenth-century Arequipa, *Landowners in Peru* (Austin: University of Texas Press, 1984), pp. 117–58; and Piel, *Capitalismo Agrario*, pp. 160–78.

also bought such lands. Elite family property had existed under the Incas, but alienable, deeded property was indeed a novelty, and created a new relationship of Indian elites to land.[38] Moreover, the existence of this category would create real tensions within communities, as elites, and especially caciques, sought to redefine communal land as their own private property.

Finally, how Andean elites organized and reproduced themselves also changed, dramatically, in the two centuries after the conquest. In one particular custom, the Spanish insistence on eradication and conversion was spectacularly successful: Indian noblemen abandoned polygamy for monogamy.[39] We have so little information on the ideology of stratification and domestic organization in provincial preconquest societies (and, for that matter, colonial societies) that evidence of the impact of this change is lacking, but the implications are clear and enormous.[40] The prize of male authority in Andean society was no longer reproduction. Elite polygamy had enabled a curaca to leave ten or twelve children, some to be married into the ayllu to reproduce the lineage's authority, others to marry out to create ties with other ayllus. Now cacical couples left a few children – in exceptional cases, five or six; usually, two or three; often, none. Lineage remained extremely important, but reckoning of kinship changed as the basic unit of the elite became the monogamous household. Elite polygamy stressed the creation of kinship ties between the curaca and large swaths of the community; rankings depended on hierarchies *within* this kin group. In contrast, the marriage logic of colonial elites became exclusionary: elite families sought to limit marriages with commoners.[41]

The one group for whom we have considerable evidence about preconquest organization is the Incas of Cusco. As the imperial power, the Incas were of course atypical, but the enormity of the changes in their organization suggests the scope of the restructuring. Again, the particulars of Inca organization remain the subject of considerable debate, but the broad contours in the two or three generations before the conquest are well established.[42] Pachacutec, Tupac Yupanqui, and Huayna Capac successively founded their own *panacas*; they married scores or hundreds of women, from throughout the empire, from within the different ayllus of the Cusco area, and above all

---

38 See Chapter 4, pp. 128–131, for private property in eighteenth-century Indian communities.

39 Caciques and Indian nobles had children out of wedlock, but this conformed to Spanish patterns of marital and extramarital relations. It appears that no stigma was attached to parents of such children. For Cusco nobles who recognized their illegitimate children in their wills, ARC, NOT, Villagarcia, Leg. 280, 130 ff., July 12, 1788 (Pablo Soria Condorpusa) and ARC, NOT, Zamora, Leg. 294, 360ff., November 24, 1788 (Isidora Auccatinco).

40 D'Altroy, *Provincial Power*, pp. 62–7, for the concentration of female productive (and, presumably, reproductive) power in elite Wanka compounds.

41 For eighteenth-century marriage patterns, see Chapter 3, pp. 97–102, 110–111.

42 Chapter 1, n5.

from the descendants (matrilineally and patrilineally) of Manco Capac.[43] Within this last group, rankings were contested – this was the stuff of Inca dynastic politics. But in the decades before the Spanish any "legitimate" claimant to imperial authority needed to be overwhelmingly "capac": to have as ancestors almost exclusively those descended from the panacas (Table 1.1). The imperial Incas were also clearly divided into two moieties, Anan and Urin, with the former of greater "capac" status. The civil war between Atahuallpa and Huascar did not deny this logic: the battle was over who was more "capac," and thus the rightful successor. But with the execution of Atahuallpa this logic had immediately begun to unravel.

Several factors contributed to this. First was the Spanish failure or refusal to recognize the particularities of Inca dynastic politics. In recognizing Paullu, they appear to have violated the "capac" principle, as Paullu's mother, although undisputedly of high birth, was not Inca at all.[44] In this they followed Spanish ideals of succession, which emphasized the father. The Spanish certainly insisted that both parents be noble for the status to pass on, but they drew no distinction between the daughter of a central Peruvian lord and a very "capac" woman from one of Cusco's panacas. Indeed, Inca Garcilaso – actively hispanicizing the Incas – insisted that "the female line is ignored by the Incas."[45] Of course, the Spanish failure to observe Inca hierarchies does not mean that the Incas themselves abandoned them.[46] But the Incas were no longer the sole arbiters of status in Cusco. Even when they had been, decisions had been bitterly contested – hence the civil war. Now, rivals could appeal to Spanish governors and judges to adjudicate claims. This did not necessarily destroy Inca reckonings of hierarchy and status, but it did modify them: descent from Paullu – and thus Huayna Capac – would become a real mark of standing among the Incas by the eighteenth century.

Other, more structural, factors worked against the preservation of pre-conquest organization and reckonings of status. The most important was simply the imploding population. In 1609 Inca Garcilaso claimed that there were 567 Incas left in Cusco.[47] The largest panaca was Sucso (that of Viracocha), with 69; most of the earlier had 40–50. The civil war left its mark: the descendants of Tupac Yupanqui and Huayna Capac numbered just 40 (18 and 22). These figures raise enormous problems, as it is by

43 Julien, *Reading Inca History*, pp. 17–8, 22–48.
44 Ibid., pp. 43–4.
45 *Royal Commentaries*, p. 626. Strikingly, just before, he denied Atahuallpa's claims on the basis that his mother was not "capac"; p. 615.
46 Julien, *Reading Inca History*, p. 48. David Cahill, "The Inca and Inca Symbolism in Popular Festive Culture: The Religious Processions of Seventeenth-Century Cuzco," in *Habsburg Peru: Images, Imagination and Memory*, eds. Peter T. Bradley and David Cahill (Liverpool: Liverpool University Press, 2000), pp. 124–44, for seventeenth-century processions and the possibility of cultural reproduction.
47 *Royal Commentaries*, p. 626.

no means clear who is included in them. However, the scale is telling. The organization of imperial Inca society had been aggressively expansionist; the attempts to limit authority to those of high "capac" status helped to create hierarchies in a rapidly growing population of Incas.[48] Between the demographic crisis, the effects of the civil war, and the introduction of monogamy, the colonial Incas faced the opposite problem: they had to negotiate collapse. After Toledo, they also confronted a loss of political authority around Cusco itself. The Incas of the panacas – those with "capac" standing – had always formed only a part of the population in the thousand or so square miles around the Huatanay, albeit the dominant part. By the end of the sixteenth century, the relation of the "capac" Incas and the so-called "Incas by privilege" itself had changed; necessarily, the organization of the Inca elite had to change.

The result was two somewhat contradictory responses in the organization of the "capac" Incas. When, precisely, these changes occurred is not clear, but certainly by the early eighteenth century, those who were universally recognized as the heirs to the "señores Yngas" were structured very differently than in the sixteenth century, without having lost a clear sense of shared identity. The "earlier" panacas were reduced during the late sixteenth century in the suburban parishes of Belén, San Sebastián, and San Gerónimo, southeast of the city along the Huatanay.[49] As a result, these parishes, and in particular San Sebastián, were home to Inca ayllus in the colonial sense: self-governing, landholding corporations that, in this case, were composed largely of Inca nobles.[50]

In contrast, the descendants of the great emperors – Huayna Capac, Tupac Yupanqui, and Pachacutec – had been transformed into a number of noble lineages. They remained among the most powerful Inca families in Cusco throughout the colonial period, but no longer formed coherent ayllus recognized by the Spanish. To be sure, the parishes of San Blas and San Cristóbal, into which these panacas had been reduced, had Inca noble populations in the eighteenth century (16 and 22, respectively, in 1765).[51] But by the eighteenth century the Inca ayllus in San Cristóbal and San Blas, now urbanized parishes, no longer had the communal lands that formed the material heart of the suburban panaca–ayllus. Moreover, descendants of Tupac Yupanqui and Huayna Capac were also scattered in the surrounding pueblos as caciques. Don Toribio Tamboguacso serves as an example. Undeniably Toribio was viewed as "Inca" by his peers in the late eighteenth

---

48 Indeed, the insistence on maternal "capac" status appears to have been an imperial innovation.

49 For Incas and the parish reductions, Catherine J. Julien, "La organización parroquial del Cuzco y la ciudad incaica," *Tawantinsuyu* 5 (1988): 82–96.

50 See Tables 1.1, 3.1, and 3.2.

51 See Table 3.2.

century. The son of the cacique of Taray, Toribio had succeeded his father as an elector of the Inca cabildo. Toribio claimed descent from Pachacutec, Mayta Capac, and Huayna Capac, but he never mentioned any affiliation with their panacas or ayllus.[52] He was, rather, a Tamboguacso, from the great ruling family of Taray: here, colonial lineage had replaced panaca affiliation. Certainly the legitimation of his Incaness resonates with the panaca organization and "capac" hierarchies of the early sixteenth century, but nearly three hundred years later, the structures of Incaness had been radically reworked.

The information about Toribio's ancestry comes from the electoral records of Cusco's Inca cabildo, and these give a clear sense of the changes in Inca organization over the centuries of Spanish rule. The Inca cabildo was an honorific institution founded in the late sixteenth century to elect from among the Inca nobility a bearer of the royal standard – an *alférez real* – for the annual procession of Santiago. The alférez predated the cabildo by nearly half a century: the post was established by royal decree on May 9, 1545.[53] This office well captured the Incas' ambiguous colonial position. The main performance of their continued precedence was to carry the king's banner in honor of the patron saint of Spanish conquest, who had miraculously appeared during the 1535 siege to wrest Cusco from Inca control.[54] At first the alférez real was chosen from and by the descendants of Huayna Capac who had supported the Spanish against Manco Inca; one of the first to serve was Paullu Ynga. By the 1570s the election of the alférez had been extended to the various Inca panacas – perhaps a return to a more Inca understanding of status, perhaps a response to the rapidly dwindling population. Moreover, curacas and nobles of other indigenous ethnic groups who had been settled in Cusco by the Incas in the preceding century contested Inca dominance, and sought to occupy the *alferezgo real*; no doubt they were aided in this by Toledo's anti-Inca campaign in the 1570s. In the 1580s the Inca nobility complained that non-Incas were usurping the office. In response, Cusco's judge for Indians ordered each Inca moiety to present twelve representatives to elect the alférez – thus was founded Cusco's cabildo of twenty-four Inca electors.[55]

From its foundation to the end of Spanish rule in 1824, the Inca cabildo served as the most important manifestation of Inca privilege and corporate identity. The earliest account of the cabildo's organization comes from the

---

52 In the 1799 presentation of his son, Don Manuel Asencio Tamboguacso. ARC, COR, Civ., Leg. 29, Exp. 620.

53 Donato Amado Gonzales, "El alférez real de los Incas: resistencia, cambios y continuidad de la identidad indígena," in *Incas e indios cristianos*, pp. 221–50; and J. Uriel Garcia, "El alferazgo real de indios," *Revista Universitaria* 26 (1937): 193–208.

54 Betanzos, *Narrative*, p. 290.

55 Amado Gonzales, "El alférez real," pp. 223–4.

1595 election of the alférez real. The twenty-six electors were organized by moiety and ayllu, although the reorganization of Cusco into parishes was beginning to make itself felt.[56] By the election of 1598, the electors were no longer listed by ayllu or moiety, although it was noted that "in this present year the said alférez came from the Hurincuzcos of the Ayllu Uscamaita."[57] The organization of the cabildo varied over the seventeenth century, generally grouped by ten to thirteen royal ayllus, sometimes referred to as the "grandsons" of each Inca king; at times other electors represented "all the Hatun Cuzcos."[58] The waning of Hanan/Hurin division is made clear by its absence; and in the eighteenth century Inca nobles never referred to a moiety affiliation. Following the 1720 epidemic, cabildo organization was standardized into twelve "houses," representing the panacas of the twelve Incas recorded by Inca Garcilaso; this organization lasted until the cabildo's abolition at independence.[59] By the eighteenth century the Incas' principal ceremonial institution had been reworked to conform to the idealized, hispanicized view of Inca history presented by the Incas' own Renaissance historian, a view that in turn structured their perception and presentation of their own genealogies.[60] Most importantly, while "house" and ayllu appear to have overlapped for some of the earlier panacas, by the 1700s the electors for the "houses" of Huayna Capac, Tupac Yupanqui, and Pachacutec were not affiliated with a particular ayllu in the colonial sense.

That said, concerns about "capac" status, and hierarchies among Manco Capac's "descendants," continued. In 1655 two descendants of Huayna Capac appealed to the Lima Audiencia to prevent the sale of the alférez real in perpetuity to Don Francisco Suta Yupanqui, cacique of Ayllu Sucso (Viracocha's panaca) in San Sebastián.[61] Huayna Capac's descendants opposed the sale, insisting that the choice of alférez real rested with the Inca cabildo, and that only descendants of Huayna Capac be given the honor. In the first they were successful; in the second, Incas from all panacas continued to occupy the post. Later, the Incas united to

---

56 Twelve electors came from Hanan Cuzco, and 14 from Hurin Cuzco; parish and ayllu affiliations were given. ARC, BE, I, 290–2; Amado Gonzales, "El alférez real," pp. 224–5, 239.

57 ARC, BE, I, 294.

58 Amado Gonzales, "El alférez real," pp. 240–6. Hatun Ayllu, or Iñaca Panaca, were the descendants of Pachacutec; although the electors also included an elector for "Pachacutic Ynga," and another "nieto de Pachacutic"; ibid., p. 241.

59 ARC, COR, Civ., Leg. 29, Exp. 620.

60 For Inca Garcilaso's recreation of Inca history according to the paradigms of Renaissance and Christian humanism, see Margarita Zamora, *Language, Authority, and Indigenous History in the Comentarios Reales de los Incas* (Cambridge: Cambridge University Press, 1988); Aurelio Miró Quesada, *El Inca Garcilaso* (Lima: Pontificia Universidad Católica del Perú, 1994); MacCormack, *Religion*, pp. 332–82; David Brading, *The First America: The Spanish Monarchy, Creole Patriots and the Liberal State* (Cambridge: Cambridge University Press, 1991), pp. 255–72.

61 Amado Gonzales, "El alférez real," pp. 227–8.

repel attempts by those with little or no "capac" status to carry the standard. In the 1680s members of the cabildo opposed the election of Don Francisco Uclucana Sahuaytocto – the non-Inca hereditary cacique of Ayllu Chachapoyas in Santa Ana parish – even though his wife was a descendant of Huayna Capac.[62] Perhaps in response, in 1691 a Royal Decree ordered that "the Corregidor . . . not consent that any Indian who has not qualified and proven his nobility wear the *mascapaycha*."[63] Similarly, in 1756 Don Diego Ninancuyuchi of the Hospital parish was elected to the office. Son of a cacique in Cotabambas and married to an Inca noblewoman, Diego was a prominent merchant.[64] He appears to have been of Inca ancestry patrilineally; however, from a provincial family, he quite probably was not matrilineally Inca.[65] Nonetheless, the election for the following year began with a striking statement, that "the election must be made of a worthy person who is of the royal lineage of the Inca kings who were of these kingdoms according to the established custom," suggesting that the Inca cabildo did not wish Ninancuyuchi's election to set a precedent.[66] Others of doubtful "capac" status served as alférez on occasion, but overall the descendants of Manco Capac maintained their monopoly on this honor.[67]

Of course, it was only a ceremonial honor. That the Incas were so openly recognized as an elite, indigenous group by the Spanish was remarkable, but it is telling that only in the narrow sphere of electing a standard-bearer were they granted wide autonomy in establishing and enforcing their own hierarchies. The cabildo had no real authority, and the Incas were as localized as all other Andean societies by the *reducciones* and Toledan reforms. The monopoly on power around Cusco that had been the presupposition of imperial Inca rankings and organization was utterly destroyed; and if in the eighteenth century a real sense of "capac"-ness remained, the structures of late colonial Inca organization were utterly different than those of the sixteenth century. Again, in their organization the Incas were unique, but overall the types of reorganization they underwent are representative of those of other complex, preconquest elites. The loss of indigenous extralocal

---

62 Ibid., pp. 228–31.

63 ARC, BE, I, 810.

64 For his family, ARC, COR, Civ., Leg. 33, Exp. 708. For his economic activites, see Chapter 4, p. 134.

65 For Ninan Coyochi, Julien, *Reading Inca History*, p. 73. In the end, Ninancuyuchi did not serve. Elected on June 28, he was taken ill and died four days later; the cabildo elected another alférez. Diego noted in his deathbed will that his replacement should repay his estate the 100 pesos he had already spent on expenses for the office, suggesting that choice of the alférez preceded the formal election. ARC, NOT, Domingo Gamarra, Leg. 126, 701ff, June 30, 1756.

66 ARC, COR, Civ., Leg. 29, Exp. 620.

67 Don Vicente Choquecahua held the office in the 1770s (ARC, NOT, Juan Bautista Gamarra, Leg. 144, 398); in 1802, Mateo Pumacahua (ARC, COR, Civ., Leg. 29, Exp. 620).

political authority wore down the formal relations of provincial elites, as the Spanish courts did not recognize them and some – like Paullu – sought to reorganize them. More fundamental still, the successful imposition of monogamy redefined kinship and domestic units, and introduced an ideal of elite organization that emphasized the lineage, not as the means of reckoning status in a larger, closed group, but as the primary source of elite identity.

As a result, Cusco's eighteenth-century Indian nobility bore far less resemblance to their preconquest forebears than to their creole peers – differing from the latter above all in their self-identity as "indios nobles" or "yngas nobles" and their language (and, indeed, Cusco's "Spaniards" were as likely to speak Quechua as Spanish).[68] This created a cultural divide within Indian society, between a hispanicized elite and a more "Indian" commons. But indigenous Andean societies had also undergone staggering changes. Whole societies collapsed, and new communities were created. Parish churches had replaced *ushnus*. Ayllus were grouped into pueblos, *alcaldes* and caciques had become integral parts of local politics. All tributaries understood the meaning and value of silver coins, and so on. The colonial Indian elite was divided from the commons by cultural as well as material capital, and in the colonial Andes the former had a distinctly Spanish face. But the question whether the provincial curaca, educated and Inca-fied at the royal court in Cusco, returning to his ayllu to collect tribute for the imperial authorities, living in a large compound with a number of wives, was "closer" to the community under his rule than was the cacique, educated at San Borja, returning to his pueblo to collect tribute for the crown, living in a sizable house on the *plaza* and married to the daughter of a cacical dynasty in a neighboring town, is unanswerable. What is certain is that colonial, indigenous Andean communities were internally stratified, and that their upper ranks both sought to reproduce the distinction between themselves and commoners, and defined themselves as part of the Indian republic.

The Spanish Republic

The Indian republic was only half – albeit by far the larger half – of colonial society. The long seventeenth century witnessed an enormous expansion of both Peru's Spanish population and the viceregal market economy. As a result of this growth, by the time of the Bourbon reforms both Indian society and its nobility would exist in a social and economic landscape dramatically different from that in which the royal bureaucrats of the sixteenth century had instituted their reforms. When Toledo visited Cusco in the 1570s, Spaniards made up scarcely 1 percent of Peru's population,

68 Ignacio de Castro, *Relación del Cuzco*, ed. Carlos Daniel Valcárcel (Lima: Universidad Nacional de San Marcos, 1978), p. 44.

Table 2.1. *Population of the Bishopric of Cusco, by Province and República*

Province	1689, Non-Indian	1689, Indian	1689, Total	1792/1807 Non-Indian	1792/1807, Indian	1792/1807, Total
Cusco Cercado	2,512	8,322	10,834	17,746	14,254	32,000
Abancay	1,354	13,734	15,088	6,840	18,419	25,259
Oropesa/Urubamba	693	6,199	6,892	4,086	5,164	9,250
Calca y Lares	160	6,009	6,169	680	5,519	6,199
Paucartambo	180	4,668	4,848	1,744	11,229	12,973
Quispicanchis	500	12,997	13,497	4,390	19,947	24,337
Paruro	403	11,759	12,162	5,202	15,034	20,236
Tinta	206	12,229	12,435	5,923	29,045	34,968
Aymaraes	437	9,540	9,977	4,499	10,782	15,281
Chumbivilcas	150	6,434	6,584	4,471	11,475	15,946
Cotabambas	150	6,954	7,104	1,587	18,237	19,824
Lampa*	575	9,390	9,965	6,820	34,851	41,671
Azángaro*	300	8,712	9,012	3,259	28,844	32,103
Caravaya*	269	4,940	5,209	2,526	17,941	20,467
TOTAL	7,889	121,887	129,776	69,773	240,741	301,514

Note: Figures for 1689 are derived from the bishop's survey (*Cuzco 1689*). Although informative, the survey was not systematic. For the Indian population I have used the figures derived by Wightman, *Indigenous Migration*, p. 200. I have calculated the non-Indian figures; as some priests spoke of adults, others of "almas," and others did not differentiate between absentee landowners and residents, these are less reliable. Unless noted, 1792/1807 data is from Unanue, *Guía*, pp. 89–93. "Totals" are the sums of the figures given in the preceding two columns. Figures for Azángaro are from 1798, in Nils Jacobsen, *Mirages of Transition: The Peruvian Altiplano, 1780–1930* (Berkeley: University of California Press, 1993), p. 22; those for Lampa and Caravaya are from the Intendants' reports of 1807: BNP, Man., D-10473 and D-10474. Because of jurisdictional differences between the Marquesado of Oropesa and the subdelegado of Urubamba, for 1689 Ollantaytambo is included under Calca y Lares, and in 1793 under Urubamba. Vilcabamba's 2 parishes (with 973 Indians, 41 Spaniards) are included under Oropesa for 1689.

and were concentrated in Lima.[69] By 1690 the bishopric of Cusco had almost 8,000 people of European and African ancestry (often mixed with Indian), who together constituted the *república de españoles*; with the fall in the indigenous population, the Spanish republic comprised 6 percent of the bishopric's people. Both the absolute and the relative numbers grew in the next century, as the Spanish republic increased eightfold while the Indian population did not even double, so that by the 1790s more than one fifth of the bishopric's population was Spanish or mestizo. Table 2.1 shows both the scale of the eighteenth-century expansion of the "non-Indian" population, and also the enormous provincial variety. Of course, the categories of "Indian" and "non-Indian" are themselves problematic, an issue that will be discussed below. However, the overwhelming concentration of the bishopric's "Spanish republic" in the city of Cusco, and the dramatic expansion

69 Lockhart estimates the Spanish population of Peru in 1555 at 10,000. *Spanish Peru*, pp. 135–6.

of that republic in all provinces during the eighteenth century, does emerge clearly.

But long before the growth of the Spanish population it already exerted great influence on the Indian republic. Spanish colonization in highland Peru took two forms: the expansion of Spaniards' economic control into the Indian countryside, and physical settlement by those in the Spanish republic.[70] The first occurred long before the second. From the capture of Cusco onward, Spaniards enjoyed privileges that allowed them to rework the Andean economy in their favor. The crown and church bureaucracies placed Spaniards at the heart of pueblo economies. The gradual abolition of the *encomienda* took away private Spaniards' direct access to Indian labor, but another mechanism allowed them to tap into the rural economy: the purchase of land alienated from Indian communities. While overburdened communities sold or rented land to help meet their obligations, far more important was the transfer of surfeit pueblo lands, which the ever-bankrupt crown claimed as vacant and sold in *composiciones de tierras*.[71] This transfer of ownership introduced novel forms of organization into rural Andean society, and created institutions that enabled Spaniards to extend control of production and expropriation far beyond the colonial cities (Table 2.2). Measuring the extent of Spanish property-owning in the bishopric is enormously difficult, as often the bishop's survey makes no mention of size, thus not distinguishing between a ranch with 10,000 sheep and one with 100. Similarly, eighteenth-century figures vary from total numbers of properties to tributary rolls that only record haciendas and ranches with resident tributaries (and, of course, how reliable such rolls are is itself unclear). Nonetheless, a clear sense of the scale and distribution of such holdings does emerge. According to the 1689 survey, Spanish-owned property in rural Cusco included 500 haciendas and 150 coca and sugar plantations, over 200 ranches, 8 large textile factories, and more than 50 mines. These rural holdings allowed the creole elite of Cusco to attract Indian migrants, and with their labor to produce goods – sugar, coca, and cloth – to market in the mining cities of the Altiplano.[72]

Sugar production was concentrated in the warm valleys of Abancay, fifty miles west of Cusco.[73] The Paucartambo valley, forty miles east of

---

70 For demographic changes and hacienda expansion in Cusco, Magnus Mörner, *Perfil de la sociedad rural del Cuzco a fines de la colonia* (Lima: Universidad del Pacífico, 1978).

71 Davies, *Landowners*; Piel, *Capitalismo Agrario*, pp. 160–78. For sale by community, *Cuzco 1689*, p. 48.

72 For the creole economy, Gibbs, *Cusco*; Mörner, *Perfil*; Glave and Remy, *Estructura Agraria*; Piel, *Capitalismo Agrario*; Laura Escobari, de Querejazu, *Producción y comercio en el espacio sur andino en el siglo XVII: Cuzco-Potosí, 1650–1700* (La Paz: Embajada de España, 1985) Kathryn J. Burns, *Colonial Habits: Convents and the Spiritual Economy of Cuzco, Peru* (Durham: Duke University Press, 1999).

73 *Cuzco 1689*, pp. 208, 176–83, 196–9.

Table 2.2. *Haciendas in the Intendancy of Cusco, Late Seventeenth and Late Eighteenth Centuries*

Province	# Hazdas (a) 1689	# Hazdas (b) 1786	# Hazdas (c) 1788/92	1–5 Tribs	6–14 Tribs	15–29 Tribs	30+ Tribs	Avg. per Hazda	Biggest Hazda
Abancay	180	81	44	18	9	12	5	13	53
Urubamba	93	61	19	3	5	6	5	23	58
Calca y Lares	46	38	24	7	11	3	3	13	61
Paucartambo	76	106	73	11	30	24	8	16	117
Quispicanchis	77	116	9	0	5	2	2	19	44
Tinta	12	39	0	0	0	0	0	n.a.	n.a.
Paruro	121	43	42	18	17	6	1	9	39
Chumbivilcas	45	57	37	19	11	4	3	10	41
Cotabambas	41	22	3	0	0	1	2	38	57
Aymaraes	14	11	10	4	2	4	0	12	22
TOTAL	705	574	261	80	90	62	29	14	117

Note: "Hazda (a)" is a tally of haciendas, mines, obrajes, and ranches in the 1689 survey (*Cuzco 1689*). "Hazda (b)" lists the number of haciendas reported in the 1786 *Estado de las provincias del Cusco*. "Hazda (c)" gives the number of haciendas listed in the tributary rolls of 1788 or 1792 for the various provinces; it therefore includes only haciendas on which tributaries were matriculated. The fifth through ninth columns show the distribution of the haciendas listed in column four [Hazda (c)], by number of tributaries matriculated on the hacienda. The tenth column contains the average number of tributaries per hacienda in the province; the eleventh column, the number of tributaries on the largest hacienda in each province. For columns 2 and 3, see Mörner, *Perfil*, p. 32. For columns 4–11, see the provincial tribute tables (in the order in which the provinces are listed), ARC, INT, RH, Legs. 194 (1792); 163 (1785); 196 (1792); 186 (1787); 185 (1787); 195 (1792); 198 (1792); 196 (1792); 194 (1792); 194 (1792).

the city, was the major center of coca cultivation.[74] The bishopric also had a strong textile industry, employing a myriad of social relations, from cottage weaving to guild production in Cusco to factory production in the countryside near the city. The last – dominated by huge *obrajes* – fed the Altiplano market.[75] In the pastoral pueblos of the highlands, Spaniards purchased pasturage for sheep ranches.[76] Finally, in the temperate valleys around Cusco, hundreds of properties supplied the mundane necessities of any early modern city.[77] Much royal agricultural land in the Inca heartland had been seized and divided; as a result, while all pueblos near Cusco had

74 Ibid., pp. 253–69. For the Cusco-Potosí coca trade, Glave, *Trajinantes*, pp. 79–116; Escobari, *Producción*, pp. 85–6.

75 *Cuzco 1689*, pp. 156, 161, 166, 173. Escobari, *Producción*, pp. 78–84. For eighteenth-century *obrajeros*, Neus Escandell-Tur, *Producción y comercio de tejidos coloniales: los obrajes y chorrillos del Cusco, 1750–1820* (Cusco: Centro Bartolomé de las Casas, 1997), pp. 71–134.

76 Azángaro, Lampa, and Chumbivilcas had the largest numbers of these ranches: 63, 42, and 32 respectively. *Cuzco 1689*, passim.

77 Ibid., passim.

some Spanish properties, landowning was concentrated in parishes founded in Inca-dominated communities.[78]

The largest Spanish holdings were vast, with resident populations of up to 500 people – the size of many pueblos.[79] These made up scarcely one tenth of Cusco's Spanish properties, and were clustered in a few provinces and parishes. But by 1689 four-fifths of the bishopric's parishes had at least one Spanish property, and roughly one in four of the Indian population had settled on them.[80] Sugar and coca plantations reigned supreme in lowland areas peripheral to the Indian societies of the bishopric: here the creole economy created new communities rather than displacing the old. Elsewhere the effects of Spanish properties varied from one parish to the next.[81] Almost half of the bishopric's 135 parishes had fewer than three Spanish-owned properties in 1689; in 6 of the 15 provinces, this was true for more than half of all parishes.[82] Only in the provinces around Cusco – Abancay, the Marquesado of Oropesa, Calca y Lares, and Chilques y Masques – did every parish have at least three properties. And their presence did not necessarily undermine Indian communities, or their elites. Landowners required seasonal labor, and where Spanish properties existed alongside Indian communities, the latter offered an obvious source. For Indians, such labor brought cash to pay tribute.[83] Nor were absentee landowners necessarily hostile to Indian elites, to whom they looked for stability in the communities where their assets were located. Thus, the relationship between Spanish properties and Indian communities could be symbiotic as well as hostile, with Spanish landowning buttressing elite control.[84]

More generally, these properties were the products and the underpinnings of the highland market economy, whose effects were felt all through the Andes. One of the most significant changes in the colonial Andes was in long-distance exchange, as its organization moved from control of political

---

78 The greatest concentrations were in Anta, Zurite, Oropesa, Pisac, Ollantaytambo, Urubamba, Yucay, Guanoquite, Paruro, Yaurisque, and Accha Urinsaya. *Cuzco 1689*, passim. For the seizure of imperial lands by the Spanish, Sempat Assadourian, *Transiciones*, pp. 92–150.

79 David T. Garrett, "Descendants of the Natural Lords Who Were: The Indian Nobility of Cusco and the Collao under the Bourbons" (Ph.D. diss., Columbia University, 2002), pp. 136–9; ARC, COR, Civ., Leg. 41, Exp. 871, for the estate of the Marquis of Casa Xara.

80 *Cuzco 1689*, passim.

81 Ibid., p. 117, for Chupa, with three-fifths of Azángaro's private ranches, and one-fourth its Spaniards.

82 Cotabambas, Tinta, Caravaya, Azángaro, Chumbivilcas, and Aymaraes. Ibid., passim.

83 For symbiotic exploitation between hacendados and Indian communities in central Mexico, John Tutino, *From Insurrection to Revolution in Mexico: Social Bases of Agrarian Violence, 1750–1940* (Princeton: Princeton University Press, 1986), pp. 143–8. Also *Cuzco 1689*, p. 168; for Upper Peru in the eighteenth and nineteenth centuries, Klein, *Haciendas and Ayllus*.

84 Opposition to abuses by Spanish landowners could also buttress the position of caciques in their communities. AGI, Escribanía, Leg. 1058C, Exp. 29 for Quiquijana in the 1720s.

authorities (under the Incas) to the domain of the market.[85] Silver production in Alto Peru supported a vast market network, dominated by the Lima–Potosí axis, which linked Peru's cities and certain industrial and agricultural enclaves. This market economy was a hybrid creation, utterly dependent on the variegated tributary economy of the Andes to sustain it in the face of enormous inefficiencies imposed by terrain, geographic size, sparse population, and the fiscal demands of the crown.[86] Rural properties played a dual role in this economy. They provided the profits by which urban *rentiers* (and rural landowners) became consumers, stimulating a population of artisans and wage laborers, who in turn became a market for necessities; they also produced many of the goods required by this market – sugar, coca, and textiles – and also foodstuffs grown around Cusco, Arequipa, Cochabamba.[87]

Although Spanish Peruvians dominated the highland market economy, they did not monopolize consumption, production, or transportation. Indian laborers in highland cities turned to the urban markets, and caciques and rural villagers acquired their luxuries through the market. Peasant plots, communal lands, and cacical properties all produced goods for sale.[88] In the seventeenth century the Indian nobility of the southern highlands dominated the transport business, as their llama and mule trains carried goods across the Titicaca basin.[89] These dealings could be enormous: in his 1673 will Don Gabriel Fernandez Guarachi, cacique of Jesús de Machaca, declared as his property 2,250 llamas, 1,000 of which were to carry "wine from the valleys of Moquegua."[90] Peru's market economy thus created Indian fortunes as well as Spanish. Those at valuable positions in the market benefited greatly from its expansion. More generally, the cacique stood at the intersection of the highland market economy and the subsistence economy of the Indian community, and profited from the location. Thus, by the 1700s a vibrant Spanish republic and market were as essential to the Indian elite as were the communal economies over which it presided.

The economic colonization of rural Cusco was mirrored by physical settlement, although Tables 2.1 and 2.2 show that the two did not occur simultaneously. The removal of lands into Spanish freehold was underway

85 With the significant exception of the *reparto*; Chapter 4, pp. 122–123.
86 Especially Sempat Assadourian, *El sistema*; also Larson, *Cochabamba*; Glave, *Trajinantes*; Andrien, *Andean Worlds*, pp. 73–102; Escobari, *Producción*.
87 Larson, *Cochabamba*, pp. 51–91; Davies, *Landowners*. For Cusco, see n72 above.
88 Spalding, "Kurakas and Commerce"; Glave, *Trajinantes*, pp. 20–176; Choque Canqui, *Sociedad*, pp. 109–58; John V. Murra, "Aymara Lords and Their European Agents at Potosí," *Nova Americana* [Turin] 1 (1978): 231–43.
89 Glave, *Trajinantes*, pp. 20–176, 279–304.
90 Silvia Rivera, "El Mallku y la sociedad colonial en el siglo XVII: el caso de Jesús de Machaca," *Avances* (La Paz) 1 (1978): pp. 7–27; Choque Canqui, *Sociedad*, pp. 109–58.

by the 1550s and expanded in the seventeenth century; but the rural Spanish population remained tiny until the 1700s, when Spaniards and mestizos began to constitute an appreciable part of most pueblos. Three factors contributed to this expansion: immigration, natural growth, and intermarriage. Immigration from Spain was the least important, at a few dozen a year after the decades of conquest.[91] The growth of creole Cusco was due to creoles' ability to reproduce themselves. But the growth of the república de españoles owed much to the inclusion of mestizos therein. Although as Andean in their ancestry as Spanish, legally mestizos belonged to the lower ranks of Spanish society, and the growth of this group created a sizable class of rural and urban poor outside the ayllus of Indian society, who competed with them for resources.[92]

Spanish Andeans were strikingly urban: in 1690 almost one in three of the bishopric's non-Indians lived within a twenty-minute walk of the Cusco cathedral; nor were those outside the city evenly distributed through the bishopric (Table 2.1). Six of the fourteen rural provinces did not have a single parish with 100 Spaniards, while five (out of 126) parishes were home to one-third of the rural "republic of Spaniards."[93] In the temperate and semitropical valleys closer to Cusco, Spanish settlement was concentrated in areas producing sugar and coca, in pueblos founded atop royal Inca communities, and along the Vilcanota within thirty miles of Cusco.[94] Four of the twelve parishes with Spanish populations of more than one hundred were in this Inca heartland: Urubamba, Maras, Ollantaytambo, and Oropesa. All four shared a similar history, as sites of large, royal Inca landholdings that had passed intact to Spaniards, stimulating Spanish settlement and landowning.[95] This relative density of Spanish settlement close to Cusco was in marked contrast to the highlands to the west and south. There, a century and a half of Spanish rule had produced almost no Spanish settlement. In Canas y Canchis, fifty-nine of every sixty people were Indian. Only in Caravaya, Lampa, and Aymaraes did the república de españoles make up 5 per cent of the population, and these three had substantial deposits of silver and gold. Four of the twelve parishes with more than 100 non-Indians were in these provinces; three of the four were mining centers.[96] Elsewhere in the highlands, small numbers of Spaniards lived in overwhelmingly Indian communities.

91 Nicolas Sánchez-Albornoz, "The Population of Colonial Spanish America," in *The Cambridge History of Latin America*, ed. Leslie Bethell (Cambridge: Cambridge University Press, 1984), II, 16–35.
92 In 1790 the intendency of Cusco had 23,104 mestizos. Unanue, *Guía*, p. 178.
93 Curaguasi, Limatambo, Maras, Urubamba and Oropesa. *Cuzco 1689*, passim.
94 Ibid.; Glave and Remy, *Estructura agraria*, pp. 58–63.
95 *Cuzco 1689*, pp. 156–8.
96 Pucará, Sandia, Soraya; ibid., pp. 89–91, 105–6, 352.

Where these rural Spaniards stood in colonial society is difficult to gauge. They ranged from impoverished migrants to miners, landowners, and traders of provincial importance and with close ties to Indian elites. At the bottom were landless squatters, a group composed largely of mestizos who resembled the *indios vagos* wandering the Andes in huge numbers during the seventeenth century. Better-heeled creoles disavowed any relation. The priests of the parishes of Umachire and Macarí made typical comments in their 1689 reports to the bishop. The former reported that Umachire had five hundred Indians, and "eight married persons called Spaniards, who are not"; his neighbor, that "the pueblo of Macarí has five or six Spaniards, all mestizos who, for being children of Indian women and wearing the costume of the Spanish enjoy that title."[97]

The number of these "españoles de la tierra" (as they were derisively called by well-educated priests) increased dramatically in the eighteenth century, with significant repercussions for rural society.[98] In every province of the bishopric the non-Indian population grew at least fourfold; in all but the six provinces around Cusco, it grew at least tenfold, while the number of Spanish-owned properties underwent no similar expansion (Tables 2.1 and 2.2). A comment from Copacabana in 1805 suggests the position of impoverished mestizos in the late colonial highlands. Remarking on the distribution of communal land, witnesses observed that "... these lands sustain, in addition to the families of the originarios and forasteros who make up the moieties and ayllus, more than one hundred people of the mestizo class, including both sexes, to whom is permitted their use, by immemorial custom, out of Christian and fraternal charity. They sow a few bits [of land], with the obligation to help with the functions of the pueblo."[99] Exempt from tribute burdens, mestizos of this ilk were a rootless and mobile group, united by a shared imputation of mixed ancestry, and prevented by the extent of Indian commons from acquiring property either in freehold or through guaranteed hereditary access. In itself, the growth of this class undermined Indian noble power since, by law, the Indian elite who presided over rural Indian life had no authority over those in the república de españoles, no matter how base.[100] In practice, the caciques of rural pueblos dominated all in their communities but the most powerful Spaniards; but as poor, rural non-Indians grew in numbers, they could form a power base for provincial creole elites.

97 Ibid., pp. 60 and 80. Such observations can be found in most entries from the Collao.
98 Ibid., 237; it is a play on the Spanish term for llamas, "carneros de la tierra."
99 ANB, Ruck, Exp. 217, 125.
100 Although Indian alcaldes could hold blacks and mestizos "hasta que llegue la justicia real." *Recopilación*, Book VI, Title III, Law 17.

Those creole elites were of considerable importance in rural areas, although they ranked far behind the bishopric's true elite, the city's aristocratic houses and other well-to-do Spaniards. Provincial Spaniards prospered as ranchers, mine owners, *hacendados*, and merchants, and by the end of the seventeenth century they were to be found in every province, if not in every pueblo. Their impact on Indian society was in part a factor of their numbers. In 1689, perhaps twenty parishes had a Spanish community of more than a dozen households; by 1800 almost all did. These local Spaniards required negotiation by Indian elites. By no means was that negotiation always peaceful: legal and open conflicts between caciques and Spanish landowners were a common feature of rural society.[101] But the interests of rural creoles and Indian nobles were also likely to converge, and together they could form a united local elite, better able both to control the Indian commons and to check the power of the corregidor and the priest. Indeed, in his decrees relating to caciques, Toledo included two laws that forbade caciques to give banquets for or presents to Spaniards, and required permission from the corregidor before they entered into business dealings.[102] Certainly these decrees had little effect on pueblo alliances. Reporting to the bishop in 1689 the priest of Anta bemoaned "... the molestations and damage that [the tributaries] receive from the Spaniards and mestizos, in particular the Rosas, who live among them. And also the Governors, principal caciques, and *mandones* who are no less [eager] to increase the hurt and sufferings of tributary Indians to take over their lands, livestock, and houses in order to rent them to the mestizos."[103] Poorer mestizos provided a rental market for communal property, whereby Indian officials could profit at the expense of the tributaries. Richer creoles and mestizos had the power to abuse tributaries directly, often in league with the cacical elites. Indian and Spanish elites of rural pueblos were divided by their positions in both the colonial economy and the colonial polity, but united by the shared interests of those with power.

Often, they were united by matrimony as well. Ninety years after the priest penned these complaints, the "cacique principal" of Anta was a Rosas, married to the daughter of the former cacique, Don Mateo Quispeguaman.[104] The Quispeguaman and Rosas families were following an established practice. From the time of the conquest, Spaniards and Indian noble families had sought to strengthen their position in colonial society through intermarriage. Both Ñusta Beatriz and Melchor Carlos Ynga had married Spaniards, and the unions of their female cousins with *conquistadores*

---

101 For example, that in Quiquijana in the 1720s: AGI, Escribanía, Leg. 1058C, Exp. 29.
102 Ballesteros, *Ordenanzas*, Book II, Title 6, Laws 20 and 22.
103 *Cuzco 1689*, p. 195.
104 ARC, NOT, Tapia Sarmiento, Leg. 258, 376 ff., July 7, 1770.

established some of Cusco's most prominent creole families.[105] Within a few generations the upper reaches of Cusco's creole elite had stopped inter-marrying with Indians, instead marrying among themselves, with creoles from other cities, or with immigrants from Spain. However, among the rest of colonial society such unions were common – witness the bishopric's large mestizo population and the frequent mentions of mestizos in the 1689 survey. Many of these unions took place among the Spanish and Indian masses, but they also occurred between the Indian and creole elites of the countryside.

At present, only anecdotal evidence is available. In 1689 Guaquirca had a sizable Spanish population, of thirty-eight adults and thirty-eight children; forty-four of these came from just four families. These in turn were tied by marriage to Guaquirca's formidable cacical family. The patriarch of the pueblo's Spaniards, Diego Garcia Contreras, was 60 years old; he had children by an earlier marriage, both of whom had married Spaniards and settled in the pueblo. However, in 1689 he had been married for 20 years to the 40-year-old Doña Ana Maria Ayquipa Arcos Guachaca, "heiress to the cacique and governor of this Pueblo"; the couple had six children.[106] She was almost certainly the sister of the current cacique, Don Francisco Ayquipa Arcos Guachaca, so that the hereditary lords of Collana Aymara had close ties of kinship to the small cluster of Spaniards settled among them.

Such marriages formed bonds between the two republics within the pueblo. Indeed, despite Philip II's 1576 prohibition "that caciques not be mestizos," a number of cacicazgos passed through such alliances.[107] The existence of such "mestizo" caciques indicates the general failure to enforce many of the crown's decrees. But it also suggests how family alliances could supersede ethnic distinctions, so that, in the end, the Ayquipa Arcos Guachaca and Contreras cousins formed an interethnic ruling clan in Collana Aymara. Just as the Incas had intermarried with the nobilities of the societies they conquered, so did the Spanish, creating mixed local elites. They were united by need: the Spaniards, for access to the local economies controlled by the Indian nobility; the latter, for the connections that even rural Spaniards had to the political and economic networks of Spanish Peru. At the same time, these local elites were by no means unified: Spaniards and Indians remained divided legally, culturally, and economically. In 1689 in most communities in the bishopric, the Indian component of these local elites was still dominant, although the growth of Spanish Peru over the next

---

105 Temple Dunbar, "Don Carlos Inca," especially pp. 144–5 and 170.
106 *Cuzco 1689*, pp. 397–9.
107 *Recopilación*, Book VI, Title VII, Law 6. For intermarried cacical families, ANB, EC, 1793–11 [Chucuito], and ANB, EC, 1796–97 [Laja].

century would shift the balance of power until, following the Tupac Amaru rebellion, provincial Spaniards increasingly won control of rural society.

In 1759 the corregidor of Lampa set out for Ñuñoa to name a new cacique after Don Ramon Basques had resigned, unable to make tribute payments. The corregidor appointed the 43-year-old Don Antonio Guaman Tapara, whose family had emerged from the pueblo's late seventeenth-century wreckage as local leaders. Antonio had served as the mita captain in the 1740s; his parents were described as "descendants by direct line from caciques of this pueblo."[108] After choosing Tapara, the corregidor assembled the village officers, Indian principales and commoners, and Spanish residents and charged them

... to obey [Tapara], maintaining his privileges and exemptions while at the same time providing him with the services and assistance that he ought to enjoy as cacique, as Your Majesty has disposed and ordered in His Royal Ordinances, and [that] the said Don Antonio Tapara will perform the greatest efficiency in the collection of the Royal tributes under his charge in order to make the payments at their required times, and at the same time he will take care, as his obligation, that the Indians attend church and mass the days on which they should, so that they can be instructed in the mysteries of Our Sainted Faith; he is charged to ... maintain them in peace, and good conduct treating them with love, and equity. ...[109]

The official description of the cacique was unchanged since the time of Toledo. This simple performance of colonial authority serves as testimony to the continuity that two centuries of Spanish rule had brought to Andean society, as an ideal of pueblo politics codified in the sixteenth century saw itself reproduced in the eighteenth.

But that appearance of continuity was deceptive. The seventeenth century brought enormous changes to Andean society, and the Indian elite. The collapse of the indigenous population produced widespread migration and the reconstitution of pueblos and ayllus. Monogamy, new understandings of property, and cultural hispanicization all reworked the relationship between the Indian nobility and the commons, and the internal organization of elite groups. The larger colonial society within which the Indian republic existed also changed dramatically. The rise of a market system, the expansion of Spanish property-owning in rural regions, and the growth of the Spanish population created their own pressures and opportunities for Indian communities and their elites. The ideal of Indian pueblos set apart from Peru's Spanish population and ruled by Indian nobles under the watchful gaze of the parish priest proved unsustainable. By the eighteenth century colonial rule had done much to transform the economic

108 According to Antonio's description; ARC, RA, Adm., Leg. 167 (1808–9).
109 See Appendix.

relations between cacique and community, and to create local elites that spanned the legal divide between the two ethnic republics. Nonetheless, the sixteenth-century legislation continued to define the organization of the Indian republic. The localized dialectics of colonialism in the Andes undermined particular pueblos and their elites, while affirming overall the central position of both in the organization of society, so that the Indian elites of eighteenth-century Cusco were simultaneously a relic of the Inca empire, the creation of sixteenth-century laws, and the product of two centuries of colonial rule.

PART II

The Indian Nobility of Bourbon Cusco

3

Cacical Families and Provincial Nobilities

The colonial Indian elite – part nobility of blood, part nobility of office – received recognition of its privileges as individuals, families, and even *ayllus*. But the Indian elite had no official role in the governance of Peru above the level of the pueblo: no *cortes* or assemblies bound them together. Nor did such institutions bind together creole Peru, but urban, provincial, and viceregal offices in the church and royal government helped to forge a more unified Spanish elite that ruled Peru. The Spanish had usurped imperial, and even provincial, government from the indigenous elite. However, extralocal alliances of Indian elites did not vanish altogether. Some sense of a shared identity, rooted in Inca ancestry, may have bound together a broad Andean elite, although archival evidence for this is very thin. Economic currents did draw migrants across the viceroyalty – with Incas from Cusco moving to Potosí and nobles from Azángaro settling in Lima.[1] Presumably they maintained familial ties with their native communities, although these do not appear to have been sufficiently dense to create the solidarities that would emerge among creoles in the late eighteenth and early nineteenth centuries.[2]

Rather, at the provincial level, localized Indian elites throughout the Andes created their own networks of marital alliances that spanned pueblo, and provincial, frontiers. The result was a series of regional nobilities, in which interrelated cacical families held sway over large swaths of the highlands. In examining the organization of these nobilities, this chapter focuses on the survival or production of provincial Indian elites, the organization of cacical succession in the bishopric, and patterns of marriage alliances. Three caveats are necessary. First, the geography of these groups and alliances changed over time: patterns from the middle of the eighteenth century are not normative for earlier eras. Nor did every province

---

1 ARC, NOT, Acuña, Leg. 10, 367 ff., January 19, 1774, for Don Joseph Poma Ynga. BNP, Man., C-3315, for Don Fernando Mango, of Azángaro, in 1797 a tailor in Lima.
2 Benedict Anderson, *Imagined Communities: Reflections on the Origin and Spread of Nationalism*, 2nd edn. (London: Verso, 1991), pp. 47–66.

or region have a network of interrelated cacical families. Finally, in positing the existence of "provincial nobilities" I do not suggest that these were coherent, organized groups in which the maintenance of collective authority played a role in individuals' decisions. Certainly the Inca nobility around Cusco had a group consciousness, although the intense competition among them was not always conducive to group solidarity. In the Titicaca basin, marriage alliances between cacical dynasties ended immediately after the Tupac Amaru rebellion, when the logic of Indian power changed dramatically. From then, cacical families sought alliances with Spaniards to preserve familial power and showed no commitment to an Indian "cacical class."

The Colonial Incas

Over the sixteenth and seventeenth centuries, the Inca colonies that had spanned Tahuantinsuyu were absorbed into the provincial societies of the colonial Andes. But the Inca nobility around Cusco remained a cohesive group for the length of the colonial period and received unique recognition from the royal government. Although the Spanish understood the distinction between the Incas and other Indians as one of nobility, not ethnicity (a reinterpretation that in no way displeased the Incas), the crown conceded to them a corporate identity. Inca exceptionalism manifested itself in many ways, all of which interacted to reinforce Inca preeminence in Indian Cusco, and a position of privilege in the area more broadly. The sixteenth-century concessions of nobility to large numbers of Inca men and their descendants created a noble Indian caste in and around the city, numbering one to two thousand in the eighteenth century. This nobility demanded, and generally received, deference and privileges on the basis of their Inca ancestry. They also had an officially sanctioned institutional presence: the Inca *cabildo*, responsible for the annual display of the Incas' special position in Cusco, the carrying of the royal standard by an Inca noble in the procession of Santiago. Less formally, Inca nobles prospered as urban merchants and artisans. Most importantly, the combination of the Incas' legal privileges, and their traditional dominance in the provinces around Cusco, left them the ruling caste of the region's Indian republic, as Inca nobles filled most of the ayllu and pueblo *cacicazgos* within twenty miles of the city.

Examination of the colonial Inca nobility's internal organization confronts several challenges. The first is simply a dearth of information. Although the Inca nobility of Cusco Cercado left a relatively rich trove of documentation in notarial and court records, such sources are far rarer for the outlying pueblos. Thus, the following account of cacical organization in rural Inca pueblos is necessarily a sketch, gleaning what information it can from wills and lawsuits. Other difficulties are inherent in the category "Inca" itself. Inca Garcilaso and others divided the "Incas" into "Incas by blood" and "Incas by privilege." These terms were colonial innovations, but they reflected the very real divide between those with "capac" status, that is, those who claimed descent from Manco Capac, and other groups "descended" from his siblings.[3] How these hierarchies corresponded to those of eighteenth-century Cusco and its hinterland is unclear. Even the undeniably "capac" – those of the *panacas* – were, by the 1700s, divided by the colonial categories of noble and tributary. Distributed throughout the Cusco area at the time of the conquest, only some had been ennobled by the Spanish. Cusco's parishes of San Sebastián and San Gerónimo were unique: while Incas with patents of nobility lived throughout the area, nowhere else had entire ayllus exempt from tribute and recognized as noble (Tables 3.1 and 3.2). Even there, not all panacas had noble status, and in others only some members were so recognized. In 1785 all in San Sebastián's Ayllu Sucso were legally noble, but none in San Gerónimo's Ayllu Sucso.[4] Conversely, three of the seventeen men in San Sebastián's Ayllu Aucaylli were noble, but all twenty-three were noble in San Gerónimo's Aucaylli. In Belén, just four of the thirty-eight men in Ayllu Uscamayta had noble status. Whether the tributaries of these "royal" ayllus considered themselves "Incas," or were considered so by their noble neighbors, is not clear.

A substantial majority of the Inca nobility of Cusco Cercado were "capac" or "dynastic" Incas – "descendants" of Manco Capac. The main exception were the nobles of Ayarmaca in San Sebastián. The Ayarmacas (reduced in San Sebastián, Pucyura, and Chinchero) were the most important group other than the Incas in the Cusco area before the imperial expansion; they were also clearly linked to the Incas through marriage, and many accounts have one or more of the earlier Incas' principal wives coming from this group.[5] To Inca Garcilaso these were Incas by privilege; the nobility of the ayllu in San Sebastián is a reminder that the colonial Inca elite was not composed solely of "capac" Incas. This becomes clearer outside Cusco Cercado, where other groups – of "nondynastic" Incas, or Incas by privilege – had long been intimately linked with the descendants of Manco Capac. Among these there were nobles and cacical lineages.[6] In his 1768 guide to the viceroyalty, Cosme Bueno observed of Urubamba province that it contained "many Indian families of noble origin, but very poor."[7] The large

---

3 Bauer, *Development*, pp. 21–2; Julien, *Reading Inca History*, pp. 233–53.
4 ARC, INT, RH, Leg. 175.
5 Julien, *Reading Inca History*, pp. 68–72; María Rostworowski de Diez Canseco, "Los Ayarmaca," *Revista del Museo Nacional* {Lima} 36 (1969–70), pp. 58–101.
6 For example, the Callapiñas and others of Pacarectambo; Gary Urton, *The History of a Myth: Pacariqtambo and the Origin of the Inkas* (Austin: University of Texas Press, 1990), pp. 42–60.
7 Cosme Bueno, *El conocimiento de los tiempos. Efeméride del año de 1768* (Lima, 1767).

Table 3.1. *Adult Male Indian Population, Selected Parishes in Cusco Cercado, 1768*

Parish/Ayllu	Cacique	Noble[a]	Originario	Forastero
San Blas		*16*	*61*	*80*
Capac	Chrispin Tintacana	3	6	24
Urincosco	Lazaro Yllaguaman	3	0	31
Collana	Bartolome Pomalondo	5	24	15
Hatan Yngacona	Nicolas Camacondori Ynga Yupanqui	5	31	10
San Cristóbal		*22*	*62*	*111*
Collana	Sebastian Guambotupa	6	4	40
Cayhua	Antonio Chiguantito	0	45	32
Suna	Antonio Pilcotupa	11	7	14
Hanancusco	Phelipe Puma Ynga	5	6	25
Belén		*24*	*59*	*99*
Collana	Ramon Henrriques	6	2	26
Quesco y Maras	Marcos Maigua	6	23	31
Sutec Uscamayta	Marcos Pumayauarina	12	3	22
Urinsaya Altomirano	Tomas Astopoma Ynga	0	31	20
Santa Ana		*0*	*94*	*69*
Chachapoya y Yanacona	Pablo Condorpusa	0	13	26
Chinchaysuio Chasqui	Simon Ninancuro	0	6	15
Callas Quispeguana	Melchor Quispe	0	17	13
Anansaya Collana	Carlos de Alanya	0	19	12
Cinquenta Uguriche	Mathias Tupa Apo Suma Yanyachi	0	39	3
Matriz (excluding guilds)[b]		*13*	*27*	*66*
Yanaconas	Lucas Poma Ynga	13	27	66

[a] Excluding cacique.
[b] 1765.
Source: From tribute rolls and appeals by Indian nobles matriculated as tributaries. ARC, COR: Adm., Leg. 94 (1767–84); Civ., Leg. 46, Exp. 1024.

pueblo of Maras, in particular, was known for its large nobility and numerous cacical lines. The Maras themselves, by some counts, came with Manco Capac and his brothers on the journey from Pacarectambo; the pueblo's main ayllus – Mullacas and Maras – were probably subjected to the Incas in the generation before Pachacutic's imperial expansion.[8] Its cacical families traced their ancestry to Sancho Uscapaucar, a *curaca* in the mid-1500s who does not appear to have been part of the "capac" Incas; however, in the seventeenth and eighteenth centuries Maras' nobles routinely took "Ynga" as part of their family names, and at least line one claimed Paullu Ynga as

8 Julien, *Reading Inca History*, pp. 238–9.

Table 3.2. *Male Indian Population, San Sebastián and San Gerónimo, 1768*

Parish and Ayllu	Noble	Originario	Forastero	Total
San Sebastián	403	303	77	783
Sucso Collana Pachaca, "que son de los Nobles que no pagan tributos"	120	–	–	120
Aucailli, "nobles"	31	55	20	106
Apomaita y Quecaquirau	2	18	2	22
Rauragua	7	49	28	84
Chima, "nobles y originarios"	42	41	9	92
Ayamarca y Pumamarca, "nobles en la que se comprehenden varios aillos y tributarios"	171	47	18	236
Yacanora Puyan Aucaguaqui y Caias, "nobles y originarios"	28	2	–	30
Yanaconas	2	51	–	53
Tributaries on various haciendas	–	40	–	40
San Gerónimo	131	554	44	729
Collana	1	80	10	91
Chavincosco	1	41	6	48
Callanpata	–	21	3	24
Sucso de Nobles	74	–	–	74
Aucailli de Nobles	45	–	17	62
Orcon	1	49	–	50
Andamachay	1	52	8	61
Apomaita	1	56	–	57
Quecaquirao	2	31	–	33
Raurau	1	44	–	45
Anaguanque	1	105	–	106
Soroma	1	56	–	57
Collana	2	19	–	21
TOTAL	534	857	121	1512

Note: Includes all males; 281 were listed as sons of nobles not of tributary age. At the time of the matriculation, roughly 250 adult noblemen were exempted from tribute.

Source: From tribute rolls and appeals by nobles matriculated as tributaries. ARC, COR: Civ., Leg. 49, Exp. 1129 [San Sebastián]; Adm., Leg. 94 (1767–84) [San Gerónimo].

an ancestor.[9] And, like Cusco Cercado, the pueblos of the Marquesado de Oropesa had their own "Ynga *alférez real*."[10]

At the same time, many rural cacical families proudly asserted their descent from Inca emperors; often these lines were the product of colonial alliances between local ruling lineages and the surviving lines of

9 For Maras' cacicazgos, ARC: RA, Ord., Leg. 27 (1798); COR, Ped., Leg. 90 (1753–65). For the Cusipaucar, INT, Gob., Leg. 145 (1792–3).

10 ARC, COR, Civ., Leg. 45, Exp. 976 (1762), for Viñapi Autapaucar.

Inca royals. Moreover, these areas had their own clusters of "Inca nobles" who claimed descent from Manco Capac.[11] By the eighteenth century, all of these groups were intermarried. Patrilineally Chinchero's eighteenth-century cacical dynasty, the Pumacahuas, were not from the "capac" elite; but in 1777 Don Francisco Pumacahua was married to a descendant of Huayna Capac, and his successor, Mateo Pumacahua, often added "Ynga" to his name.[12] By the seventeenth century prominent lineages of groups broadly affiliated with the descendants of Manco Capac – that is, the Incas by privilege, or nondynastic Incas – asserted their own "Incaness." They had, in fact, become more "Inca," as descendants of Tupac Yupanqui and Huayna Capac sought to retain their privileged place in a changed world by marrying into these families. Also, the Spanish endowed being "Ynga" with symbolic authority. By "Ynga" or "orejón" sixteenth-century narrators had narrowly meant the "dynastic" Incas; Inca Garcilaso used the division of "blood" and "privilege" to differentiate the panacas from the other groups with whom their history was closely linked.[13] But as control of cacicazgos in the surrounding provinces became more important to status and wealth than did "pure" dynastic ancestry, the hierarchies within this larger "Inca" group changed.

Perhaps the most difficult question is to what extent tributaries in the former Inca heartland considered themselves "Incas." Yucay and Ollantay-tambo had Ayllus Cusco, as did Calca, Lamay, Coya, and Pisac. In Paruro, the pueblos around Pacarectambo – Paruro, Yaurisque, Guanoquite, Coror, and Capi – all had Ayllus Yngacona ("Inca people"). Where these stood in the hierarchies of the eighteenth-century Indian republic is unclear: whether the tributaries of Guanoquite's Ayllu Yngacona saw their caciques from the Borja Quispe Carlos Ynga family (descendants of Huayna Capac) as kin or as a distinct nobility – or somewhere in between. Nor do we know the hierarchies between the ayllus of Yngacona and other ayllus they lived among.

But whatever the difficulty in defining precisely who was "Inca" in eighteenth-century Cusco, their presence is clear. Their privilege was rooted in their exceptional history, as the descendants "of the Yngas, natural lords of our kingdoms of Peru," an ancestry that the government recognized, the people of Cusco acknowledged, and the Inca nobility aggressively performed.[14] In virtually every narrative of Cusco's, and Peru's, history they occupied a special role. To the Spanish they symbolized the just transfer of

---

11 For example, Acos and Acomayo: "Indios de Sangre Real," pp. 207 and 226, and ARC, RA, Ord., Leg. 76 (1812), for Rimachimayta lands.

12 "Indios de sangre real," p. 217.

13 Julien, *Reading Inca History*, p. 29.

14 In the Poma Ynga petition, ARC, INT, RH, Leg. 202 (1796), 5r. Also ARC, COR, Civ., Leg. 47, Exp. 1036, 1.

dominion from Inca to Castilian lordship. To this narrative Cusco's Incas added their loyalty to the Spanish crown in the civil wars of the 1540s. To all in Cusco, the Incas symbolized the city's proud history, and its rightful (if unacknowledged) precedence over Lima. And by the eighteenth century, among the indigenous societies of the highlands the Inca past had come to symbolize a utopian era of benevolent rule, promoting a popular understanding of Inca authority that lent support to the colonial Incas' privileged position in and around Cusco.[15]

The Incas performed that privilege in the religious processions at the center of colonial civic life. Befitting its size, history, and wealth Cusco had many processions, but those of Corpus Christi and Santiago dominated the city's calendar.[16] The Inca nobility marched in both, led by the caciques of the city's Inca ayllus and parishes, and dressed in "traditional" Inca costumes – themselves evolving over the centuries of Spanish rule.[17] Inca noblemen marched in headdresses adorned by the *mascapaycha*, the scarlet fringe that had been the hallmark of Inca imperial authority; noblewomen dressed as Inca princesses, or *ñustas*.[18] Like the Inca nobles themselves, these costumes and the venues were colonial creations by which a privileged stratum of Cusco's Indian republic assumed and performed its ancestry to assert its position in contemporary society.

The Incas also asserted their peculiar and close tie to the Jesuits, created by the marriage of Sayri Tupac's daughter and granddaughter to Martin Garcia Loyola and Juan de Borja. Those unions had great symbolic importance in colonial Cusco, and a large seventeenth-century painting of the ceremonies still hangs in the Jesuit church.[19] In 1777, among the possessions of Doña Josefa Villegas Cusipaucar Loyola Ñusta was a painting of "St. Ignatius, St. Francis Borja, and the marriage of Doña Beatriz," which affirmed Josefa's membership in the Inca elite, and her close, if ambiguous, relation to the creole elite.[20] More generally, these depictions of the marriage served as a cultural bond between Spanish Catholicism and the

---

15 Flores Galindo, *Buscando un Inca*; Burga, *Nacimiento*; O'Phelan Godoy, *La Gran Rebelión*, pp. 21–45; Rowe, "El movimiento"; and Jan Szeminski, *La Utopía Tupamarista* (Lima: Pontificia Universidad Católica del Perú, 1993).

16 Dean, *Inka Bodies*; Amado, "El alférez real"; Manuel Burga, "El Corpus Christi y la nobleza inca colonial: memoria e identidad," in *Los conquistados: 1492 y la población indígena de las Américas*, ed. Heraclio Bonilla (Bogotá: FLACSO, 1992), pp. 317–28; David Cahill, "Popular Religion and Appropriation: The Example of Corpus Christi in Eighteenth-Century Peru," *Latin American Research Review* 31:2 (1996): 67–110.

17 Dean, *Inka Bodies*, pp. 122–59.

18 Ibid., pp. 110–20, and 130–1. ARC, NOT, Quintanilla, Leg. 237, 260 ff., May 30, 1759, for Doña Antonia Loyola Cusitito Atauyupanqui.

19 José de Mesa and Teresa Gisbert, *Historia de la Pintura Cuzqueña*, 2nd edn. (Lima: Fundación Augusto N. Wiese, 1982), I, 180; II, 246–7.

20 The daughter of Doña Antonia Loyola Cusitito Atauyupanqui (n18 above). ARC, NOT, Juan Bautista Gamarra, Leg. 133, [ ], February 12, 1777.

Incas and creoles of Cusco, just as huge murals of Inca and Habsburg kings created idealized political ties.[21] Cusco celebrated Castilian rule on the day of Santiago, and remembered its special relationship to the Jesuits on St. Francis Borja's day. Esquivel left a description of the pageant of 1741: "[I]n the morning a representation of the marriage of Don Martín García Loyola and the daughter of Don Felipe Túpac Amaru was presented in the church of the Company, conforming to that painted on a canvas at the entrance of the church. A son of Don Gabriel Arguelles, called Pedro, played the husband; and a daughter of a cacique of [blank], named Narcisa, played the wife."[22] Of course, Beatriz was the daughter of Sayri Tupac, not Tupac Amaru – a reminder that the particulars of Inca history were secondary to colonial Inca privilege generally.

Esquivel noted the presence of the Marquis of Valleumbroso and the Corregidor at the tableau. That he did not name the cacique (in a chronicle full of names) suggests that not all in Cusco conceded to the Incas the standing they sought. By the eighteenth century, even humbler Spaniards were contesting Inca precedence, foreshadowing the racialized hierarchy of the next century. A complaint to Cusco's cabildo suggests both the performance of Inca nobility and the reluctance of some to concede it. In October 1741, Don Andres Cachagualpa Navarro Cayanchara, "[a] noble descendant of the royal line of Manco Capac and as such Captain of the Infantry of Nobles . . . in Chilques y Masques" complained that "a woman named Andrea Garay, [wife] of a mestizo whose name I do not know" had assaulted his wife, "Doña Pasquala Quispe Sucso, without heed [that] she is . . . a known Ñusta of royal blood, legitimate sister of the current alférez real."[23] "Andrea de Aranibar, legitimate wife of Don Juan Garay," answered his complaint, arguing that "Andres Navarro, an Indian . . . , and his wife" had attacked her in the street. Both Andres and Andrea sought to assert their own standing and undermine that of their opponent. He described his Inca ancestry and that of his wife, and denied Andrea's status by not using the honorific "Doña," and associating her with *mestizaje*. She argued that "Navarro" – without his Inca surnames – was simply an "Indian."[24]

Spanish officials also tried to eliminate the privileges of Cusco's Inca nobles – above all, their tribute exemption. Don Diego Manrique y Lara, corregidor of Cusco in the late 1760s, launched a particularly aggressive campaign against them.[25] As they had for centuries, the city's Inca nobles

21 Mesa and Gisbert, *Historia de la pintura*, I, 283–6; II, 503–5.
22 Esquivel, *Noticias Cronológicas*, II, 434.
23 ARC, CAB, Crim., Leg. 94 (1740–59).
24 For Cachagualpa and Quispe Sucso's wealth, ARC, NOT, Acuña, Leg. 3, 509 ff., October 7, 1764.
25 Also documents in postrebellion nobility suits; see Chapter 7, n73, n74, n77. For those presented from 1766 to 1768, ARC, COR: Civ., Leg. 46 (Exp. 1023); Leg. 47 (Exps. 1036, 1037, 1038); Leg. 49 (Exps. 1098, 1109, 1122, 1123, 1124, 1125, 1126, 1127); Leg. 50 (Exp. 1147); and Adm., Leg. 94 (1767–84), for the Inga Roca and Cayo Gualpa.

presented their documents, and then appealed to Lima when he did not accept them. Ultimately, it was royal support that preserved the Incas' privileged position. In 1768 Lima confirmed the Incas' privileges against Manrique, as the Audiencia upheld 200-year-old concessions against the efforts of a provincial governor to expand his tax base. The recognition granted to the Incas by Charles I's patents of nobility placed them in a unique position in Bourbon Peru. The exemptions from tribute and personal service were substantial privileges; but just as important, the patents of nobility differentiated a swath of Cusco's indigenous population from the rest of the Indian republic, and gave them a weapon with which to force Spanish officials to recognize that they were not simply Indian, but Inca.

Greatly reinforcing their legal privileges was the Inca nobility's institutionalized role in Cusco's ceremonial life. Here the Inca cabildo's monopoly on the election of the alférez real was a constant reminder to all Cusqueños of their special standing. That said, the significance of the Inca cabildo is hard to gauge. Whatever the intention of the crown at its creation in the 1580s, by the 1700s the Inca cabildo had no political, judicial, or administrative authority, and at times even the Incas themselves appear to have treated it with ambivalence. Many electors did not appear for the annual election, and from 1767 to 1777 the electors " ... voted in the said elections without that previous formality [of corregidor and notary], as the successors do not have confirmation from the Royal and Superior Government, on account of finding themselves poor and destitute, without the means to pay for their titles, equally for the duties of the elected alférez real ... "[26] However, in 1777 the corregidor revitalized the cabildo, and except for a brief dissolution after the Tupac Amaru rebellion, it functioned until independence. And despite the apparent disregard for the elections, disputes broke out over open seats, suggesting that the offices were prized.[27] Electors invariably claimed their status when presenting themselves in writing before the crown's officers, courts, and notaries; so did former *alféreces*. The cabildo conferred standing on electors and gave them the power to determine the status of Inca nobles by appointing them alférez. Moreover, the cabildo did occasionally act as a body in lawsuits and petitions to protect Inca privileges, providing an institutional mechanism by which the Inca nobility could act collectively. Thus, the existence of the cabildo helped preserve the legal recognition of the Inca nobility as a privileged group, recognition that was crucial to the maintenance of an Inca identity through centuries of Spanish rule.

Other urban institutions promoted Indian noble standing more generally; given the uniqueness of Cusco's Indian nobility, these necessarily

---

26 ARC, BE, I, 671. From 1740 to 1766, the average number of electors present at the elections was just 12. ARC, COR, Civ., Leg. 29, Exp. 620.
27 Ibid., for 1789.

reproduced Inca privilege. Religious brotherhoods in the city's parishes had Inca majordomos.[28] The especially prestigious office of "cacique" of the cathedral's sacristans was chosen from the electors of the cabildo, "according to ancient and observed custom, in virtue of a Royal Provision published by the excellent lord viceroy ... Don Francisco de Toledo."[29] The city also had a regiment of Indian nobles, largely ceremonial until it defended the city from Tupac Amaru II. Indian nobles occupied its honorific offices, again claiming their titles whenever they presented themselves in the written record. The regiment also created a ceremonial space for nobles of only partial Inca ancestry who were excluded from the cabildo: Don Pablo Soria Condorpusa, Don Vicente Choquecahua, and Don Mateo Pumacahua were all officers.[30]

The College of San Borja was also a prominent mark, and producer, of Indian noble privilege. Few records of San Borja's financing, curriculum, and organization survive, but rosters from the middle and late 1700s show the size of the school: in 1762 it had twenty-one students, and in 1773 twenty-three Indian nobles were studying there.[31] By then the college drew only from the bishopric. San Borja was not an exclusively Inca institution, and had students from non-Inca and mixed-ancestry cacical families from Tinta, Chumbivilcas, Aymaraes, and Cotabambas. But these were invariably sons of caciques, while numerous Inca nobles with no cacical claims also studied there.[32] For the Incas, noble privilege bred privilege more generally, as their sons were ceded a position of authority in Indian society and educated to assume it.

The city's urban economy also reinforced the Indian nobility's standing and wealth. Cusco's Indian population played a central role in its market and industry, but the better positions went to Spaniards and Indian nobles; the latter amassed respectable fortunes as merchants and the owners of textile factories (*chorrillos*). A 1759 inventory put Doña Antonia Loyola Cusitito Atauyupanqui's worth at 7,500 pesos.[33] A descendant of Yahuar Huaccac, she was the widow of Don Tomas Cusipaucar Villegas (an alférez real). But

28 Don Josef Ramos Tito Atauchi, Don Antonio Guamantica, Don Juan Carlos Llanac Ponca, and Don Silvestre Guaypartupa Ynga. ARC, NOT: Vargas, Leg. 243, [ ], December 30, 1813; Rodriguez Ledezma, Leg. 201, 643 ff., May 21, 1813; Quintanilla, Leg. 237, 144 ff., February 10, 1756. ARC, CAB, Civ., Leg. 97 (1770–3).

29 BNP, Man., D-6047.

30 For Choquecahua ARC, NOT, Juan Bautista Gamarra, Leg. 146, 398 (1782). For Soria Condorpusa, ARC, RA, Adm., Leg. 149 (1789–90). For Pumacahua, Chapter 7, pp. 239–241.

31 ARC, CC, Leg. 11, Cuaderno 57 (1765–73); "Indios de Sangre Real," pp. 207–9. A 1793 roster lists 127 students; by then the college was also educating Spaniards. Seven are listed as "Los Caciques"; by their family names another 16 were Inca nobles. AAC, XI, 6, 109.

32 In the 1760s and 1770s, one in six of the students for whom there is information was a noncacical Inca noble. "Indios de sangre real."

33 ARC, NOT, Quintanilla, Leg. 237, 260 ff., May 30, 1759.

her wealth resembled that of any well-to-do woman in a Spanish city. The bulk of her property was three substantial, urban houses worth 6,500 pesos. She also had 600 pesos of cloth-processing equipment, including dying vats and presses, and owned five *chicherías*. The baldly economic aspects of her Inca legacy were limited to a share in six *topos* of family land in San Sebastián.

Inca nobles also ranked prominently among the city's skilled artisans.[34] Don Agustin Condemayta, master candlemaker with a public shop, was an Inca elector in the 1760s, as was the blacksmith Don Francisco Pumayalli; two other Pomayalli brothers were master candlemakers.[35] Don Geronimo Orcoguaranca of San Gerónimo operated a tannery in San Blas brought by his wife (Doña Josefa Cusilloclla) as her dowry; he was alférez real in 1736, and an elector from 1741 until his death.[36] Doña Bernarda Ramos Tito Atauchi (a descendant of Paullu Ynga) and Don Pablo Soria Condorpusa established their son Miguel as a master silversmith in the 1770s.[37] And so on.[38] Inca nobles remained important in the city's guilds after the Tupac Amaru rebellion. Don Diego Cusiguaman – Inca elector, alférez real in 1789, cacique in San Gerónimo, colonel and commissary of the regiment of Indian nobles from the early 1790s until 1805 – was also a "master tailor with a public shop."[39] Don Francisco Xavier Guamantupa, accepted as a "proto-barber" into the barbers' guild in 1785 (and later its alcalde), was alférez real in 1804 and elected to the Inca cabildo in 1809.[40] Don Antonio Guamantica, elected to the cabildo in 1789, was a master silversmith and served as the guild's alcalde in 1796.[41]

The interaction of the symbolic capital and legal privileges of the "descendants of the natural lords of these kingdoms in their gentility" with the economic opportunities of one of Peru's largest cities enabled a colonial, urban Inca nobility that survived for two centuries. Their local standing did not have a solitary base. Rather, from its formal foundation the Spanish city included a ceremonial role for the Incas; Cusco's guild industry and market provided them a degree of material wealth as members of the city's

34 Cusco's guilds left few records; see Ramón Gutiérrez, "Notas sobre organización artesanal en el Cusco durante la colonia," *Histórica* [Lima] 3:1 (July 1979): 1–15; Jesús Covarrubias Pozo, *Cusco colonial y su arte* (Cuzco: Editorial Rozas, 1958); Mesa and Gisbert, *Historia de la pintura*, I, 139–91.

35 ARC: CAB, Ped., Leg. 113 (1760–73); NOT, Chacon y Becerra, Leg. 72, 383 ff., October 26, 1782; NOT, Quintanilla, Leg. 237, 257 ff., May 10, 1759.

36 ARC, NOT, Juan Bautista Gamarra, Leg. 133, [ ], August 25, 1751.

37 ARC, NOT, Arias Lira, Leg. 39, [ ], August 22, 1778; Justo Sahuaraura, *Recuerdos de la Monarquia Peruana, o Bosquejo de la Historia de los Incas* (Paris: Rosa, Bouret, 1850), pp. 43–7.

38 Garrett, "Descendants," p. 185, n75.

39 See Bernardo Achacasa's complaint in ARC, INT, Crim., Leg. 107 (1787–9).

40 For the barbers' guild, ARC, INT, Gob., Leg. 131 (1784–5); for service as cacique, the case of Jose Balverde, ARC, INT, Gob., Leg. 146 (1794–5).

41 ARC, INT, Ord., Leg. 39 (1796), on the guild's feast.

respectable classes; and through institutions like religious brotherhoods, the Indian regiment, the college of San Borja, and ayllu cacicazgos this noble caste maintained its authority within Cusco's Indian republic. This complex interplay created a sizable group of Indian nobles who occupied numerous positions of standing and authority.

Inca Cacicazgos

Although Inca nobles served as caciques in the city's ayllus, these cacicazgos were relatively unimportant to their authority and wealth. Symbolically and historically, Cusco had been the center of Inca rule; but it was one of the most aggressively colonized spaces in the Andes. The great plaza, imperial palaces, and temples of Inca Cusco became the Cathedral parish, the center of Spanish settlement and rule. By the mid-1700s the surrounding "Indian" parishes of San Blas, San Cristóbal, and the Hospital were urban neighborhoods with mixed populations, their small ayllus little more than administrative, tax-collecting units, with little communal land and largely populated by migrants (who were notoriously reluctant to pay tribute). These cacicazgos appear to have operated on an interim basis; at least, the 1726 tribute roll for San Cristóbal noted the custom of appointing Inca nobles from outside the ayllus as caciques.[42] Temporary offices with limited opportunity for acquiring wealth, they contributed little to the fortunes of the city's Incas.

That is not to say that cacicazgos were unimportant to the Incas as a group: the suburban and rural cacicazgos within twenty miles of Cusco were central to the group's material privilege and status. However striking the Inca ceremonial presence in Cusco, the key to their reproduction as the ruling caste of the surrounding area's indigenous communities was their near-monopoly on cacical office. The pueblos of the Marquesado de Oropesa had their own electors and alférez real, as did those of Chilques y Masques, but cacicazgos were the foundation of the rural Incas' wealth and political authority.[43]

The description of Melchor Carlos Ynga's baptism in 1571 listed thirty-three "pueblos that the Incas inhabit" within thirty miles of Cusco.[44] Here the Incas had established their regional dominance long before the Spanish conquest, and these bonds were sufficiently strong that two centuries later most of the communities had as caciques either "capac" Incas or Incas by

---

42 In the 1768 tribute rolls. ARC, COR, Adm., Leg. 94 (1767–84).

43 For Urubamba, see the 1761 dispute involving Don Alfonso Paucar Cusco Ynga; ARC, COR, Prov., Civ., Leg. 71 (1752–65). For Paruro, Navarro Cachaguallpa's petition, ARC, COR, Ped., Leg. 91 (1766–84).

44 Ocampo Conejero, quoted in Temple Dunbar "Don Carlos Inca," p. 163.

privilege. Men who claimed descent from the Inca panacas occupied cacicazgos in all nine parishes of Cusco Cercado; in Guanoquite, Ccorca, Colcha,
Araypalpa, Paruro; in Anta, Pucyura, Zurite, Guarocondo; Yucay, Maras,
Guayllabamba; Coya, Pisac, Taray, Lamay, San Salvador; Caycay, Colquepata,
Guasac; Oropesa and Quiquijana.[45] Together, in the mid-eighteenth century in Cusco, on the Anta plain, in the Vilcanota valley from Quiquijana
to Urubamba, and in the Yaurisque valley, many thousands of Indians lived
under the rule of Inca caciques.

But if Inca rule in the pueblos around Cusco is clear from the surviving
record, how that rule was organized is not. Or, more accurately, there was no
clear, uniform organization. Nor is that surprising. From sixteenth-century
accounts, the complex organization of the preconquest Incas does emerge,
albeit fitfully. Faint echoes of this can, perhaps, be found in the distribution
and affiliations of eighteenth-century Inca caciques.[46] However, colonial
rule created its own logic and networks of affiliation that supplanted and
overlaid earlier structures of authority. To some extent this occurred through
Spanish imposition, but it also occurred through Inca adoption. Succession
patterns, and the relations between a pueblo's ayllus, were open to contestation, even if witnesses might describe them as existing "desde la gentileza."
If Inca nobles challenged one another for the honorific privileges of the Inca
cabildo, they were certainly willing to fight over cacicazgos. As a result,
succession patterns and internal hierarchies varied greatly, the product of
intra-Inca politics as much as the hand of colonial authorities, and efforts to
provide a "model" of Inca cacical succession or organization would give an
erroneous impression of homogeneity. But some broad observations about
Inca cacicazgos, cacical succession, and the internal organization of the
pueblos of Cusco in the mid-1700s are possible.

First is the nature of the unit over which the cacique exercised authority. By the eighteenth century the pueblos created around Cusco in the
1500s were recognized and functioning communities. But these pueblos
were composed of constituent ayllus, which often had their own caciques.
Even the presence of a dominant "cacique principal" did not eliminate
the authority of the ayllu caciques. Such fractured pueblo governance was
common in communities with large noble populations. San Sebastián, San
Gerónimo, Pucyura, and Maras all had four or more ayllu caciques – in San
Sebastián, closer to ten.[47] This was in part a factor of size; with populations ranging from 1200 to 5000, these were larger than most other Inca
pueblos. But the organization of these pueblos suggests that one prize of

45 Garrett, "Descendants," pp. 588–642, *passim*.
46 The ties between the cacical families of Pucyura and Belén are suggestive. AGN, DI, Exp. 413 (1785)
   for the Alferez Poma Orcosupa, and ARC, RA, Adm., Leg. 156 (1797) for the Quispe Uscamayta.
47 Garrett, "Descendants," pp. 596–606, 611–6, 620–3.

nobility was ayllu autonomy, and these heavily "Inca" communities resisted the administrative conflation of ayllus in the pueblo.

In contrast, along the Vilcanota from the Huatanay downstream to Calca the pueblo had become the dominant unit of administration, and just one cacique ruled.[48] In these villages with populations under one thousand, the constituent ayllus survived as units of internal organization, but the pueblo was the level at which royal officials took notice of and interacted with the community.[49] Other pueblos and parishes remained divided into discreet portions, each with its own cacique and with no overarching pueblo cacique.[50] In Oropesa during the mid-1700s, the Cusipaucar Mayta lineage held the cacicazgo of Ayllus Huascar and Moina; the Yauric Ariza held that of Ayllu Cuzco. The marriage of Don Jose Cusipaucar Mayta and Doña Melchora Ariza united the two cacicazgos in one couple, but this was a union of crowns, not ayllus. On Jose's death the Cusipaucar Mayta cacicazgo went to a daughter by a previous marriage, while Jose and Melchora's son-in-law took over Ayllu Cuzco. Finally, a few caciques ruled in more than one pueblo, usually through marriage.[51] The son-in-law of the Oropesa cacical couple was Don Pedro Sahuaraura Ramos Tito Atauchi, heir to an ayllu cacicazgo in Santiago; as a result, he served as cacique of half of Oropesa and half of Santiago.[52]

No individual or lineage had a recognized claim to precedence over the Incas as a whole. Indeed, even in particular pueblos authority was often shared among numerous elite families. San Sebastián had dozens of noble lineages.[53] In Pucyura, men from the Alferez Poma Orcosupa, Ñancay, Corimanya, and Quispe Uscamayta lineages held the pueblo's ayllu cacicazgos.[54] Which, if any, of these families was the "dominant" one in Pucyura is unclear; certainly they intermarried, and local power moved among them over generations.[55] On a larger scale, in neighboring Anta the pueblo's *cacicazgo principal* moved between three families in the first half of the

---

48 Lamay, Coya, Pisac, Taray, Caycay, Guasac, Ibid., pp. 626–33.

49 See tribute rolls from the 1780s and 1790s; sources in Table 2.2.

50 Colquepata, Oropesa, Santiago, Garrett, "Descendants," pp. 609–11, 636–8.

51 Don Bernardo Xaime Guambotupa of Caycay and Guasac, BNP, Man., C-4218 (1767). In the 1730s Don Marcos Chiguantupa was cacique of Colquepata and, through his wife, of Guayllabamba; ARC: BE, III, 534–7; and NOT, Garcia Rios, Leg. 178, 1101 ff., May 30, 1756.

52 ARC: NOT, Joseph Bernardo Gamarra, Leg. 121, 662 ff., October 11, 1796; and COR, Civ., Leg. 59, Exp. 1338.

53 Table 3.2 for the noble population; Garrett, "Descendants," pp. 596–606.

54 "Indios de Sangre Real," pp. 211–4; AGN, DI, Exp. 413; ARC, INT, RH, Leg. 211 (1800); and ARC, RA, Adm., Leg. 156 (1797).

55 Don Miguel Ñancay, cacique of Ayllu Ayarmaca in the mid-1700s, married Doña Lucia Corimanya; their sons did not become cacique. One, Eusebio, served as alcalde; his daughter, Doña Marcusa Ñancay, married Don Blas Quispe Uscamayta, cacique from the 1770s until 1800. Their son Lucas was alcalde in the 1840s. ARC, JC, Leg. 47 (1841); "Indios de Sangre Real," p. 211.

eighteenth century.[56] Don Pedro Carlos Ynga Llanac Ponca held the office around 1700; two generations of Poma Ynga men succeeded him, and by the 1740s Don Mateo Quispeguaman held it. The latter Poma Ynga (Julian) married Doña Martina Quispeguaman, and Mateo Quispeguaman had held several ayllu cacicazgos under Julian, suggesting multiple, intermarried, cacical lineages. This multiplicity produced considerable competition, which raises three issues of cacical authority in the Inca-controlled pueblos: whether cacicazgos were hereditary or elective; how succession was organized; and the relationship between the localism of cacical office and the larger, intercommunity nature of the Inca nobility as a whole. The variety of particular cases and the fragmentary nature of the evidence make broad conclusions impossible, but it is clear that precisely these issues were the object of conflict and concern among the eighteenth-century Inca nobility.

The only categorical observation supported by the archival record is that authority in rural, Inca-dominated communities was largely hereditary. Almost universally, the Inca ayllu and pueblo caciques in the half-century before the Tupac Amaru rebellion came from lineages that had held cacical office in previous generations, and many traced their descent from preconquest royalty. In Anta and Pucyura, the Poma Ynga, the Alferez Poma Orcosupa, and the Ñancay descended from Tupac Yupanqui, the Quispe Uscamayta from Huayna Capac. The Corimanya claimed descent from the "Inca kings," as did the Guamantica of Guarocondo. The Tamboguacso of Pisac and Taray counted several Inca monarchs as ancestors, including Huayna Capac; so did Chiguantupa of Colquepata. The Cusipaucar of Araypalpa and Maras traced their ancestry to Paullu Ynga, while Chillitupa men, from Viracocha's panaca, occupied cacicazgos in Oropesa and Zurite. While detailed information on the ancestry of many cacical families does not survive, many caciques in Inca pueblos share the lineage names of urban Inca electors.[57] Cacical authority around Cusco was vested in a small noble caste that traced its ancestry to "la gentileza," comprised just a few percent of the area's Indian population, and successfully passed its collective authority across the generations.

More narrowly, in the eighteenth century cacical office in these communities was often hereditary from parent to child, although numerous *caveats* are necessary. There has been a tendency to accept that the Royal Decree of 1614 imposed male hereditary succession on the Andean cacicazgo.[58] And, indeed, a number of claims by Inca caciques appear to support that

---

56 Garrett, "Descendants," pp. 611–6. Pucyura was an annex of Anta.

57 For particular pueblos, ibid., pp. 588–642.

58 Díaz Rementería, *El cacique*, pp. 111–24; Silverblatt, *Moon*, pp. 150–3; Spalding, "Social Climbers"; Wightman, *Indigenous Migration*, pp. 16 and 80; Rasnake, *Domination*, p. 116.

conclusion. But those seeking royal recognition of their claims tailored their representations to the prejudices of the courts. As the Audiencias recognized hereditary possession in principle, those who held an office were wont to style themselves "proprietary" occupants. As a result, they routinely asserted that their families had proprietary claim to an office when in fact a pueblo had several rival (usually interrelated) cacical lineages.[59]

Evidence from the eighteenth century suggests that proprietary possession of cacicazgos was common, but not universal, among the Incas. The smaller pueblos of the Vilcanota valley (Pisac, Taray, Coya, Lamay) had cacical dynasties that stretched back at least into the seventeenth century; their rule was generally uncontested.[60] The two ayllu clusters of Oropesa both had cacical families with dynastic pretensions who, in their own statements, had proprietary rights to their offices, and whose claims went unchallenged.[61] In Santa Ana, the Uclucana's cacical monopoly began to erode in the middle of the eighteenth century, but they were nonetheless recognized as proprietary caciques.[62] Similarly, in Santiago the two main ayllu cacicazgos passed hereditarily; the Sahuaraura, the Inca caciques of Ayllu Cachona, claimed their rule dated to the sixteenth century.[63]

Elsewhere, direct succession was less firmly established. The most detailed information comes from San Sebastián, which, as the most noble parish in the bishopric and home to half the royal panacas, cannot be viewed as typical. Rather, it is the extreme of the spectrum, a community in which a large, fractious Inca nobility competed among themselves for dominance. The endless lawsuits of the 1760s and 1770s make clear the importance of ayllu cacicazgos, that the parish had a principal cacique, and that this office – and apparently many ayllu cacicazgos – was not hereditary.[64] From the 1760s until the 1790s Don Cayetano Tupa Guamanrimachi was San Sebastián's principal cacique, an office that made him one of the most powerful, and richest, Inca nobles in Cusco.[65] Cayetano was the son of Inca nobles, but his parents had not been caciques. Rather, in 1754 he succeeded

59 For example, Guayllabamba. ARC, NOT, Garcia Rios, Leg. 182, 1101 ff., May 30, 1756; "Indios de Sangre Real," p. 229; AAC, VII-5-84; and ARC, RA, Adm., Leg. 154 (1795).

60 For Taray, see below. For the Ynga Paucar of Coya, ARC, RA, Ord., Legs. 6 (1790) and 9 (1791). For the Paucarpuña of Lamay, ARC, NOT, Pedro Joaquin Gamarra, Leg. 148, 555 ff., October 15, 1799; the 1767 appointment of Manuel Prado Sunatupa, ARC, COR, Prov., Civ., Leg. 72 (1766–9); and ARC, NOT, Tomas Gamarra, Leg. 180, 334, August 21, 1782.

61 ARC, NOT, Joseph Bernardo Gamarra, Leg. 110, 710 ff., July 3, 1785; ARC, NOT, Palacios, Leg. 230, 23 ff., November 30, 1769; ARC, COR, Civ., Leg. 59, Exp. 1338; AGN, DI, Exp. 32–643; ARC, NOT, Juan Bautista Gamarra, Leg. 133, [ ], November 22, 1770. For Cusipaucar Mayta as cacique of all Oropesa, ARC, COR, Prov., Civ., Leg. 71 (1752–65).

62 ARC, COR, Civ., Leg. 50, Exp. 1149 and Leg. 52, Exp. 1169.

63 ARC, INT, Gob., Leg. 150 (1800–2), for Francisco Alvarez's claim to the cacicazgo.

64 Garrett, "Descendants," pp. 596–606.

65 ARC, NOT, Rodriguez Ledezma, Leg. 245, 507 ff., June 27, 1790.

a male relation both to an electorship in the house of Yahuar Huacac and as cacique of Ayllu Aucaylli (Yahuar Huacac's panaca), suggesting a link between the two offices. Over the next decade Cayetano extended his rule to two smaller panacas, Apomayta and Quecaquirao. Through his marriage to Doña Asencia Quispe Sucso of Ayllu Sucso, the large panaca of Viracocha, he became its cacique. Cayetano's mother was also a Quispe Sucso: it appears that men descended from and/or married to noblewomen of Sucso served as its caciques, preventing the control of the panaca by a single male lineage.[66]

By the mid-1760s Cayetano was the parish's "cacique principal." For the next ten years, he and his faction were continually in court against a rival group of nobles, allied behind Don Lorenzo Cayo Gualpa Yupanqui Ynga, cacique *gobernador* of "Collana Pachaca" (which included the panacas of Chima and Rauraua). Lorenzo traced his descent from Viracocha and the Ayllu Sucso: that an Inca nobleman from Ayllu Aucaylli served as cacique of Sucso, while one from Sucso was cacique of Chima and Rauraua, shows the complexity of cacical politics and succession in the parish. Complicating matters further, other individuals served as caciques in other ayllus.[67] Driving much of the intraparish conflict were Tupa Guamanrimachi's efforts to replace ayllu caciques with his supporters, and efforts by his enemies to do likewise – suggesting that these cacicazgos were contestable. As a result of this conflict, Cayetano was jailed twice – in 1770 at the behest of Cusco's *alcalde mayor*, Don Bernardo Gongora, and in 1777 of the parish priest. Throughout, Inca caciques in the parish switched sides frequently: those who won cacicazgos through Cayetano's support turned against him, while those who had denounced him in the 1760s defended him in 1777 and joined in denouncing Gongora. Through it all, Cayetano maintained his position as "cacique principal" until shortly before his death in the 1790s. His sons succeeded him neither as cacique of San Sebastián as a whole nor of Ayllu Sucso (whose cacicazgo passed to an Inca noble from another ayllu whose wife was a Quispe Sucso). Far from being hereditary, this most important Inca cacicazgo was held by a combination of election, recognition by Spanish authorities, and aggressive assertion of authority by the claimant.

Cacical politics in Anta, Pucyura, and Maras were lesser versions of those in San Sebastián, with cacicazgos moving (contestedly) among various families.[68] As in Ayllu Sucso, the office often passed from one line to another through the marriage of a cacical heiress. In Santiago, Maras,

---

66 AGN, DI, Exp. 336, 1770. In the next generation, Don Jose Sinchiroca and Doña Bartola Quispe Sucso's son-in-law, Don Simon Tisoc Orcoguaranca Sayritupa Inca, became cacique of Sucso and Aucaylli (ARC, NOT, Rodriguez Ledezma, Leg. 248, 411 ff., July 8, 1797). Like Cayetano, Simon was an elector but not for the house of Viracocha.

67 For various San Sebastián ayllu caciques, see the witnesses in Gongora's suit against Tupa Guamanrimachi, ARC, COR, Crim., Leg. 81 (1766–9).

68 Garrett, "Descendants," pp. 611–16 and 620–3.

Guarocondo, Guayllabamba, Lamay, and Oropesa, nobles from outside the community married daughters of previous caciques and succeeded to the office; in Guasac the office went to the Inca husband of the previous cacique's surviving sister.[69] In Lamay, the office passed through women for most of the eighteenth century. After Don Bernabe Paucarpuña's death around 1740, his son-in-law served as cacique until his death in 1755, when Bernabe's daughter ruled as *cacica* until her death in 1767. The office passed to her sister, whose husband ruled in her name; it then passed to their daughter, and to her husband, in 1780.[70]

That the cacicazgo of Lamay passed without contest through women for three generations, and at one point passed from sister to sister, suggests a role for female succession in Inca cacical politics.[71] Pucyura's Ayllu Ayarmaca also shows that the succession of sons was not uniformly preferred.[72] In the mid-1700s, the ayllu's much venerated cacique was Don Miguel Ñancay, who traveled to Lima to defend Pucyura's mill. He had two sons, educated at Cusco's San Borja College, but he was succeeded by his grandson-in-law, Don Blas Quispe Uscamayta, who served as cacique until the early 1800s; Don Marselino Ñancay then succeeded Blas. Both the Ñancay and the Quispe Uscamayta were prominent families; the passage of the cacicazgo through a cacical heiress prevented the monopolization of power in one male line.

This reading defines cacical power as male, suggesting that the marriage politics of pueblo elites served to negotiate competition between male nobles. Female political authority was not unknown in the preconquest Andes, with some curacazgos passing through the female line or occupied by women.[73] Although the Royal Decree of 1614 clearly favored male succession, female succession remained important. Legally women were not to exercise cacical authority in their own name, but, as so often in the colonial Andes, such laws were often conspicuously violated.[74] Later cacical claims

69 Ibid., pp. 609–10, 617–8, 622, 624, 627, 632–4.
70 ARC: COR, Prov., Civ., Leg. 72 (1766–9), May 1767 (for Manuel Prado Sunatupa's appointment); NOT, Tomas Gamarra, Leg. 180, 334, August 21, 1782; and testimony in the 1790 Ynga Paucar cacical claim; ARC, RA, Ord., Leg. 6 (1790), 24–6.
71 In 1755 Don Gregorio Guallpataymo of Coya referred to the Paucarpuña when explaining that women could occupy cacicazgos. Ibid.
72 "Indios de Sangre Real," pp. 211–4; the lawsuit against Quispe Uscamayta, ARC, INT, RH, Leg. 211 (1801); Marselino Ñancay's petition, ARC, CAB, Ped., Leg. 116 (1800–9).
73 Silverblatt, *Moon*, pp. 17–9, 63–4; Rasnake, *Domination*, p. 117.
74 Thomson, *We Alone*, pp. 75–8, 303 n34. Spanish mayorazgo law would suggest that women could possess but not occupy a cacicazgo. However, the laws surrounding cacicazgo succession (*Recopilación*, Book II, Title VI, Law 7, 1–4) are not explicit on female succession, and the numerous cases of cacicas exercising power indicate that this aspect of mayorazgo law was not rigorously applied to cacical succession, at least in the bishopric of Cusco. For discussion, by witnesses in a cacical dispute, of the acceptability of women ruling in their own right, see ARC, RA, Ord., Leg. 31(1798), 67–75 of the Unzueta suit.

suggest that in the 1600s powerful Inca cacicas ruled in their own right.[75] Certainly in the 1700s a number of them did: in addition to Doña Michaela Paucarpuña in Lamay, Doña Maria Ramos Tito Atauchi served as cacica of Ayllu Cachona in Santiago for eighteen years, from the death of her son in the Tupac Amaru rebellion until her own death.[76] Doña Isidora Tupa Orcoguaranca held the cacicazgo of Coya in the name of her underage son; so too did Doña Juana Uclucana of Santa Ana, although in this case it was she, not her husband, who was from the cacical dynasty, and so on.[77] However, in all these cases the woman who occupied the office was a widow or single. By the eighteenth century cacicas were rarer than Inca noblemen occupying cacicazgos inherited by their wives, suggesting that Spanish ideals of gendered authority, if not rigorously enforced, nonetheless had worked their way deeply into indigenous society.

Thus, the principal source of tension surrounding the cacicazgo in most Inca pueblos was competition among noblemen for the office. In a sense, the core of the conflict was whether authority passed through fraternal or filial succession. Before the conquest, Inca imperial authority did pass from father to son (although to which son was a matter of contention), but ayllu authority was often understood as fraternal.[78] In that case the "brothers" (all male cousins in the paternal line) held power, and while one individual would personify it, on his death it passed to another of the same generation.[79] The imposition of monogamy, and with it early modern European family and household structure, led to the favoring of succession from father to son, and, in the absence of a son, to a daughter rather than to a brother or cousin.

This tension between fraternal and filial succession is clear in a dispute between two branches of the Tamboguacso family in Taray, one that shows the willingness of cacical claimants to adopt Spanish norms of succession when it suited their purposes, and then ignore the precedent in the future.[80] In 1761 the cacique, Don Lucas Tamboguacso, faced a challenge from his second cousin, Doña Gregoria Tamboguacso, and her husband (Chart 3.1).

75 For Doña Lorenza Cusipaucar and Doña Cathalina Sisa of Ayllus Collana and Loyola in Maras during the 1600s, ARC, RA, Ord., Leg. 27 (1798), 1. For Doña Ana Cusimayta y Espinoza, "cacica principal y gobernadora" of Paucartambo during the 1600s, the Cusiguaman nobility claim, ARC, INT, RH, Leg. 218 (1807), 6r.

76 ARC, NOT, Joseph Bernardo Gamarra, Leg. 121, 662 ff., October 11, 1796.

77 ARC, COR, Civ., Leg. 50, Exp. 1149 and Leg. 52, Exp. 1169. Doña Leonarda Tecsetupa succeeded her father as cacica of Ayllus Chima and Rauraua in San Sebastián, and Doña Martina Chiguantupa succeeded hers as cacica of Colquepata – although she was a religious recluse, and a series of creoles ruled in her name (ARC, NOT, Melendez Paez, Leg. 184, 526 ff., November 14, 1812).

78 Gibson, *The Inca Concept*, pp. 15–31.

79 Spalding, *Huarochirí*, p. 33; Díaz Rementería, *El cacique*, p. 218.

80 ARC: RA, Ord., Leg. 31 (1798) (the case by Sebastian Unzueta); NOT, Pedro Joaquin Gamarra, Leg. 169, 672 ff., June 3, 1761; NOT, Juan Bautista Gamarra, Leg. 133, 22 ff., February 20, 1781; NOT, Joseph Bernardo Gamarra, Leg. 120, 607 ff., March 11, 1795.

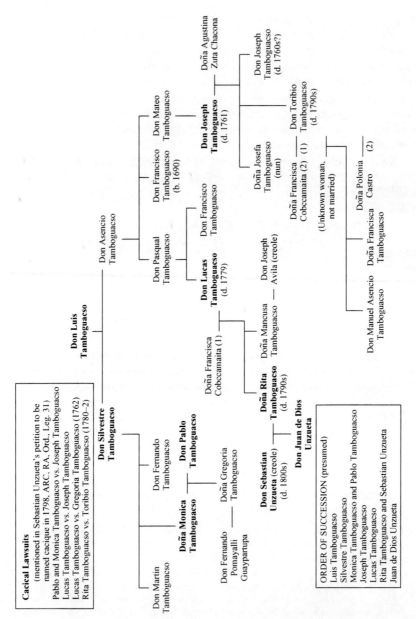

Chart 3.1 The Tamboguaso of Tiaray

Lucas and Gregoria's great grandfather, Don Luis Tamboguacso, had been cacique in the 1600s; Gregoria descended from Luis's elder son, who had left no male heirs. Lucas successfully repulsed Gregoria's claims, presenting witnesses who argued that "even though there remained daughters of Don Silbestre Tambo Guacso, it is the Incaic and immemorial custom that women do not succeed in this government" (although other witnesses presented by Gregoria noted that "she is married to a noble ... and of good custom," and pointed to Doña Micaela Paucarpuña of Lamay to suggest that women could rule in Taray).[81] Lucas died eighteen years later. A fight over the cacicazgo ensued between Lucas's daugher, Rita, and his nephew, Toribio – son of the late Don Joseph Tamboguacso, Lucas's fraternal cousin and predecessor as cacique. Rita won the cacicazgo; intriguingly, she presented witnesses arguing that female succession was widespread in the Inca provinces and utterly acceptable in Taray; among them was Gregoria's widower, Don Fernando Pumayalli Guaypartupa.[82] In this instance, female succession did prevail in the absence of sons. However, preconquest Inca kinship practices equated brother and fraternal cousin.[83] So, apparently, had the Tamboguacso earlier in the century, as the cacicazgo moved between brothers and nephews who shared the same male ancestry; 1779 saw the victory of a filial understanding of succession over a fraternal one.

But that is perhaps to read too much into a very local squabble. The conflict in Taray is also evidence of the fluidity of succession patterns, as pueblo politics, and the balance of power between different lineages, were central in determining succession. To be sure, the preferences and prejudices of the royal courts played an important role: both the dispute between Gregoria and Lucas, and that between Toribio and Rita, were decided by Lima.[84] And, without question, royal justice had a preference for direct hereditary male succession in cacicazgos. But the extent to which the courts imposed this as an absolute norm was limited, for two reasons. First, of course, neither of these cases involved direct father–son succession: mortality rates meant that this ideal often did not obtain. Second, only a limited number of such disputes made their way to Lima. A brother of Lucas Tamboguacso, Don Francisco, formally renounced his claim to the office in 1783 in front of a Cusco notary.[85] Francisco gave two reasons for his decision: "in this kingdom women succeed to cacicazgos, ... [and] his niece Doña Rita Tambohuacso

81 ARC, RA, Ord., Leg. 31 (1798), 18v, 20r, 22r, 24r, 39–40.

82 Ibid., 62–75.

83 Lounsbury, "Some Aspects."

84 Thomson, *We Alone*, pp. 73–8, for the untangling of the Spanish legal principles at the heart of the Audiencia of Charcas's decision in one succession dispute, and for an interpretation that views Audiencia jurisprudence as having greater effect on succession practice than does my interpretation here.

85 ARC, NOT, Agustin Chacon y Becerra, Leg. 73, [ ], July 11, 1783.

is a woman of judgment and talent, and treats the Indians in such a manner that she is loved by them, as is her husband as well." Quite possibly
there were other factors as well: Sebastian Unzueta was from a prominent
creole family in Calca y Lares, and could have seen his wife's claim triumph
through an expensive battle of legal attrition. And certainly Sebastian and
Rita entered into unwritten, but very real, obligations to look after her
aging uncle. In that, the family avoided yet another costly appeal to Lima
to sort out its succession.

Spanish law declared cacicazgos ideally hereditary through the male line,
but the regional variety in the distribution of cacical authority and cacical
succession was determined by the density of noble lineages fighting for a
smaller number of cacical offices, while pueblo politics produced the local
particularities. In some communities this took the form of clear, established
hereditary succession in one (male) lineage. In others, cacical offices moved
among several lineages; and in some it frequently passed through women to
their husbands. In any event, cacical succession was frequently contested.
This was true throughout the highlands, but elite competition was more
common in the Inca heartland than in other areas precisely because of the
number of potential claimants.[86]

That the rival claimants for cacicazgos in Maras, Taray, or San Sebastián
were all closely related to one another, and to the caciques of other communities, underscores the second broad conclusion possible about Inca cacical
succession: it reproduced Inca authority over the tens of thousands of members of the Indian republic within thirty miles of Cusco. The one immemorial custom that the Incas actually upheld quite successfully was their rule
around Cusco. But how that rule was organized was the object of frequent,
often hostile, negotiations among the households, lineages, and ayllus that
made up that regional Indian elite. Ultimately, such conflict around cacical
succession was not the result of efforts to preserve "Ynconcuza" custom in the
face of Spanish imposition, but rather of a much more profound transformation in colonial Inca society. A central tenet of the Toledan reforms was the
introduction of the "household" into the ayllu. The conflicts around cacicazgos and the use of contradictory rationales to justify possession reflected the
inherent contradiction within the Inca nobility, whose privileges depended
on their shared group history, but whose interests were calculated in terms
of the household or family. These tensions and interests were negotiated
through the one institution both recognized as legitimate by the Spanish
and capable of forging bonds between lineages, households, and distinct
communities: marriage.

86 ARC: COR, Civ., Leg. 59, Exp. 1338; INT, RH, Leg. 219, 1808–10 (Oropesa); CAB, Ped., Leg.
    114 (1773–86) (Zurite). Also Chapter 5, pp. 162–165.

Marriage served as the central mechanism for maintaining a family's authority across generations, reproducing the Inca nobility, and defining hierarchies within colonial society. As with cacical succession, only the broadest claims about eighteenth-century Inca marriage are possible. Inca nobles were monogamous, although they often remarried on the death of their spouse. As a result, family structure was complicated by stepchildren and half-siblings.[87] And like other Indian nobles, Inca nobles did not marry commoners. To be sure, the boundary between a prosperous *originario* and an impoverished noble in Maras was porous, and such marriages undoubtedly occurred. But among Inca nobles prosperous or self-important enough to dictate wills, engage in notarized transactions, or otherwise voluntarily leave a written record, such alliances are absent.

In pueblos with more than one cacical lineage, marriage among them strengthened the claims to authority of both lineages while negotiating potential conflict between them. Often in mid-eighteenth-century Cusco cacical couples were composed of two local nobles: in Pucyura, Blas Quispe Uscamayta and Marcusa Ñancay; in Taray, Lucas Tamboguacso and Doña Francisca Cobccamaita.[88] In this case the Tamboguacsos were the undisputed cacical dynasty of the pueblo, but the marriage to another leading Inca family of Taray served to strengthen their hold. And, in a clear indication of the perceived value of such alliances, after Lucas's death Francisca married his first cousin once removed, Don Toribio Tamboguacso.[89] The result was the lawsuit over the cacicazgo between Rita (Lucas and Francisca's daughter), and her stepfather and second cousin, Toribio.[90] Similar intermarriages between dominant Inca lineages took place in Maras, Anta, and of course San Sebastián.[91] In all of these, cacical authority was established by the creation of a cacical couple in which both members came from dominant lineages in the community, although in which the husband held the office of cacique.

---

87 Of 183 Indians with wills from 1750 to 1825 in the notary books of the ARC, on writing their last will 8 had never married, 107 had married once, 55 had married twice, 12 had married three times or more. One in eight had had children by more than one spouse; one in five living children had a living half-sibling. One in six testators had never had children; another sixth had no surviving children. Of the nearly seven hundred children mentioned in the wills, just 40% were still alive when their parent made the will.

88 ARC, NOT, Zamora, Leg. 293, 6 ff., December 7, 1783.

89 In neighboring Coya, Doña Isidora Tupa Orcoguaranca, widow of the cacique Don Sebastian Ynga Paucar, took (almost immediately) as her second husband Don Gregorio Tamboguacso, whose mother (Doña Francisca Ynga Paucar) had been Sebastian's sister. She then successfully claimed the cacicazgo for her son Miguel Ynga Paucar (who at the time was twelve and studying at San Borja), and occupied it in the interim. ARC, RA, Ord., Leg. 6 (1790), 24–7.

90 ARC, NOT, Zamora, Leg. 293, 6 ff., December 7, 1783.

91 Garrett, "Descendants," pp. 596–606, 611–5, 620–3.

Equally common were marriages between elite families in different communities. In addition to "son-in-law" caciques, male heirs married noblewomen from outside their communities. Don Bernardo Tamboguacso, cacique of Pisac, married Doña Francisca Ynquiltupa, daughter of an Inca elector and former alférez real from San Cristóbal.[92] The four daughters of Doña Paula Auccatinco and Don Pascual Quispeguaman of Belén formed marriages that effectively tied together much of the Inca hinterland (Chart 3.2).[93] Paula, from a cacical family in Quiquijana, married Pascual in the 1720s or 1730s. He was cacique of the parish's Ayllu Collana, although neither an Inca elector nor alférez real. The couple prospered: in her 1747 will Paula listed several houses and an impressive amount of silver, money, and jewelry.[94] Their daughters all married high into the Indian nobility around Cusco: Isidora to Don Antonio Quispe Tacuri, a prosperous merchant; Rosa to Don Sebastian Tupa Cusiguallpa, cacique (and alférez real) of Yucay; Rafaela to Don Juan Bautista Alferez Poma Orcosupa, a cacique in Pucyura; and Santusa to Don Vicente Choquecahua, cacique of Andaguaylillas.[95]

The first three were Inca nobles. But Choquecahua almost certainly came from a non-Inca lineage that had consolidated its control over Andaguaylillas (which, suggestively, had an Ayllu Cañari).[96] The colonial Incas readily formed marital alliances with other nobles (witness also the late-seventeenth-century marriage between Don Francisco Uclucana and a descendant of Huayna Capac); moreover, the "capac" Incas of the panacas had intermarried regularly with the ruling "Inca by privilege" lines in the neighboring provinces.[97] And provincial "Inca" nobles from much farther away (and presumably not of pure Inca ancestry) settled in Cusco and married Inca noblewomen.[98] Again, for election to the cabildo pure "capac" ancestry appears to have been a criterion (although not necessarily an absolute one),

92 ARC, NOT, Juan Bautista Gamarra, Leg. 133, [ ], September 24, 1777.

93 All generally (though not invariably) used "Auccatinco" as their family name, suggesting matrilineal affiliation. R. Tom Zuidema, "'Descendencia paralela' en una familia indígena noble del Cuzco (documentos del siglo XVI hasta el siglo XVIII)," *Fénix* 17 (1967), 39–62. But Paula Auccatinco had taken her father's lineage name, suggesting that naming patterns were fluid.

94 ARC, NOT, Juan Bautista Gamarra: Leg. 133, [ ], August 21, 1747; and Leg. 145, [ ], October 11, 1765.

95 For Isidora, ARC, NOT, Zamora, Leg. 294, 360ff., November 24, 1788. For Santusa: ARC, NOT: Juan Bautista Gamarra, Leg. 145, [ ], July 19, 1766; Vargas, Leg. 244, 336 ff., December 20, 1814; Pedro Joaquin Gamarra, Leg. 83, 577 ff., January 24, 1815; Rodriguez Ledezma, Leg. 202, 577ff., December 4, 1815; Vargas, Leg. 246, 647ff., January 4, 1816. For Rosa, the wills of Paula Auccatinco (above); for Rafaela, AGN, DI, Exp. 413 (1785).

96 For Choquecahua, ARC, NOT, Tomas Gamarra, Leg. 180, 324ff., June 15, 1782.

97 Chapter 2, p. 59, for Uclucana.

98 For example, Pablo Soria Condorpusa and Bernarda Ramos Tito Atauchi (ARC, NOT, Lamilla, Leg. 191, 251ff [1798]).

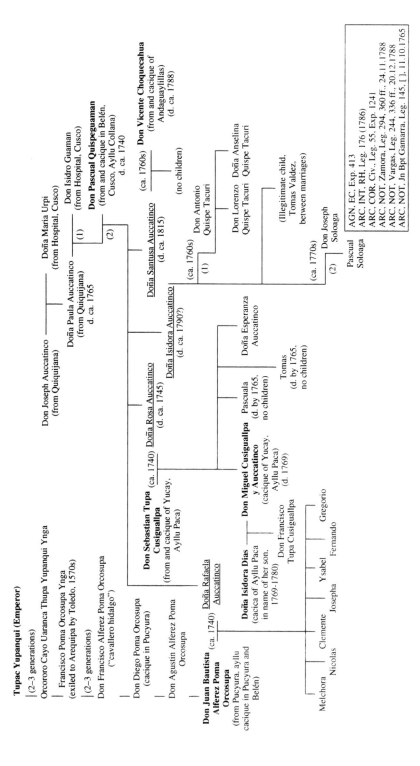

Chart 3.2 Marriages of the Four Quispeguaman–Auccatinco Sisters

and descent from one of the panacas (especially the imperial ones) certainly contributed to standing and authority. But by marriage alliances the elite lineages of both Inca and non-Inca communities in neighboring provinces created bonds to forge a colonial, but nonetheless very Inca, ruling stratum of Cusco's Indian republic.

These marriages between noble and cacical households within a pueblo or in different pueblos separated the Indian nobility from the Indian commons, and helped to reproduce the Inca nobility and its authority through a high degree of endogamy. This produced some tension among the Inca nobility, as families prominent in their own pueblos opposed the passage of cacicazgos to noblemen from other communities.[99] Such marriages asserted the primacy of the family and household in the reproduction of broader Inca authority in the Cusco area. In the absence of any obligation to forge particular alliances imposed or recognized by Spanish law, the dominant Inca families around Cusco acted in their own interest, preserving their authority by marrying with rivals in the pueblo, or other powerful cacical families from the area. While the reproduction of the Incas as a coherent noble group was one effect, it was not necessarily the principal intention. That, instead, lay in the efforts of the upper ranks of the Inca elite to maintain their privileged status not only as Incas, but also within colonial society.

This last imperative led to marriage alliances with creoles, which took place throughout the colonial period. Before the Tupac Amaru rebellion, these marriages usually united cacical or other noble lineages with prominent creoles settled in the pueblo. The Rosas family, well established in Anta by 1689, married into all three of the prominent cacical dynasties.[100] Early in 1700s Doña Marcela Rosas married Don Dionicio Carlos Llanac Ponca at a time when Don Pedro Carlos Ynga Llanac Ponca was cacique.[101] Two generations later, Doña Maria Dominga Quispeguaman, daughter of the cacique Mateo Quispeguaman, married Don Nicolas Rosas; after her death, he remarried to Doña Martina Poma Ynga, from another of Anta's cacical lineages.[102] Doña Polonia Cobccamaita of Taray, whose sister Francisca married Lucas and Toribio Tamboguacso, married two creoles from Taray.[103] Her niece Doña Rita Tamboguacso married the son of a local creole family, Don Sebastian Unzueta, who assumed his wife's cacicazgo. Inca men also married creoles: Don Luis Francisco Quispe Borja Ynga, son of a cacique in Guanoquite and a descendant of Huayna Capac, married Doña Agustina

99 For the example of Maras, see Chapter 5, pp. 162–163.

100 *Cuzco 1689*, p. 195.

101 Their son Don Juan Carlos Llanac Ponca moved to Cusco's Hospital parish, where he served as an ayllu cacique. ARC, NOT, Quintanilla, Leg. 237, 144 ff., February 10, 1756.

102 ARC: NOT, Tapia Sarmiento, Leg. 258, 376 ff., July 7, 1770; and the lawsuit against Riquelme in INT, RH, Leg. 204 (1797).

103 ARC, NOT, Chacon y Becerra, Leg. 77, 147 ff., August 23, 1788.

Castilla, "española"; after her death he married Doña Barbara Laura Tupa Ynga.[104]

As such alliances had done for two centuries, these marriages negotiated the relations between leading Inca and creole families in pueblos around Cusco.[105] However, by the mid-1700s the balance of power was beginning to shift to the creole population. It was not unheard of that the son of a creole and an Inca noble would occupy a cacicazgo.[106] But the creole husbands of Maria Dominga Quispeguaman and Rita Tamboguacso assumed pueblo cacicazgos in the name of their wives.[107] Nicolas Rosas did so in the 1760s or 1770s; Sebastian Unzueta in 1778. These individual instances do not suggest that the wholesale removal of Inca caciques that followed the rebellion had begun before Tupac Amaru marched on Cusco: the widespread alienation of Inca cacicazgos was a postrebellion phenomenon. But these occasional, Spanish caciques in Inca pueblos underscore both the fluidity of cacical succession and the expansion of creole power; and also that by the 1770s the primary commitment of leading Inca families was to the preservation of their own status and authority, not to the corporate integrity of the Incas as a collective group.

Among Cusco's most important Inca families during this period were Asencio Ramos Tito Atauchi, Maria Vazquez Obando, and their seven children who survived to adulthood.[108] Asencio was a descendant of Paullu Ynga, Maria the daughter of a cacique in Santa Ana, where the couple settled after marrying in the 1720s. One son entered religious orders; another married an Inca noblewoman from Santa Ana whose father had been an interim cacique in the parish. After she died, leaving no children, he then married the daughter of an Inca noble from San Gerónimo.[109] Of the five daughters, three married creoles, and two married caciques in Cusco Cercado: Bernarda to Pablo Soria Condorpusa of Santa Ana; Maria to Nicolas Sahuaraura, the hereditary cacique of Santiago's Ayllu Cachona. These marriages solidified the family's control over Santa Ana parish, marginalizing the historically dominant Uclucana; tied them to a powerful cacical dynasty; and created numerous bonds with creole Cusco.

The alliances of the children of Don Joseph Guamantica, cacique of Ayllu Rahuanqui in Guarocondo, followed a somewhat different pattern. Joseph married three times, always to noblewomen from the Anta plain.[110] With

104 ARC: INT, RH, Leg. 179 (1786) (for nobility petitions); and NOT, Juan Bautista Gamarra, Leg. 133, [ ], May 4, 1779.
105 Also the marriage of Doña Rosa Armendariz and Don Pascual Caceres Mango Tupa Ynga of Catca. ARC, CAB, Ped., Leg. 113 (1760–73) (January 9, 1770).
106 For example, Don Nicolas Loayza Quispetupa of Caycay; Chapter 5.
107 Also Ayllu Yngacona, in Guanoquite; ARC, NOT, Palacios, Leg. 230, 561, March 23, 1772.
108 ARC, NOT, Juan Bautista Gamarra, Leg. 133, [ ], January 9, 1749; and [ ], August 26, 1755.
109 ARC, NOT: Villavisencio, Leg. 284, 617 ff., May 2, 1769; Acuña, Leg. 6, 830 ff. [1768].
110 ARC, NOT, Arias Lira, Leg. 39, 549 ff., April 29, 1779.

his first wife he had two children who survived to adulthood, and one with his second. Of the former, his son – Don Gabriel Guamantica – married an heiress to the cacicazgo of Ayllu Choco in Santiago and served as cacique there throughout the 1770s.[111] His sister, Doña Tomasa Guamantica, married a noble from Guarocondo; but their father's cacicazgo went to their half-sister's husband, Don Lorenzo Copa Cusicondor, an Indian noble from Urubamba.[112] Here, all marriages were with prominent Indian families. The daughters remained in Guarocondo, one marrying within the pueblo, the other to a nobleman from twenty miles away who became cacique. The son married into a prominent Cusco family and assumed his father-in-law's cacicazgo. In their marriage alliances, the Guamantica and the Ramos Tito Atauchi resembled dozens of Inca families. They used their wealth and status to marry children into other cacical lines or into other prominent families in their own community, reinforcing their claim to the cacicazgos occupied by the father. The Ramos Tito Atauchi also forged links outside that nobility through marriages to local creoles, foreshadowing the alliances that would be made after the Tupac Amaru rebellion, when the creole elite overwhelmed the Indian elite of the southern highlands. And, in all cases, their marriages reinforced the divide between an Inca nobility and the Indian commons.

Inca authority in the pueblos around Cusco survived for more than two and a half centuries after the conquest, due largely to Spanish recognition of Inca exceptionalism, and the Incas' aggressive performance of it. They played a central role in Cusco's ceremonial life, and enjoyed the benefits of legal nobility. Their privileged position enabled them to benefit from the urban economy. But the urban Incas were only a part of this larger nobility. For those outside Cusco, local authority and relative wealth came from their dominance of pueblo life, above all from the control of dozens of cacicazgos. All of these served to reproduce the Incas as a noble caste in Cusco's Indian republic. So too did the actions of the Incas themselves, above all through marriage. The particulars of hierarchy and authority were ill-defined among them, and open to constant contestation and negotiation; but combined, their own self-consciousness and Spanish legitimation of it maintained Cusco's Incas as the largest and most cohesive group of Indian nobles in colonial Peru.

Highland Lords and Rural Nobles

In their history and their recognition as a noble caste, the Incas of Cusco were unique in Peru. But that the countryside around Cusco had a complex

---

111 He was deposed for abuses in 1781; Catalina Tisoc Sayritupa's suit for the cacicazgo, ARC, INT, Gob., Leg. 139 (1787).
112 ARC, NOT, Zamora, Leg. 293, 138ff., June 16, 1786.

Indian elite was not exceptional. Wherever a sizable indigenous population lived in self-governing pueblos and ayllus, an Indian elite was necessary to colonial rule. This was particularly true in the southern half of the bishopric of Cusco.[113] With relatively little Spanish settlement, the pueblos of the southern highlands and the Titicaca basin had heavy colonial burdens, sending *mitayos* up to five hundred miles to Potosí. They were also home to some of the richest cacical houses in Peru. Many dynasties traced their ancestry back to the sixteenth century and the Inca royalty, but they were not directly part of the Inca nobility of the Cusco area. Rather, in the 1700s a few dozen cacical dynasties whose wealth and power were deeply rooted in hereditary control of their pueblos intermarried among themselves and dominated the pueblos of the Titicaca basin.

Not every pueblo and ayllu had a hereditary cacical dynasty, nor were the most powerful families distributed randomly through the region. Some communities came under the dynastic rule of one family, others had multi-family elites in which none established clear dominance across the generations, while in others the more elective ideal of the Toledan pueblo appears to have held sway. And, far more so than for the Incas, evidence is scarce: most communities in the highlands left no information on internal organization and cacical succession. What exists is tantalizingly incomplete: we know of the claims of the Tapara of Ñuñoa Urinsaya, but nothing of Ñuñoa Anansaya.[114] Interpreting such *lacunae* is virtually impossible. For many communities – including important towns along the royal road – the archives contain few or no records. Overall, though, certain observations are possible about the organization of cacical elites, their history and genealogy, and the geography of cacical authority in the Vilcanota highlands and the northern Titicaca basin.

The Vilcanota Highlands

There was no clear frontier between Cusco's Inca-dominated hinterland and the highlands; roughly, the boundary lay in southern Quispicanchis and Tinta. In 1720 the ayllu caciques of Quiquijana were Don Martin Tiraquimbo, Don Francisco Niño, Don Melchor Guamansauni, Don Thomas Ramos, and Don Alonso Orcoguaranca – a mix of Spanish, Inca, and other surnames.[115] Two Cusqueño Inca nobles occupied cacicazgos on an interim basis in pueblos in Tinta. In the 1760s and 1770s, Doña Catalina

---

113 For the region's cacicazgos generally, Garrett, "Descendants," pp. 643–701; for particular caciques or pueblos, Glave, *Trajinantes*, pp. 279–304 (Asillo) and *Vida*, pp. 117–78 (Coporaque); Ward Stavig, "Eugenio Sinanyuca: Militant, Nonrevolutionary *Kuraka*, and Community Defender," in *The Human Tradition in Colonial Latin America*, ed. Kenneth J. Andrien (Wilmington: Scholarly Resources, 2002) (Coporaque); Choque Canqui, *Sociedad* and Rivera, "El Mallku" (Machaca).

114 Chapter 2, p. 70; also Appendix.

115 Stavig, *The World of Túpac Amaru*, p. 230.

Pachacutic y Salas of Zurite was a cacica in Layo, then in Yanaoca, but made no proprietary claim to either cacicazgo.[116] In Yauri Don Francisco Guambotupa, a muleteer from Caycay's cacical family, served as cacique of Ayllu Cama in the 1770s, 1780s, and 1790s.[117] These pueblos may have had historic ties to the Incas that had survived two centuries of Spanish rule.[118] The presence of interim, Inca noble caciques also suggests that the need for a cacique made possible the assumption of cacicazgos by successful, noble immigrants in pueblos along this major trade corridor.

Otherwise, in the mid-1700s the "Inca" caciques south of Quiquijana did not have close ties to Cusco's Incas. A dynasty of Inca ancestry had hereditary possession of the cacicazgos of Acos, Acomayo, and Sangarará, making the Tito Condemayta the most powerful cacical family in the area.[119] Another dynasty that claimed descent from Tupac Amaru I held the cacicazgos of neighboring Tungasuca, Pampamarca, and Surimana.[120] The Condorcanqui had been caciques of Surimana since the 1500s, and Jose Gabriel Condorcanqui was cacique of the pueblos when he launched his rebellion in 1780. But the difference between his father's family name and his adopted name of Tupac Amaru suggests the historical, linguistic, and social frontier that separated Tungasuca and Yucay.

To be sure, Inca ancestry was prized, and proudly claimed, by cacical families to the south, and there were a number of "Inca" cacical families along the ridge between Cusco and Titicaca. For at least three generations, men from the Challco family held the cacicazgo of Sicuani's Ayllu Calasaya. Clemente lost the office in the aftermath of the rebellion, and in 1792 sought restitution from Cusco's Audiencia, arguing that both Chuquisaca and Lima had confirmed his family's hereditary claim to the cacicazgo.[121] His supporters testified "that the said Don Clemente has his origin on the paternal side in the Yndios Principales and nobles of the parish of San Sebastián, on account of which they . . . were never of the tributary caste nor

---

116 ARC, NOT: Acuña, Leg. 14, 302 ff., June 17, 1779; Zamora Leg. 294, 402–13, October 21, 1785; Rodriguez Ledezma, Leg. 248, 153 ff., July 4, 1796.

117 According to Glave, the Cama were part of the Cana maximal ayllu; he describes Guambotupa as a "curaca étnica", but does not draw links to the Incas. Glave, *Vida, símbolos*, pp. 132–5. For his ties to Caycay, Sala i Vila, *Y se armó*, pp. 128–35; for the Guambotupa of Caycay and Guasac, Chapter 5, pp. 163–165.

118 Yauri had been part of Paullu Ynga's encomienda. Puente Brunke, *Encomiendas*, pp. 364, 381.

119 The pueblos had a combined tributary population of several thousands; ARC, INT, RH, Leg. 185 (1787). Don Lorenzo Tito Condemayta was the principal cacique of all in 1720. ARC, COR, Prov., Civ., Leg. 75 (1776–9), for land disputes with family information; ARC, RA, Ord., Leg. 25 (1797), for Don Evaristo Delgado's suit over the cacicazgo of Papres; ARC, BE, II, 316–21.

120 *Genealogía de Tupac Amaru por José Gabriel Tupac Amaru (documentos inéditos del año 1777)*, ed. with introduction by Francisco A. Loayza (Lima, 1946); also Chapter 6, pp. 202–205.

121 ARC: RA, Adm., Leg. 151 (1792). Calasaya had about three hundred people at the time; see the tribute list for Tinta, INT, RH, Leg. 195 (1792).

subject to servitude."[122] Challco was a common family name among the Inca nobility, suggesting that an Inca lineage had established itself in Calasaya as the ayllu's cacical dynasty.[123] Similarly, the cacical family of Sicuani's Ayllu Quehuar in the first half of the eighteenth century, the Fernandez Pillaca, claimed descent from "the Incas Orejones of this Kingdom."[124]

But that Fernandez Pillaca identified himself as descended from the "Inca Orejones" rather than tied to a specific panaca shows the divide between him and Cusco's eighteenth-century Inca nobility. Here distant Inca ancestry served to legitimate provincial cacical families; there is no mention of marriage bonds with Cusco's Incas. Similarly, while Condemayta was a common Inca surname (and Acos and Acomayo were home to a number of Inca nobles), during the 1700s the cacical family did not intermarry with Cusco's Incas.[125] Their ties were to nearby cacical families and to local Spaniards. Tomasa – cacica in the 1770s – was married to Don Tomas Escalante, from a locally prominent creole family; their daughter married Don Evaristo Delgado, who in turn held the cacicazgo of neighboring Papres.[126] Similarly, the Condorcanqui had married into two Spanish families within their parish: the Noguera (Jose Gabriel's mother) and the Bastidas (of Pampamarca, his wife). Jose Gabriel and his father also had strong ties to the Tito Condemayta: according to Tomasa, her father Sebastian had been the godfather of Jose Gabriel's father, and sent him to Cusco's College of San Borja.[127]

The strong hereditary rule of the Tito Condemayta and Condorcanqui appears to have been atypical in the Vilcanota highlands. In the 1750s the Fernandez Pillaca lost their cacicazgo to another lineage (with no Inca pretensions), the Aymituma. In the eighteenth century, Sicuani grew into the largest pueblo in the Vilcanota valley; it had eleven ayllus and no recognized principal cacique.[128] In the ayllus, cacical authority might pass from father to son or son-in-law, but often a family held onto a cacicazgo for only one or two generations. In its size and growth, Sicuani was unique: these factors might have produced a fluidity of cacical power. But although information for Tinta is scarce, what there is suggests that Sicuani was not unusual in the absence of clear cacical dynasties. The interaction of disease,

---

122 ARC, RA, Adm., Leg. 151 (1792).

123 ARC, COR, Civ., Leg. 46, Exp. 1023 (1765).

124 Testimony by Mathias Fernandez Pillaca in a 1760s dispute over land, ARC, COR, Prov., Civ., Leg. 72 (1766–9).

125 For Conde Mayta, Julien, *Reading Inca History*, pp. 205–6; ARC, COR, Civ., Leg. 49, Exp. 1098; the Guallpa *probanza*, ARC, RA, Ord., Leg. 31 (1797), 88, 101.

126 For Escalante, ARC, COR, Prov., Civ., Leg. 75 (1776–9); for Delgado, the suit over the Papres cacicazgo in ARC, RA, Ord., Leg. 21 (1795).

127 ARC, BE, II, 321.

128 For Sicuani, Chapter 5, pp. 155, 156, 160–162.

the *mita*, and tribute created periodic vacuums in cacical power. In many pueblos, several lineages could claim to be of the "blood of caciques"; and once a successful migrant or originario held the office in a moment of crisis, the community had yet another cacical line.[129]

The cacicazgo thus became a site of contestation among elite families. This was equally true around Cusco, where only a few Inca families managed to establish a monopoly on their pueblos' cacicazgos. But almost without exception, the cacical claimants there came from clearly Inca noble lines. In contrast, it appears that no overarching identity united the pueblo elites of Tinta, where claims of privilege and power were negotiated within each community.[130] Several historical factors would explain this. While the Canas and the Canchis had early allied with the Inca, their societies were less centralized than those to the south and composed of overlapping ayllu systems without an overarching political structure.[131] Tinta was also the most distant province subject to the Potosí mita, and suffered greatly from *forastaje* and migration.[132] Finally, under the Incas Tinta had formed the frontier between Quechua and Aymara.[133] There was no single boundary: the sixty miles south from Quiquijana to the La Raya pass was an ambiguous space, dividing the Quechua societies of the central Peruvian valleys from the Aymara societies of Titicaca and the Altiplano geographically, politically and culturally. In the eighteenth century the province lay between the draw of Cusco and that of La Paz, Potosí, and Arequipa; between the Inca nobility and the great Aymara caciques to the south.

The Titicaca Basin

Crossing the ridge into the Titicaca basin, the organization of Indian pueblos and of the cacical elite changed markedly. In contrast to the fractured organization of Sicuani, with its eleven autonomous ayllus, pueblos in Lampa, Azángaro, Paucarcolla, and Chucuito were more unified, as single entities or divided into moieties that came under the rule of single caciques. Cacical authority was also more clearly hereditary than in Tinta. Ruling over large pueblos in areas of little Spanish settlement and with access to

---

129 The lawsuit against Don Santos Mamani of Ayllu Lurucachi, ARC, COR, Prov., Civ., Leg. 79; also Stavig, *The World of Túpac Amaru*, pp. 196, 231–2, 251–2.

130 Cacical lines in Sicuani intermarried; ARC, COR, Prov., Civ., Leg. 76 (1780–4), for Mollo Apasa and Ayllu Anza. For the Condorcanqui, Leon G. Campbell, "Social Structure of the Túpac Amaru Army in Cuzco, 1780–81," *Hispanic American Historical Review* 61:4 (November 1981): 675–93; Scarlett O'Phelan Godoy, *Un siglo de rebeliones anticoloniales: Perú y Bolivia, 1700–83* (Cusco: Centro Bartolomé de Las Casas, 1988), pp. 249–51 and 308–20; also *Genealogía de Tupac Amaru*.

131 Glave, *Vida, símbolos*, pp. 25–56; Stavig, *The World of Túpac Amaru*, pp. 1–12.

132 Wightman, *Indigenous Migration*, p. 142.

133 Stavig, *The World of Túpac Amaru*, p. 5.

the Upper Peruvian markets, the cacical dynasties of the Titicaca basin and the Altiplano were among the richest Indian families in the Andes. Scores of pueblos from the La Raya pass south to Potosí had been founded by the Spanish in the old Aymara *señorios*. While the cacical dynasties of these communities often traced their ancestry directly to preconquest lords, they did not enjoy the corporate recognition of Cusco's Incas. As a result, there was no larger institution that united all of the Aymara cacical families. Rather, well-entrenched dynasties married with those of neighboring pueblos, or of neighboring provinces, weaving together this Indian aristocracy into larger groups united in their ancestry and their interests and, by the middle of the eighteenth century, increasingly separated from the communities over which they ruled.

The communities of the upper Ayavire had cacical dynasties in the eighteenth century, although their origins are not always clear. Just to the north of the Ayavire, in the southernmost reach of the Apurímac, Don Eugenio Canatupa Sinanyuca, from a cacical family of Coporaque's Ayllu Collana, had, by 1768, become the pueblo's interim "cacique principal."[134] The Sinanyuca had been prominent in Coporaque for generations, although how far back their dominance stretched is not clear. The same problem confronts the reconstruction of cacical succession and authority in Macarí and Umachire, which were under the rule of powerful caciques by the 1760s: Don Gabriel Cama Condorsayna in the former, Don Bernardo Succacahua in the latter. But neighboring pueblos did have well-established cacical families: in Cupi, Don Juan Guacoto Puma Caxia claimed that his ancestors had occupied the cacicazgo since the 1500s; in Santa Rosa, Ñuñoa, Pucará, and Nicacio the Guampoco, Tapara, Cota Luque, and Pachari respectively constituted cacical dynasties at least since the 1600s.[135]

These dynasties reproduced their authority through strategic marriages, although data is extremely scarce. In the 1760s Bernardo Succacahua of Umachire married Doña Teresa Garcia Cotacallapa, daughter of the cacique of Usicayos, in Caravaya.[136] His brother, Francisco, married the daughter of Don Antonio Solis Quivimasa Ynga and Doña Ignacia Auccatinco, Quiquijana's principal cacical couple.[137] In this, though, the two appear to have been exceptional. Most marriages that united cacical houses spanned just ten or twenty miles. Cacical alliances here were with local lineages, or Spaniards. The Sinanyuca are a good example. In the mid-1700s, they intermarried with the Hilaguamanchuco (cacical family of another of Coporaque's ayllus); but Don Eugenio Canatupa Sinanyuca was the son

---

134 Glave, *Vida, símbolos*, pp. 136–152, and Stavig, "Eugenio Sinanyuca."
135 Garrett, "Descendants," pp. 663–71.
136 ARC, NOT, Joseph Bernardo Gamarra, Leg. 124, 233 ff. [1799].
137 ARC, NOT, Villavisencio, Leg. 288, 352 ff., February 27, 1778.

of Don Jose Canatupa Sinanyuca and Doña Alfonsa Estrada. He married two Spanish women; but in the 1770s his son Asencio married Doña Tomasa Cama Condorsayna, the daughter of Gabriel of Macarí, fifteen miles to the south.[138] It is thus difficult to make out a single trajectory for cacical alliances. Asencio was technically just one-quarter "Indian," but to those in Coporaque and Macarí he was clearly an Indian noble: married to an Indian noblewoman, heir to one cacique and son-in-law to another. From the evidence available for the 1760s and 1770s, it appears that pueblo caciques along the ridge frequently had as parents two nobles from the same pueblo.[139] The mothers and wives of caciques were invariably awarded the honorific "Doña," while their surnames usually do not correspond to caciques in neighboring pueblos. The two central points of tension to negotiate were relations among the Indian elite of a community and those with local Spaniards. If no one pattern of alliance emerges as dominant, it is because the dynamics of local power varied by community.

Further south the provinces around Titicaca had an Indian aristocracy composed of cacical dynasties tracing their ancestry to before the Spanish conquest. In Azángaro Anansaya the Choquehuanca claimed to have held the cacicazgo since Inca rule.[140] Charles I had recognized a son of Huayna Capac as cacique, and with his marriage into a ruling lineage in Azángaro the office passed through the Choquehuanca for 300 years. In Azángaro Urinsaya, the Mango Turpa, who also claimed Huayna Capac as an ancestor, held the cacicazgo at least from the mid-seventeenth century. A third Inca–Aymara dynasty, the Chuquicallata (also claiming descent from Huayna Capac), ruled San Taraco at least from the mid-seventeenth century through the eighteenth century and extended their rule to Saman at some point in the mid-1700s. West of the lake, Don Ambrocio Quispe Cavana, the proprietary cacique of Cavanilla, claimed Inca ancestry through his mother; the paternal surname suggests the ruling lineage of the Cavana ethnic group.[141] Just to the south the Cutimbo had hereditary control of Anansaya in Chucuito: they descended from Apo Cari, a Lupaqa curaca at the time of the great 1567 census.[142] The Catacora held cacicazgos in Acora at least since the early seventeenth century (claiming descent from "the noble Catacoras, [who were] honored by the King for some great services").[143] For two centuries several interrelated families battled over the cacicazgos of Juli, the largest

138 For Eugenio, ARC, NOT, Vargas, Leg. 236, 357 ff., November 27, 1804. For Asencio and Tomasa, ARC, CSJ, Leg. 30 (1829).
139 Appendix, for Guaman Tapara of Ñuñoa Urinsaya; ARC, NOT, Joseph Bernardo Gamarra, Leg. 124, 233 ff. [1799], for Succacahua of Umachire.
140 For cacical families in Azángaro, Garrett, "Descendants," pp. 675–87.
141 ANB, EC, 1785–23; RREE, PRA, Exp. 186.
142 ANB, EC, 1793–11; Thomson, *We Alone*, pp. 71–5.
143 ARC, INT, Ord., Leg. 97 (1797–9), for Doña Ignacia Catacora's estate.

Lupaqa town. One claimed as their ancestor Don Domingo Llaglla, a curaca of Conda in 1568. Described at the time as a "good Christian, married [and] of good life, form, and example," Llaglla was the descendant of the "gentile Ynga Caroma, lord who was of Conda."[144] No less impressively, the progenitor of the Chiqui Ynga Charaxa was "the Indian Charaxa, named as the true cacique by the Ynga Guaina Capac, last king and natural lord."[145] Similar lineages were important in the bishopric of La Paz: an Inca lineage of the Tito Atauchi – intermarried with Aymara cacical lines – ruled the sanctuary pueblo of Copacabana (an important Inca colony) until 1778.[146]

Not all caciques near the lake traced their ancestry to before the conquest. In eastern Huancané, Spanish–Indian noble families had held the cacicazgos since the late 1600s.[147] In the old Lupaqa pueblo of Ilave, two Spanish brothers took over the cacicazgo in the 1760s, suggesting that Spaniards were beginning to dislodge the Indian elite.[148] And, as elsewhere, the pueblos around Titicaca were composed of ayllus and moieties, with their own offices and hierarchies.[149] How the lesser elite of the Aymara pueblos understood their genealogy, and their relations to the great cacical dynasties, is harder to establish than in the Inca-dominated pueblos. The use of "Don" in legal documents, assertions by ayllu principals of their own nobility, and the elaborate Inca surnames of some pueblo prominents do, however, show the existence of local nobilities.[150]

Structurally the main differences in the organization of cacical rule between the Titicaca basin and the Inca hinterland were the presence of well-established dynasties in the cacicazgos principales of large communities and a clearer division between them and the secondary local elite. Choquehuanca rule over Azángaro Anansaya made the family one of the richest families in Indian Peru and one of the most powerful families – Indian or Spanish – between Cusco and La Paz. The prized Inca cacicazgos – those over the whole parish of San Sebastián, or the pueblo of Anta – were not the monopoly of individual families; in the Titicaca basin, they generally were.

Well-established dynasties did not prevent competition for cacical office: cousins here went to court just as they did in Cusco.[151] Moreover, succession

---

144 ARC, RA, Adm., Leg. 161 (1801–2), 65v.

145 ARC, RA, Ord., Leg. 33 (1799), 67v.

146 ANB, EC, 1773–83 and AGN-A, IX, 31–3–4 Exp. 103 (1778). See also Thomson, *We Alone*, pp. 32–4.

147 Garrett, "Descendants," pp. 688–92.

148 ANB, EC, 1797–56.

149 The Arevilca of Cavanilla (RREE, PRA, Exp. 189 (1793)); also, the Atamas Mamani of Azángaro, Chapter 4, p. 132.

150 AGN-A, IX, 31–3–4 Exp. 103 (1778), for Inca family names among Copacabana's *principales*.

151 Earlier lawsuits in ANB, EC, 1793–11 [Chucuito]; ARC, RA, Ord., Leg. 30 (1798) [Juli].

could be confusing. Among the Choquehuanca, the office apparently went from father to son; among the Mango Turpa, sometimes sons, sometimes nephews succeeded.[152] The demographic crises made impossible any single rule of succession. It was not uncommon for cacicazgos around Titicaca to pass through women to their husbands. Nor were women ruling in their own right unheard of, although this appears to have been less frequent than in the Inca-dominated communities around Cusco, perhaps because of differences in indigenous gendering of political authority or perhaps because the Spanish ideals (and laws) of male succession and rule had taken deeper root here.[153] Thus, while the cacicazgos of the large Aymara pueblos around the lake generally passed through generations in one line, the surviving record suggests no hard and fast rules of succession: rather, a complex interplay (and manipulation by various actors) of legislation, indigenous custom, local politics, and mortality determined each succession. But it is clear that in the decades before the rebellion, most of the largest pueblos in the Azángaro valley and on the western and southern sides of the lake had as their caciques descendants of preconquest lords, and the Indian elite of the Collao retained their power to an extent as remarkable as the Incas of Cusco.

By the eighteenth century, these great cacical families married within their own region, or to the south; no marriages bound them directly to Cusco, more than a hundred miles to the north. That had not always been the case: several ruling dynasties had been formed in the early sixteenth century through Inca–Aymara marriages, and similar alliances were made in the seventeenth century.[154] But in the 1700s, these families married among themselves or with Spaniards. They forged long-distance ties, but with other cacical houses around Titicaca, on the Altiplano, or in the Chilean highlands. Don Blas Choquehuanca, son and cacical heir of Diego Choquehuanca (whose own wife, Doña Manuela Bejar, was from a creole-Inca–Aymara family in neighboring Putina), married Doña Marta Siñani Fernandez Chuy, the daughter of the cacique of Carabuco, 100 miles from Azángaro on the eastern shore of Titicaca.[155] She, too, came from an impressive alliance, between Don Agustin Siñani of Carabuco and Doña Anastasia Fernandez Chuy, daughter of Don Carlos Fernandez Chuy, the hereditary

---

152 Gilberto Salas Perea, *Monografía Sintética de Azángaro* (Puno: Editorial Los Andes, 1966), pp. 20–3.

153 See above, n74. Doña Bernarda Pachari of Nicacio; ARC, RA, Ord., Leg. 28 (1798); Doña Felipa Campos Alacca of Laxa (ANB, EC, 1796–97); Doña Juliana Tico Chipana of Zepita (BNP, Man., C-1705, 1791); Doña Maria Teresa Choquehuanca of Azángaro Anansaya (ARC, RA, Adm., Leg. 156, 1797).

154 ANB, EC, 1785–23, 69v. Quispe Cavana claimed descent from Don Felipe Tupa Yupanqui and Don Gonzalo Picchi Guallpa Ynga; for them, ARC, COR, Civ., Leg. 50, Exp. 1147. Also Glave, *Trajinantes*, pp. 281–8, for Don Bartolome Tupa Hallicalla of Asillo Urinsaya.

155 Leonardo Altuve Carillo, *Choquehuanca y su Arenga a Bolívar* (Buenos Aires: Planeta, 1991), p. 64.

cacique of Laxa. The Fernandez Chuy intermarried with the Tito Atauchi of Copacabana and other cacical dynasties around the southern edge of the lake; so this marriage linked the Choquehuanca to the important cacical dynasties on the southern side of the lake.[156] Don Ambrocio Quispe Cavana of Cavanilla married Doña Maria Chique Ynga Charaxa, heiress to Pomata's cacicazgo and linked to Juli's cacical lineages, where her brother was a cacique.[157] And so on.[158] In the mid-eighteenth century, the ruling dynasties around Titicaca were producing themselves as a regional aristocracy.

As a result, in the decades before the rebellion, the great cacical houses of the Titicaca basin eschewed marriage with the second tier of their pueblos' Indian nobility. Of Diego Choquehuanca and Manuela Bejar's other children, two entered the church and two daughters married Spaniards.[159] Such intermarriage, creating alliances between local Spanish families and cacical dynasties, was common around Titicaca, and their offspring at times succeeded to cacicazgos.[160] They might also have been a recent phenomenon. Diego and Manuela's daughters married far more "Spanish" spouses than their parents, and Diego's sister, Doña Josefa Choquehuanca, had married Don Luis Chuquimia, presumably from the Copacabana lineage. Josefa was the daughter of a Choquehuanca–Mango Turpa marriage.[161] Similarly, Don Cristóbal Mango Turpa, cacique of Azángaro Urinsaya in the 1730s and 1740s, married Doña Ana Atamas Mamani, from another Azangareño cacical line; one of their daughters married a Choquehuanca.[162] In contrast, the decades before the rebellion saw a shift in marriages, now uniting well-entrenched cacical dynasties with those of other pueblos, and with provincial Spaniards.

---

156 ANB, EC, 1761–87 and 1807–11. Marta died in childbirth and Blas remarried, to Doña Brigida Sagastigua; their son Manuel became cacique of Azángaro Anansaya in 1797: ARC, RA, Adm., Leg. 166 (1808).

157 ANB, EC, 1785–23, 11r; and the suit over Juli's cacicazgos in ARC, RA: Ord., Leg. 33 (1799) and Adm., Leg. 161 (1802).

158 Don Domingo Mango Turpa, of Azángaro Urinsaya, and Doña Antonia Chuquicallata of San Taraco and Saman; ARC, RA, Ord., Leg. 14 (1794); Don Fausto Xauregui Colque of Pucarani and Doña Rafaela Tito Atauchi of Copacabana; ANB, EC, 1773–83; Doña Catalina Chuquimia Tupa Yupanqui of Juli and Don Pheliciano Lupistaca of Ilabaya (Chile); Jorge Hidalgo Lehuede, "Indian Society in Arica, Tarapaca, and Atacama, 1750–1793, and Its Response to the Rebellion of Túpac Amaru" (Ph.D. diss., University of London, 1986), p. 65.

159 RREE, PRA, Exp. 105. For Maria Manuela Choquehuanca, ARC, NOT, Pedro Joaquin Gamarra, Leg. 79, 10ff., January 15, 1808. For Maria Teresa Choquehuanca, ADP, INT Leg. 3, Exp. 51; *CDBR*, I, pp. 512–23; ARC, RA, Ord., Leg. 36 (1800).

160 As examples, the Alacca of Laxa, ANB, EC, 1796–97; and the mixed-blood lineages in eastern Paucarcolla; Garrett, "Descendants," pp. 689–92.

161 In the Mango Turpa claim to an estancia, ARC, RA, Ord., Leg. 9 (1791).

162 Salas Perea, *Monografía*, pp. 20–1. Chapter 4, p. 132, for the Atamas Mamani.

The colonial Andes had thousands of caciques, ranging from ayllu leaders to the hereditary lords of large towns. In the bishopric of Cusco more important cacicazgos were generally held by elite families, whose status and privilege spanned generations, and through intermarriage, these families created sizable, if ill-defined, provincial nobilities. In many areas, preconquest elites retained power in Indian society for more than two centuries after the conquest. Both the Incas around Cusco and the cacical dynasties of the Titicaca basin self-consciously asserted their ancestry, and through marriage reproduced familial claims to elite standing. But not all hierarchies were static. In the upper Vilcanota and Ayavire valleys families consolidated their authority during the colonial era; at any rate, they made no effort to trace their authority to before the conquest. The internal and dynastic politics of these highland pueblos shifted with broader demographic, economic, and political changes in the region, while from one generation to the next a clear bias toward hereditary authority contributed to hereditary rule. And even where late colonial Indian elites had recognizable links to preconquest elites, they were radically different: by the 1750s the Inca nobility of Cusco were a product of colonial rule in the nature of their noble privileges, in their organization, and even in their history. Yet the colonial Incas understood themselves to be, and were understood to be, the direct descendants of the "natural lords who were," who had dominated the indigenous societies in the region around Cusco for the past four centuries.

Equally important, by the early eighteenth century the Incas and other well-entrenched ruling elites understood their own immediate affiliations within the paradigm of the monogamous household and lineage, and conceived of themselves as part of, yet discreet units within, the larger community. One much cited result of this change, coupled with the Royal Decree of 1614, was the adoption of Spanish ideals of cacical succession, particularly of male primogeniture. In fact, in the bishopric of Cusco this appears to have been far from universal. Certainly in the mid-1700s cacicazgos were overwhelmingly held by individuals whose families had some ancestral claim to authority in their communities, whether it stretched back to Inca rule, or just to one or two generations. However, the oft-invoked rhetoric of hereditary succession and proprietary rights belies the fluidity of authority in Indian communities, in which cacical authority moved among numerous elite lineages, passing through daughters, sisters, brothers, nephews, as well as (and at times in preference to) sons. While a number of pueblos did have clear cacical dynasties, by no means did all. The organization of cacical authority varied considerably from region to region, and pueblo to pueblo, underscoring the importance of local dynamics, and not simply crown policy, in pueblo politics.

This fluidity of succession owes itself in part to preconquest political organization, but contradictions inherent in the colonial organization of the república de indios also contributed greatly. Most importantly, the presence of numerous ayllu cacical lineages often prevented the emergence of a ruling dynasty in a particular pueblo. Both the Inca-dominated areas around Cusco and some of the larger Vilcanota valley communities (such as Quiquijana and Sicuani) had complex cacical elites, producing a constant negotiation of pueblo hierarchies and authority. The interaction of preconquest social organization and the dynamics of colonial rule also produced considerable regional variety in the organization of these elites. Unique in the Andes, the colonial Inca around Cusco remained a coherent noble caste, translating their position as an ethnic ayllu into a paradigm of blood nobility comprehensible to, and endorsed by, the Spanish. Around Titicaca, ruling lineages of the Aymara meta-ayllus reproduced their privilege through dominance in particular communities, then forged a regional aristocracy through marriage. In between, the colonial Indian elites of the Vilcanota highlands were rooted in particular communities and generally reproduced their authority through local alliances. The localization of Indian societies pursued by the crown succeeded to differing degrees in different areas. Certainly no provincial cacical network bound together more than a few provinces: the Inca and the Titicaca basin lords were at one extreme. But they show the existence of extralocal dynastic politics, and alliances, among Indian elites.

In sum, the organization of highland cacical authority and succession varied considerably. The interaction of several forces produced this variety: preconquest social organization, the extent to which elite privilege had been recognized by the Spanish, the effects of the social dislocations of the seventeenth century, the particulars of inter-ayllu relations, and the competition for authority among Indian elites and between them and Spaniards. As a result, while Spanish rule maintained, transformed, and produced stratification in Indian pueblos, the organization of local cacical authority was usually open to challenge and change. Cacical succession was thus dynamic and inextricably intertwined with pueblo politics and those of local and provincial Indian nobilities.

4

Communal Economies and Indian Fortunes

When Lampa's corregidor appointed Antonio Tapara as cacique of Ñuñoa Urinsaya, he articulated the cacique's three responsibilities: tribute collection, Christian rule, and good government.[1] He started with tribute collection: he had ridden forty miles across the mountains because the earlier cacique had failed in what was, to crown officials, the cacique's central duty. What mattered most was that twice a year the cacique collected his community's tribute and delivered it to the corregidor (and, in *mita* areas, that he delivered his corvees). This was no easy task. Many tributaries were reluctant to pay; others fled or died, leaving the cacique to cover the shortfall. Moreover, in many areas tributaries lacked access to cash. A complex market tied together the highland cities, but barely penetrated Indian pueblos. Caciques often had to convert their tributaries' labor or produce into cash for tribute, which allowed caciques to dominate local economies, making them the nexus between the community and the colonial market. Caciques also enjoyed usufruct of communal land and used their personal wealth to dominate capital-intensive factors of production in their communities.

Cacical houses were thus by far the richest segment of Indian society. Not all accumulated wealth: the obligation for communal debts made the *cacicazgo* a perilous position. But successful caciques funneled the profits of office into private wealth. This created a structural conflict between communities and a cacical elite committed to familial property, and historians have argued that cacical wealth produced class stratification, and conflict, in the colonial pueblo.[2] At the same time, the foundation of cacical wealth remained in control of the communal economy. The interests of cacique and community thus frequently came together, and the economic position of the cacical elite differed markedly from that of their creole

---

1 Chapter 2, p. 70; and Appendix.
2 Stern, *Peru's Indian Peoples*, pp. 158–83; Spalding, "Social Climbers," and "Kurakas and Commerce"; Silverblatt, *Moon*, pp. 109–24; Sánchez-Albornoz, *Indios*, pp. 99–107; Piel, *Capitalismo Agrario*, pp. 207–12.

neighbors.[3] The result was a cacical class divided from the commons by its wealth and by its familial strategies, but to whose fortunes the Indian community was of the greatest importance, and who in turn played a central role in the smooth working of the communal economy.

Despite the general structural similarity of their position, economically the members of highland Peru's cacical elite reflected the enormous variety within the Indian republic, just as they did in their ancestry and the nature of their cacical claims. Many of Cusco Cercado's Inca nobles – whether caciques or not – were as tied to the city's artisanal and mercantile economy as they were to the rural economy of the Indian pueblo, and as guildmasters and merchants they resembled their urban creole counterparts in the nature of their wealth and their economic activities. Even the rural Inca nobility operated in the city's economic orbit. The heavy colonization of the Inca heartland by Spanish Peru, above all through the establishment of haciendas and other rural properties, created competition for control of the rural economy and prevented rural Inca caciques from acquiring the wealth of their peers to the south. So too did the small size and fractured organization of the agricultural pueblos in the temperate valleys around the city: few caciques here controlled villages with more than a few hundred people. Even as the direct sway of urban Cusco and the old Inca nobility diminished, up the Vilcanota valley in Canas y Canchis, cacical wealth generally remained modest, again limited by the small size of most communities. However, further south, above all in the Titicaca basin, the strong hereditary control that some families exercised over large communities, with little Spanish settlement or private property yet with very strong ties to the monetized economy through the mita and the sale of crops and basic products to the highland cities, produced some of the richest indigenous houses in Peru. Thus, while all caciques operated in the liminal space between the economies of the Spanish and Indian republics, between the market and the pueblo, that space itself differed dramatically across the bishopric, and with it the wealth and activities of the indigenous elite.

The Cacique and the Pueblo Economy

To sixteenth-century reformers, the ill-defined boundary between the communal economy and the *curaca's* domestic economy was the hallmark of cacical tyranny. As they understood it, the lands of the curaca were not distinguished from the community's, while communal surplus for tribute and exchange was assessed and transported by the curaca, who also controlled any imports. Various laws sought to change this, placing

---

3 Pease, *Curacas*, pp. 154–71; Choque Canqui, *Sociedad*, pp. 27–85; Glave, *Trajinantes*, pp. 281–304; Spalding, *Huarochirí*, pp. 209–38.

lands in the possession of the community, fixing tribute per capita, and freeing commerce for the Indians.[4] To some extent they succeeded. By the eighteenth century the cacique did not have a monopoly on any aspect of the communal economy other than tribute collection. The growth of the rural Spanish republic created numerous points of contact between the Indian household and the market. Caciques also had limited control over communal land, distributed by the *alcalde* and other village officials.[5] Finally, a century and a half of *composiciones de tierras* and private lands had produced prosperous tributary households somewhat independent of the communal economy. By the eighteenth century the economies of the cacical house and the community were no longer indistinguishable.

Nor were they entirely separate. Despite these reforms and the growth of an Andean market economy, the cacique continued to occupy a central position in the communal economy. Several factors contributed to this, the most important of which was tribute collection.[6] From 1680 to 1720 the bishopric's annual tribute payments ranged from 40,000 to 60,000 pesos. In the 1740s and 1750s they had risen to between 60,000 and 80,000 pesos, spiking to 100,000 pesos by the late 1770s. Less than one peso per person in the Indian republic, in large communities annual tribute came to over a thousand pesos, huge sums for pueblo economies. Tribute's size relative to these is hard to determine, as detailed information on pueblo production is very rare. In 1807, the subdelegates of Caravaya, Huancané, and Lampa filed reports of the annual value of their provinces' exports (Table 4.1). In addition to the obvious problems of examining tribute rates from the mid-eighteenth century in the light of later production figures, these were remote provinces with relatively little Spanish settlement, whose *pueblos* were agricultural, pastoral, and mining communities rather than urban markets, and so cannot be taken as normative for the bishopric. Nonetheless, they do give some idea of the scale of the Indian economy: in all three provinces, the value of goods exported came to no more than ten pesos per capita of the Indian population, and in Caravaya was scarcely four pesos. In both Lampa and Huancané more than half the exports were silver and gold from local mines, an industry generally under Spanish control. These exports accounted for most of the circulation of specie within Indian communities, either directly through the sale of domestic produce or indirectly through wages (particularly in the mining industries in Lampa and Huancané). As a result, the tens, hundreds, or thousands of pesos that flowed through the

4 *Recopilación*, Book VI, Title I, Law 25.
5 For alcaldes and land distribution, see the lawsuits against Riquelme of Anta, ARC, INT, RH, Leg. 204 (1797); Nuñez de la Torre of Urubamba, ibid., Leg. 195 (1792); and ANB, Ruck, Exp. 217 (1802–7).
6 TePaske and Klein, *The Royal Treasuries*, I, 109–223.

Table 4.1. *Production for Export in Caravaya, Huancané, and Lampa, 1807*

Province and Commodity	Annual Value of Exports (pesos of 8 reales)
Caravaya [population: 20,467; 88% Indian]	TOTAL: 82,600
• Coca	40,000
• Other agricultural harvest	11,300
• Sheep	6,000
• Manufactures	8,500
• Gold	16,800
Huancané [population: 23,986; 88% Indian]	TOTAL: 241,709
• Agricultural harvest	20,984
• Livestock	86,150
• Manufactures, nontextile	15,400
• Manufactures, textiles	21,175
• Silver	98,000
Lampa [population: 41,671; 84% Indian]	TOTAL: 363,523
• Harvest (includes cheese and wool)	29,782
• Livestock	85,792
• Manufactures, nontextile	34,320
• Manufactures, textiles	24,056
• Silver	189,573

Source: From subdelegates' reports on provincial economies. BNP, Manuscritos, Exps. D-10474 (Caravaya); D-9555 (Huancané); and D-10473 (Lampa).

hands of a community's cacique as tribute constituted a substantial portion of the surplus production that was sold through the market.

Thus, collecting tribute entailed much more than gathering coins from every tributary. Many did pay in cash, earned by personally entering the monetized realm of the colonial system. By the 1750s most pueblos had a few Spanish traders, and every community had prosperous Indian households who owned draft animals and perhaps an oven. This was the ideal Toledo had fostered, and it had taken root. But each community also had those who met their obligations with lambs, crops, and cloth, or labored for the cacique or on haciendas, their wages paid to the local lord.[7] Evidence is frustratingly thin: there are no known cacical "account" books, listing who paid in cash and who in kind; which *ayllu* met its payment with the communal harvest; and so on. No doubt these were factors of local custom and of the accessibility of markets, and no doubt they varied within given communities. But anecdotal evidence gives insight into how responsibility for tribute collection allowed the cacique to extend control over local production.

7 ARC, NOT, Acuña, Leg. 10, 401 ff., December 6, 1774.

Most simply, certain fields and flocks were dedicated to tribute payment.[8] In 1771, Don Alexo Orcoguaranca Ynga collected and sold the harvests of such fields in Guayllabamba for 300 pesos, or roughly 30 percent of the pueblo's tribute.[9] The year before, Don Nicolas Rosas, cacique of Anta through his wife Doña Maria Dominga Quispeguaman, signed a note to the corregidor of Abancay to liquidate the pueblo's tribute and *reparto* debts. Anta was the largest pueblo near central Cusco and its markets, and its ayllus' lands came to 2,000 acres, three-fifths of them irrigated.[10] The debt was correspondingly impressive, at 8,199 pesos. To meet it the couple pledged personal property, but above all crops: 4,000 pesos for that year's harvest of corn, wheat, and beans from Anta's lands.[11] How the relation between communal harvests and individual tribute was calculated is unclear. But in marketing sizable portions of their communities' harvests, caciques added to their authority in both the pueblo and the regional economy.

Farther from Cusco, the absence of nearby markets further contributed to cacical control.[12] In 1788, the subdelegate of Azángaro described a provincial economy in which production for urban markets was well established: "[t]hey are in the custom of weaving *bayetas* . . . from the wool of sheep, that they sell to *vecinos* and *forasteros* who travel with them to the cities of Cusco, Arequipa, and La Paz, where they sell them, and dye them all colors. . . . And there is the custom that the caciques take them as tribute, and send them to be sold in these cities."[13] But the description makes clear the difficulty of transport: the cities were all more than a week's journey from Azángaro, and tributaries depended on middlemen, among whom the cacique figured prominently. More than two centuries after Toledo had instituted tribute assessed per capita in cash, in the well-populated but remote provinces of the Titicaca basin the Indian peasantry continued to pay its obligations in kind.

Indeed a decade later, in February 1798, the caciques of Azángaro asked to delay December's tribute payment until April, because ". . . the great poverty to which these times have reduced the miserable Indians being well known, we have found ourselves compelled and obliged by force to collect tribute in the goods of their industries, since they have no other means to exchange these goods for cash." This, they argued, was customary: the caciques then sold the goods in the highland cities. Unusually heavy rains had flooded the roads, and so their agents had not yet returned with the cash.

---

8 In 1774 the possessions of Gabriel Cama Condorsayna, cacique of Macarí, included "quatrocientos borregos de los tributos . . . en las tierras del comun." ARC, JC, Leg. 18 (1830).

9 AAC, VVI-5-84. For the annual tribute, Garrett, "Descendants," p. 251, n15.

10 ARC, INT, RH, Leg. 204 (1797), "Contra Don Ramon Riquelme," pp. 3–18.

11 ARC, NOT, Tapia Sarmiento, Leg. 258, 376 ff., July 7, 1770.

12 *Cuzco 1689*, p. 168; ANB, Ruck, Exp. 217, 125v (1805).

13 RREE, PSG, Exp. 146 (1788).

The subdelegate supported their claim and added that the province usually paid its December tribute in April and June tribute in October. However, this arrangement troubled the reformist Bourbon officials as much as it had their Habsburg predecessors. The royal treasury's lawyer opposed the postponement: using language that could have been excerpted from one of Toledo's reports, he attributed the problem "... to the abuse that [caciques] have introduced, of charging tribute in goods, of blankets, baskets, homespun, sheep, etc., carrying on a type of commerce or trade which is of no little value to [the caciques], since they remit the goods to the cities of Cusco, Arequipa, La Paz, Cochabamba, and Moquegua...."

By then Don Fermin Mango, cacique of Azángaro Urinsaya, had joined his peers, and he replied to these charges with a fuller description of tribute collection: "[t]he customary collection is made ... in each ayllu, when they gather the people ... and the greater part of the tributaries absent themselves for not having at hand anything with which to satisfy this just contribution, until by means of the greatest exertions, one catches them, with no way to acquire their share, so that the poor cacique is obliged to pay for them, and to receive payment, with great hardship ... in scrawny lambs, baskets, rope, and other goods that the region produces, which it is necessary to convert into money...."[14] The descriptions are mirror images. To the Spanish bureaucrat, the Indian lord was a corrupt official extorting labor and goods from the community to sell at a profit in urban markets. The cacique saw himself as a noble supervising his community's participation in the colonial system. Both views reflect the same material truth. Because the crown demanded tribute in cash and the southern highlands' market economy generally operated far from Indian pueblos, caciques stood at the nexus between local production and the colonial market, one of the greatest prizes the rural Andes had to offer.

Caciques enjoyed other privileges that entitled them to a disproportionate share of communal resources.[15] Most importantly, they received communal land (and labor) to defray the burdens of their office. Toledo set the amount of cacical lands at twelve topos.[16] In practice there was no standard figure, but the ubiquity of cacical land is clear. These lands were not property of the cacique: they were commons whose harvest was ceded to him (or her). The 1765 inventory of the goods of Don Narciso Carillo Pomayalli, the cacique of Colquepata, gives an idea of how cacical land functioned. Like many Inca caciques in the pueblos near Cusco, Narciso left a modest estate — his only real property were undescribed "lands" in

14 RREE, PRH, Exp. 108.
15 Caciques also received a salary. Díaz Rementería, *El cacique*, pp. 85–9. In the province of Chucuito in 1766, cacical pay varied dramatically, from nothing to 8% of tribute. AGI, Charcas, Leg. 591.
16 Sala i Vila, *Y se armó*, pp. 65–6.

Calca.[17] Of equal value was the harvest of cacical lands, yet to be realized: a dozen *estancias* and ayllus had set aside the harvest of specific fields for him.[18] Together, these were sown with 130 cargas of seed, worked by the communities on their land for their cacique.

The portion of Colquepata's labor and land dedicated to Narciso is not stated; nor was it in dispute. But communities often accused their caciques of usurping communal land.[19] Caciques took more land than the community deemed appropriate, or grazed private flocks on communal pastures. Also, communities dedicated the harvest of lands worked communally to cover specific burdens – particularly, in mita regions, the cost of supporting the families of *mitayos* or paying for shortfalls. The boundary between these communal and cacical harvests was often the subject of conflict. Caciques' desire to claim communal property as private property drove this conflict, but feeding it was the ill-defined distinction between different sorts of communal land.

The lengthy lawsuit against the cacique of Copacabana, Don Manuel Antonio Chuquimia, provides unusually detailed information on the allocation of communal land. The officials of both moieties were called to give testimony on the subject and declared that "[both moieties] have that which corresponds to them [divided] by turn every 6 years . . . in which each Indian *originario* receives 14 *brazadas*, and each *forastero* 12; the cacique receives 40 *brazadas*, and the priest 30, in consideration of the burdens of benefice, by ancient established custom in which nothing has been innovated. To the mitayos, too, they assign lands, giving them seeds of 50 cargas of potato and a half carga of quinoa, to work them."[20] Mitayos in Potosí remained part of the communal economy, their share of land planted and worked by the rest of the community. The cacique and the priest, simultaneously part of and set above the community, had larger shares and received land in both moieties. As important as the land was labor, also supplied by the community. Most *jilakatas* reported that their ayllus had sown roughly forty bushels daily for three days: one for the community, one for the cacique, and one for the mitayos.

The differences in the testimony of Chuquimia and Copacabana's jilakatas are telling (and not simply for their disagreement over Chuquimia's "abuses," with the jilakatas insisting that Chuquimia had taken communal harvests beyond those allocated). The jilakatas distinguished between land sown and harvested for the cacique, the community, and the mitayos, but

17 RREE, CN, Exp. 110.

18 RREE, CN, Exp. 166.

19 For prerebellion complaints of cacical usurpation, ANB, EC, 1762–144; and RREE, PRH, Exp. 184.

20 ANB, Ruck, Exp. 217, 125.

Chuquimia did not: to him, the various community lands and harvests were interchangeable. Most striking in different testimonies was the distinct reckoning of communal harvests: the jilakatas provided information on the amount of land dedicated to various purposes, the amount of seed sown, and the number of days worked. In contrast, Chuquimia reckoned in pesos. He listed his expenses for the community between 1803 and 1807, which ran 300–350 pesos a year, and included bread for the poor, paper for the community's legal dealings, and candles for Holy Thursday. The greatest share of expenses was for the mitayos, to whom Chuquimia made gifts in cash, food, coca, and liquor. Central to Chuquimia's defense were his claims of the value of the harvest: in 1806, 115 pesos of chuño and 45 pesos of quinoa.[21] Two aspects of these differences are striking. First, quite literally, Chuquimia personified the monetization of communal production, the point at which it went from being reckoned in land and labor to being calculated in pesos. Second, to Chuquimia, the claim (true or not) that his cacical expenses were greater than the income of the communal lands assigned to him shows an understanding of the cacicazgo as an office which should turn a legitimate profit, utterly distinct from that of the jilakatas, in which the cacique's respect for communal property and its complex allocation should take precedence.

The distinction between cacical lands, lands dedicated to mitayos, and those used to pay tribute was important, and this lawsuit shows that it was an area of concern and conflict between cacique and community. But whether it was Orcoguaranca selling the pueblo's corn for tribute money, Mango and his peers gathering Azángaro's household production for sale in distant cities, or Chuquimia taking the harvest of designated fields to defray mita expenses, the cacique turned communal produce into cash, which was then used to meet the obligations of the community. At issue was not whether the cacique should serve as the conduit of Indian produce into the viceregal market, but how much he should profit from this role.

Tribute and mita ensured that Indian communities were overwhelmingly net exporters. But they were not entirely self-sufficient: highland pueblos created a market for the necessities and luxuries of Indian society, which in turn presented other opportunities for cacical control. The negotiation of exchange between communities had been a central role of preconquest elites, and Andean society had established mechanisms for distributing these goods that long predated Spanish rule and the advent of colonial markets.[22] In his defense, Chuquimia presented accounts of his expenses on behalf of Copacabana. These included thirty to forty pesos a

21 ANB, Ruck, Exp. 217, 2.
22 Pease, *Curacas*, pp. 91–145

year for coca and *ají* – products of the warmer valleys – given to the trib-utaries of Copacabana when they performed the communal labor.[23] These distributions performed two ideals of the relationship between the cacique and the pueblo: first, that a logic of gifting, and not of monetized relations, characterized exchange within the community; and second, that the cacique controlled the juncture between Copacabana's economy and those of other communities, ensuring that the community received what it could not produce.

Other colonial methods of distribution also served to cement the caci-cal hold on local markets; testimony against Chuquimia provides glimpses of these. Mariano Ensinas, a vecino of Copacabana and son of Doña Fran-cisca Cusiguaman Pomaatagualpa, claimed that his mother had had a shop of which Chuquimia's wife, Doña Maria Josefa Salinas, had taken con-trol.[24] Numerous *principales* alleged that Chuquimia had established an illegal monopoly on the sale of liquor within the pueblo.[25] With the liquor monopoly and Salinas' shop, the Chuquimia household placed itself between a large pueblo and the rest of the viceroyalty. Nor were they unique: many caciques also profited from the sale of liquor and other goods to their com-munities, owning the *chicherías* and *pulperías* in which liquor was made and sold.[26]

Finally, caciques played a crucial role in the reparto, the forced sale (at inflated prices) of mules, manufactured goods, coca, and other products by the corregidor to the communities in his province. The reparto became widespread, if illegal, by the late seventeenth century.[27] Supporters argued that the reparto increased economic activity in Indian pueblos, although almost all in rural society viewed it with hostility.[28] But despite com-plaints by priests, ayllus, and caciques, the crown would not abandon the reparto, which increased corregidores' compensation without reducing trib-ute income. Instead, as part of the reforms of the mid-eighteenth century, an effort was made to regulate the reparto, in a (patently futile) attempt to make it less abusive and a more successful effort to increase its value.

23 ANB, Ruck, Exp. 217, 1–4.
24 Ibid., 9–10.
25 Ibid., 132–3.
26 Fernandez Cutimbo, ANB, EC 1793–11; Pachacutic y Salas, ARC, NOT, Zamora, Leg. 282, 402 ff., October 21, 1785; Cama Condorsayna, ARC, JC, Leg. 18 (1830); Guampoco, ARC, RA, Ord., Leg. 8 (1791), 1.
27 Moreno Cebrián, *El corregidor*; Javier Tord Nicolini, "El corregidor de indios del Perú: comercio y tributos," *Historia y Cultura* {Lima} 8 (1974): 173–210; Jürgen Golte, *Repartos y rebeliones: Túpac Amaru y las contradicciones de la economía colonial* (Lima: Instituto de Estudios Peruanos, 1980); Thomson, *We Alone*, pp. 106–39. For a revisionist view of the Mexican reparto, Jeremy Baskes, *Indians, Merchants, and Markets: A Reinterpretation of the Repartimiento and Spanish Indian Economic Relations in Colonial Oaxaca 1750–1821* (Stanford: Stanford University Press, 2000).
28 Jacobsen, *Mirages*, p. 96; *Cuzco 1689*, pp. 37, 293.

Legalized and formalized in 1751, the reparto then expanded until it was curtailed following the Tupac Amaru rebellion.[29]

The reparto's logic was tributary: purchasers received goods in return for their payments, but these exceeded the market value of the merchandise. Indeed, at the local level the reparto was organized much like tribute: the corregidor distributed goods to caciques and other notables; these middlemen then allocated the burden of the reparto among their communities and paid the corregidor. Some caciques turned profits on the reparto and undertook their own forced sales to their tributaries.[30] But the reparto also threatened cacical fortunes, especially as burdens increased in the 1760s and 1770s, and caciques sought to shield themselves and their heirs from corregidores' demands for these debts. On June 13, 1761 the cacique of Taray, Don Joseph Tamboguacso, made a hurried power of attorney to his wife to make his will; he died days later. The posthumous will listed his assets; the power of attorney, in contrast, concentrated on essentials: his claim to the cacicazgo, recognition of his three children as his legitimate heirs, and an insistence that "to the [corregidor] General Don Santiago Mateo Urdapileta he owes nothing for tribute nor for the reparto."[31] In so doing Tamboguacso sought to protect his family from the corregidor's demands at the most precarious moment in its fortunes.[32]

Burdensome though they could be, these forced sales also reinforced cacical authority. In 1782, Don Lorenzo Copa Cusicondor of Guarocondo complained to the Cusco *cabildo* about the former corregidor, Miguel Navarro, who had done a reparto, though not through Cusicondor: he had taken over because the debt collector was so abusive.[33] Navarro claimed that Cusicondor still owed him 1,056 pesos, which the latter disputed. It was a substantial, though not crippling, sum; its assumption by Cusicondor reinforced his position as the intermediary between the viceregal market, crown officials, and his community. On a grander scale – befitting a Titicaca Basin cacique – Don Agustin Siñani of Carabuco was responsible for a reparto of some 12,000 pesos.[34] Once again, this transaction reaches our attention only because it was contested; countless others have left no record. But certainly Siñani's sale of 251 mules and thousands of pesos of cloth and knives reinforced his dominant role in the economy.

29 Golte, *Repartos*, pp. 79–125; O'Phelan Godoy, *Un siglo*, pp. 117–73. Reparto burdens varied greatly by region; in the bishopric of Cusco the average was two pesos a year per capita.
30 ANB, EC, 1762–144, 18v; also ARC, NOT, Villagarcia, Leg. 280, 267 ff., January 24, 1789, for Juana Vilcapi of Toro.
31 ARC, NOT: Domingo Gamarra, Leg. 129, 514, June 3, 1761; and Pedro Joseph Gamarra, Leg. 169, 672 ff., June 13, 1761.
32 ARC, COR, Civ., Leg. 55, Exp. 1241 (1746–65), for Tupa Cusiguallpa's estate.
33 ARC, CAB, Ped., Leg. 114 (1773–86).
34 ANB, EC, 1761–97.

Caciques also exerted control over local production. They had a right to labor from the community, beyond that used to cultivate cacical lands. Don Blas Quispe Uscamayta, cacique of Pucyura's Ayllu Ayarmaca in the 1790s, was assigned a couple of shepherds and muleeters, along with "two women with the title of *mitani*" who wove in his house.[35] In larger communities, caciques claimed dozens of workers: from shepherds, agricultural laborers, and muleeters to tributaries who turned cacical houses into small factories.[36] A 1774 inventory of the possessions of Macarí's cacique gives an idea of the magnitude. Don Gabriel Cama Condorsayna's mansion was the imposing seat of Macarí's ruling family, with well-furnished rooms around the front patio. But the second patio served as a processing plant for local textiles, with forty dying vats, two large cauldrons, 100 lb. of soap, a quantity of dye, and several hundred yards of cloth.[37] Here the cacique washed and processed the rough-weave received in lieu of tribute, adding value with tributary labor as the pueblo's manufactures passed through his house.[38]

Cama Condorsayna's possessions show a second way in which caciques extended their control over various aspects of the economy: capital investment beyond the ability of the tributary household. Given the poverty of the Indian commons, this threshold was easily reached. Indeed, the cacical monopoly on marketing tribute paid in kind owed itself to this poverty. For tributaries in Colquepata, Macarí, and Azángaro, converting harvests or cloth into cash was no easy task. Cama Condorsayna owned 17 mules, 70 mares, and 200 llamas, a reminder of the unique position in the highland economy of cacical houses along the royal roads linking Lower and Upper Peru.[39] By the 1700s the cacical monopoly on fleeting this long-distance trade had passed, although it remained the basis of some fortunes, most famously that of Jose Gabriel Tupac Amaru.[40] But even caciques uninvolved in this portage owned animals to carry their communities' harvests to market: Carillo Pomayalli of Colquepata had forty donkeys. He also owned twelve "master plow oxen" to plow the village fields.[41] Other village prominents had oxen as well, but the cacique owned far more than needed

---

35 Mitanis were women performing labor to meet communal obligations. ARC, INT, RH, Leg. 211 (1801), 1–3.

36 ARC, COR, Civ., Leg. 45, Exp. 976.

37 In the dispute over his son's estate; ARC, JC, Leg. 18 (1830). Catalina Pachacutic y Salas constructed a chorrillo. ARC, NOT, Acuña, Leg. 14, 302 ff., June 17, 1779.

38 In 1779 Don Gaspar Altamirano advanced Jose Gabriel Tupac Amaru of Tungasuca 2,062 pesos; he was to deliver 180 finished cloths and 660 varas of rough-woven cloth to the obraje of Taray for processing. ARC, NOT, Palacios, Leg. 232, 80, February 21, 1779.

39 ARC, JC, Leg. 18 (1830). Xauregui and Tito Atauchi of Pucarani had twenty-four pack mules, eight donkeys, five saddle mules, and six horses. ANB, EC, 1773–83.

40 Stavig, *The World of Túpac Amaru*, pp. 155–7.

41 RREE, CN, Exp. 348, 1765. ARC, NOT, Tapia Sarmiento, Leg. 258, 376 ff., July 7, 1770: Rosas and Quispe Guaman had twenty-six oxen.

to tend his modest lands: a dozen animals underscored his importance and authority in the pueblo economy.

Caciques controlled other capital items essential to the daily life of the ayllu or pueblo: mills and ovens. The latter were mentioned often in the wills of rural caciques.[42] Similarly, in grain-growing communities, control of the mill expanded the cacique's role in the local economy.[43] The Pucyura mill shows the coincidence of political and economic authority in caciques' hands. In the mid-1700s the pueblo's cacique, Don Miguel Ñancay, made two journeys to Lima to claim ownership of the mill for the community, in opposition to the priest (who claimed it for the parish church).[44] Ñancay won, and from then until well after independence the mill remained the property of Pucyura, and was leased to the Ñancay for 200 pesos a year – 100 to the parish church for its maintenance, 100 to help with Pucyura's tribute – reinforcing their importance in the pueblo's economy.[45]

It was the multiplicity of caciques' activities in the local economy that strengthened their control. They collected the crown's tribute and conducted the forced sales of the corregidor. They ground the village's grain and baked it into bread; they controlled much of the market for imported goods; they received a sizable portion of the communal harvest to sell in urban markets, and in addition received labor in their own households as tribute. The short will of Don Gregorio Mamani, cacique of two ayllus in Tinta, nicely captures these numerous roles of the cacique.[46] Tinta was not under the rule of a single family; nor did Mamani claim hereditary rights to these cacicazgos. But he was from a prominent family, describing both his parents and his wife as "indios principales." Almost every item in Mamani's will involves the ayllu economy. He owed the corregidor 100 pesos for tribute debts and 26 pesos for the reparto; but "various Indian tributaries from his ayllu owe him small amounts on their tribute," and a creole *hacendado* owed him 90 pesos for the Indians from the ayllu who had worked his lands. Mamani owned four teams of oxen, ten mares, and five donkeys; he had built an oven in Machacmarca. The material interdependence of the cacique's domestic economy and the ayllu economy is

42 ARC, NOT: Joseph Bernardo Gamarra, Leg. 115, 570 ff., December 20, 1788; Zamora, Leg. 294, 402 ff., October 21, 1785; Acuña, Leg. 10, 401 ff., December 6, 1774; Tomas Cardenas, Leg. 65, November 26, 1752; Rodriguez Ledezma, Leg. 248, 411 ff., July 8, 1797.

43 Lucas Poma Ynga had a mill in Quiquijana. *CDBR*, IV, p. 11.

44 See Chapter 5, pp. 171–172; also "Indios de sangre real," pp. 211–12.

45 ARC, NOT, Villavisencio, Leg. 288, 4ff., January 14, 1778. Ñancay's grandson-in-law, Blas Quispe Uscamayta, served as tribute collector and had the rental of the mill. ARC, NOT, Pedro Joaquin Gamarra, Leg. 77, 584 ff., August 16, 1804.

46 ARC, NOT, Acuña, Leg. 10, 401 ff., December 6, 1774. In 1792, the two ayllus combined had 134 tributaries. ARC, INT, RH, Leg. 195 (1792).

nowhere clearer. That interdependence went largely unchallenged, in principle, until the Tupac Amaru rebellion. Indian communities contested the actions of their caciques, but over matters of practice, over what share of local labor and land particular caciques deserved. In mid-eighteenth-century Cusco, neither the crown nor the Indian commons denied that the cacique should occupy a dominant position in the pueblo economy, for caciques played too crucial a role in the colonial system generally, as the most important intermediary between the economies of the two ethnic republics.

Private Wealth in the Indian Republic

The cacicazgo played an even more important role in the household economies of the colonial Indian elite. Some idea of the potential for profit emerges from the dealings of Doña Catalina Pachacutic y Salas, the Inca noblewoman who served as cacica of Layo and Yanaoca in southern Tinta. She insisted that she had acquired her impressive fortune through her own work: in thirty years she purchased a ranch worth 6,000 pesos; constructed a *chorrillo, pulperías*, and an oven; and received lands from Layo's Ayllu Urinsaya in recompense for her services.[47] Her estate grew to ten thousand pesos; by the time of her death late in the 1790s she was one of the richest Indian women in the bishopric and an important figure in the economy of the upper Vilcanota.

But the cacicazgo was also economically perilous. Caciques were responsible for tribute and reparto debts, and corregidores were unforgiving. Caciques' property was seized to make up for shortfalls, and just as the cacique beat and jailed tributaries to extract their payments, so did corregidores beat and jail caciques to do the same.[48] The migrations and epidemics of the seventeenth century had made the burden of many cacicazgos untenable; even in the eighteenth century, with a demographic and economic expansion, caciques renounced office because of the burdens.[49] Twenty-five years before tribute shortfalls forced Don Ramon Basques to resign as cacique of Ñuñoa Urinsaya, Don Antonio Cota Luque of Pucará wrote to Lima that the tribute rolls listed twenty-five more tributaries than were in the pueblo, and that he owed the corregidor eighty-four pesos on a reparto of mules. As a result, complained Cota Luque, "in the pueblos there are not Indian principales, nor a mestizo nor a Spaniard who wants to be

---

47 ARC, NOT: Acuña, Leg. 14, 302 ff., June 17, 1779; Zamora, Leg. 294, 402 ff., October 21, 1785; Rodriguez Ledezma, Leg. 248, 153 ff., July 4, 1796.

48 Saignes, *Caciques*, p. 9; ARC, CAB, Civ., Leg. 49, Exp. 1164; Stavig, *The World of Túpac Amaru*, p. 132.

49 ANB, EC, 1793–11, 74v for Chucuito Anansaya.

cacique."[50] When Lampa's corregidor rode to Ñuñoa to replace Basques, he called together the "Indian principales and the plebeians" and ordered that they propose three men for the office. The community proposed only two: Basques and Antonio Tapara. The moiety maneuvered so that the corregidor had no choice but to appoint their candidate; but the record of the election suggests that caciques could, in fact, be hard to find.

And yet they were found. The information about Pucará and Ñuñoa comes from claims to the cacicazgos made by descendants of those who took over the offices. In the absence of more comprehensive evidence, it is unclear whether caciques as a class periodically faced economic crises, or whether the particular dynamics of individual pueblos would sporadically make the office untenable.[51] However, the Indian nobility continued to take on these offices and, once acquired, sought to maintain them in their families. For despite its pitfalls, the cacicazgo remained the most important position in Indian society. Its occupant enjoyed great power and authority within the community and had the opportunity of acquiring wealth, although this could entail violating Spanish law and the sensibilities of Indian communities.[52] Caciques could hide people when the new tribute rolls were prepared, but later collect from them and thus profit handsomely.[53] Indeed, tacitly caciques were expected to collect from those not on the rolls to make up for those who had died or moved away. When this practice became an abuse was determined as much by local politics as by the actual actions of the cacique; but complaints suggest the wealth that caciques could accumulate.[54] In 1755 tributaries from Lampa launched a suit against their cacique, Don Diego Pacoricona.[55] According to the tributaries Diego usurped communal lands dedicated to the community's mitayos; he forced tributaries to work for free on his own lands; he made them work his mule and llama trains without pay, and from this alone had made 1,500 pesos; he had a liquor monopoly and forced those who owed tribute to work in his tavern; and he hid tributaries.

One did not have to be as abusive as Pacoricona to profit from the cacicazgo, and many well-off caciques did not face legal challenges from their communities. But accusations against caciques underscored tensions

---

50 ANB, EC, 1775–176, 7v and 8v.

51 O'Phelan Godoy argues that the replacement of proprietary caciques with Spaniards increased with the legalization of the reparto; Stavig observes that this was uncommon in Quispicanchis and Tinta before the rebellion. O'Phelan Godoy, *Kurakas*, pp. 17–28; Stavig, *The World of Túpac Amaru*, p. 126.

52 For more on complaints about cacical abuses, see Chapter 5 generally; n32 for specific cases.

53 This accusation figures prominently in complaints against caciques, no doubt because it was sure to attract the attention of crown officials.

54 ANB, Ruck, Exp. 217, 12, for Chuquimia of Copacabana's fortune.

55 RREE, PRH, Exp. 184. A prominent cacical family in eighteenth-century Lampa, the Pacoricona served as caciques in Lampa and Calapuja. ADP, INT, Exp. 35.

between caciques and communities. Most caciques played several essential economic roles in their communities that made possible the accumulation of private wealth. In turn, this wealth created economic possibilities and imposed an economic logic different from those of the rest of the Indian republic, and divided the upper ranks of the cacical elite from their communities. No other segment of Indian society was able to embrace so strongly Spanish forms of property and instruments like chaplaincies and dowries. Because of these private assets, the familial economies of the Indian elite's top stratum resembled those of creole society and stressed the preservation of family wealth and status over generations. The liminal position of the cacique in the colonial economy reproduced itself in the cacical elites' domestic economies, as they negotiated a fundamental material dialectic of colonial society: between the communal economies of Indian Peru and the private economies of the Spanish republic.

Cacical families were not alone in the Indian republic in acquiring private lands and livestock. To the sixteenth-century Habsburg reformers the apparent lack of private property in Andean society was a compelling indication of Inca tyranny, and the Spanish quickly introduced deeded, alienable titles, monetized value, and relatively open sales of private land. These, combined with preconquest customs of recognizing elite lineages' hereditary claims to land, created Indian households who were set apart from the majority of their community by their property. Only a minority of Indian households had such claims to land. Nonetheless, private or household property played an important, if secondary, role in local production and a primary role in marking and preserving stratification. Records of private property among the Indian kulak or yeoman class are rarer than those for the great cacical families who, like their creole peers, repeatedly left their mark in Cusco's notary books and court records. But enough information survives to suggest the type and magnitude of private property in the eighteenth-century Indian republic.

Land was alienated from the commons in two ways: through concession of the community and by royal sale in *composición*. This created two sorts of property in Indian pueblos. Those who had rendered some service might receive lands from the commons – for example, the concession of an *estancia* on communal land to a nobleman who had performed the onerous job of captain of the mita contingent to Potosí.[56] Widows and children of caciques might be given lands and houses in the community, in "composición del cacique."[57] So too were sacristans and cadet lines of cacical families. Most property claims in Indian communities functioned thus: every village had

---

56 RREE, PRA, Exp. 90 (1793); also ARC, COR, Prov., Civ., Leg. 75 (1776–9) for the Hancco dispute in Sicuani.
57 ARC, NOT, Joseph Bernardo Gamarra, Leg. 110, 107 ff., July 3, 1785, for Yauric Ariza of Oropesa.

bits of land conceded to individuals on a quasi-permanent basis, and often this land had been improved, with orchards or sheep folds, to produce the small wealth of ayllu notables. That a particular family had a claim to it was not in dispute; at question were the length and limits of such claims.[58]

They could last for generations. In the Ayllu Cupi of Huancané, the Estancia Sincara first appears as private property in 1634, when Pedro Guancollo presented witnesses to support his claim that the small ranch belonged to him absolutely and not to the ayllu commons. In 1698, Francisco Guancollo was in court defending the estancia against Eugenio Camasa, and in the 1780s Antonio Guancollo appeared before the Cusco Audiencia, complaining that Don Alonso Camasa, the "curaca and *segunda* of another ayllu" was trying to dispossess him. Soon after (in 1792), Antonio and his brothers launched another complaint, this time against Mateo Quispe, who was serving as Ayllu Cupi's tribute collector and argued that the land belonged to the ayllu, not the Guancollos.[59] That the Guancollos had retained control of Sincara for a century suggests that they ranked among the ayllu's most important lineages. That they had a century-long feud with the Camasas over the land suggests that the latter, too, were local prominents, and in 1787 Don Eugenio Camasa was Huancané's Indian alcalde.[60] The history of the estancia shows the points of conflict within Indian pueblos: between a prominent ayllu lineage and the man appointed to collect tribute, over whether the yield of the ranch should go to the family or to help with the ayllu's obligations; and between two Indian families, both of some rank, over who had claim to this bit of land long since marked off from the commons.

It is not clear whether the Guancollos retained their claim to the estancia. What is noteworthy is that they appealed to the newly founded Cusco Audiencia. Usually, private and familial claims to communal property operated below the level of the royal courts, and we have only occasional anecdotal records. Just as important, the division of Peru into ethnic republics and the insistence by colonial officials that property in Indian pueblos was communal meant that claims within the community did not have the same status that property sold by the crown did. As a result, pueblo prominents were often eager to convert the former into the latter through composición.[61] In 1780 Don Agustin Pachari and his sons prepared a petition to the royal courts, asking that the lands of Queela, in Nicacio, be confirmed as family property, "as Indios Principales and heirs to the cacicazgo of the pueblo . . . as

---

58 ARC, RA, Ord., Leg. 34 (1799) for an informative dispute in Colquemarca; for others, Garrett, "Descendants," p. 279, n82.

59 ARC, RA, Ord., Leg. 10 (1792).

60 RREE, PC, Exp. 1.

61 ANB, EC, 1761–102 for a case from Azángaro.

descendants of those who previously possessed this government." The current cacique supported their claim, and the "judge delegated for the visitation, sale, and composition of lands" confirmed Agustin's possession: the land was transformed into private property recognized by the crown.[62] The legal papers that accompanied such land brought protection from the colonial courts, solidifying the standing of prominent families by placing their land outside the community's reach.[63]

Privately owned livestock also featured prominently in pueblo economies. In sheep, cattle, and mules – introduced by the Spanish – private ownership was the rule. In pastoral communities, ayllus and pueblos owned large common flocks to help to defray communal obligations.[64] But individuals also amassed holdings: that of a prosperous household might reach two hundred sheep, or fifty cows, and a few oxen or mules.[65] Such holdings were important in village life. Oxen and mules were invaluable in labor-starved communities, while sheep and cattle formed a productive store of wealth.[66] Such property was also the mark of status and wealth within the Indian community, playing an important role in local stratification. Owners often described themselves as nobles or principales, used the honorific "Don" in their documents, and claimed privileges by blood or by service to the community. They were a minority in every pueblo.

How common such lands and flocks were in the colonial pueblo is impossible to gauge. A handful of provincial notary books from the agricultural pueblos of Urubamba and Calca survive in the Cusco archives; they contain seventeen Indian wills from the 1770s to the 1810s. While only three are of caciques, all but one mention property.[67] Indeed, a purpose of the wills was to stake a cross-generational claim to bits of land, explaining how they came into the testators' possession. Don Blas Serban Cusipaucar had an adobe house roofed in tile, along with two topos of wheat land, which he had inherited from his mother; four more topos of wheat land, which had come to him after he paid for his brother's funeral; a small house roofed with tile from his mother-in-law; another house with two irrigated topos of corn land that he had purchased for 180 pesos; and a small salt pan that he had

62 ARC, RA, Ord., Leg. 4 (1789), 2.
63 ARC, CAB, Civ., Leg. 33, Exp. 837.
64 For example, the description of Langui in *Cuzco*, 1689, p. 245.
65 The "richest" tributaries in Copacabana in 1805 had flocks of 100 sheep. ANB, Ruck, Exp. 217, 125. Also Colquemarca, *Cuzco 1689*, p. 313; for others, Garrett, "Descendants," p. 283, n92.
66 ARC, NOT: Joseph Bernardo Gamarra, Leg. 118, 405 ff., July 29, 1793; Chacon y Becerra, Leg. 79, 103 ff., September 9, 1792; Quintanilla, Leg. 237, 62 ff., September 4, 1755; Tomas Gamarra, Leg. 180, 354–6, July 10, 1783.
67 ARC, NOT: Tomas Santos Gamarra, Leg. 181; Moya, Leg. 229; Forton, [ ] [Urubamba, 1802–18]; Grajeda, [ ] [Urubamba, 1827–34]. Twelve testators used "Don."

also bought.[68] Blas was quite prosperous by pueblo standards: most of the noncacical wills mention smaller estates. Although such holdings made up only a small part of the land in Indian pueblos, by the 1700s almost every community had land set apart from the common by tradition or on the basis of a faded deed, and privately owned flocks of animals. Their owners were the local elites of the Indian republic, their wealth insignificant in the larger economy but of great importance within the community.

Thus, caciques and the great Inca nobles were not the only Indians to acquire private property. But distinguishing their property were both its magnitude and the economic logic of cacical families. The wealth of prosperous tributaries and lesser Indian nobles was not of a scale to separate them from the communities in which they lived: as a rule such household property never reached more than a few hundred pesos.[69] In contrast, the fortunes of the richest caciques in Bourbon Cusco surpassed 10,000 pesos.[70] These paled next to those of Cusco's creole aristocrats, but towered over those of other Indian prominents in their pueblos.[71] With such fortunes these families had different horizons than those over whom they ruled, and their wealth tended to draw them away from the community and into networks of provincial elites – both Indian and creole.

The estate of Don Diego Choquehuanca, cacique of Azángaro Anansaya, is illustrative. The Choquehuanca had ruled this large community since the time of the conquest.[72] At the time of his death in 1792, Diego was one of the most powerful men around Lake Titicaca. His two-story house was worthy of a corregidor, with eleven rooms, two patios, and two kitchens.[73] In its furnishings it resembled an aristocratic mansion in Cusco far more than the three-room hut of a prosperous tributary. Diego owned a bed with all the trappings, nearly twenty paintings (ten in gilt frames), half a dozen statues of saints, several tables, chairs, and benches, two rugs, and four wooden doors. He left six trunks of clothing, of the most impressive variety: European and Andean vestments of velvet, brocade, wool, and alpaca, trimmed with gold and silver thread. He had sixteen pounds of silver hollowware, and

---

68 ARC, NOT, Grajeda, Leg. s/n, 696 ff., May 14, 1790. [Urubamba, 1827–34, sic].

69 For others, RREE, CRA, Exp. 237 (1805); ARC, INT, Ord., Leg. 76 (1816) for the possessions of Don Manuel Chalco, of Santo Tomás.

70 None of the bishopric's eighteenth-century caciques approached the wealth of Ñusta Beatriz or Melchor Carlos Ynga. The 1673 will of Gabriel Fernandez Guarachi of Machaca describes a fortune of tens of thousands of pesos, suggesting that La Paz's cacical elite was richer than Cusco's. Rivera, "El Mallku."

71 In 1755 the assets of Cusco's Don Agustin Xara, the Marquis of Casa Xara, were valued at more than 215,000 pesos. Like most creole fortunes, the value of his estate was reduced by debts, for a net worth of 50,000 pesos. ARC, COR, Civ., Leg. 41, Exp. 871.

72 For a 1789 description of Azángaro, RREE, PSG, Exp. 146.

73 ADP, INT, Exp. 46, April 10, 1802; ADP, INT, Exp. 51, October 30, 1802.

two pounds of gold in assorted forms; the remainder of his jewelry had been given as collateral for a 300-peso loan. Above all, he had livestock: more than 14,000 sheep on several estancias, worth 14,000 pesos.

In such pueblos the concentration of wealth was striking. Azángaro was also home to other noble Indian families that dominated local offices below the moiety cacicazgos, and their relative poverty highlights the wealth gap. Don Toribio Atamas Mamani's 1748 will clearly indicates his local standing. Toribio, his wife, and his adult children all enjoyed the honorific "Don," and his will names his father (Don Francisco), makes hereditary claims to communal land, and leaves instructions to bury him "in the chapel of Our Lady of the Rosary which my grandparents and ancestors built for this purpose."[74] Atamas Mamani belonged to a lineage that had once occupied a cacicazgo in the pueblo. Acknowledged as "hijos d'algo" in Azángaro, they carefully perpetuated their position of honor.[75] But this principal of Urinsaya had only modest possessions.[76] His wife had brought a dowry of six cows, and the herd had increased to thirty. Toribio owned a house and two estancias that had long been possessed by his family; he also owned fifteen mules. By local standards Atamas Mamani was fairly well off (although, with ten children, he was quick to lament his poverty); but in comparison to those of the cacical family of Anansaya his possessions were paltry.

Atamas Mamani had peers in most highland pueblos, ayllu caciques who controlled wealth that put them at the top of their community, but did not remove them from it. In contrast, few Indian families in the bishopric equaled the Choquehuanca. Those who did were concentrated in the major pueblos of the Titicaca basin and on the Altiplano, as a group the richest concentration of Indian families in Peru.[77] By the eighteenth century Inca caciques around Cusco were noticeably poorer. Inventories and wills from the 1760s and 1770s suggest that the personal worth of prominent caciques there ran from two to three thousand pesos. The nature as well as the scale of the property varied, with farmland playing a more important role than livestock in temperate agricultural regions. In 1782, Vicente Choquecahua of Andaguaylillas owned twenty-eight topos in the pueblo, worth some 2,000 pesos.[78] With his wife he also owned a house and a bit of land in her parish (Belén), as well as several mules. Joseph Tamboguacso of Taray

74 ANB, EC, 1759–13, 1r.

75 ADP, INT, Exp. 69.

76 ANB, EC, 1759–13.

77 Eugenio Sinanyuca of Coporaque was worth more than 10,000 pesos (ARC, NOT, Vargas, Leg. 139, 357 ff., November 27, 1804), as were Bernardo Succacahua of Umachire (ARC, NOT, Joseph Bernardo Gamarra, Leg. 124, 233 ff. [1799]) and Ambrocio Quispe Cavana of Cavanilla (ANB, EC, 1785–23, 6v). For others, see Garrett, "Descendants," p. 288, n106.

78 ARC, NOT, Tomas Gamarra, Leg. 180, 324 ff., June 15, 1782.

and his wife owned farmland worth 1,350 pesos and houses worth 1,450 pesos, all in the neighboring parish of San Blas.[79] They also had a couple of modest houses in Taray, four mules, and a fair amount of silverware and elegant clothing (though nothing like Choquehuanca). Other caciques had similar holdings: one to two thousand pesos in land; a few modest houses in their communities; the silver, furnishings, and clothing required of their rank; and a bit of livestock.[80]

For Cusco, these were rich caciques who ruled entire pueblos.[81] Below them were Inca ayllu caciques who, despite their imperial ancestry, resembled the village notables described above. In the 1790s Don Blas Quispe Uscamayta and Don Manuel Corimanya served as ayllu caciques in Pucyura, which had 250 tributaries in all.[82] Quispe Uscamayta claimed that "my ancestors were commonly considered descendants of the Uscamaytas . . . and of the Incas Huayna Capac and Mayta Capac"; he had studied at San Borja.[83] Corimanya, who also claimed Inca ancestry, could sign with a legible, if not polished, hand.[84] Yet their property was modest. In 1801, they both owned respectable houses in Pucyura: two stories, four rooms, of adobe with tile roofs and wooden doors. Corimanya had 225 pesos of livestock, plus the communal harvest; Quispe Uscamayta had 50 pesos of livestock, 4 topos of land, and the communal harvest.[85] Married to Miguel Ñancay's granddaughter, Quispe Uscamayta also had the leasehold on Pucyura's mill.[86] By the standards of Pucyura the two were prosperous, but of no more than local importance. Some caciques around Cusco had more substantial fortunes – for example, Rosas and Quispeguaman of Anta. But Anta was atypical in its size and its history as an important indigenous community long before the conquest.[87] In general, with their large, fractious nobility and relatively small pueblos, the valleys around Cusco offered less opportunity for cacical enrichment than the provinces to the south.[88]

Indeed, the richest Incas in eighteenth-century Cusco and its hinterland were closely tied to the urban economy. Although they aggressively identified themselves as Indian nobles, their economic activities resembled those

79 ARC, NOT, Pedro Joseph Gamarra, Leg. 169, 672 ff., June 2, 1761.

80 For Inca caciques' livestock holdings, see Garrett, "Descendants," p. 289, n110.

81 Around 1790, Taray had 190 tributaries; Andaguaylillas had 115. ARC, INT, RH: Leg. 196 (1792–3) and Leg. 185 (1788), respectively.

82 ARC, INT, RH, Leg. 194 (1792–3).

83 ARC, RA, Adm., Leg. 156 (1797), 47; "Indios de sangre real," p. 226.

84 See Corimanya's complaint against Don Vicente Ladron de Guebarra. ARC, INT, Ord., Leg. 39 (1796); for his Inca ancestry, INT, RH, Leg. 211 (1801).

85 ARC, INT, RH, Leg. 211 (1801), 19–22.

86 ARC, NOT, Pedro Joaquin Gamarra, Leg. 77, 584 ff., August 16, 1804.

87 Also Mateo Pumacahua's equally atypical fortune, acquired after the rebellion; Chapter 7, pp. 239–241.

88 ARC, INT, Ord., Leg. 4 (1785) for Pumahuallpa Garces Chillitupa of Zurite.

of the city's well-to-do creoles; as with their creole peers, their preferred investment was urban real estate.[89] Antonia Loyola Cusitito Atauyupanqui was worth some 7,500 pesos; Diego Ninancuyuchi left a similar estate on his death in 1756, which he had acquired as a merchant and the owner of a chorrillo.[90] In addition to his chorrillo, its presses and vats, and 1200 yards of cloth (half of it processed, half of it still rough), his will lists debts and contracts amounting to several thousand pesos, for lambs, soap from Cochabamba, and the ubiquitous "efectos de Castilla" (imported goods). Otherwise, his principal assets were two houses in the Hospital parish and the impressive clothes and furnishings of an urban noble. Don Asencio Ramos Tito Atauchi and Doña Maria Vasquez Obando had an estate worth almost 10,000 pesos in houses, furnishings, debts, clothing, silver, jewelry, and some agricultural lands.[91]

Ramos Tito Atauchi was the cacique of two ayllus in Santa Ana; Ninancuyuchi, of Ayllu Collana in the city's Hospital parish. But these cacicazgos were not the source of their wealth. Indeed, for Ninancuyuchi the opposite was true: his wealth had led to his appointment, which was a financial drain. The Hospital was the most urban of Cusco's eight Indian parishes, with no communal land and an Indian population consisting largely of rootless laborers, from whom it was difficult to extract tribute. Such cacicazgos were generally forced on Indian nobles, for whom the office was an expensive burden. Ninancuyuchi tried, unsuccessfully, to renounce the office, as did others.[92]

For the urban Indian nobility, the sources of wealth were trade, industry, and the crafts, not the cacicazgo.[93] Urban Indian nobles were prominent in the butcher's guild and the lucrative trade in lambs with the Collao.[94] Their dealings could be substantial: in 1776 Don Ventura Caguatupa (a cacique in Santa Ana) and Don Ignacio Apocmayta ("indio noble del Cusco") signed a 2,000-peso contract for the purchase of 4,000 lambs.[95] Indian nobles also traded in grain: in her 1758 will Asencio's daughter, Doña Tomasa Ramos Tito Atauchi, noted that she owed 2,000 pesos for a shipment of corn.[96] And like Ninancuyuchi, a number owned chorrillos along the small Sapi

89 Also AAC, II.7.128 for the inventory of the goods of Doña Ygnacia Cusigualpa.
90 For Loyola Cusitito Atauyupanqui, see Chapter 3, p. 84. For Ninancuyuchi, ARC, NOT, Diego Gamarra, Leg. 126, 701 ff., June 30, 1756. For his family, and his election as alférez real, see Chapter 2, p. 59.
91 ARC, NOT, Juan Bautista Gamarra, Leg. 133, [ ], January 9, 1749; and [ ], August 2, 1755.
92 ARC, CAB, Civ., Leg. 26, Exp. 678. For others, Garrett, "Descendants," pp. 590–1.
93 Chapter 3, p. 85, for Indian noble artisans.
94 ARC, CAB, Civ., Leg. 25, Exp. 669.
95 ARC, NOT, Juan Bautista Gamarra, Leg. 145, [ ], March 16, 1776; for others, Garrett, "Descendants," p. 293, n127.
96 ARC, NOT, Juan Bautista Gamarra, Leg. 133, [ ], August 23, 1758; for others Garrett, "Descendants," p. 293, n128.

and Tullumayo rivers.[97] The Indian noble fortunes that these activities produced were by no means insignificant; in some sense they were also "cacical" fortunes, in that almost all of Cusco's richest Indian nobles served as caciques. But these urban nobles were economically far closer to Cusco's better-heeled creoles than to their rural peers. This did not make them less "Indian": they remained the most self-conscious and organized group of Indian nobles in Peru. However, it underscores the complexity of the bishopric's Indian nobility, adding an urban–rural dichotomy to the ethnic distinction between the Incas and the Aymara lords and that between the agricultural valleys and the pastoral highlands.

This variety in the magnitude and nature of Indian fortunes is a reminder of the dangers of treating what was essentially a noble estate as a unified economic class. Both within and between regions there were marked differences in the economies of noble families. Where there were little Spanish settlement and long traditions of complex indigenous societies – coinciding with the areas of mining mitas – cacical families of considerable wealth dominated provincial society. In Cusco and its agricultural hinterland, rural caciques were of more modest wealth (if impressive lineage); on the other hand, the urban economy of Cusco created its own Indian rich, largely drawn from the Inca nobility. Not all communities and cacicazgos within each region conform to these patterns. Both renunciations of office mentioned above occurred in Lampa: the burdens of office in the mita area could bankrupt as well as enrich caciques. The highlands also contained hundreds of small hamlets, sometimes under the effective control of a nearby pueblo and its cacique, sometimes with their own, humble caciques. Large highland pueblos with clearly established *caciques gobernadores* or principales had ayllu caciques below them. Conversely, one of the richest Inca nobles was Cayetano Tupa Guamanrimachi, principal cacique of San Sebastián parish. During his more than thirty-year rule he acquired forty topos of land in the parish, worth several thousand pesos.[98] But certainly in the mid-1700s the descendants of the Aymara lords surpassed their erstwhile rulers in wealth and power; while among the Incas those in the city of Cusco and involved in its trade and industry were often richer than rural cacical houses.

Many factors contributed to this variety. The legacy of Inca imperial rule and of Spanish recognition of Inca nobility was the concentration of noble families around Cusco, who generally moved with some facility in the colonial system. Their men were more likely to be literate than most Indians; they often had ties of real or fictive kinship with Spaniards; and, as a tangible legacy of former greatness, many had a few topos of land in freehold,

97 For Narciso Carillo Pomayalli, ARC, NOT, Domingo Gamarra, Leg. 129, 500 ff., January 2, 1761; for others, Garrett, "Descendants," p. 293, n129.
98 ARC, NOT, Rodriguez Ledezma, Leg. 245, 507 ff., June 27, 1790.

long ago bought from or conceded by the crown. In many of these pueblos, interrelated lineages of Inca nobles vied for the cacicazgos, generally serving as a check to the power and wealth of any one in particular. In contrast, the pueblos formed in the pastoral highlands, and especially in the Titicaca basin, were often larger and under more concentrated rule, either as single entities or divided into moieties. Preconquest political history played a role. While the Cusco region had had its complex political geography of panacas, Incas by blood and Incas by privilege, in Collasuyo and Condesuyo the Incas had recognized local and provincial ruling dynasties, and in many colonial pueblos their descendants were still ruling in the mid-1700s.

Other factors distinguished the area around Cusco from the rest of the bishopric. The market economy of Spanish Peru entered far more deeply into daily life here. The city created a market for the produce of peasant plots, while the hundreds of Spanish-owned properties located in the Inca pueblos of the Anta plain and Vilcanota valley created a market for tributary labor, which could be negotiated individually. The economic role of caciques was far from negligible: they collected and sold communal harvests and were responsible for tribute and reparto payments. But caciques around Cusco had neither the near-monopoly on the sale of Indian produce of those in more remote areas nor the economic importance in the regional economy. Economically Tamboguacso, Carillo Pomayalli, and their peers ranked below many of creole Cusco's *hacendados*, professionals, and merchants, let alone its titled aristocrats.[99] At the same time, the city presented economic opportunities for Indian nobles as skilled artisans and merchants. Few had the economic success of Loyola Cusitito Atauyupanqui, but the city was home to scores of Indian noble merchants and artisans with property of 1,000 or so pesos.

In contrast, the cacical dynasties in the highlands south of Cusco often held near-monopolies on the interaction between local and regional economies and dominated the provincial economies: few if any Spaniards in Lampa and Azángaro rivaled the wealth, let alone the power, of Quispe Cavana, Succacahua, and Choquehuanca. The heavy communal burdens placed on these societies by the Potosí mita also reinforced the centrality of the communal economy, which the absence of nearby markets did little to erode. Nor did the numerous Spanish properties in the region: those near Indian pueblos were usually sheep ranches, which provided little market for labor. The coca plantations and gold mines of the eastern yungas had a voracious appetite for workers, but were far from the highland pueblos,

---

99 Above, n71; also Don Agustin Chacon y Becerra, a senior notary for the government and descendant of conquistadores. His *escribanías* alone were valued at 32,000 pesos; his real property at over 30,000 pesos but mortgaged for 21,000 pesos. ARC, NOT, Chacon y Becerra, Leg. 65, 442 ff., December 22, 1803.

and often supplied by corvées. The result, generally though by no means universally, was that in the Indian communities of the Titicaca basin, material stratification was far more pronounced than within those around Cusco, and it is not surprising that here the rebellions of 1780–3 most resembled class wars.

These variations in cacical wealth produced distinct strata within the bishopric's cacical class. In smaller communities the material difference between the cacique and other village prominents could be quite small: the modest wealth of a Quispe Uscamayta could not translate standing within the community to standing in viceregal, or even provincial, society. That of a Choquehuanca certainly did; so, to a lesser extent, did that of the Tamboguacso. Families such as these, from the upper ranks of Cusco's Inca nobility and the great cacical dynasties to the south, made up a distinct upper class within the Indian republic. It was not evenly distributed, nor did it have members in every community. Composed of a few score families, this provincial elite was separated from the Indian republic that it ruled by the scale of its wealth, by the different opportunities that this wealth brought, and by the different strategies these opportunities required.

What most distinguished this regional Indian elite from local pueblo elites were its different horizons, geographic and ethnic, that allowed it to move beyond the confines of the pueblo. To be sure, this cacical aristocracy did not give up economic domination of their communities. Invariably the most significant assets cacical families possessed were lands and livestock in their pueblos or in adjoining parishes. Here the scale of property distinguished them from humbler caciques: Quispe Uscamayta had four topos in Pucyura, while Choquecahua owned twenty-eight topos in Andaguaylillas. Similarly, many of Bernardo Succacahua's 10,000 sheep were pastured on an estancia that he bought in composition from the crown (formalizing ownership of these "lands that he has possessed since his ancestors under sufficient superior protection").[100] At the western edge of the bishopric in Toro and Cotaguasi, the cacica Doña Juana Vilcapi left twenty-eight topos of land in the two communities on her death in 1788.[101] These included the Hacienda Pampacocha, which Juana had inherited from her parents. In 1689 the priest had reported that Pampacocha was owned by "an *indio principal* named Don Joseph Vilcapi" – a reminder of the importance of private property to the transmission of authority across generations.[102]

But unlike their humbler peers, these caciques also owned property outside their communities. Among the Inca nobility, who intermarried between communities, the possession of a topo or two of land in another

---

100 RREE, PRA, Exp. 9.
101 ARC, NOT, Villagarcia, Leg. 280, 267 ff., January 24, 1789.
102 *Cuzco 1689*, p. 316.

pueblo was common, and Choquecahua's house and lands in Belén fit that
pattern, albeit on a scale worthy of an alférez real. And, highlighting the
uniqueness of the Inca elite, urban nobles invested in rural real estate by
buying small haciendas around the city.[103] Caciques in the southern highlands were both richer and in less ecologically and economically diverse
regions. They used their wealth to acquire land in temperate areas, in a way
using cacical property to reproduce the preconquest system of vertical integration. Succacahua owned an agricultural hacienda, valued at 1,200 pesos,
in the lower valleys near Arequipa.[104] In 1756 Don Agustin Cava Apasa,
the cacique of Juliaca, bought the Hacienda Paca in Urubamba.[105] Paca
gave Cava Apasa a presence in Cusco, access to cash through the reliable
corn-market of the city, and a source of corn for his highland pueblo. Of
course, there was an enormous difference between these eighteenth-century
economic colonies and preconquest ecological colonies: the Hacienda Paca
was the property of Cava Apasa, not of Juliaca. Cacical wealth thus allowed
communities like Juliaca to maintain long-distance networks of exchange
and supply, but defined them as the domain of the cacique, not the community.

Spanish colonialism had also created new imperatives of integration:
now the pueblos of the Titicaca basin needed to be linked not only to
the temperate and semitropical lands of the Andean valleys, but also to the
markets, courts, colleges, and notaries of the colonial cities. Cacical families
bought townhouses in Cusco, with those from the southern reaches of the
bishopric preferring Limacpampa, the large plaza at the eastern edge of
the city from which the royal road headed to the Collao.[106] Those from
Chucuito, Omasuyos, Pacajes, and southward instead gravitated to La Paz,
seat of their bishopric and within the jurisdiction of their *audiencia*.[107]
These properties served as small urban colonies of the highland pueblos.
Again, they were the personal property of the caciques, underscoring the
importance of cacical wealth to the community and the economic and legal
logic that placed that wealth in the hands of the ruling family.

This concentration of wealth within cacical families tended to draw the
richest away from their communities. While certain elements of cacical
wealth – for example, cacical lands – were inseparable from the office,
private lands, flocks, houses, and movables were the personal estate of the
cacique. By Spanish law, testators had the right to dispose of one-fifth of

103 ARC, NOT, Villagarcia, Leg. 281, 130–3, July 12, 1788, for a hacienda purchase by Bernarda
      Ramos Tito Atauchi and Pablo Soria Condorpusa.
104 ARC, NOT, Joseph Bernardo Gamarra, Leg. 124, 233–7 [1799].
105 ARC, NOT, Juan Bautista Gamarra, Leg. 133, [ ], September 23, 1756; the value was 5,324 pesos.
106 For example, the Sinanyuca of Coporaque, and next door the Mango Turpa of Azángaro. ARC,
      NOT, Zamora, Leg. 293, 155 ff., September 22, 1786; also ARC, COR, Civ., Leg. 56, Exp. 1300.
107 For houses in La Paz, ANB, EC, 1807–11 (the 1779 Siñani will); also ANB, EC, 1773–83, 50.

their estate as they wished and could "improve" one child's share with one-third of the remainder. Otherwise, the estate was shared equally among all legitimate children, with the surviving spouse retaining half of the property acquired during marriage.[108] Such partible inheritance was widely adopted by Indian elites, with two principal effects: it prevented the passage of cacical fortunes intact across generations, and it created Indian noble heirs and heiresses with some wealth but no prospects of succeeding to their parents' office. Fausto Xauregui and Raphaela Tito Atauchi of Pucarani left an estate of 12,000 pesos in 1756; their children inherited just 3,000 pesos each. The latter was a respectable sum, but also a reminder that colonial fortunes often lasted no more than a generation.[109]

This highlights both the cacicazgo's potential for the generation of private wealth and its central role in the fortunes of Indian noble families. While most substantial cacical fortunes were in the hands of hereditary caciques, they were amassed during the rule of a single cacique: inherited property was not the dominant factor. Vicente Choquecahua had purchased, not inherited, his land in Andaguaylillas.[110] As we have seen, Catalina Pachacutic y Salas also made her own fortune (which fragmented at her death: she left no children and her estate was divided among nine relatives).[111] These were the norm: caciques inherited offices more than fortunes. At the same time, the inheritances of the cacical children were often large enough to place them above the level of the communal economy. This was less true around Cusco, where the children of prominent Inca caciques might inherit just a few hundred pesos. However, with 3,000 pesos each, the Xauregui Tito Atauchi children would have found no suitable partners among the indigenous population of Pucarani. Instead, they turned outside the community; the one child whose spouse is named in the probate dispute had married Don Ildefonso Fernandez Chuy, hereditary cacique of Laxa.

Other mechanisms reinforced this division of cacical wealth. Although the formal dowry never became as ubiquitous in Indian society as did private property (indeed, many Indian wills explicitly mention that the bride brought no dowry), it played a part in the financial strategies of great cacical families. Lesser pueblo elites also embraced this transfer of property between households and lineages, but the difference in quantity created a difference in quality. When, in 1722, Doña Constansa Puraca brought six cows as her dowry to Toribio Atamas Mamani, she affirmed their

108 Susan Kellogg, "From Parallel and Equivalent to Separate but Unequal: Tenochca Mexica Women, 1500–1700," in *Indian Women of Early Mexico*, ed. Susan Schroeder et al. (Norman: University of Oklahoma, 1997), pp. 133–9.

109 ANB, EC, 1773–83, 68–75. Also ARC, JC, Leg. 18 (1830) for Cama Condorsayna's estate: 10,000 pesos were divided among six children; a son inherited the cacicazgo.

110 ARC, NOT, Juan Bautista Gamarra, Leg. 146, 432 ff., October 1, 1778.

111 ARC, NOT, Rodríguez Ledezma, Leg. 248, 153 ff., July 4, 1796.

standing in Azángaro Urinsaya.[112] When, a few decades later, Doña Maria Teresa Choquehuanca – the daughter of Diego Choquehuanca – brought 3,000 pesos in dowry to Don Domingo Yrastorre, she asserted the family's standing in provincial society, strengthened its ties to the creole community, and served as a conduit drawing wealth from the Indian community into the creole economy.[113]

Women from other important cacical families had similar dowries. In 1773 Doña Maria de la Nieves Quispe Cavana, illegitimate daughter of the priest Don Marcos Quispe Cavana and the niece of Ambrocio Quispe Cavana (cacique of Cavanilla), brought a dowry of about 3,000 pesos to her marriage to Don Pasqual Diaz Calisaya, from the cacical family of Tiquillaca.[114] The two Succacahua brothers of Umachire received similar dowries from their in-laws, caciques of Usicayos and Quiquijana.[115] Throughout the highlands, interrelated cacical families forged bonds not only through the exchange of men and women, but also through the flows of wealth accompanying them. In Cusco, well-to-do urban noble families also endowed their daughters.[116] Those of Asencio Ramos Tito Atauchi and Maria Vazquez Obando received houses, jewelry, and money worth more than 1,000 pesos each.[117]

These dowries had legal advantages. They remained the property of the wife and could not be seized against the debts of the husband. Given the threat of tribute and reparto debts, dowries helped preserve a household's fortune. In 1754, when after the death of Sebastian Tupa Cusigualpa of Yucay, "the corregidor seized all [of his possessions] for tribute and reparto [debts]," Paula Auccatinco successfully demanded the return of her late daughter's dowry to her grandchildren.[118] But that the cacical household had property that could not be seized for communal debts (for which the cacique was personally responsible) shows how the familial economies of the upper ranks of the Indian nobility had become detached from communal economies.

Indeed, the relationship of the great cacical families to their pueblos' economies was somewhat paradoxical. A cacicazgo was essential to the

---

112 ANB, EC, 1759–13, 1v.

113 Although in 1802 Maria Teresa insisted that the dowry had never been paid. ADP, INT, Exp. 51; Yrastorre had died in 1761.

114 ARC, INT, Prov., Ord., Leg. 97 (1797–9), 17–20.

115 Bernardo's wife (a Garcia Cota Callapa) brought a ranch (ARC, NOT, Joseph Bernardo Gamarra, Leg. 124, 233ff. [1799]); Francisco's, Doña Polonia Solis Quivimasa Ynga, brought 2,000 pesos (ARC, NOT, Villavisencio, Leg. 288, 352 ff., February 27, 1778).

116 Paula Auccatinco and Pascual Quispeguaman's daughters also received dowries; ARC, NOT, Juan Bautista Gamarra, Leg. 133, [ ], August 21, 1747.

117 ARC, NOT, Juan Bautista Gamarra, Leg. 133, [ ], January 9, 1749.

118 ARC, COR, Civ., Leg. 55, Exp. 1240 (1773). Also the dispute over the Quispe Cavana dowry: ARC, INT, Prov., Ord., Leg. 97 (1797–9).

formation of family wealth. Other activities, like long-distance trade, could bolster it, but rural Indian nobles with fortunes of more than a thousand pesos were almost invariably no more than one generation removed from a cacicazgo. However, the formation of a cacical fortune often forced the following generation to marry out of the pueblo, transferring some of the pueblo's wealth to another family and another community. Of course, the larger economy of the cacical elite meant that money flowed into communities as well, especially among the Incas. Rosa Auccatinco's dowry transferred wealth from the Spanish-dominated urban economy to the Indian economy of Yucay; such flows of wealth also reinforced the dominance of the interpueblo Inca nobility.[119] Whether in Yucay or Azángaro, the cacicazgo remained essential to the ruling class of the Indian republic: it was the principal source of its wealth and power. But the creation of private cacical fortunes, and their distribution to children, created a cacical elite whose economic, as well as dynastic, aspirations drew them away from the communities that they ruled and forged them into a thinly distributed, provincial ruling class.

The outflow of wealth from Indian communities had its parallel in the outflow of wealth from the Indian republic. Spanish men marrying Indian heiresses were common in colonial society, and Indian noblemen also married Spanish women; here, the women tended to bring less wealth to the marriage, and the families were more likely to remain identified as Indian nobles. In the eighteenth century marriage to a cacique's daughter was one of the surest mechanisms by which a Spaniard could acquire wealth and standing in an Indian pueblo. Starting in the 1760s and 1770s, one effect was the occupation of cacicazgos by Spaniards married to cacical heiresses.[120] More broadly, such marriages extended the Spanish republic's influence in Indian pueblos. Wealth again drew cacical families away from their communities, but now away from their ethnic, rather than geographic, communities. Such was the case with Maria Teresa Choquehuanca's marriage to Yrastorre. In the absence of any detailed or systematic information, it is impossible to assess how common marriages between rural Spanish and Indian elites were becoming in the middle of the eighteenth century, although surely the growth of the rural Spanish population brought an increase. Certainly following the Tupac Amaru rebellion, alliances between Spaniards and cacical heiresses became the norm. However, the roots of this change, in which the long-standing separation between the two republics, always violated but nonetheless real, collapsed and was replaced by a more vertical hierarchy of ethnic classes, were evident in the royal policy of the mid-eighteenth century.

119 ARC, NOT, Juan Bautista Gamarra, Leg. 133, [ ], August 21, 1747.
120 See Chapter 3, pp. 100–101.

Under the Bourbons, royal offices that had been the stronghold of Spanish Peru began to admit Indian nobles.[121] A 1735 royal decree ordered that the *protectores* and *procuradores de naturales* – the lawyers and scribes whose salaries were paid by the crown, and whose job was to represent Indian interests – be Indians, since ". . . they are more apt for this office."[122] This decree notwithstanding, in Cusco the first Indian procurador (Don Jose Agustin Guamantupa) was not appointed until the early 1800s; and not until after the Tupac Amaru rebellion did a few Indian nobles appear as officials of the tobacco monopoly, the mails, and other branches of government in the southern highlands.[123] But in one bastion of Spanish authority the Bourbon reforms made themselves felt well before the rebellion. With major repercussions for the economies of cacical families, the church opened its offices to the Indian nobility.

Charles II had ordered that "Indians be able to ascend to Ecclesiastic posts" in 1697. The royal decree explicitly observed that ". . . there is a distinction among the Indians and Mestizos, either as descendants of the Indian principales, who are called caciques, or as those who proceed from Indians less principal, who are tributaries and who in their Gentility knew vassalage; it is considered that to the first, and their descendants, are owed all the privileges and honors . . . that it is customary to confer on the nobles *hijosdalgo* of Castile, and they can participate in whatever communities [that] by statute require Nobility, since it is certain that they were Nobles in their Gentility. . . ."[124] Once again, Indians of noble blood were to be separated from the Indian commons; now they were to be considered the equals of Spaniards. This decree remained a dead letter in Peru until the 1730s, but from then the church accepted Indian nobles into orders and began to loom large in the family strategies of the upper ranks of the Indian nobility.[125]

Indian noblewomen and -men had very different positions in the second estate. Since the sixteenth century the former had entered Cusco's convents in tiny numbers, where they were limited to the lower ranking white veil.[126] The white-veil dowry was more than 1,600 pesos, a huge

---

121 O'Phelan Godoy, "Repensando el movimiento nacional inca," and *La Gran Rebelión*, pp. 47–68.
122 AGN, DI, Leg. 18, Exp. 311 (1762).
123 Don Luis Ramos Tito Atauchi succeeded him; and Don Mariano Guamantica held the position in the early 1820s. ARC, RA, Ped., Leg. 181 (1788–1824) generally.
124 Antonio Muro Orejón, "La igualdad entre indios y españoles: la real cédula de 1697," in *Estudios sobre la política indigenista española en América*, 3ras Jornadas Americanistas de la Universidad de Valladolid (Valladolid: Universidad de Valladolid, 1975), I, 365–86; for the decree itself, pp. 379–81.
125 O'Phelan Godoy, *La Gran Rebelión*, pp. 47–62.
126 Burns, *Colonial Habits*, pp. 15–40, 123–5.

sum for the Indian nobility, and only a handful of Indian women took it.[127] Among those who did were Josepha Tamboguacso (daughter of Joseph Tamboguacso and Agustina Chacona of Taray) in Cusco's Santa Catalina, and Diego Choquehuanca's daughter Dionisia, in Arequipa's Santa Catalina.[128] When her parents died in 1756, Doña Josepha Xauregui Tito Atauchi of Pucarani was being educated at the "monasterio de las consebidas" in La Paz, where her parents owned a cell worth 400 pesos.[129] But female religious never figured as prominently in the strategies of the Indian nobility as in those of the creole elite. For the latter, daughters in convents limited the number of heirs, preserving the estate for other children; but the Indian nobility had less property, and the dowry could consume far more than a child's share.[130]

In contrast, the opening of the church to Indian noblemen greatly affected the Indian elite. Beneficed clergy enjoyed very high salaries – up to one thousand pesos a year. The church thus exercised an enormous draw on the creole elite, and Indian nobles also felt its attraction. In Cusco the bishopric's secular hierarchy was initially unwilling to award the prizes of colonial society to Indians. In 1761 Diego Choquehuanca appealed to Spain for intervention, as the bishop of Cusco would not appoint his son to a benefice, even though he was already ordained as a priest. The Royal Council's decision from Madrid, in December 1762, clearly set forth the new ideal of an Indian clergy: "[t]he reverend bishop fails in the fulfillment of his duty, and deprecates [the Choquehuanca] for being Indian, when he cannot ignore that their quality, far from excluding them from the enjoyment of benefices, gives them a known preference,... being in conformity to all equity and justice that as naturals and natives of that country they be preferred to Spaniards..., since the income is the product of their native soil, and also because the native language is a very effective medium for aiding the souls of the parishes."[131] The decision continued that the problem

---

127 AAC, XXIII-3-58 for Francisca de Jesus Quispeguaman (of Anta), in Santa Clara. A number of Indian noblewoman entered the Nazarrenas beguinage; Garrett, "Descendants," p. 311, n169.

128 ARC, COR, Civ., Leg. 61, Exp. 1400; ADP, INT, Exp. 51. Choquehuanca's niece was in the same convent; ARC, INT, Ord., Leg. 78 (1818).

129 ANB, EC, 1773–83, 16v and 73r. Doña Francisca Cama Condorsayna inherited a cell in Cusco's Santa Catalina convent. ARC, CSJ, Leg. 18 (1830).

130 Nuns also gave creole families access to the largest concentrations of capital in colonial Peru: those who rose high in their convents could direct loans to their relatives. The white veil prevented Indian noblewomen from reaching such positions. Burns, *Colonial Habits*, pp. 146–52. Bernardo Succacahua of Umachire did have such a relationship with the beguinage of Nazarrenas (where his wife was educated and his daughter secluded). ARC, INT, Ord., Leg. 44 (1798–9).

131 AGI, Charcas, Leg. 463, Exp. 19.

was not the aptitude of Indian nobles for the church, but simply that few "dedicate themselves to the study of letters." The Royal Council then ordered the bishop of Cusco to provide a benefice for Choquehuanca's son.

This decision was restricted to Choquehuanca, but the mid-1700s saw a modest opening of benefices to the Indian nobility. No systematic records were kept, and Indian nobles made up a tiny fraction of the bishopric's nearly 800 men in religious orders – certainly less than 5 percent.[132] But many of the great Inca and cacical families had sons in the church by 1800. The case of the Ramos Tito Atauchi is the best documented. In the 1750s Don Fernando Ramos Tito Atauchi (son of Asencio and Maria Vasquez Obando) entered orders; from 1778 until his death in 1806 he was priest of Umachire.[133] Two of his nephews followed him into the church: Jose Rafael Sahuaraura and Gregorio Soria Condorpusa.[134] Jose Rafael's half brother, Don Leandro Sahuaraura, had also taken orders, as did his nephew Justo Sahuaraura, who spent the last twenty years of his life as the treasurer of the Cusco Cathedral.[135] The Ramos Tito Atauchi were exceptional, but by 1780 many leading Indian families had a son in the clergy: among them were the Poma Ynga of Anta, the Orcoguaranca of Guayllabamba, the Solis Quivimasa of Quiquijana, the Quispe Cavana of Cavanilla, the Choquehuanca of Azángaro, and the Chuquicallata of San Taraco.[136]

The eighteenth-century entry into the church had serious consequences for Indian noble families' finances. Benefices brought large salaries, but required substantial investment: ordination generally required an endowed chaplaincy with a capital of 4,000 pesos, a huge sum for even the richest Indian families.[137] Nonetheless, it was an expense they undertook.[138] *Capellanías* were not alienated from the family's control. The right of appointment passed through the founding family, and when no one in the family could use it to enter the church, it could be passed to someone eager for ordination, in exchange for the cession of the income.[139] And, once they

132 In 1792, the bishopric had 789 men in the clergy; Unanue, *Guía*, p. 178.

133 See the dispute over his *capellanía*, in ARC, CSJ, Leg. 103 (1852).

134 For Jose Rafael, see his *Estado del Perú*, ed. Francisco A. Loayza (Lima: Librería D. Miranda, 1944). For Gregorio, ARC, NOT, Arias Lira, Leg. 39, [ ], August 22, 1778.

135 ARC, NOT, Gonzales Peñalosa, Leg. 190, [ ], October 3, 1752; for Justo, *Recuerdos*, pp. 45-7.

136 Respectively, Jorge Armando Guevara Gil, *Propiedad agraria y derecho colonial: los documentos de la Hacienda Santotis, Cuzco (1543–1822)* (Lima: Pontificia Universidad Católica del Perú, 1993), p. 528; ARC, CAB, Civ., Leg. 39, Exp. 952; AGI, Cuzco, Exp. 80; Altuve Carrillo, *Choquehuanca*, pp. 77–110; RREE, PRA, Exp. 170 (1792); earlier, for Quispe Cavana.

137 ARC, NOT, Arias Lira, Leg. 39, [ ], August 22, 1778, for Gregorio Soria Condorpusa's capellanía: his parents insisted he support his sister Melchora from the chaplaincy's income.

138 In the Ramos Tito Atauchi capellanía dispute; ARC, CSJ, Leg. 103 (1852). For other Indian capellanías, ARC: NOT, Quintanilla, Leg. 237, 144 ff., February 10, 1756; Pedro Joaquin Gamarra, Leg. 85, 34, January 30, 1818; CAB, Civ., Leg. 39, Exp. 952; INT, Prov., Ord., Leg. 97 (1797–9) (for that founded by Ysidora Catacora); *CDBR*, III, p. 51.

139 ARC, NOT, Pedro Joaquin Gamarra, Leg. 79, 475, July 10, 1809.

obtained a salaried benefice, senior members of the family could pass their capellanías to those entering orders. Having been named priest of Yanaoca, in 1806 Gregorio Soria Condorpusa relinquished his capellanía in favor of his nephew, Manuel Soria Condorpusa, so that he could be ordained.[140]

By mortgaging family property, the upper Indian nobility sponsored their sons for careers in the ecclesiastical bureaucracy that was a foundation of creole wealth and authority. The wealth produced by large cacicazgos – and by the urban economy of Cusco – led the richest Indian nobles to adopt economic strategies similar to those of well-to-do creole families. By the mid-1700s the upper ranks of Cusco's Indian nobility resembled the highland creole elite more closely than at any prior point. To be sure, they identified themselves as Indian nobles, the proud, self-conscious descendants of Aymara lords and Inca emperors. But Indian nobles also owned haciendas, estancias, and townhouses; they engaged in the long-distance trade of the highland markets; and they endowed their daughters and made priests of their sons.

Still, the economic convergence of creole and Indian noble was extremely uneven. By the mid-1700s, the main economic difference between Cusco's urban, Inca nobility of Cusco and its creole "gente decente" was the obligation of the former to take on the cacicazgos in the city's Indian parishes. In contrast, despite their wealth, the rural Indian nobility – from ayllu elites to great cacical houses – remained structurally distinct from their creole peers. Control of cacical office was central to the continued power and wealth of any Indian family. The division of cacical fortunes by inheritance required that they be reproduced through the cacicazgo itself. In 1780 rural creoles (as well as the rentiers of Cusco) lived by manufactures; by trade; by the bureaucratic offices of the church, the *corregimiento*, and the courts; and from the income of land alienated from Indian communities. The cacical elite also lived from manufactures and trade. However, their bureaucratic offices were those of the Indian pueblo, and their wealth depended, ultimately, on their control of Indian land and labor.

Standing on the frontier between peasant production and larger systems of exchange (both tribute and market) that bound together the Peruvian highlands, the cacique was essential both to the local economies of Indian communities and to the viceregal economy. The two reinforced each other, so that the collection and sale of goods for tribute expanded caciques' role in the market economy, generating wealth that strengthened their hold on the local economy. The crown and its officials depended on the cacique to ensure the flow of pesos through tribute and the reparto; but so too did the community. Caciques owned factors of production and transport beyond the

---

140 ARC, NOT, Pedro Joaquin Gamarra, Leg. 78, 52, March 15, 1806.

reach of the tributary household and negotiated the community's imports and exports. The concession of cacical usufruct of substantial portions of communal land, and the control of many communal resources, reinforced this dominant role in the communal economy.

The impact of cacical office on personal fortunes varied considerably. Caciques could see the wealth accumulated over decades lost in one or two years of poor harvests, or when a corregidor was unwilling to defer payments. Moreover, the vast majority of officials who collected tribute and negotiated economic relations between the ayllu and colonial society did not control economies large enough to propel them into the provincial elite. For the dozens of families who controlled the cacicazgos of larger communities, however, the profits of cacical office could be enormous. Indian nobles who served as caciques of pueblos and moieties around Titicaca accumulated estates far in excess of 10,000 pesos, making them among the richest in Indian Peru. In contrast, the cacical elite of the Cusco area, ruling over smaller communities and with less control of market and communal exchange, were generally poorer than those to the south, although some amassed fortunes of a few thousand pesos, separating them from more local, if equally Inca, ayllu caciques worth a few hundred pesos.

Nonetheless, cacical office was the essential foundation of great wealth in the Indian republic. Laws of partible inheritance meant that cacical fortunes were rarely transmitted intact across generations, but when cacical families managed to establish hereditary control over their office, the cacical fortune could be repeatedly replenished. Dowries and inheritances reinforced the creation of broader, provincial cacical elites, particularly in the Titicaca basin and among the Incas of the Cusco area. At the same time, the division of wealth among children also produced structural similarities between Indian noble families and their creole counterparts. Most importantly, it furthered the distinction between the communal economy and the cacical household, as the latter sought to position its members well in colonial society – through entry into the church, marriage to cacical families in other communities, and marriage to Spaniards.

The period under study in this chapter – the middle of the eighteenth century – ended with the Great Rebellion, a social explosion unequaled in Spanish America from the conquest to independence. Recent scholarship has rightly focused not only on the relations between Spanish and Indian, but also on the dynamics within the Indian republic, to assess the causes of the violence of the early 1780s. Those focusing on Upper Peru have suggested a breakdown in cacical authority, both as established cacical families collapsed in the face of economic pressures and the antagonism of Spanish governors and as the material interests of cacique and community came increasingly into conflict.[141] The information from the bishopric of Cusco presented here and in the previous chapter suggests the need for caution in positing a widespread crisis in the "moral economy" of the Indian republic, or a collapse of the "legitimate" indigenous elite. While some cacical families died out or faced financial ruin in the mid-1700s, this was an integral pattern of indigenous society for the length of the colonial period, and as Chapter 3 showed, by no means was there a widespread collapse of the hereditary indigenous elite in the decades before 1780. Moreover, while Indian nobles were more "hispanicized" at this point than earlier in the colonial era, and more likely to intermarry with Spaniards and adopt Spanish financial strategies, so too was the entirety of the Indian republic more hispanicized, as the Spanish population, and the market economy, expanded, and elite intermarriage and private property were well-established by the seventeenth century. Certainly class differentiation between caciques and the commons was pronounced, especially in the Titicaca basin, but this was hardly novel; if anything, the richest Indian nobles were poorer in the eighteenth century than they had been before.[142] That is not to deny widespread social tension in the Indian republic in the eighteenth century; rather, it calls into question the assumption that this was novel or particularly threatening to the larger social order established in the late 1500s. The next chapter turns to the politics of the cacicazgo, examining the role of the cacique, and opposition to cacical authority, in local politics and also the mechanisms by which caciques sought to legitimate their power and wealth. In so doing, it shares with the discussion of ancestry and wealth the interpretation that, while the mid-eighteenth-century changes in highland society produced many tensions in the bishopric of Cusco, the breakdown of the colonial hierarchies internal to the Indian republic – above all of noble privilege and cacical wealth and authority – were results, not primary causes, of the rebellions discussed in Chapter 6.

---

141 Especially Serulnikov, *Subverting Colonial Authority*; Thomson, *We Alone Will Rule*; for southern Cusco, Stavig, *The World of Túpac Amaru* and O'Phelan Godoy, *Kurakas sin sucesiones*, make related arguments.

142 For example, compare the 10,000–20,000 fortune of Diego Choquehuanca, to that of Gabriel Fernandez Guarachi, cacique of Machaca in the late 1600s, worth perhaps four times as much. Rivera, "El Mallku."

5

The Politics of the Cacicazgo

The most lucrative and powerful position in the Indian republic, the *caci-cazgo* was the object of considerable competition and conflict. As all cacicaz-gos ultimately fell in the crown's gift, corregidor and *audiencia* courts pre-sented an obvious venue for battles between a community's rival claimants or factions. Such complaints and lawsuits offer an important window into pueblo politics, and have not gone unnoticed by historians. Focusing on the cacicazgo as the nexus between Spanish and Indian society, scholars have viewed accusations by "indios del común" of abuses by their cacique, or the appointment of an illegitimate cacique by the corregidor, as testimony not only against individuals, but also against the corrosive effects of Span-ish colonialism.[1] Complaints of land usurpation and excessive demands for labor by caciques highlight how the emergence of an Andean form of mar-ket capitalism, and the co-option of indigenous elites in the exploitation of the Indian peasantry, created class conflict within the pueblo. Spanish interference in cacical appointments underscores the erosion of local auton-omy within Indian society, and hence Spanish disregard for material and power relations understood as legitimate within Indian communities. Join-ing dependency theory and studies of moral economy, these works have exposed how Andean commoners challenged local aspects of Spanish impe-rialism and actively sought redress.[2]

While legal and physical conflict – invariably charged with the rhetoric of illegitimacy and abuse – were a constant of colonial Andean society, in

---

1 Stern, *Peru's Indian Peoples*; Powers, *Andean Journeys*; Stavig, *The World of Túpac Amaru*; Glave, *Vida, símbolos*; Silverblatt, *Moon*; Spalding, *Huarochirí*; Sánchez-Albornoz, *Indios*; Burga, *Nacimiento*; Ras-nake, *Domination*. For anticacical lawsuits as opposition to the post-Tupac Amaru reorganizations of pueblo government, O'Phelan Godoy, *Kurakas*; Sala i Vila, *Y se armó*; and Charles F. Walker, *Smol-dering Ashes: Cuzco and the Creation of Republican Peru, 1780–1840* (Durham: Duke University Press, 1999).

2 E. P. Thompson, "The Moral Economy of the English Crowd in the Eighteenth Century," *Past and Present* 50 (February 1971): 76–136. For the "moral economy" in the eighteenth-century Andes, Ward Stavig, "Ethnic Conflict, Moral Economy, and Population"; Serulnikov, "Customs and Rules."

the past two decades scholars have focused on the period from 1740 to 1780, analyzing local unrest in the Indian republic to elucidate loci of conflict, and indigenous political ideals and strategies, in the decades preceding the Great Rebellion. Golte and O'Phelan have viewed the increasing incidence of riot and rebellion in these decades as a response to the Bourbon Reforms – Golte, to the *reparto*, while O'Phelan has shown a stronger correlation in the 1770s between a dramatic rise in unrest and the division of the viceroyalty, with the related implementation of new internal duties and the increase in the *alcabala*.[3] Both have stressed the reactive character of these rebellions, as collective, popular violence is seen as a response to new demands by the state. More recently, working on Upper Peru, Thomson, Serulnikov, and Penry have exposed how the mass rebellions of 1780–2 were produced by the interaction of profound transformations in relations of power and local governance within indigenous societies, with the sweeping reforms attempted by the crown.[4] In particular, they have emphasized a "crisis of the cacicazgo" and of the indigenous nobility in the mid-1700s. This break-down of established social hierarchies produced a democratic revolution within Aymara communities, one which yielded radicalized politics within the Indian republic. In that, the increased unrest and challenge to cacical authority in the decades preceding the rebellions are not simply a reaction to demands by the state. At the same time, they serve as causal factors of the rebellions, which become the *telos* of mid-century indigenous politics.

However, it is not clear that, in the bishopric of Cusco, legal and physical opposition to cacical rule in the decades preceding 1780 represent a crisis of indigenous elites, nor a profound shift of village politics. As Chapter 3 showed, control of cacical office remained vested within a largely hereditary class. Certainly families died out, usurpers gained office, and so on, but this had happened throughout the length of the colonial era, and one generation's usurpers were the next generation's hereditary lords. The case of the Incas around Cusco is certainly unique, but elsewhere in the bishopric the widespread collapse of hereditary elites, and/or the passage of office to Spaniards, appears to have been a postrebellion phenomenon.[5] That indigenous elites retained office does not, of course, require that they retained legitimacy, and Stavig has suggested increasing conflict within indigenous communities of the Vilcanota highlands as caciques acquired greater wealth

---

3 Golte, *Reparto y Rebeliones*; O'Phelan Godoy, *Un siglo*.
4 Thomson, *We Alone*; Serulnikov, *Subverting Colonial Authority*; Penry, "Transformations."
5 Although O'Phelan Godoy interprets the situation differently, suggesting a rise in "mestizo" caciques in mid-century with the reparto. Stavig, however, argues that the widespread alienation of cacical office from the Indian republic occurred after the rebellion in Quispicanchis and Canas y Canchis. O'Phelan Godoy, *Kurakas*, pp. 17–28; Stavig, *The World of Túpac Amaru*, p. 126.

and sought to usurp, or render as their personal property, communal hold-ings.[6] However, this chapter argues that, while social conflict was endemic in the Indian republic of Cusco in the mid-1700s, that conflict did not indi-cate the degree of internal crisis posited by Thomson and Serulnikov in Upper Peru. Rather, such conflict exposes the sites of tension within the pueblo, the complexity of local politics, and the strategies employed by indigenous elites to reproduce their authority.

The difference in local, indigenous politics between Cusco and Upper Peru reflects broader social, economic, and historical differences. The large Inca nobility did not, as a group, acquire the wealth of the great cacical houses of the south, and agricultural communities – pueblos or *ayllus* – around Cusco were generally much smaller than the great Aymara commu-nities, and thus less internally stratified. Also, the "Incaness" of the indige-nous elite in Cusco appears to have legitimated their political authority within their communities. Strikingly, the northern Titicaca basin resem-bled Upper Peru ethnically and economically far more than it did Cusco; yet, unlike in La Paz and especially Potosí, the cacical elites here also appear to have consolidated their local control under the Bourbon Reforms, rather than have lost it. Indeed, the very different trajectories of the rebellion in the Vilcanota valley and the Titicaca basin, discussed in the next chapter, suggest that social and economic tensions were far stronger in the south than around Cusco. Nonetheless, the histories of these communities in the decades before the rebellion differ from those in Upper Peru precisely in the survival of the indigenous elite, a reminder of the importance of region and locality in the multiple indigenous histories of the colonial Andes.

While the bishopric of Cusco's Indian nobility and cacical elite as a group faced less challenge from within their communities in the decades before the rebellions, cacical politics there were far from pacific: the works of Stavig and Glave have, in particular, exposed the intensity of local conflict in cacical battles in Canas y Canchis.[7] In this chapter, I similarly attempt to eludicate the *loci* of conflict in the mid-eighteenth-century pueblos of Cusco. Arguing that the indigenous elite managed to preserve its authority despite the challenges of the Bourbon Reforms, I then examine the mecha-nisms by which they legitimated that authority. Throughout, I focus on the interaction of the community and the state, and in particular the attempts by local actors to use the institutions of the state to further their own goals. Legislation and policy were decreed in Spain or Lima, but implementation and negotiations within their broad parameters were the domain of local politics. Communities and caciques turned to the royal courts to challenge the role of corregidores, priests, and private Spaniards in cacical affairs and

6 Stavig, *The World of Túpac Amaru*, pp. 111–28, 207–56.
7 Glave, *Vida, símbolos*; Stavig, *The World of Túpac Amaru* and "Eugenio Sinanyuca."

thereby to defend the boundary between Spanish and Indian in rural Peru; communities called on the courts to limit the cacique's authority. Phrased in universalized terms of cacical tyranny, such suits also expose both the particularity of local politics and the structural tensions within the late colonial pueblo. Caciques were not oblivious to these tensions: they sought to defuse opposition and reinforce the legitimacy of their rule in both Indian and Spanish eyes. How challenges to, and the reproduction of, the authority of the established indigenous elite themselves reproduced the broader political order of the late colonial pueblo in Cusco is the subject of this chapter.

The Cacicazgo and Local Conflict

Colonial Andean pueblos were not monolithic communities whose residents' interests coincided harmoniously. The incidence of rural riot and rebellion increased substantially in the middle of the eighteenth century, coinciding with the recovery of the Indian population, the expansion of the rural Spanish population, and fiscal reforms aimed at making the viceroyalty more profitable for the crown.[8] While complaints by priests and corregidores about the drunkenness and violence of Andean fiestas bear the prejudices of their authors, they show the central role of local celebrations in negotiating and resolving – often with bloodshed – pueblo conflicts and tensions.[9] These were not the only such arena: tributaries, *principales*, and caciques also sought to rearrange or affirm the balance of power within their communities by winning – or staving off – the intervention of royal justice. Much of this legal conflict centered on the cacicazgo, and the surviving lawsuits about claims to and abuse of cacical office expose the loci of intrapueblo conflict on the eve of the Great Rebellion.

Several patterns stand out. First, caciques and their supporters appealed to the courts to oppose intervention by Spaniards in cacical politics; such conflicts tested the boundaries between Spanish and Indian power. Second, communities launched lawsuits against their own caciques. At the base of such disputes were contradictions inherent in the organization of the colonial pueblo itself. The contradiction, between the aristocratic ideal of pueblo governance implicit in the cacicazgo and the more democratic ideal of the *cabildo* and *alcalde*, remained strong in the eighteenth century, and caciques' central but ill-defined role in the economy, and efforts

---

8 O'Phelan Godoy, *Un siglo*, pp. 53–206; Golte, *Reparto*; Steve J. Stern, "The Age of Andean Insurrection, 1742–1782: A Reappraisal," in *Resistance, Rebellion*, ed. Stern, pp. 34–93; Glave, *Vida, símbolos*, pp. 93–152; Stavig, *The World of Túpac Amaru*, pp. 212–24.

9 Taylor, *Drinking, Homicide*; Stavig, *The World of Túpac Amaru*, pp. 212–24; Penry, "Transformations," pp. 25–118, for anticacical and communal violence in Upper Peru.

to expand their own fortunes, provoked opposition. The aggregation of numerous communities – ayllus and annexes – within the jurisdiction of a single pueblo or parish provoked tensions between the different groups, and communities launched lawsuits against caciques as a way of asserting autonomy within the larger pueblo or parish. Finally, within communities different elite households vied for control of the cacicazgo. Battles between rival claimants or families make up the largest portion of these lawsuits, and challenges about the legitimacy of a cacique's claim to office, based on birth, feature in almost every case discussed hereafter.

Complaints about the interference of Spaniards in local politics have caught the attention of historians.[10] Corregidores notoriously interfered in cacical selection, deposing those who failed to meet payments, or challenged the governor's authority. Although the courts had recognized the hereditary claims of many cacical families, in practice the corregidor exercised enormous authority in the countryside, and used it to intervene in pueblo politics and to expand his own property.[11] Corregidores also had a recognized role in the election of interim caciques: in that of Tapara in Ñuñoa the corregidor's authority over the appointment of the new cacique was carefully performed.[12] While the community manipulated the selection to leave the corregidor with only one candidate, the role of the Spanish governor was explicitly acknowledged.

How often corregidores deposed caciques to install allies is unknowable. For richer caciques, the privilege that their disputes be heard by an audiencia was a valuable protection. One case from Chucuito shows that corregidores did remove well-entrenched caciques, but that ultimately the caciques could triumph. As Chucuito's corregidor from 1762 to 1764, Don Juan Joseph de Herrera aggressively meddled in local politics, prompting a riot in Puno. According to Don Fermin Garcia Llaglla – from one of Juli's cacical families – Herrera had read the assembled caciques of the province a letter "from the viceroy" that purported to give him enormous power, and then "deposed seven caciques, when in no case was there a shortcoming in the royal tribute, the royal *mita* of Potosí, or any vice whatsoever."[13] This testimony was given to Herrera's successor, who was investigating Herrera's short, and tumultuous, rule: by 1766 Herrera was in Spain defending himself against charges of defrauding the treasury and abusing his office. Herrera made a fortune as corregidor, and he provoked crises in the pueblos over which he ruled. But, strikingly, within five years the seven caciques were all

10 See Chapter 2, n26.
11 Karen Spalding, *De Indio a Campesino: Cambios en la estructura social del Perú colonial* (Lima: Instituto de Estudios Peruanos, 1974), pp. 31–60. Also the 1720 will of Don Pedro Carlos Ynga Llanac Ponca, of Anta, in the dispute over the Hacienda Llaulloque. ARC, INT, Ord., Leg. 35 (1795), 19–22.
12 See Appendix.
13 AGI, Charcas, Leg. 591.

back in office, while Herrera had left Peru. The corregidor who removed a well-to-do cacique with strong claim to the office might well find the royal courts allying with the latter.[14]

But a corregidor's intervention could be decisive when cacical claims were weaker or contested. In 1757 Paucartambo's governor removed Don Nicolas Loayza Quispetupa, the interim cacique of Caycay, and then named the cacique of neighboring Guasac, Don Bernardo Xaime Guambotupa, to the office. Both descended from Cusco's Inca nobility: the corregidor deposed one member of the local elite to appoint another, and Nicolas complained that Bernardo was a close ally of the corregidor.[15] In San Sebastián, opponents of Tupa Guamanrimachi argued that his rise to power owed much to his ties of *compadrazgo* with the city's corregidor.[16] During a lengthy campaign against Don Santos Mamani, cacique of Ayllu Lurucachi in Maranganí, his opponent claimed that the corregidor had confirmed Mamani because of personal ties.[17]

In these cases, corregidores were taking sides in existing battles. Guambotupa, Tupa Guamanrimachi, and Mamani were all viable candidates for the offices to which they were appointed. Like the appointment of Tapara in Ñuñoa, these episodes suggest that corregidores could determine who would occupy a cacicazgo, but in general made choices from within the pueblo elite. Nor is this surprising: the corregidor's main concern was collecting communal obligations, on which his own fortunes depended. Caciques with some legitimacy in tributaries' eyes presumably had better chances of success in these duties. Thus corregidores had incentive both to become involved in pueblo politics and to limit that involvement so as to maintain the stability of the community's government, and thereby the prompt payment of obligations.

But allegations of favoritism and collusion show that Indian communities viewed the involvement of Spanish officials in pueblo politics as problematic. Nor was the corregidor the only official who aroused complaint. Allegations that priests had agitated against the cacique were common. Indeed, the potential for conflict between cacique and priest was perhaps greater than that between cacique and corregidor, if only for reasons of proximity. Corregidores ruled over provinces of hundreds of square miles and up to a dozen parishes. Many caciques saw the corregidor only twice a year, to pay tribute. In contrast, priests were expected to reside in their parishes, and as a result they had daily interactions with the local Indian elite. Often

14 Also the 1720s case by Don Joseph Chuquiguanca of Azángaro Anansaya (father of Diego), against the corregidor; the case worked its way to Madrid. JCB, B729-M827s.
15 RREE, CSG, Exp. 31 (1767).
16 AGN, DI, Exp. 336 (1770).
17 ARC, COR, Prov., Crim., Leg. 84 (1745–73); Stavig, *The World of Túpac Amaru*, pp. 231–2.

this could produce close ties: a number of caciques and other Indian nobles appointed priests as executors of their estates.[18] At the same time, such closeness, and the inherent rivalry over precedence between priests and caciques, could also lead to open conflict, which in turn manifested itself in legal battles.

The best-studied conflict was between Don Eugenio Sinanyuca, cacique of Coporaque, and its priest, Don Vicente de la Puente.[19] The Sinanyuca family accused de la Puente of excessive charges for a funeral. When Tinta's corregidor sided with them, the priest turned to Cusco's corregidor and cabildo, accusing the Sinanyuca of inciting a mob against him and of stealing his possessions and distributing them to the crowd. But de la Puente did not topple Eugenio Sinanyuca. The cacique's alliance with the corregidor led him to take the loyalist side during the Tupac Amaru rebellion, and in the end it was de la Puente who was removed; Sinanyuca remained cacique until his death in 1804.[20] In Macarí, hostility between the priest and the cacique, Don Gabriel Cama Condorsayna, led to the latter being jailed at the insistence of the former. Principales from Macarí appealed to the Cusco cabildo, charging that the priest "has the intention of increasing his own fortune and in various ways has sought the ruin and destruction of our cacique."[21] Like Sinanyuca, Cama Condorsayna – the well-established cacique of a substantial pueblo – proved equal to the priest, and remained in office. In Verenguililla, however, the priest succeeded in toppling the cacique, Don Gregorio Ticona, in the late 1770s.[22] The priest was clearly caught up in local politics. Ticona won the office in the 1760s, after a suit against the interim cacique, Don Thomas Cornejo; following Ticona's removal, Don Rafael Cornejo became cacique. As when corregidores removed a cacique from one prominent family in favor of another, the intervention of Verenguelilla's priest proved decisive because the local elites had a history of conflict over the cacicazgo.

The events in Verenguelilla also show how battles between Spanish officials played out in the arena of local Indian politics. When Ticona was deposed, the priest of neighboring Vilque appointed him as the parish's chapel master; the fight between Ticona, Cornejo, and the two priests would have wound through the courts had the Tupac Amaru rebellion not

---

18 Rural caciques with priests as executors included Don Miguel Tupa Cusiguallpa, of Ayllu Paca, Yucay (ARC, NOT, Juan Bautista Gamarra, Leg. 145, [ ], January 10, 1766); and Don Bernardo Succacahua of Umachire (ARC, NOT, Joseph Bernardo Gamarra, Leg. 124, 233 ff. [1799]).
19 ARC, COR, Civ., Leg. 57, Exp. 1300; CAB, Ped., Leg. 114 (1773–86). Glave, *Vida, símbolos*, pp. 136–53; Stavig, *The World of Túpac Amaru*, pp. 240, 252–4; O'Phelan Godoy, *Un siglo*, pp. 228–30.
20 ARC, NOT, Vargas, Leg. 236, 357 ff., November 27, 1804.
21 ARC, CAB, Crim., Leg. 97 (1770–3).
22 Ticona Sanchez Larico's claim to the cacicazgo, ARC, INT, Prov., Ord., Leg. 99 (1802–3).

broken out. Priests also defended caciques and communities from corregidores, as the politics of the Spanish republic found their way into the Indian.[23] Taken together, these complaints reflect structural tensions in colonial rule, as Indian communities sought to limit the authority of the two colonial officials actively engaged with the pueblo, the corregidor and the priest, but also turned to them as allies in pueblo conflicts. Documents make clear that such conflict was a constant of the colonial period.

These eighteenth-century lawsuits expose another area of conflict between Indian and Spanish: private Spaniards' role in rural pueblos. The small clusters of Spanish families that had raised priests' concerns in 1689 grew steadily in the eighteenth century, and their comments echoed later in communities' complaints: those who lived in these villages were well aware of how dangerous alliances between Indian and Spanish elites could be. The eighteenth century brought a new threat: Spanish caciques. Under the Bourbons, rural Spaniards – creole and mestizo – were increasingly appointed to fill vacant cacicazgos, although this did not become the norm until after the Tupac Amaru rebellion.[24] Not all Spanish caciques were opposed by their communities, but as a group they met widespread distrust. When the corregidor of Lampa appointed Tapara in Ñuñoa Urinsaya, the representatives of the community specifically asked "... that for no reason should I name a cacique who was not Indian, because those who have had mestizos have received many wrongs, and if such were to occur ... they would see themselves compelled to abandon their houses and the pueblo of their origin."[25] Cases directed against Spanish caciques in the 1750s, 1760s, and 1770s focus more on abuses than on ethnicity, but the appointment of Spaniards was troubling to communities and judges. In 1751 when Don Antonio Cota Luque sought restitution to a cacicazgo in Pucará, the *oidores* in Chuquisaca ordered the immediate removal of the current cacique, a Spaniard, because "the exercise of this office is prohibited by his nature."[26] In May 1778 the Indians of the Ayllu Chumo in Sicuani won the removal of their Spanish interim cacique, Faustino Mexia, after charging him with abuses so enormous that "there is not time nor paper to present [them all]." They requested instead a cacique "of our ayllu ... our blood."[27] He was replaced, with the ayllu's consent, by Don Bernardo Ñaupa Lucana.

These complaints point out a fundamental contradiction of Bourbon rule: by the 1700s the legal division between ethnic republics no longer

---

23 ARC, COR, Ord., Leg. 45, Exp. 965; also the 1797 complaint against Tinta's subdelegate by the priest of Sicuani, ARC, INT, Gob., Leg. 147 (1796–7).

24 Stavig, *The World of Túpac Amaru*, p. 126.

25 See Appendix.

26 ANB, EC, 1775–176, 13r.

27 ARC, COR, Prov. Crim., Leg. 86 (1776–84). Quoted in Stavig, *The World of Túpac Amaru*, pp 126–7.

paralleled the political reality of most pueblos. Spaniards became involved in the politics of the Indian communities in which they lived, indirectly through alliances with Indian factions and directly by the assumption of cacicazgos. In 1786, while defending a Spanish cacique in Quiquijana against charges of abuse, Quispicanchis's subdelegate complained that "often the Spaniards of the pueblos are those who support the Indians, so that complaints resonate"; he claimed that the cacique's real enemies were the pueblo's other Spaniards.[28] Such complaints reveal changing political frontiers within Andean society as the rural Spanish population grew, and it was precisely along this frontier that the major legal battles after the Tupac Amaru rebellion would be fought.

But the Spanish–Indian divide was just one of many faultlines visible in prerebellion lawsuits, and other divisions could prove more important. A year before Mexia was deposed, tributaries from Ayllu Sinca – Sicuani's largest ayllu, with 1,000 people – launched a complaint against their cacique, Don Miguel de Zamalloa, "whose bad government and excesses we are suffering, with well-known and grave damage."[29] The legal battle that ensued reveals the complex internal politics of the ayllus themselves. An array of "Indian nobles, principales, caciques, *segundas*, and past *alcaldes ordinarios* of the Ayllu Sinca" – including the former cacique, Don Ramon Surco – countered the complainants, supporting Zamalloa and testifying that the suit was an attempt by Don Simon Callo, cacique of Ayllu Palla, to have himself named cacique of Sinca as well.[30] Here, one faction of the ayllus's "principales" rallied behind a Spanish cacique to defeat the alliance of another faction and Sicuani's most powerful Indian noble.[31]

The cases against Mexia and Zamalloa show Indian alcaldes and "principales" turning to the courts in the name of the "común," to depose their caciques. Not only mestizo and creole caciques were objects of such complaints: given the ill-defined role of the cacique in the local economy and the administration of justice, the exact extent of the cacique's authority was a matter of constant contestation in the courts. Communities' efforts to remove Indian caciques were infrequent, but not extraordinary, in mid-century Cusco. The detailed complaint of the community of Muñani to the Audiencia in Chuquisaca serves as a good example.[32] An annex of Azángaro, Muñani also came under the jurisdiction of the Choquehuanca. In 1762 the

---

28 In the suit against Don Rafael Bravo, ARC, INT, Gob., Leg. 137 (1786).
29 ARC, COR, Prov., Crim., Leg. 86 (1766–84). In 1791 Sinca had 249 tributaries. ARC, INT, RH, Leg. 195.
30 Palla was the second largest ayllu in Sicuani, with 239 tributaries in 1791. Ibid. Twelve men signed (all using "Don"). For Surco, ARC, NOT, Juan Bautista Gamarra, Legajo 145, [ ], May 17, 1761.
31 Zamalloa retained the cacicazgo until the rebellion; O'Phelan Godoy, *Un siglo*, p. 316.
32 ANB, EC, 1762–144, 18–9, for the charges. For others, RREE, PRH, Exp. 184; RREE, CRA, Exp. 410; ARC, COR, Civ., Leg. 59, Exp. 1338; ARC, COR, Civ., Leg. 57, Exp. 1300; also Chapter 3, pp. 90–91.

leaders of several *ayllus* and *estancias* charged the cacique, Diego Choque-huanca, and his children with an array of abuses. They alleged that Diego had jailed Don Andres Mullisaca when he was alcalde of the pueblo, ripping out Mullisaca's hair and taking three pregnant cows under the pretext of a shortfall in tribute. They charged that the Choquehuancas forced Muñani's tributaries to work without pay as *trajinantes* and on the family's estancias, grazed sheep on communal pastures without paying rent, claimed forty leagues of communal pasture as cacical property, and stole sheep. According to the witnesses, Choquehuanca had carried out his own reparto, forcing tributaries to buy knives for one peso and cloth from his *chorrillo*, and he had beaten three tributaries to death. Finally, he had hidden tributaries during the matriculations, thereby defrauding the crown of its due.

Two centuries later it is impossible to assess Choquehuanca's guilt, and only a portion of the suit survives in the Bolivian archives. Certainly he retained the cacicazgo and the family continued to rule Muñani: thirty-five years later the principales of the pueblo were again in court seeking to depose the cacica, Diego's daughter Doña Maria Teresa Choquehuanca.[33] But the 1762 lawsuit does make clear points of tension between the cacique and his subjects. The principales of Muñani sought to limit the cacique's control of communal land and labor, drawing distinctions between communal and cacical land and challenging the demands on tributary labor that Azángaro's cacical dynasty made on this outlying annex. The principales also sought to enforce a regard for their own private property and, in opposing the reparto, for the profits of their own domestic economies. Such were the material values of the Andean moral economy after two centuries of Spanish rule, which demanded the defense of both the commons and the modest private wealth of the tributary from cacical expansionism.

Other aspects of the complaint reflect the community's political values – especially that the cacique owed respect to lesser local officials, like the alcalde – and sought to place limits on Choquehuanca's power of corporal punishment. Complaints that caciques abused lesser officials are ubiquitous in suits against caciques.[34] The role that public, and painful, humiliation of lesser officials played in the cacique's authority exposes a structural tension in pueblo organization. Within a community subject to a larger moiety or pueblo, tribute collection (and the organization of other communal burdens) as well as day-to-day governance fell to lesser officials – the "segunda persona," alcalde, or perhaps an ayllu cacique. These individuals served as agents of the "cacique principal," or "cacique gobernador," who was ultimately responsible to the corregidor for tribute payment, mita contingents,

---

33 Then they were successful in their request that she be removed in favor of her nephew, Don Manuel Choquehuanca. RREE, PRA, Exp. 343, 1797.

34 Rasnake, *Domination*, pp. 127–30, for late-seventeenth-century Yura [Potosí].

and so on. Relations between pueblo or moiety caciques and those beneath them could be quite tense, as the former squeezed the latter for payment, and sought to profit at their expense. Thus it was Mullisaca, the former alcalde, who spearheaded the case against Choquehuanca. Such pueblo officials were almost always party to complaints about cacical abuse (although in larger communities like Sicuani's Ayllu Sinca, principales were themselves often split between opponents and supporters of the cacique).[35] Inextricably linked with complaints about a cacique's violation of property rights and communal assets were complaints about the cacique's violation of the persons of other officials, and illegitimate control of the pueblo polity.

Thus, Muñani's lawsuit shows a community trying to establish, and enforce, limits to cacical power over the local economy and over the community's other officers. What is striking is the extent to which the ideals advanced by the Habsburg reformers of the sixteenth century had worked themselves into the values of the Indian community. To be sure, the pursuit of royal justice influenced how complaints were presented: testimony was tailored to be persuasive to royal justices. Complaints about cacical abuse do reflect the reality of communal conflict in Indian pueblos; those reflections are simply refracted so as to arouse the suspicions of cacical power that had been deeply held by Spanish officials since the first decades of the conquest. Nonetheless, the details suggest that Muñani concurred with the crown's goal of circumscribing the cacique's role in the communal economy, and his executive powers; of defining and protecting the property rights of community and household; and of establishing the crown as the ultimate arbiter of disputes between the community and its cacique.

Testimony by Muñani's leaders suggests that they not only accepted but also insisted on this role for the crown. The witnesses stressed the shared interests of the king and his most humble vassals: the allegation that Choquehuanca defrauded the crown of tribute asserted that his malfeasance harmed both the royal treasury and the community. By making tributaries work as shepherds for his flocks, Choquehuanca was "preventing that they go on the mita to the city of Potosí."[36] Finally, in charging Choquehuanca with usurping ayllu land, the principales claimed that official documents gave them ownership. Here they called upon the Spanish regard for written title in seeking the intervention of the courts. All of these are reminders of the dynamism of moral economies, as demands and relations viewed as abusive in the sixteenth century became accepted and even normative two centuries later. But the appeal to the audiencia also brings to the fore two key aspects of highland society in the eighteenth century. The first was the

---

35 Don Lucas Mango Turpa, a noble of Azángaro Urinsaya, launched another complaint against Blas Choquehuanca in 1762. ANB, EC, 1762–18.
36 ANB, EC, 1762–144, 18v.

weakness of royal justice in rural areas, made clear by caciques' frequent violations not only of communal norms, but also of royal law. Testimony in the many such cases suggests that the royal laws protecting communities from their caciques often went unenforced. At the same time, Muñani's call for redress underscores the extent to which royal justice was recognized and sought by Indian communities. The lawsuit by Mullisaca and the rest of Muñani attempted to reject a particular relation within the colonial order as a whole; in so doing it affirmed other colonial relations, and upheld the ultimate authority of the king.[37]

Muñani's lawsuit also exposed tensions over the definition of community. The aggregation of ayllus and annexes into larger pueblos and parishes did not end solidarities based in smaller communities, although of course communal identity and the desire for autonomy evolved over time: as ayllus and pueblos expanded or contracted or became more established, their relations with others changed. Muñani's lawsuit was a bid for independence from Azángaro. The Choquehuanca held the cacicazgo of Azángaro Anansaya from the conquest to independence, and amassed large properties in the area. In 1689, according to Azángaro's priest, the cacique (Don Manuel Chuquiguanca) owned four estancias in the parish. The parish also had four estancias owned by Spanish miners in Caravaya, who used them to supply their workers with food; one of these was Muñani.[38] By 1760 Muñani had become a pueblo in its own right, including within its jurisdiction the Choquehuanca estancia of Nequenque. How Muñani had changed from a Spanish-owned estancia to an Indian community is not clear; that the community had written title to the land suggests that they had bought the estancia, forming an Indian corporation from a defunct Spanish property.[39] Twenty miles from Azángaro, Muñani was nonetheless an annex of the larger pueblo. By seeking to limit the power of Azángaro's cacical dynasty over its daily life, Muñani was also attempting to declare its autonomy within Azángaro parish.

That Muñani – a smallish pueblo legally bound to a larger one a full day's walk away – developed a distinct corporate identity is hardly surprising, but this component of community–cacique conflict was not unusual. Many attempts to remove caciques, or to prevent their accession to office, charged that the cacique should not rule because he was an outsider to the community. To be sure, "outsider" and "community" were open to competing

---

37 For how communities' recourse to Spanish courts strengthened the rule of the crown, Stern, *Peru's Indian Peoples*, pp. 114–37, and Woodrow Borah, *Justice By Insurance: The General Indian Court of Colonial Mexico and the Legal Aides of the Half-Real* (Berkeley: University of California Press, 1983).

38 *Cuzco 1689*, p. 112.

39 ANB, EC, 1762–144, 22r (although no witnesses knew exactly what the titles were, or where they were at the moment).

interpretations. In their efforts to remove Don Santos Mamani from the cacicazgo of Ayllu Lurucachi in Maranganí, both local Spaniards and members of the ayllu insisted that Mamani could not hold the cacicazgo because his parents had been *forasteros*; but Mamani's father had been cacique before him.[40] Perhaps the charges were false; or perhaps the Mamanis had settled in Lurucachi and assumed control over the cacicazgo, control that was repudiated only when the son tried to make it hereditary.[41] In any case, the language shows that these were battles about the definition of community, over the degree to which the ayllu was subsumed in the larger pueblo, and whether the cacique of an ayllu or pueblo should be drawn from its own dominant families or from outside. There was no single pattern: many pueblos came under unified cacical rule, others were agglomerations of quasi-autonomous ayllus, and organization was not static. Nor was there necessarily solidarity within these associations: factions within ayllus and pueblos made alliances across such boundaries in efforts to improve their own positions.

Another example from Sicuani illustrates this complexity. Sicuani grew rapidly in the eighteenth century to become the largest town on the royal road between Cusco and Puno: its Indian population quintupled between 1689 and 1792, to roughly 5,000.[42] Because of this rapid growth, Sicuani differed from other large pueblos with entrenched cacical elites and established hierarchies between groups. Instead, Sicuani was the site of constant conflict; indeed, in 1770 Indians from surrounding ayllus invaded the center of the pueblo.[43] Cacical politics were correspondingly contentious. Throughout the 1770s Don Christobal Aruni Mollo Apasa and Don Miguel Zuñiga disputed the cacicazgo of Sicuani's Ayllu Anza.[44] From a noble family, Aruni Mollo Apasa claimed a proprietary right to the cacicazgos of Anza and Canacagua. In 1779 he complained to Lima of the terrible treatment that he had received from Zuñiga. Five years earlier Aruni Mollo Apasa had renounced the cacicazgos to his relative Pedro Quispe. Pedro then died, and the corregidor named "as interim cacique a mestizo named Miguel Zuñiga who does not have . . . any claim to this office."[45] To remove Aruni Mollo Apasa from Sicuani, Zuñiga sent him to Potosí as mita captain; while he was gone, claimed Aruni Mollo Apasa, Zuñiga had abused the ex-cacique's wife

---

40 ARC, COR, Prov., Crim., Leg. 84 (1745–73).
41 Also the denunciation against Don Dionicio Pacoricona as "governador intruso" of Lampa. RREE, PRH, Exp. 184. For others, O'Phelan Godoy, *Kurakas*, pp. 17–28.
42 For 1689, *Cuzco 1689*, pp. 242–3. In 1792, Sicuani had 1,270 tributaries. ARC, INT, RH, Leg. 195 (1792).
43 O'Phelan Godoy, *Un siglo*, p. 302.
44 ARC, COR, Prov., Ord., Leg. 76 (1780–4).
45 The testimony of Aruni Mollo Apasa, ibid.

and children and had stolen his property. On Aruni Mollo Apasa's return, the Spanish alcalde imprisoned him at Zuñiga's behest; after his release, when the former cacique headed to Cusco to seek justice, Zuñiga had him assaulted by two Indians, who stole his documents and locked him in an *obraje*. Lima was understandably troubled by these claims, and ordered the corregidor to go to Sicuani to depose Zuñiga and investigate.

Testimony in colonial depositions is usually contradictory, and this case was no exception. Ayllu members testified that they loathed Aruni Mollo Apasa, who, they claimed, was abusive and was not from their ayllu. Spanish *vecinos* were more sympathetic to him: all acknowledged hearing about Zuñiga's abuse of him, the robbery of his papers, and his recent imprisonment in the obraje. Don Tomas Perez Gondifuela insisted that Aruni Mollo Apasa was noble and had served as cacique of Canacagua and later taken over Anza from his father-in-law, Don Felipe Aroni. The most intriguing testimony, by two tributaries, asserted that the Indians who had robbed Aruni Mollo Apasa were Bentura and Simon Aymituma of Ayllu Quehaur, under the rule of Don Juan Aymituma.[46] The two brothers were presumably his sons, and the Aymituma were the ayllu's dominant family. By 1785, Don Simon Aymituma was cacique of both Quehuar and Canacagua, whose tributaries denounced him for abuses.[47] By the 1790s Simon had perhaps died: his name does not appear in the large case brought against the new interim cacique of Ayllu Quehuar, Don Francisco Martinez. The case was spearheaded by none other than Don Bentura Aymituma; the *alcalde mayor* of the pueblo was by then Miguel Zuñiga.[48]

Thus, what appears to be a dispute between an Indian noble cacique and a mestizo usurper unfolds into a multifaceted battle: between Spanish and Indian, between two noble lineages (the Aymituma and the Mollo Apasa) as the former entered an alliance with a mestizo to extend its influence over another ayllu, and finally between members of Ayllu Anza and the man who had assumed its cacicazgo by marrying its heiress. Moreover, that battle spanned decades; indeed, here the Tupac Amaru rebellion scarcely registers, as many of the same families and individuals continued to fight through the courts (and undoubtedly in other arenas as well) from the 1760s through the 1790s. To some extent Sicuani was an exceptional community because of its ill-defined hierarchies and the rapid growth of both its Spanish and Indian populations. But in their broad outlines the conflicts in and

46 ARC, NOT, Juan Bautista Gamarra, Leg. 145, [ ], May 17, 1761. Aymituma had sons studying at San Borja in Cusco in 1775; "Indios de sangre real," p. 228.

47 ARC, INT, Gob., Leg. 132 (1785).

48 ARC: INT, RH, Leg. 201 (1795), and RA, Ord., Leg. 25 (1797). Arriaga had not removed Zuñiga in 1780, citing insufficient evidence.

between Ayllus Anza, Canacagua, and Quehuar reflect those throughout the Indian communities of the bishopric in the mid 1700s: between cacique and community, Indian and Spaniard, and ayllu and ayllu.

The conflict between Aruni Mollo Apasa and the Aymituma also exposes the competition between leading families in a community. These conflicts took many forms: efforts by one Indian noble to dislodge another as interim cacique, battles over succession to vacant cacicazgos between branches of the same family, rivalry between the caciques of different ayllus to be named "principal cacique" of a pueblo. At heart, all were battles for local supremacy. Like communities' lawsuits against their caciques, these disputes were conscious attempts to draw royal intervention into pueblo politics (and the two sorts of suit were often intertwined); here, however, the goal was to elevate, or humble, a particular claimant or family. Lawsuits over succession rights thus employed different rhetorical strategies than those waged by communities against their caciques. The latter appealed to the crown as the righteous defender of aggrieved vassals suffering under a local tyrant, while succession disputes appealed to the royal courts to uphold the rights of a noble family or to expose the pretensions of usurpers – that is, to ensure legitimate succession. Thus, the charges by cacical claimants seek to invalidate rival claims by impugning the birthrights or challenging a family's claim to hereditary control of office.[49]

Such succession battles were particularly common in the Inca-dominated communities around Cusco, with their many noble lines. In 1756, as part of the battles for dominance in Maras, Don Pablo Llanac Paucar Aucapuma, the "cacique principal y gobernador" of Ayllu Mullacas, appeared before the corregidor to complain that

... Antolin Usca, a tributary from Anta ... having contracted matrimony with Juliana Uscapaucar, daughter of Don Francisco Sancho Uscapaucar and Doña Maria Sinchiroca, has attained, through sinister and false relation ... an investigation of the cacicazgo, by saying that the parents, grandparents, and ancestors of the said Juliana were proprietary caciques of the ayllus of Maras and Mullacas, not being in truth more than a mere intruder ... and [there is] not conceded to the said Antolin any right or action in place of the said Juliana[;] this has been prohibited by the insurmountable defects that [the claim of] her parents suffered, since they never were [caciques] of Mullacas, ... and [I am] in current possession of the cacicazgo of the Ayllu Mullacas by provision of the government of Your Lordship ... having justified [possession] since the [time of] gentility, which moved Your Superior Greatness to pronounce the expressed title on September 22 [1755] ... and more

49 See Chapter 6, pp. 204–205, for aspersions on Tupac Amaru's ancestry. Also ARC, INT, Ord., Leg. 34 (1794) for Don Fermin Mango vs. Don Tomas Mango (Azángaro); ANB, EC, 1793–11, 2; ARC, COR, Civ., Leg. 47, Exps. 1043 and 1060.

so, being the said Antolin [given] to vices that render him ineligible for any office . . . "⁵⁰

Llanac Paucar pursued five lines of attack in just one paragraph. As a tributary from another community, Antolin Usca was ineligible to rule in (heavily noble) Maras; he was also morally unfit for the office. The family of his wife, the putative cacical heiress, were not who they claimed to be; or if they were, their claim did not extend to Ayllu Mullacas, for Llanac Paucar's ancestors had ruled the ayllu since the time of the Inca empire. Llanac Paucar presented these charges to raise the concern of royal judges: they should not be taken at face value. Antolin Usca and his wife referred to him as "Don Antolin Quispe Uscamayta," part of the prominent Inca lineage from Pucyura. And Maras' cacicazgos were notoriously contested among the pueblo's nobility: just as Llanac Paucar deprecated the couple's claims, he exaggerated the strength of his own to Mullacas.⁵¹

At the heart of such battles was competition within the Indian elite. But they involved the broader politics of rural Peru. The Tamboguacso dispute over Taray's cacicazgo shows changing patterns of succession and legitimacy – or, at least, appeals to custom and against innovation.⁵² A 1722 suit by Don Lucas Fernandez Cutimbo of Chucuito Anansaya pitted a member of the cacical dynasty against a provincial Spaniard who claimed descent, several generations back, from a cacical heiress: here, writ small, was the conflict between Indian and Spanish elites for control of Indian communities.⁵³ Similarly, elites of different ayllus and factions within a pueblo sought to prevent particular families, or outsiders, from assuming control of their ayllus: the battle between Llanac Paucar and Uscamayta in Maras is as much a battle over ayllu autonomy as those between the principales and caciques of Sicuani's Ayllus Sinca and Anza. Indeed, succession battles and lawsuits against abusive caciques are best viewed as different arenas in which the basic issues of local power were contested. Succession disputes simply placed at the fore the question of "legitimacy."

The complexity of pueblo politics emerges in the cacical disputes of Caycay and Guasac. Neighboring Inca-ruled pueblos, Guasac was the annex of Caycay. In the late 1750s Don Bernardo Xaime Guambotupa served as cacique of both – according to his heirs, as their "proprietary and legitimate principal cacique and governor."⁵⁴ Whether they were historically united is unclear. Bernardo certainly came from prominent Inca lineages and was already cacique of Guasac when, in 1757, he launched a legal challenge

---

50 Llanac Paucar's complaint, in ARC, COR, Ped., Leg. 90 (1753–65), 1–2.
51 For conflict over Maras' cacicazgos, Garrett, "Descendants," pp. 620–5.
52 See Chapter 3, pp. 93–96.
53 ANB, EC, 1793–11, 1–15.
54 BNP, Man., C-4218 (1767).

against the interim cacique of Caycay, whom Bernardo called "Don Nicolas de Loayza, Spaniard."[55] Nicolas described himself as "Don Nicolas Loayza Quispethupa," the interim cacique but with a maternal blood right to the cacicazgo.[56] Nicolas fought the suit, but Bernardo won and ruled the pueblos until his death in the mid-1760s. In his will he left the cacicazgo of Guasac to his sister, Doña Martina Xaime Guambotupa, and that of Caycay to his cousin, Don Marselino Xaime Guambotupa.[57]

Martina and her husband, Don Thomas Tupa Orcoguaranca (an Inca elector from Cusco), occupied the cacicazgo of Guasac unchallenged. But that of Caycay was soon the object of legal battle. In 1766 Loayza Quispetupa, now a *"vecino* and *hacendado* of Caycay," charged that the corregidor had appointed Bernardo unjustly, so Marselino should not inherit the cacicazgo.[58] He was unsuccessful: the extant complaint ends with a call for documents but no further action. However, in March 1767 Martina and Thomas launched their own suit against Marselino, which progressed little for two years.[59] Then, in January 1769, the "principales" of Caycay – including the two sacristans of the pueblo church, the alcalde, and others whose Inca family names and use of "Don" suggest their standing – complained to the corregidor of Cusco about abuses they suffered from Marselino. The complaints resemble those of all such *denuncias*: Marselino usurped ayllu lands and water; beat the tributaries; seized private houses, land, and livestock; and charged tribute "even from boys seven years old." Also active in the lawsuit was the parish priest, who lodged an initial complaint that compared his parishioners' lot unfavorably to that of Barbary slaves, as "although [the Indians of Caycay] have liberty, it should not be called such, since they are subjected to such hardships."[60] More denunciations streamed in until, in July, Thomas and Martina reasserted her claim to the cacicazgo of Caycay, arguing that Bernardo had not had the right to separate the two cacicazgos, and that as his sister Martina had the stronger claim.

Whether the complaints against Marselino reflected widespread disaffection with his rule, or simply an effort to further Thomas and Martina's claims, is unknowable. But the whole range of conflicts and actors present in the Bourbon pueblo played parts in the battle for Caycay's cacicazgo. It began with the corregidor's removal from office of a member of the local creole, land-owning elite with some Inca ancestry, in favor of the Inca cacique of a neighboring pueblo, who then consolidated his control over the two

55 For Bernardo's genealogy, see Don Juan Cusiguaman's nobility claim, ARC, INT, RH, Leg. 218 (1807), 6r.
56 RREE, CSG, Exp. 31 (1767).
57 RREE, CRA, Exp. 249.
58 RREE, CSG, Exp. 31.
59 BNP, Man., C-4218 and C-4222.
60 RREE, CRA, Exp. 410.

communities until his death seven years later. At that point, after a futile effort by Loayza Quispetupa to regain the cacicazgo, the contest shifted to two cousins; the priest and a number of Caycay's local prominents then intervened on the side of one candidate, and did so by appealing to Spanish concerns about cacical tyranny.

The legal record gives no decision about Caycay's cacicazgo, but in 1805 a son of Marselino and a granddaughter of Thomas and Martina were in court over the office.[61] Their resort to royal justice is a reminder that few, if any, court verdicts were final. The battles of the grandparents would be revisited decades later; or a cacique deposed in the 1750s might seek restitution in the 1760s. Competition surrounding cacicazgos is illuminating because it could be so enduring: corregidores and priests came and went, but the elite lineages of a pueblo lasted for generations, even centuries. Spanish officials were drawn into local battles – and often provoked them. But the decades-long conflicts between the noble cousins of Caycay, and the factions in Sicuani, show the dynamism and the continuity of conflict in colonial Indian communities. The specifics of each dispute are as rooted in local politics as in the dialectics of colonialism, but overall, these lawsuits and complaints expose the politics of the Bourbon pueblo.

Underlying such conflicts were the broader divisions of the pueblo, and of colonial rule generally: between cacique and community, Indian and Spanish, ayllu and pueblo. Interacting with these was the competition among local elites. Of course, cacical disputes were taken to royal courts, or presented to other Spanish officials. Not all local conflicts took this form. Denuncias of caciques for abuses make clear that the politics of the pueblo were violent, and extended to disputes over precedence in church or in crossing the plaza, and insults hurled between enemies were the stuff of daily conflict.[62] But anti-cacical lawsuits provide invaluable windows into pueblos' political histories, although they must be approached with caution. The system of Spanish advocates for Indians created a mechanism by which Indian communities could articulate their political grievances and visions, but only in certain forms. By affirming the ideals of pueblo autonomy, the just cacique, and legitimate succession, Indian communities and their elites sought to manipulate royal justice and use it as part of local

---

61 ARC, INT, Gob., Leg. 152 (1806–9); ARC, INT, RH, Leg. 218 (1807); RREE, CRA, Exp. 249. After the rebellion Caycay had a creole cacique (ARC, INT, Ord., Leg. 3, 1785), but Tomas was named *"alcalde mayor* and receptor of tributes" of Guasac. Don Juan Cusiguaman, ARC, INT, RH, Leg. 218 (1807).

62 AGN, DI, Exp. 336 for Cayetano Tupa Guamanrimachi against San Sebastián's priest for insults in 1778; RREE, PRA, Exp. 236 for insults hurled at Doña Antonia Chuquicallata as she crossed the plaza in Azángaro; and ARC, RA, Crim., Leg. 103 (1789) for the violence and court battles that followed scuffles over precedence in Azángaro.

politics. In doing so they made the cacicazgo a central site of contention within the Indian pueblo.

The Performance and Production of Cacical Legitimacy

The competition for cacicazgos, and challenges to their rule, did not go unmet by caciques. They responded to lawsuits in kind, disparaging the claims of their opponents and presenting their own witnesses and documents. With their greater wealth cacical families were generally better equipped to wage such battles than were their opponents. But a lawsuit was a sign that cacical legitimacy was already under threat. To avoid such challenges caciques performed their authority in a myriad of ways, and used the privileges of wealth, education, and status to reinforce the legitimacy of their rule in the eyes of two audiences: their communities, and Spanish officials and courts.

To both his subjects and Spanish officials, the cacique was the chief intermediary between the community and the networks of Spanish rule. Located on the frontier of the two republics, the cacique needed to appeal to both.[63] Different values and criteria for selection could lead corregidores and audiencia judges to impose caciques that communities viewed as usurpers, and "caciques intrusos" were stock figures of cacical disputes throughout the colonial era. In the early 1600s Guaman Poma lamented "how the principal caciques are not obeyed nor respected because they are not true lord[s] by lineage nor do they do good works."[64] Historians have echoed this plaint, seeing the introduction of such intruder-caciques as a corrosive effect of colonialism in Andean society, contributing enormously to the rise of class conflict and the erosion of cacical legitimacy in the Indian republic.[65]

That such an erosion has been dated variously to the late 1500s, the middle of the seventeenth century, the early 1700s, and the 1750s highlights the regional variations in the history of Indian Peru under Spanish rule. But the variety also suggests that the effects of usurpation and illegitimacy have been overstated. For more than a century and a half after Guaman Poma's letter to the king, caciques continued, as a group, to be respected and obeyed. The first half of this chapter stressed the complexity of pueblo politics,

63 Thierry Saignes, "De la borrachera al retrato: Los curacas andinos entre dos legitimidades," *Revista Andina* 5:1 (1987): 139–70.

64 *El primer nueva corónica*, p. 768.

65 María Rostworowski de Diez Canseco, *Curacas y Sucesiones, Costa Norte* (Lima: Imprenta Minerva, 1961); Pease, *Curacas*; Susan Ramirez, "The 'Dueño of Indios': Thoughts on the Consequences of the Shifting Bases of Power of the 'Curacas Viejos Antiguos' under the Spanish in Sixteenth Century Peru," *Hispanic American Historical Review* 64:4 (November 1987): 575–610; Powers, *Andean Journeys*; Stern, *Peru's Indian Peoples*; Glave, *Trajinantes*, pp. 302–4; O'Phelan Godoy, *Kurakas*; Spalding, "Social Climbers." See Thomson, *We Alone*, pp. 66–70, for discussion of the different criteria used to evaluate the "decline" of the cacicazgo.

and challenges to particular caciques. But it was not until after the Great Rebellion that the fundamental legitimacy and necessity of the office itself came under attack. Communities, nobles, and Spanish officials fought over who would be cacique, not whether there should be one. Moreover, within the contours defined in the late sixteenth century, over time communities rewrote their own histories: the son of a "cacique intruso" could easily become the legitimate "cacique proprietario" in the eyes of both tributaries and Spanish officials. As a result, the disruptions that toppled individual cacical dynasties, or large swaths of the cacical elite in a particular region, could give way within one or two generations to dynasties who had occupied the office "since time immemorial," and were widely reckoned the legitimate caciques of their communities.

While Spanish and Indian understandings of legitimacy often differed, they were not entirely contradictory. Both valued caciques who managed to collect tribute and assemble mita contingents without provoking local tumult; who profited enough from office to cover occasional shortfalls and to defend the community's legal claims, but not so much that they usurped communal lands and defrauded the crown; who had some familial claim to the office; and whose education and manner located them as both elite members of their own communities and peers of the Spanish officials with whom they interacted. Such caciques often enjoyed widespread recognition of their rule from both their communities and local Spaniards.

To be sure, to maintain power caciques resorted to the abusive strategies denounced in the lawsuits mentioned earlier. These received considerable attention in colonial courts, as they confirmed the stereotype of the abusive cacique; such actions also loom large in the negative portrait of the cacical class put forward by historians. Through such abuse, caciques reproduced and depended on the open violence that underpinned the exploitative relations of colonial society.[66] But such violence – often almost ritualized (at least according to legal complaints), like the pulling of lesser pueblo officials by the hair through the plaza – also won the acquiescence of Indian commoners in the fulfillment of their material obligations, and reinforced cacical authority and the hierarchies of the pueblo.[67] The power to dominate and humiliate other members of the community set the cacique apart. While such violence was open to challenge in the courts, Spanish officials gave caciques latitude to perform overt aggression, thereby legitimating their power locally. Just as the courts and officials considered paternal violence as necessary to social order, so too did they view cacical violence.

---

66 Stern, *Peru's Indian Peoples*, pp. 102–6; Díaz Rementería, *El cacique*, pp. 69–76.

67 See the complaint by Lucas Mango Turpa against Blas Choquehuanca; ANB, EC, 1762–18. Also Steve J. Stern, *The Secret History of Gender: Women, Men, and Power in Late Colonial Mexico* (Chapel Hill: University of North Carolina Press, 1995), pp. 189–213.

And the ideal of the cacique was patriarchal: separated from his tributaries by noble birth, education, and wealth, the cacique was to be as an adult among children.[68] The performance of authority by caciques, and the rewards of birth and office conceded by the Spanish, emphasized this distinction. Caciques rode mules while tributaries walked; they were literate and spoke Spanish; they took their legal cases to the royal courts, avoiding the power of the corregidor. These were ideals: many caciques were illiterate, spoke no Spanish, and had no real hope of escaping the corregidor's control; but others did. And caciques were recognized as the representatives of their communities before Spanish officials. Like the good father, the good cacique protected those under his charge from the outside world, he maintained order in his community, and he provided them with necessities otherwise beyond their reach.

Thus, while hierarchical and patriarchal, cacical authority rested on far more than violence. Caciques used their private wealth to reinforce their position by establishing themselves as patrons, asserting through their generosity their importance to the well-being of the community. Small loans to tributary neighbors, a willingness to leave tribute uncollected, perhaps after a house had been struck by tragedy – such debts created networks of obligation that reinforced caciques' position in the community. When Don Nicolas Santa Cruz of Urubamba dictated his will, various tributaries owed him a total of forty-three pesos for tribute from when he had been cacique of Ayllu Yanaconas.[69] Whether he intended his wife and children to collect these small debts is not clear; in any case, the obligation of the ayllu's poorer tributaries to his family had been noted. Doña Juana Uclucana, heiress to a cacical family in Santa Ana, simply stated that she owed no debts and that her children knew her debtors, bequeathing to her sons (one of whom assumed the cacicazgo) the debt relations that she had built up in her parish.[70] Unfortunately for the historian, these networks functioned outside the written realm, their passing mention in wills hinting at the daily negotiations of the colonial pueblo, now lost to us.

More visible two centuries later is cacical patronage of public buildings and institutions, most importantly pueblo churches.[71] Symbolically these churches occupied an ambiguous space in the colonial order. The church was the representation and the agent of Spain's Christianizing mission in the Andes. Controlled by the priest – almost always Spanish – the church

68 For the idea of Amerindians as natural children, Pagden, *The Fall*, pp. 57–108.
69 ARC, NOT, Moya, Leg. 229, 690 ff., April 13, 1785.
70 ARC, NOT, Tomas Gamarra, Leg. 180, 357 ff., August 16, 1783.
71 Caciques also constructed other buildings: Don Pasqual Uscapaucar Ynga, cacique of Maras, endowed a small hospital. ARC, CAB, Civ., Leg. 81, Exp. 2015.

signified colonial rule in its most localized manifestation. But precisely because of its towering prominence, the church also symbolized and embodied the pueblo as a community, and along with its plaza became the center of civic life. Therefore, through patronage of its construction and furnishing, the cacical and noble elites of Indian society established a privileged relation to this space, in so doing asserting and reinforcing their own privileged position within the community.

At its grandest, this patronage was impressive indeed. In the 1670s Don Gabriel Fernandez Guarachi, cacique of Jesús de Machaca, left 20,000 pesos for the construction of the pueblo's temple, whose ornaments included a 100-lb. silver chandelier and a 15-lb. silver-gilt monstrance encrusted with pearls and precious stones.[72] The grandeur of Machaca's church reflected the exceptional power and wealth of the Guarachi, but in the southern reaches of the bishopric of Cusco caciques also built pueblo churches.[73] By the 1700s Inca caciques around Cusco were not nearly so rich, and their patronage was correspondingly modest. But they too endowed their churches. In his 1745 will Don Sebastian Tupa Cusiguallpa, cacique and governor of Yucay, left thirty pesos to adorn the monstrance, while Don Joseph Guamantica, cacique of Guarocondo, "... adorned the pulpit at his own cost, in which he spent 220 pesos, and commissioned a silver bell, three robes for the priest, a cassock of *perciana*, an outfit of perciana, a candle for the Lord of the Souls, [and] a silver crown of four marks for the child Jesus."[74] Others gave gifts that placed themselves at the heart of the community's sacred space. Don Mateo Pumacahua, the leader of the royalist forces against Tupac Amaru, celebrated his victory with a mural memorializing it in his pueblo church.[75] Among the thousands of paintings adorning the walls of rural churches were votive paintings commissioned by caciques; in Azángaro, one chapel had a painting of the Last Supper, complete with portraits of the donors – two cacical couples – viewing the scene.[76] Whether through the construction of the church or the gift of its furnishings, caciques (along with rivals among the pueblo elite) performed their munificence and their

72 Roberto Choque Canqui, "Una iglesia de los Guarachi en Jesús de Machaca (Pacajes-La Paz)," in *La venida del reino: Religión, evangelización y cultura en América, Siglos XVI–XX*, ed. Gabriela Ramos (Cusco: Centro Bartolomé de Las Casas, 1994), pp. 135–49.

73 The Guampoco of Santa Rosa; ARC RA, Ord., Leg. 8 (1791) [3]. Eugenio Canatupa Sinanyuca erected a chapel in Coporaque; ARC, NOT, Vargas, Leg. 236, 357 ff., November 27, 1804. Also Altuve Carillo, *Choquehuanca*, p. 52, for Putina.

74 In his will; ARC, NOT, Arias Lira, Leg. 39, 541 ff., April 29, 1779. For Tupa Cusiguallpa, ARC, COR, Civ., Leg. 55, Exp. 1241 (1773).

75 Mesa and Gisbert, *Historia de la pintura*, II, 387.

76 Altuve Carrillo, *Choquehuanca*, p. 31. For cacical devotional paintings, Mesa and Gisbert, *Historia de la pintura*, II, 514–6; and O'Phelan Godoy, *Kurakas*, Figures 3 and 4.

position in the community by endowing it with communal treasures. They also performed their Christian devotion, demonstrating their fitness to rule to the parish priest and other Spanish officials.

The church also provided colonial Peru with its most important lay organizations, the brotherhoods (*cofradías*) in almost every church. Here caciques combined religious devotion with communal control, serving as majordomos.[77] In the 1730s Don Marcos Chiguantupa Coronilla Ynga, one of rural Cusco's most powerful Inca caciques, held the office for the brotherhood of the Puríssima Concepción in Guayllabamba.[78] The brotherhood had dozens of members, among them Spanish vecinos and Inca nobles; as majordomo, Chiguantupa asserted his rank in the pueblo. Puríssima Concepción also had seven and a half topos of land in the pueblo commons that brought in 52.5 pesos a year, paid by the renter to the pueblo's cacique, thence to the brotherhood. Chiguantupa thus extended his control over the communal property of Guayllabamba, although such economic benefits were certainly secondary to the rewards – both in the afterlife and in local status – that the office brought. Indeed, economically such service could be a burden. Don Miguel Soria Condorpusa was majordomo of the brotherhood of the Santíssima Sacramento in Santa Ana for thirty-three years, during which, according to his will, ". . . I have served the brotherhood, . . . paying from my own goods the costs of candles and music in the nights of Corpus [Christi], its eight days and Thursday of each year, the small offering that is gathered from the faithful not able to cover [the costs]."[79] In return for such economic support, Soria Condorpusa's patronage of the brotherhood brought status in his parish, in which his father, grandfather, and uncle had held cacicazgos.

The church's central role in the pueblo thus gave caciques, and cacical families, numerous opportunities for patronage.[80] Many of these – particularly the *fiestas* at the heart of communal life – have left little record; but from wills and the occasional cofradía book the presence of such patronage is clear.[81] Driving it was certainly a strong religious devotion. Andean elites embraced Christian practice in the first decades of the conquest and remained fervent devotees of the Trinity, Mary, and the saints. They filled their houses with religious statues and paintings, and joined the religious processions that were the main public ceremonies in colonial Peru. But

77 For urban Inca majordomos, see Chapter 3, P. 84. Diego Ninancuyuchi was majordomo of the brotherhood of Our Lady of Loreto in the Jesuit church; ARC, NOT, Diego Gamarra, Leg. 126, 701 ff., June 30, 1756.

78 See the book of the *cofradía* de Puríssima Concepción, extant in the AAC.

79 ARC, NOT, Bernardo Joseph Gamarra, Leg. 75, 236 ff., February 19, 1801.

80 Cacical families also had special seats in the pueblo church. Xavier Albó, "Jesuitas y culturas indígenas: Perú, 1568–1806," *América Indígena* 26:3 (July 1966): 265.

81 See Penry, "Transformations," pp. 219–69 for cofradías and community in mid-eighteenth-century Alto Peru.

votive paintings next to the altar, a private crypt in the pueblo church for a cacical dynasty, the public gifts of vestments and silver to adorn the village saints – these were also political gestures. They affirmed the wealth and importance of the cacique, and asserted a special relation of the cacical elite to both the religious space of the parish church and the statues and paintings that made up the local divinities whose worship was tolerated (indeed, encouraged) by the Spanish.

This patronage required money, and the church served as the most visible mechanism by which cacical families could return to their communities some of the wealth acquired through office. There were others as well, and of greater material importance. Above all, caciques assumed their communities' defense in the colonial courts when ayllus and pueblos sued one another, and Spanish colonists, over the possession of lands and rights to water.[82] While technically Indian commoners and communities were exempt from legal fees, in practice Spanish justice was never free, and these court cases could cost huge sums of money. In 1802 Don Luis Eustaquio Balboa Fernandez Chuy presented his accounts for his two cacicazgos, Pucarani and Laxa. He stated that the income from cacical and communal lands was tiny: just forty-five pesos a year. However, he was engaged in four lawsuits over communal land: three for Laxa, all with Spanish hacendados, and one for Pucarani, with the pueblo of Pariamanya. All told, he claimed to have spent 856 pesos in just two years, and the expense was bankrupting him.[83] Caciques' claims about the poverty of communal property are always suspect, but the legal fees are not unusual.[84]

The importance of such legal service to the community in establishing a family's claim to rule across the generations emerges in the successful defense of Pucyura's claim to its mill undertaken in the 1740s by Don Miguel Ñancay. Ñancay's sons alluded specifically to this when petitioning to study at Cusco's College of San Borja:

It is very important to make clear the services of our father Don Miguel Ñancay, who died being cacique and Governor of the Ayllu Tique Collana and Ayarmaca Tamboconga in the service of Your Majesty (may God protect Him), and who defended a mill the rent of which at present serves the Sacred Church of this pueblo and also helps with the royal tribute. Dr. Don Miguel de Hermosa attempted to appropriate the said mill, and in the two voyages that our father made to the

---

82 In addition to the cases discussed later, BNP, Man., C-4221 for Caycay; also the 1754 complaint by Don Cayetano Tupa Guamanrimachi against Don Bernardo Gongora, ARC, COR, Ped., Leg. 90 (1753–65).

83 ANB, Ruck, Exp. 217, 149v-152v.

84 Also ARC, NOT, Garcia Rios, Leg. 182, 1101 ff., May 30, 1756; ARC, INT., Ord., Legs. 33 and 34 (1794); and ARC, RA, Ord., Leg. 59 (1807) for the defense of Colquepata's lands, first by Marcos Chiguantupa and then by his daughter, Martina; and the authority that it brought.

city of Lima he won the mill for his pueblo in a countersuit. In consideration of these services the governor Don Pedro Julian Puma Ynga, principal cacique and proprietary governor of Anta, never allowed that we be burdened with the payment of tribute as is well-known in the pueblo.[85]

In undertaking the defense of the mill, Miguel Ñancay confirmed his family's claims in a number of arenas. Pucyura acknowledged the deference owed to the Ñancay throughout the next century, as Miguel's descendants and their spouses occupied important offices in the pueblo and held the lease on the mill.[86] The powerful cacique of Anta – of which Pucyura was an annex – also affirmed the family's special standing, and the support of such a cacique could be decisive in local struggles. Finally, that the sons of Ñancay made so much of their father's lawsuit in their petition to enter San Borja reminds us that to Spanish officials such service was an ideal performance of cacical authority. The journey and the lawsuit cost hundreds of pesos, a large sum for an ayllu cacique (albeit with an Inca pedigree). But it was a wise investment. Ñancay became the cacique who had appeared before the royal audiencia of Lima and successfully defended his community. In the eyes of all, he had behaved as the perfect cacique, a fact the family was quick to point out in their successful bid to retain authority in Pucyura.

Caciques could also use the defense of communal property to cripple rivals by reclaiming lands ceded in earlier generations. In 1767 Don Juan Aymituma of Sicuani's Ayllu Quehuar went to court against Don Mathias Fernandez Pillaca over the lands of Aguascalientes.[87] Mathias, the former cacique and, according to himself, a legitimate claimant to the office, had inherited the lands from his father, Francisco, to whom the corregidor of Canas y Canchis had awarded them in 1713, after he had defended them from Don Manuel Solorzano, a cacique of Ñuñoa. Aymituma argued that Francisco had received the land as cacique, and that it now should pass to him; Mathias claimed that the land had gone to his father as private property, thence to Mathias. The conflict was not about the cacicazgo per se: Mathias made no claim to the office. However, by turning to the courts as the defender of the commons, the current cacique could impoverish a rival family, with a strong claim to the cacicazgo should Mathias's heirs choose to seek it.

Whatever the specific motives driving a cacique's defense of communal lands, that they took charge of their communities' legal disputes is a reminder that caciques were among the few Indians in rural communities with the requisite literacy, and knowledge of Spanish courts and laws, to

---

85 "Indios de sangre real," pp. 211–12.
86 Chapter 4, p. 125.
87 ARC, COR, Prov., Civ., Leg. 72 (1766–9).

undertake such an effort. That the information about Miguel Ñancay's journey to Lima is found among the proofs of nobility presented by students at Cusco's San Borja College points out the close tie between cacical authority and Spanish education.[88] Many of the caciques discussed in this work were alumni of San Borja – above all, those drawn from the Inca lineages around Cusco. A number of cacical families from the southern reaches of the bishopric also sent their sons to the college.[89] In the mid-eighteenth century cacical families from more than 100 miles from Cusco turned elsewhere to educate their sons – to non-Indian colleges in Cusco, or to La Paz or Chuquisaca.[90] The effect was the same: caciques educated in the highland cities' colleges served the goals of Spanish colonialism by the example and the enforcement of reasonably orthodox religious practice, and by their knowledge of the basic laws of Spanish Peru. The organization of colonial society thus confirmed the legitimacy of an educated Indian elite by making it simultaneously an instrument of Spanish colonialism and the mechanism by which Indian communities – whose preservation was essential to their continued exploitation – were defended.

The unusually detailed inventory of the possessions of the cacical couple of Pucarani, Don Fausto Xauregui Colque and Doña Rafaela Tito Atauchi, lists their library.[91] With fifty volumes their holdings were exceptional among the cacical elite.[92] They do, however, shed light on the intellectual world of the highest ranks of the Indian elite, and of the colonial highlands generally. Above all, the couple's books showed the still-central role of the Spanish counter-Reformation in colonial intellectual life. Three quarters of the books were religious: breviaries, lives of saints, missals, St. Augustine's *Confessions*. The couple had two lives of St. Ignatius (one in Latin), a life of

---

88 The urban Incas were fairly literate: eighteen of the twenty-four electors assembled for the 1789 cabildo election could sign their names, the majority with an educated hand. ARC, COR, Civ., Leg. 29, Exp. 620. Also ARC, CAB, Civ., Leg. 44, Exp. 1056, for a document witnessed and signed by five Inca noblemen from Maras. RREE, PRA, Exp. 342, for a 1797 request by nobles and principales of Azángaro; half a dozen signed, some illegibly.

89 For San Borja, and student lists, see Chapter 3, n31.

90 Apolino Xavier Xauregui Colque of Pucarani studied in Chuquisaca; his sister at a convent in La Paz. ANB, EC, 1773–83, 16v. Pedro Mango Turpa of Azángaro Urinsaya studied at San Antonio Abad in Cusco; Gregorio Choquehuanca of Azángaro Anansaya at Cusco's San Bernardo. RREE, PSG, Exp. 149; Altuve Carillo, *Choquehuanca*, p. 67.

91 ANB, EC, 1773–83, 22–50.

92 Only one of more than 150 Indian wills from Cusco between 1750 and 1825 lists books; intriguingly, it is of Martina Chiguantupa, the cacica of Colquepata. She was educated in Cusco's Santa Teresa convent; as she proudly noted in 1785, "... estoi instruida en ambas idiomas indico y español, y saber leer y escribir por la buena educcacion que me dieron mis padres." According to an 1801 will, she owned seven religious books. ARC, NOT: Ayesta, Leg. 46, 405 ff., December 7, 1801; Arrias Lira, Leg. 41, 540 ff., September 24, 1785. Gabriel Cama Condorsayna, cacique of Macarí, owned "quatro libros de varios autores." ARC, JC, Leg. 18 (1830).

Santa Teresa, Mother Agreda's *Mystical City of God*, and, most strikingly, "a book of the life of Christ in Aymara," illustrating their role as the connection between the Latin of Peru's classrooms, the Spanish of its administration, and the Aymara of the pueblo church.[93]

Not all of their books were religious: the couple's library also shows the cacique's role as the community's legal defender.[94] These included three works of composition and rhetoric, allowing them to move more gracefully and persuasively in literate Peru and to distinguish themselves from the semiliterate Indian officials whose petitions and complaints could verge on incomprehensible. The couple also owned the standard four-volume Laws of the Indies, a book of Royal Ordinances, and one of laws of jurisprudence in Latin. With these Xauregui Colque could mount defenses against attempts to collect alcabala on the sale of the communal harvest, or against a corregidor's interference in cacical succession. The well educated among the Indian elite had not only the basic tools with which to appeal to the courts, but also a knowledge of the privileges and protections that colonial law afforded them and their communities.

Nor did educated caciques defend only their communities' interests. Spanish society and courts in colonial Peru gave enormous deference to legal and notarized documents. While such papers never entered the lives of the great majority of colonial Peru's Indian population, for the nobility and cacical elite these documents were crucial to their self-definition and their privileged position. Patents of nobility issued by Charles I (and their notarized copies), wills, deeds, confirmations of office, and bits of lawsuits all served to confirm the legal and material position of the Indian nobility. This was as true for the Inca blood nobility of Cusco as for cacical families, and a number of wills make specific mention of titles of nobility.[95] For both nobles and caciques, such documents asserted their claims in an idiom and through a medium that were singularly persuasive to Spanish judges. But for caciques, the possession and management of documents relating to communal claims also bolstered their position in their pueblos.

Most wills and inventories simply mention "instrumentos" and "papeles" in passing, but those who made the Xauregui Colque–Tito Atauchi inventory were meticulous, detailing over five hundred separate lots including papers.[96] In addition to records of debts, the couple had a forty-one-page

93 ANB, EC, 1773–83, 39–40.
94 Ibid. They also had a book each of music, arithmetic, and comedies; and the works of Quevedo.
95 For example, Don Miguel Quispe Amau and Doña Polonia Ynquiltupa. ARC, NOT: Rodriguez Ledezma, Leg. 246, 546 ff., March 1, 1793; Garcia Rios, Leg. 182, 1067 ff., May 13, 1759. For others, Garrett, "Descendants," pp. 373–4, n112.
96 ANB, EC, 1773–83, 31–3.

confirmation of Fausto's claim to the cacicazgo and another seven pages declaring him *maestre de campo* in the provincial regiment. They had titles to their private properties (houses in La Paz and ranches in Omasuyos), confirmed both by notarized sales and, for one ranch, by a thirty-six-page *composición de tierras*. Other family papers included a copy of the cacical papers of Raphaela's father, Don Guillen Tito Atauchi, as well as an inventory of Guillen's estate and one of Fausto's father's estate. A clear reminder of the Tito Atauchi's illustrious ancestry, they also had three pages of "testimony that speaks of the privileges of the Yngas of this Realm." Finally, they had in their possession a royal provision exempting Pucarani's Indians from tithes, and papers that confirmed the restitution of the estancia of Chipamaya to the commons of the pueblo. Armed with these papers, the couple and their heirs could prove their claim to rule Pucarani and their privileges as Incas; they could defend their legitimacy within the pueblo by proving its exemption from tithes and its possession of Chipamaya; and they could maintain their own claims to property throughout the bishopric. Such written documents made it far easier to preserve property, office, and status across generations. Indeed, it is small wonder that these bundles of paper were a target when rebel forces, and local mobs, stormed cacical mansions during the Great Rebellion.

The various cacicazgo titles and the recognition of Inca privilege did more than simply affirm the legal rights of Xauregui Colque and Tito Atauchi: they confirmed their noble – indeed, royal – ancestry. Certainly cacical families' insistence on their hereditary claims to office aimed to sway Spanish judges. But the Indian societies of the highlands also had a clear regard for lineage and hereditary hierarchies. The frequency of calumnies against the ancestry of rival claimants for cacicazgos, or caciques accused of abuses, suggests that a crucial source of legitimacy within Indian communities came from the family into which one was born. The 1800 case against Blas Quispe Uscamayta and Manuel Corimanya, ayllu caciques in Pucyura, shows the power of ancestry in local politics. In describing their position in the pueblo, the subdelegate of Abancay reported that ". . . the two are related to all of the principales [of Pucyura] and are almost worshipped by the commoners, on the strength of certain documents of nobility . . . of which they boast vainly, and in particular [Corimanya] . . . Corimanya, [though] of a humble and inconsequential exterior, it would seem is of a character too proud and self-important, [and] has managed to win for himself among his people the renown of "Inca" . . ."[97] Both Quispe Uscamayta and Corimanya claimed descent from the Inca emperors.[98] In 1800, the subdelegate

97 ARC, INT, RH, Leg. 211 (1801), 35–6.
98 ARC, RA, Adm., Leg. 156 (1797); ARC, NOT, Pedro Joaquin Gamarra, Leg. 77, 584 ff., August 16, 1804.

viewed this as reason to depose them: just twenty years after the highlands exploded in revolt behind the self-proclaimed "Inca" Tupac Amaru, any governor was wary of those who boasted of Inca ancestry. However, from the sixteenth century until 1780 such ancestry bolstered cacical pretensions in Spanish eyes. According to the subdelegate, it also bolstered them within the community. Strikingly, the performance of ancestral authority involved the display of documents of nobility.

Disputes over succession make clear the importance of ancestry to cacical legitimacy. When Francisca Chuquimia belittled the claims of Copacabana's cacique, Don Manuel Chuquimia, insisting that "he has taken the name Chuquimia without being one, but rather the descendant of some Uros Indian fishermen who since their ancestors would not even have dreamed of being *principales* [and] *jilakatas* of Indians," she exposed indigenous hierarchies that coexisted with Spanish understandings of rank.[99] While no others matched the displays of Cusco's Inca nobility, throughout the highlands caciques stressed the birthright of their noble ancestry. In the Choquehuanca mansion in Azángaro a stone tower reputedly built by a preconquest lord and ancestor of the family stood in the front patio.[100] This affirmation of a family's timeless rule was probably unique, but throughout the southern highlands caciques routinely referred to their descent from Huayna Capac or from one of the Aymara lords: Apo Cari for the cacical houses of Chucuito, Apo Guarachi for the Fernandez Guarachi of Machaca. The Guarachi also claimed descent from Huayna Capac; a 1734 Guarachi will mentions a painting of the Inca and Spanish monarchs of Peru, and later in the century the family commissioned a series of the twelve Inca monarchs.[101] Along with the repeated affirmations that the family's rule stretched back centuries, portraits of the Incas that awed petitioners in the cacical mansion affirmed the Guarachi's power before their community just as the wills, patents of nobility, and notarized genealogies affirmed it in the eyes of Spanish officials.

Cacical ancestors and noble blood were not sufficient in themselves to guarantee possession of a cacicazgo. Many communities had more than one such family who might produce a claimant, and these could themselves change: the seventeenth-century dislocations created considerable dynamism within the social hierarchies of the Indian republic. For every cacical house that could document its descent from preconquest *curacas* or the Inca royalty, there was another whose claims became quite murky when traced back just two or three generations. But assertions of hereditary

99 ANB, Ruck, Exp. 217, 17. For an Aymara noble, there was no greater insult.

100 Altuve Carrillo, *Choquehuanca*, pp. 31, 81–2.

101 For Apocari, ANB, EC, 1793–11, 1. For Apo Guarachi, Diane Fane, ed., *Converging Cultures: Art and Identity in Spanish America* (New York: Harry N. Abrams, 1996), p. 238.

nobility, whatever form they might take, served to set the cacique, and other nobles, apart from the community as a whole.[102] As we have seen, this genealogical distance between the Indian commons and the nobility was then reinforced by the marriage patterns of the latter.

Finally, the Indian elite set itself off from the Indian commons by the conspicuous possession and consumption of elite goods, and the hosting of celebrations. Cacical houses' huge flocks of sheep and holdings of land served as stores and producers of wealth, and economically were the most important parts of their property. But other forms of cacical property had considerable symbolic value. Once again, the detailed inventory of Xauregui Colque and Tito Atauchi provides an excellent window into pueblo life and the manner in which the cacical elite displayed their wealth.[103] When the couple died in 1756, they left an estate worth 12,000 pesos, which included some 700 pesos in clothing. By the 1750s, the garb of a rich cacique was virtually interchangeable with that of a wealthy hacendado or provincial governor: Fausto had a beaver hat trimmed with silver, several jackets of high quality wool, wool breeches, and so on. Indian noblewomen wore a mixture of Spanish and Indian vestments in lavish fabrics. Raphaela had many skirts of velvet, wool, and taffeta, along with *llicllas* embroidered with silver and gold thread.[104] To this was added jewelry.[105] Any Indian woman used a large brooch (topo) to close her lliclla. Those of pueblo elites and poorer nobles were of silver, those of the high nobility were of gold. Earrings, rosaries, crucifixes, rings, and brooches of gold and silver set with emeralds, diamonds, topazes, pearls, and glass also made the standing and wealth of the Indian nobility clearly visible to all.

Caciques also owned saddle mules, which served as transportation but also to display authority and wealth. Xauregui Colque and Tito Atauchi had a silver-trimmed saddle and silver stirrups worth 200 pesos, the entire wealth of a prosperous tributary. Xauregui Colque also owned three muskets, whose possession and use clearly set the upper reaches of the Indian

---

102 For an idea of how the Indian nobility internalized this division, see the letter by Don Felix Tupa Guamanrimachi, an Inca cacique in San Sebastián, to his son Mariano (a painter), in jail for his "bad nature and criminal deeds" – and not for the first time. Felix forgave him, but urged him "que te portes como Yndio Noble ... dejando tus malos bisios." ARC, RA, Crim., Leg. 129 (1803).

103 ANB, EC, 1773–83, 38–51. ADP, INT, Exp. 51, for Choquehuanca.

104 Wealthy urban Incas dressed even more grandly. Among Doña Josefa Cusipaucar Loyola's clothes were a skirt appraised at 130 pesos and a velvet *lliclla* worth 100 pesos. ARC, RA, Ord., Leg. 22 (1796).

105 Xauregui Colque and Tito Atauchi had three gold crucifixes, three coral rosaries (one with pearls), a gold topo, three pairs of gold and pearl earrings, and two gold rings. Josefa Cusipaucar Loyola owned two gold topos, three pairs of gold earrings, two gold clasps, two chokers, a gold cross, and eight rings.

nobility apart from their pueblos.[106] So too did cacical mansions, their size and grandeur reflecting the power of the family as well as the size and wealth of the community. Around Titicaca two-story houses had ten or more rooms, two patios, and internal balconies. They were modestly furnished: that in Pucarani had a dozen chairs, several benches and tables, a bed (with valuable bedclothes), and many chests and small writing boxes. The most important household furnishings were religious paintings and statues: roughly two dozen paintings in gilt frames and a statue of Our Lady of the Conception housed in a mirrored niche and appraised at 100 pesos. The expense of such images showed the family's wealth; more importantly, to Spaniards they indicated their Christian faith. To the people of Pucarani, the canvases and statues were the semidivines that protected families and ayllus from the harshness of life in the colonial Andes; the number and lavishness of those in the cacical house gave the family a privileged position in the pueblo's religious geography.[107] Finally, the couple owned twenty-two pounds of silverware, which, in the cash-starved Titicaca basin, was widely used in lieu of cash to settle debts and secure loans. Such grandeur was exceptional, the prerogative of only a few dozen Indian households in the bishopric. But all cacical couples displayed the marks of their status: with a velvet jacket, a lliclla embroidered with silver thread, a tile roof on a two-story, four-room adobe house, a few gilt frames with paintings of the saints. Clothing and furnishings were the material marks of nobility, reinforcing the rank and privileges of the Indian elite in the eyes of Spaniards as well as of Indians.

The wealth accumulated by cacical families also allowed – required – them to assert their importance in the public celebrations of familial events: above all funerals and weddings. For the nobility there was no more important or opportune moment to assert standing than a funeral. Certainly priests used funerals to extort money from their parishioners; the subject was a matter of endless complaint.[108] However, those with money spent lavishly on the ritual: the funeral of Xauregui Colque and Tito Atauchi cost 400 pesos.[109] This paled next to the rites for Asencio Ramos Tito Atauchi in Cusco in 1750, which cost 1,000 pesos: one-tenth of the couple's fortune.[110] The greater expense reflects the social competition of the city, where many Inca nobles competed among themselves, and with the

---

106 Joseph Tamboguacso of Taray had a sword, two pistols, and two muskets. ARC, Pedro Joseph Gamarra, Leg. 169, 672 ff., June 3, 1761. Don Esteban Pumahuallpa Garses Chillitupa of Zurite owned an "espadin viejo de fierro." ARC, INT, Ord., Leg. 4 (1785).

107 The quantity of religious paintings and statues listed in almost any Indian will suggests continuity between these and *conopas* of Andean religion. For conopas, Mills, *Idolatry*, pp. 75–100.

108 AAC, VI-I-18b, for an exceptionally interesting case.

109 ANB, EC, 1773–83, 63v.

110 ARC, NOT, Juan Bautista Gamarra, Leg. 133, [ ], August 26, 1755.

city's creole population, for standing. As the principal cacique in the parish of Santa Ana, a Sergeant Major in the Indian regiment, an Inca elector, former *alférez real*, and descendant of Huayna Capac, Asencio required such an extravagant funeral.[111] So did his family, to show its wealth and assert its importance at its most vulnerable moment, the death of its patriarch. Weddings also involved a costly show. When the couple's daughter Maria married Nicolas Sahuaraura, the festivities cost 200 pesos.[112] Sahuaraura was also from the upper ranks of the Inca nobility: the heir to a cacicazgo in Santiago parish, he would succeed his father-in-law as the commissioner of Cusco's regiment of Indian nobles. Their union demanded such pomp.[113]

Lavish weddings and funerals, bonds of kinship with Spaniards and other Indian nobles, dress and household furnishings, ease at communicating in Spanish and knowledge of Spanish law, patronage and defense of their communities – all of these set the upper ranks of the Indian elite apart from the Indian commons. Historians have argued that in asserting this difference through Spanish education and the use of Spanish luxury goods and Spanish dress, caciques became increasingly hispanicized, thereby producing a cultural conflict between cacique and commons that mirrored the class conflict implicit in the organization of the pueblo economy.[114] This discussion suggests a more complex process. Social hierarchies and material stratification had been integral to Andean society long before the arrival of the Spanish.[115] Colonialism created a new logic for this stratification and provided new forms of material and symbolic capital to underpin it. This did not undermine the authority of local elites or the legitimacy attached to it. The remarks by Abancay's subdelegate about Quispe Uscamayta and Corimanya show the complex hierarchies of the late colonial Andean pueblos. These were not only material: the property of Quispe Uscamayta and Corimanya made clear their rank as pueblo prominents, but did not set them above their community in wealth.[116] Rather, their lineages, their marriages, their histories of service to and authority in the community, their literacy, and the respect given to them by Spanish officials and other Indian nobles, coupled with material display, reinforced their rank in Pucyura.

---

111 For detailed accounts of funeral expenses, see the 1808 dispute over the estate of Doña Francisca Xaviera Asarpay. ARC, INT, Ord., Leg. 65 (1808). Also ARC, CAB, Civ., Leg. 51, Exp. 1189, for Don Jose Flores Apotumayo's funeral.

112 Maria Vazquez Obando's will. ARC, Juan Bautista Gamarra, Leg. 133, [ ], August 26, 1755.

113 ARC, NOT, Acuña, Leg. 10, 383 ff., September 11, 1774, for Flores Apotumayo weddings.

114 Stern, *Peru's Indian Peoples*, pp. 167–72; Virgilio Galdo Gutiérrez, *Educación de los curacas: una forma de dominación colonial* (Ayacucho: Ediciones Waman Puma, 1970); Rasnake, *Domination*, pp. 121–3; Spalding, "Social Climbers."

115 D'Altroy, *Provincial Power*; Bauer, *Development*.

116 For Quispe Uscamayta's and Corimanya's property, see Chapter 4, p. 133.

The same was true throughout the bishopric, as every pueblo had its Indian elite. Their authority and privilege did not go uncontested. However ancient his lineage, no cacique was above challenge either from within his community or from Spanish officials; conversely, the able performance of cacical duties could strengthen the hereditary claims of a new family. The dynamism of cacical succession and local hierarchies did not in itself render illegitimate cacical authority. The structural role of the cacique in the colonial pueblo made the office necessary, while creating expectations and possibilities of cacical performance that themselves produced and legitimized power. At the same time, this discussion of cacical authority has drawn its evidence from the three or four decades preceding the Tupac Amaru rebellion of 1780–3. The sources precluded examination of the legitimacy of the office itself. The royal courts upheld the office of cacique, and so plaintiffs did not argue that a community ought not to have a cacique; they simply argued about who should be cacique. This does not mean that the existence of a privileged Indian elite was universally accepted in the Indian republic. In the Titicaca basin, the rebellions of the early 1780s ignited smoldering class conflicts within Indian communities. The Indian nobility and the cacicazgo, seemingly timeless parts of Andean society, would come under direct attack, never to recover. To this crisis of the colonial order we now turn.

PART III

Crisis and Collapse

6

From Reform to Rebellion

On November 4, 1780, Don Jose Gabriel Tupac Amaru seized Don Antonio de Arriaga, Tinta's corregidor, as he passed through Tungasuca, of which Tupac Amaru was cacique. For the next six days Tupac Amaru imprisoned Arriaga, while a huge crowd assembled in the pueblo; proclamations were read denouncing Arriaga and claiming that "[t]hrough the King it has been ordered that there no longer be sales tax, customs, or the Potosí *mita* and that Don Antonio Arriaga lose his life because of his harmful behavior."[1] Tupac Amaru forced the corregidor to send for weapons and money so that the cacique and his followers were well armed; then, on November 10, Arriaga was hung in front of the crowd. Tupac Amaru and his troops headed north down the Vilcanota valley, reaching Quiquijana in two days and sacking the *obraje* of Pomacanchis on their way. Caciques from nearby pueblos actively joined, or were caught up in, the rebellion, and the forces grew dramatically as they went.[2] The upper Vilcanota was in open rebellion.

Receiving news of Arriaga's execution on November 12, the Cusco *cabildo* sent a regiment to quash the rebellion. At the forefront were Cusco's Inca nobles, who rejected Tupac Amaru almost to a one; so too would their peers around Titicaca.[3] Indeed, the irony of Inca (and other Indian noble)

---

1 Quoted in Walker, *Smoldering Ashes*, p. 35. For accounts of the Rebellion, ibid., pp. 16–54; Boleslao Lewin, *Túpac Amaru el rebelde: su época, sus luchas y su influencia en el continente* (Buenos Aires: Editorial Claridad, 1943); Lillian E. Fisher, *The Last Inca Revolt, 1780–1783* (Norman: University of Oklahoma Press, 1966); O'Phelan Godoy, *Un siglo*, pp. 223–87; and AGI, Cuzco, Leg. 63.

2 Almost all caciques in the bishopric of Cusco implicated in the rebellion were from neighboring parishes: Tomasa Tito Condemayta of Acos, Acomayo, and Sangarará (the only Indian noble executed along with Tupac Amaru and his family), *CDBR*, III, pp. 324–65; Lucas Collque of Pomacanchis; *CDBR*, III, pp. 935–55; Joseph Mamani of Tinta; *CDBR*, IV, pp. 515–55; Fernando Urpide and Agustin Aucagualpa of Pirque; *CDBR*, IV, pp. 477–513; Miguel Zamalloa of Sicuani; *CDBR*, V, pp. 395–428. For those prosecuted for the rebellion, O'Phelan Godoy, *Un siglo*, pp. 308–20.

3 Almost no Inca nobles were implicated in the rebellion; the principal exception, Luis Poma Ynga of Quiquijana, was hung by del Valle when Tinta fell. *CDBR*, III, pp. 300–1, 448; AGI, Cuzco, Leg. 63, 2. Only two of Cusco's Inca nobles were tried. Juan de Dios Inca Roca was accused of gathering recruits for Tupac Amaru. Inca Roca and San Sebastián's priest both testified that he was simply an Inca noble involved in the lamb trade caught in Sicuani at the outbreak of the rebellion; he had told

loyalty to the crown is striking, and this chapter attempts to explain it. That loyalty was not for want of appeals from Tupac Amaru: as he marched down the Vilcanota he sent letters – alternately cajoling and threatening – to leading Inca nobles and highland caciques asking them to join him.[4] Pedro Sahuaraura, a cacique in Oropesa and the commissary of the Indian nobles, immediately forwarded his to the bishop, saying that "I leave marching with my people in search of the rebel, the infamous Jose Tupa Amaro, cacique of Tungascua, who deserves an exemplary punishment for the perpetual discouragement of others."[5] Sahuaraura and the city's Indian nobility joined royalist forces led by Don Tiburcio Landa and met Tupac Amaru at Sangarará on November 19. The rebels routed the royalists; Sahuaraura was killed, and the pueblo church was torched, killing those who had sought refuge inside. So began the largest rebellion against Spanish rule in the Americas between the conquest and the wars of independence. The rebellion started by Tupac Amaru lasted three years, largely because it converged with and fed an interrelated series of rebellions in Upper Peru, first sparked in Potosí in 1780.[6] When royalist troops crushed the last remnants in 1783, tens of thousands were dead; the destruction of property was correspondingly great. The rebellion provoked a rethinking of the colonial order by Spanish officials, with disastrous effects for the Indian nobility. More broadly, the forces and fears unleashed by the rebellion are viewed, variously, as prime factors in the highland struggles for independence in 1810 and 1815, or for the failure of these struggles.

Over the past half-century, while differing on its causes and goals, historians have agreed in viewing the rebellion as an extraordinary rupture in the colonial order and as both product and cause of social and economic transformation.[7] Generally the "Great Rebellion" or series of rebellions from Cusco

---

Micaela Bastidas that he was an Inca cacique and would rally troops only so that she would release him. He received a year of exile in Callao. *CDBR*, IV, pp. 188–208. Jacinto Inquiltupa, a cacique in Santa Ana accused of receiving letters from Tupac Amaru, was absolved. *CDBR*, III, pp. 820–30.

4 *CDBR*, I, pp. 455–6, 513–23; III, pp. 122, 127.

5 *CDBR*, I, p. 111.

6 Thomson, *We Alone*; Penry, "Transformations"; María Eugenia del Valle de Siles, *Historia de la rebelión de Túpac Catari, 1781–2* (La Paz: Editorial Don Bosco, 1990); O'Phelan Godoy, *Un siglo*, pp. 257–87; Leon Campbell, "Ideology and Factionalism during the Great Rebellion, 1780–1782," in *Resistance, Rebellion and Consciousness in the Andean Peasant World, 18th to 20th Centuries*, ed. Steve J. Stern (Madison: University of Wisconsin Press, 1987), pp. 110–39.

7 For literature reviews, Jean Piel, "Cómo interpretar la rebelión panandina de 1780–1783," in *Tres Levantamientos Populares: Pugachöv, Túpac Amaru, Hildago*, ed. Jean Meyer (Mexico: CEMCA, 1992), pp. 71–80; Walker, *Smoldering Ashes*, pp. 17–22. For interpretations of Tupac Amaru and the rebellion as precursors of independence, Lewin, *Túpac Amaru*; Jorge Cornejo Bouroncle, *Túpac Amaru, la revolución precursora de la emancipación continental* (Cusco: Universidad Nacional San Antonio Abad, 1947); Daniel Valcárcel, *Túpac Amaru, precursor de la Independencia* (Lima: Universidad Nacional de San

to Chuquisaca is seen as the culmination of decades of profound social change and growing discontent. The groundbreaking studies of Golte, O'Phelan Godoy, and Stavig located causation in the increased tributary demands and economic disruption of the Bourbon Reforms, and in the disruption of an established Andean "moral economy."[8] More recently, Thomson and Serulnikov have argued that change and conflict within indigenous communities in the mid-1700s were at least as important as a sense of grievance at the state's material demands.[9] Such findings also highlight the pronounced difference in the distinct geographical and temporal stages of "the" rebellion, particularly between the traditional goals of Tupac Amaru's rebellion and the more radical agenda of the Tupac Catari rebellion in La Paz, which took on the characteristics of a social revolution by targeting rural elites and their property.[10]

Recent scholarship has also exposed the complexities of allegiance among the indigenous population and problematized the simple Indian–Spanish dichotomy. O'Phelan Godoy, Mörner, Trelles, and Campbell first demonstrated that much of the leadership of the Peruvian (Tupac Amaru) stage of the rebellion was creole, and that the overwhelming majority of the Indian elite, along with much of the Indian peasantry near Cusco, did not join in the rebellion.[11] Several works have since directly addressed the role of indigenous elites in the rebellion, and in so doing have expanded our understanding of the complex dynamics that drove it, and the hierarchies and tensions of Bourbon society more generally. O'Phelan's work has posited a

---

Marcos, 1977); Luis Durand Flórez, *Independencia e integración en el plan político de Túpac Amaru* (Lima: Editorial P.L.V., 1974). In contrast, John Rowe and others have viewed the rebellion as an indigenous rejection of both colonial and Spanish–American rule. John H. Rowe, "El movimiento" and *Quechua Nationalism*; L. E. Fisher, *The Last Inca Revolt*; Alberto Flores Galindo, *Buscando un Inca*; Jan Szeminski, *La Utopia Tupamarista* and "Why Kill the Spaniard? New Perspectives on Andean Insurrectionary Ideology in the 18th Century," in *Resistance, Rebellion*, pp. 166–92; Leon Campbell, "Ideology and Factionalism." Building on this, others place the rebellion as the culmination of an "Age of Andean Insurrection" when violent rejection of the colonial order by Peru's indigenous peoples was endemic, which stands in counterpoint to the creole anticolonialism of the wars of independence. O'Phelan Godoy, *Un siglo*; Stern, "Age of Andean Insurrection"; Spalding, *Huarochirí*, pp. 270–93; Walker, *Smoldering Ashes*, pp. 50–4.

8 Golte, *Repartos*; O'Phelan Godoy, *Un siglo*. Stavig, *The World of Túpac Amaru*, especially pp. 207–56. Also, John R. Fisher, "La rebelión de Tupac Amaru y el programa imperial de Carlos III," in *Túpac Amaru II – 1780: sociedad colonial y sublevaciones populares*, ed. Alberto Flores Galindo (Lima: Retablo de Papel, 1976), pp. 109–28.

9 Thomson, *We Alone*; Serulnikov, *Subverting Colonial Authority*; also Penry, "Transformations."

10 Campbell, "Ideology and Factionalism"; O'Phelan Godoy, *Un siglo*; Thomson, *We Alone*; Serulnikov, *Subverting Colonial Authority*; Penry, "Tranformations."

11 O'Phelan Godoy, *Un siglo*; Campbell, "Social Structure" Magnus Mörner and Efraín Trelles, "The Test of Causal Interpretations of the Túpac Amaru Rebellion," in *Resistance, Rebellion*, pp. 94–109.

loyalism (and rejection of "the Inca Nationalist Movement of the eighteenth century") among the indigenous elite that she attributes to royal recognition of claims of Inca ancestry and proprietary rights to cacicazgos, as well as entry into the church and military by Indian nobles.[12] Glave and Stavig have focused on the particular case of Eugenio Sinanyuca, the powerful loyalist cacique of Coporaque, and in so doing revealed the central importance of Tinta's provincial politics in the development of a "pan-Andean" rebellion.[13] Working on the bishopric of La Paz, Choque Canqui and Thomson have also examined the pronounced loyalism of the cacical elite there; in particular, Thomson has analyzed the radicalization of the Tupac Catari rebellion in light of the region's socioeconomic structure, and the resultant division between the cacical elite and their communities.[14]

In that, while acknowledging larger structural preconditions that united the regions involved in the "Great Rebellion," such studies have moved to the fore the variety of local and regional politics in the indigenous societies of the late colonial south Andes, and their centrality to the development and trajectory of the rebellion. Most significantly, Thomson, Serulnikov, and Penry have exposed the complex dynamics of popular politics in Upper Peru. This chapter focuses instead on Cusco, and on elite, indigenous politics before and during Tupac Amaru's great challenge to Spanish authority. In particular, it explores the political beliefs and practices of the Inca nobility in the mid- to late-eighteenth century, examining their own complex relationship to royal authority and its agents and competing ideologies of Inca privilege and exceptionalism within the bishopric. Such a focus on politics and ideology within the Indian republic helps to illuminate the social geography of the rebellion, and to expose the interaction of local politics and the larger regional political economy in a way that highlights the political complexity of the Indian republic.

In its organization, initial success, and scope, the Great Rebellion stands apart; and certainly by Sangarará the enormity of the uprising was apparent. But in its initial stages the rebellion followed a pattern increasingly common in the bishopric during the preceding decades. Arriaga was not the first corregidor to lose his life to an angry crowd of his subjects: O'Phelan Godoy has counted more than 100 riots and rebellions in the viceroyalty of Peru from 1700 to 1780.[15] Most resemble the Mexican village riots described by Taylor, which were directed against specific grievances (and

12 O'Phelan Godoy, "Repensando" and *La Gran Rebelión*, pp. 47–68.
13 Glave, *Vida, símbolos*, pp. 136–52; and Stavig, "Eugenio Sinanyuca."
14 Roberto Choque Canqui, "Los caciques frente a la rebelión de Túpak Katari en La Paz," *Historia y Cultura* 19 (Lima, 1991): 83–93; and Thomson, *We Alone*, especially pp. 222–31.
15 In 1777, the corregidor of Chumbivilcas was killed when he jailed a cacique, and Urubamba had anti-corregidor riots; in 1770 the house of Arriaga's predecessor was burned by an angry mob. And others: O'Phelan Godoy, *Un siglo*, pp. 296–305.

particular officials) but not intended, nor understood by the crown, as challenges to Spanish rule.[16] In Upper Peru, caciques were frequent targets of this violence, but in Cusco it was directed more against corregidores and their assistants, a sign of widespread anger at the *reparto* and the expansion of tributary rolls in the 1760s and 1770s. Indeed, such riots could enjoy the tacit support of local elites, suggesting a widespread sympathy in rural society for opposition to these exactions and the existence of a "moral economy" that united broad sectors of rural society.[17] Decrying perceived abuses of power by royal officials, these rebellions nonetheless did so through appeals (however violent) to the crown to redress grievances. To the extent that the Tupac Amaru rebellion was a local riot spun out of control, these are its forebears.

Whatever its Andean aspirations, the rebellion was also driven by the particular frustrations of the highlands south of Cusco. The provinces at its core – Quispicanchis, Tinta, and Chumbivilcas – were uniquely illserved by the Bourbon Reforms, and it is telling that the rebellion failed to take hold closer to Cusco, where the same conditions did not apply. All three contributed to distant mining mitas; indeed, the rebellions from 1780 to 1783 were a mass rising of the area subject to the Potosí mita. Adding the reparto and tribute, the colonial burdens on these provinces were unusually heavy. Tinta and Chumbivilcas had grown disproportionately in the eighteenth century, with the Indian population doubling and the Spanish increasing thirtyfold.[18] The 1776 division of the viceroyalty hurt the trade with Altiplano markets that was the compensatory benefit of the annual migrations to Potosí, and the rebellion drew heavily from *arrieros*.[19] While the 1760s and 1770s saw an increase of open discontent, the Vilcanota and Apurímac highlands were a focal point; as we saw in Chapter 5, cacical politics there were particularly contentious. From 1768 to 1780, all but two riots in the bishopric were in these three provinces, and each had at least one substantial anti-corregidor riot.[20] Conflict was also building within communities. Sinanyuca's appointment as cacique had provoked tumult in Coporaque in 1768, and through the 1770s terrible relations between Sinanyuca and the priest kept the town tense.[21] Similarly, the largest pueblo

---

16 Taylor, *Drinking, Homicide*, pp. 113–70; Thomson, Penry, and Serulnikov have challenged treating such rebellions as discrete episodes and have instead explored the larger anticolonial projects they suggest.

17 Priests were notoriously active in local tumults. Glave, *Vida, símbolos*, pp. 117–52; and David Cahill, "Curas and Social Conflict in the Doctrinas of Cuzco, 1780–1814," *Journal of Latin American Studies* 16:2 (November 1984): 241–76.

18 See Table 2.2.

19 O'Phelan Godoy, *Un siglo*, pp. 308–17.

20 Ibid., pp. 296–305.

21 Stavig, "Eugenio Sinanyuca"; Glave, *Vida, símbolos*, pp. 117–52.

in the area – Sicuani – was the site of constant legal battles and of internal violence.[22]

But its planning and organization make clear that Tupac Amaru envisioned a much more sweeping challenge to the organization of Spanish rule in the rural Andes. Two closely related aspects differentiate it from these earlier local riots and rebellions. The first was simply the presence of Tupac Amaru and his wife Micaela Bastidas. Recent work has rightly criticized how the focus on elite leadership in popular insurgency attributes political agency to disaffected elites rather than to the popular masses. But the central role of the cacical couple of Tungasuca in the rebellion, particularly in its initial stages, is undeniable. Caciques (and priests) might sympathize with, and even incite, an angry crowd; Tupac Amaru and Bastidas kidnapped a corregidor, held him prisoner for six days while gathering forces, and then publicly tried and executed him. While the rebels were as unruly and disorganized as any informal, early modern army, the course of the rebellion showed a well-developed strategy. In all, their leadership was essential to the movement from local riot to Great Rebellion.

Second, the Rebellion's organization and its considerable support from the nearby provincial elite – Indian as well as creole and mestizo – suggest that Tungasuca was the opening salvo in a larger conspiracy. Here, too, Tupac Amaru had recent Andean predecessors. Stern's assertion, that from 1742 to 1782 colonial authorities "contended with the more immediate threat or reality of full-scale civil war, war that challenged the wider structure of colonial rule and privilege," exaggerates the situation, but in the decades before 1780 opposition to the colonial order was increasingly conceived on the extralocal level.[23] In their articulation, however, these conspiracies had been far less successful. The one prolonged anticolonial insurgency before Tupac Amaru had taken place in the central sierra from the 1730s into the 1750s. Juan Santos Atahuallpa, who claimed descent from the emperor, had established a raiding "kingdom" in the semijungle eastern slopes of Tarma and Xauxa provinces.[24] Unlike pueblo riots, this insurgency did have a discernible anticolonial ideology, articulated through an anti-Spanish, Inca messianism. At the same time, Santos Atahuallpa established a territory outside Spanish hegemony by moving to the fringes of Spanish rule, not by overthrowing Spanish authority in the colonized territories of the Andes.

Santos Atahuallpa's insurgency was known in Cusco: Esquivel mentioned it in his *Noticias cronológicas*, and we can only guess at this anticolonial warrior's reception in the oral culture, perhaps aiding the conceptualization of

---

22 Chapter 5, pp. 155, 156, 160–162; O'Phelan Godoy, *Un siglo*, p. 302.
23 Stern, "The Age of Andean Insurrection," p. 35.
24 Francisco A. Loayza, ed., *Juan Santos, el invencible* (Lima [Editorial Miranda], 1942); and Stern, "The Age of Andean Insurrection."

alternatives to Spanish rule. Closer to Cusco, Azángaro rose in riot in 1737.[25] In response, the people of Cusco assembled a troop and marched south, to be joined by Indian nobles from the Titicaca basin.[26] The troop returned a month later with thirty-nine prisoners, who were taken to Lima.[27] The scale of the response, and the number and social rank of those taken prisoner, suggest a far larger insurgency than the almost routine pueblo assault against the corregidor. But the unrest in Azángaro remained an isolated phenomenon: while local conflict rose dramatically, not for another generation would the bishopric be the site of far-reaching conspiracies.

Two were exposed in Cusco in the years just before Tupac Amaru seized Arriaga, although the first, in 1776 and 1777, appears to have been more the intersection of Inca messianism and a local riot against the corregidor in Urubamba than a full-fledged conspiracy.[28] As 1777 approached, talk of a prophecy by Santa Rosa, that in the year of the three sevens an Inca would be crowned as king of Peru, was widespread. In 1776 Don Domingo Navarro Cachaguallpa – from a prominent Inca noble family in urban Cusco – was arrested along with Juan de Dios Espinoza Orcoguaranca for plotting rebellion.[29] In turn, they said that "one named Sierra" had told them that "...[in] the year of the three sevens, which is that of 1777...all of the Indians of this kingdom must rise against the Spaniards and kill them, beginning with the corregidores, alcaldes and other people of white faces and blond hair, that there is no doubt since the Indians of Cusco have named a king who will govern them."[30] This "plot" came to nothing, and it is not clear that Navarro Cachaguallpa and Espinoza Orcoguaranca were punished.[31]

In the following year a "Don Josef Gran Quispi Tupa Ynga" wrote to the captains of the Indian militia in Urubamba, advising them that "...he had to crown himself [king] because the time in which the prophecies of Santa Rosa and San Francisco Solano would come true was arriving."[32] In a reminder of the complexity of Inca identity – even in its millenarian

---

25 Esquivel, *Noticias cronológicas*, II, p. 261; Thomson, *We Alone*, p. 316, n64.

26 Don Ylario Garcia Llaglla Ynga of Juli claimed to have gone with the Indians of Chucuito to suppress it; in the Juli cacical dispute, ARC, RA, Ord., Leg. 33 (1799), 105.

27 Esquivel, *Noticias cronológicas*, II, p. 261; O'Phelan Godoy, *Un siglo*, p. 104.

28 For prophecy and Inca messianism in the 1770s, Ramón Mujica Pinilla, *Rosa limensis: Mística, política e iconografía en torno a la patrona de América* (Lima: IFEA-FCE-BCRP, 2002), pp. 335–60; O'Phelan Godoy, *La Gran Rebelión*, pp. 21–45; Jorge Hidalgo Lehuede, "Amarus y cataris: aspectos mesiánicos de la rebelión indígena de 1781 en Cusco, Chayanta, La Paz y Arica," *Chungará* 10 (March 1983): 117–38; and Szeminski, *La Utopia Tupamarista*.

29 He was the son of Andres Navarro Cachaguallpa and Pasquala Quispe Sucso; Chapter 3, p. 82.

30 *CDBR*, II, p. 229.

31 In 1783 Navarro Cachaguallpa was described as an "indio principal de la parroquia de Hospital" in a lawsuit over family land. ARC, JT, Leg. 89 (1770–1815), 35.

32 *CDBR*, II, p. 242.

form – he continued that if the English invaded Quito, it was essential "...to contradict and oppose whomever that wanted to crown himself, because there they had known Atahuallpa as their king, and he was not the legitimate descendant of the Inca emperors and on that account, [Josef Quispi Tupa] being a descendant of Huayna Capac and Viracocha Ynga, the kingdom belonged to him...."[33] The effect of Quispe Tupa's appeal is unclear. That a riot against the corregidor of Urubamba began in the Inca stronghold of Maras in November 1777 is certain, and remarkable, as such riots were almost unheard of in Inca pueblos.[34] From Maras's jail Quispe Tupa confessed to a massive plot, and numerous letters had been sent.[35] But the actual tumult did not spread beyond Urubamba, and in its events and trajectory resembled other local riots – with the corregidor's house and furniture burned along with grain he had collected from the province. The Spanish population participated along with the Indian, and the uprising did not draw much support from the Inca nobility.[36] Despite widespread talk of an apocalyptic return of Inca authority, Cusco's Inca nobles appear to have been uninterested in fostering the prophecy's fulfillment.

Cusco's Silversmiths' Conspiracy of 1780 drew from a more elite swath of society and was overwhelmingly urban and creole, but had an Inca at its head and manifested a creole–Inca political identity.[37] Spearheaded by members of the Silversmiths guild, the conspiracy was betrayed by a conspirator in confession to his priest. Hung alongside prominent creole conspirators was Don Bernardo Tamboguacso Pomayalli, the twenty-four-year-old Inca cacique of Pisac, who was married to Doña Francisca Ynquiltupa, daughter of a former *alférez* of Cusco's Inca cabildo.[38] What provoked Tamboguacso to participate in the conspiracy is unclear.[39] But like all whose interests were tied to Cusco's trade in grain, coca, and sugar, he suffered from the introduction of the La Paz customs and the increase in the *alcabala*. Tamboguacso himself stated that these created common cause between creole and Indian,

33 *CDBR*, II, p. 243.

34 O'Phelan Godoy, *Un siglo*, pp. 188–95; *CDBR*, II, pp. 235–42.

35 Mujica Pinilla, *Rosa limensis*, pp. 344–7; and AGI, Lima, Leg. 1044.

36 Only a few Cusipaucar were implicated. O'Phelan Godoy, *Un siglo*, pp. 188–95.

37 O'Phelan Godoy, *Un siglo*, pp. 207–17; Víctor Angles Vargas, *El Cacique Tambohuacso: Historia de un proyectado levantamiento contra la dominación española* (Lima: Industrial Gráfica, 1975).

38 Ibid., pp. 158–75; for Francisca, ARC, NOT, Juan Bautista Gamarra, Leg. 133, [ ], September 24, 1777.

39 In December 1779, he had been jailed at the request of the church for a matter involving his wife. He was quickly released because, as the Protector of Indians observed, "segun el testimonio presentado de las Reales Cedulas los de su clase gosan de mas altas preminencias que los Yndios tributarios y como que disfrutan de todas las prerrogativas concedidas a los hijos dalgo de Castilla deve a amparselos con mas justa rason; respecto de que estos no deven ser presos sin por delitos graves plenamente justificado." ARC, COR, Civ., Leg. 59, Exp. 1346.

and led him to conspire, if not against the crown, at least against the reformed Bourbon order in Cusco.[40]

Thus, the Tupac Amaru rebellion clearly built on eighteenth-century traditions of protest and resistance. But it moved dramatically beyond these earlier insurrections, above all by moving from local uprising to widespread rebellion, challenging not simply particular officials but colonial rule generally, and not from the margins of colonial Peru but from its very heart. This success gave Tupac Amaru and Bastidas the opportunity to articulate a political ideology. For the earlier insurgencies in the bishopric had met with little success. The talk of Santa Rosa's prophecy and the return of Inca rule had yielded, if anything, an anti-corregidor riot in Urubamba, and the Silversmiths had been discovered before their conspiracy took any action. As a result, neither succeeded in igniting the highlands, nor in leaving a clear record of the goals of the movement.

In contrast, Sangarará was the most significant defeat dealt to Spanish rule by Indian forces since the 1530s, and it shook Cusco's colonial society correspondingly. Tupac Amaru next turned south into Lampa, then west to Velille, in Chumbivilcas. By early December the rebellion had engulfed Tinta, Quispicanchis, Chumbivilcas, Lampa, Azángaro, Caravaya and reached the city of Puno. Victory brought recruits: the rebel forces rose to perhaps fifty thousand.[41] A few Indian nobles were among them. Pedro Vilca Apasa (long a foe of the Choquehuanca) became a rebel commander.[42] Among Tupac Amaru's most fervent Indian noble followers was Don Juan Pablo Huaman Sullca of Crusero. Huaman Sullca wrote to Tupac Amaru on December 9, advising him to beware of Spaniards, and sending a book that showed the Spaniards had killed Tupac Amaru I.[43] From a prominent cacical lineage, Huaman Sullca asked that "as I am favored by nobility, . . . [you] give me some title in the militia, since I enjoy such privileges as a descendant of Tupac Yupanqui"; he also requested guns for his followers. Intriguingly, these he wanted so that they might "make war against the infidel Chunchos in the pueblo of Inabari," not against the Spaniards of the highlands.[44]

But Huaman Sullca was the exception.[45] Few others heeded Tupac Amaru's calls, and the cacical elite of the Titicaca basin remained resolutely loyal. As news of Sangarará reached Lampa, the province's caciques arrived in its capital with armies of tributaries to defend the crown. Quispe Cavana

---

40 O'Phelan Godoy, *Un siglo*, p. 212.

41 Walker, *Smoldering Ashes*, p. 40.

42 *CDBR*, III, p. 591, and ANB, EC, 1762–144, 10, for Vilca Apasa. In Asillo a cacical family, the Guaguacondori, supported the rebels; Sala i Vila, *Y se armó*, p. 118.

43 *CDBR*, III, pp. 51–2.

44 Ibid.

45 Indeed, other Huaman Sullcas fought for the crown. ARC, DZ, Leg. 36 (1787–8); RREE, PRA, Exp. 461 (1797).

of Cavanilla brought seven hundred and Succacahua of Umachire brought eight hundred; the Choquehuanca followed from Azángaro with some two thousand.[46] In Lampa, Succacahua, Cama Condorsayna, Pachari, Tapara, Cava Apasa, Quispe Cavana; in Huancané, Calisaya, Viamonte, Cornejo, Mendoza Tatara, Ticona; in Azángaro, Choquehuanca, Chuquicallata, Mango Turpa, Uisa Apasa; in Chucuito, Fernandez Cutimbo, Catacora, Chique Ynga Charaxa, Garcia Llaglla – all remained loyal to the crown.[47] With their families and loyal tributaries, they fled west to Arequipa, or east to Sorata, later to return with loyalist troops.

The Titicaca campaign slowed the drive north: not until late December did the rebels move closer to Cusco. By then, although their armies remained dominant Tupac Amaru and Bastidas's elite support was evaporating. In late November Don Antonio Solis Quivimasa Ynga, of Quiquijana, fled to Cusco.[48] He confessed that he had blocked the roads at the rebel's orders, but claimed to have complied from fear.[49] His son-in-law, Don Francisco Succacahua, assumed his *cacicazgo*. At first Francisco tried to stave off Tupac Amaru, asking that he not seize Quivimasa's property as Francisco was his son-in-law, and because they had a religious mortgage.[50] But on December 10 Bastidas had him arrested for not complying with orders.[51] Nor was he alone: in their defense at later trials, those who supported Tupac Amaru in November insisted that they had done so only under duress. Such testimony is naturally suspect; however, when she wrote to Tupac Amaru of Succacahua's arrest, Bastidas lamented that ". . . Sucacagua has betrayed us, and the rest, as the attached will impress on you, and so I am not myself because we have very few people."[52]

But the loyalists had not recovered from the defeats of November, and the rebels remained in control of Tinta, Chumbivilcas, Lampa, and Quispicanchis. In late December, they began a siege of Cusco itself from the Vilcanota valley. By then, royalists troops began to arrive from Lima; Cusco's militias – including that of Indian nobles – went into battle, joined by loyalist caciques leading their tributaries. Mateo Pumacahua of Chinchero stopped the rebels at Guayllabamba, blocking the Urubamba–Cusco road and keeping them from the Anta plain. Ill-trained, poorly armed, and losing momentum, the rebel forces began to drift away, and by January 10 the

46 *CDBR*, I, p. 337.

47 See n72 for requests for *premios*; Sahuaraura, *Estado del Perú*; RREE, PRA, Exp. 505 (1798); O'Phelan Godoy, *La Gran Rebelión*, pp. 63–7.

48 He was later captured and killed by the rebels. AGI, Cuzco, Leg. 80.

49 *CDBR*, III, p. 122.

50 *CDBR*, III, pp. 50–1.

51 *CDBR*, IV, p. 23. Succacahua later testified that he and his brother-in-law, the priest Pedro Solis Quivimasa Ynga, had plotted (unsuccessfully) to kill Tupac Amaru and Bastidas. Ibid., V, p. 171.

52 *CDBR*, IV, p. 23.

siege ended. Tupac Amaru's cousin, Diego Christobal Tupac Amaru, led a campaign to the Paucartambo valley, causing considerable destruction, but by February the focus of the rebellion had moved south up the Vilcanota. On February 24 Marciscal Jose del Valle arrived with an army from Lima; on March 19 they marched against Tupac Amaru and his command at Tinta.[53] After a siege of the town, on April 6 Tupac Amaru and his family were captured. They were tried and sentenced, and on May 18 executed in Cusco's main plaza; they were then dismembered, their body parts sent for public display to pueblos that had rebelled.[54]

The execution of Tupac Amaru did not end the rebellion, although the arena of action now moved south to Titicaca and the Altiplano. November's events in Tungasuca had had a parallel hundreds of miles to the southwest, in Macha, near Potosí.[55] There Tomas Catari, a claimant to the cacicazgo, had been battling the corregidor since 1779, appealing to the Audiencia in Chuquisaca. In August 1780 he and his followers seized the corregidor, although he was soon released. In January Catari was murdered, and his brothers launched a rebellion that, later under the leadership of Julian Apasa (or Tupac Catari), engulfed the Altiplano. In February the one urban uprising in the larger rebellion took place in Oruro.[56] The Catarista troops then laid siege to La Paz from late March until late June when the city was relieved by troops from Buenos Aires.

Meanwhile, the area from Tinta to La Paz had seen almost continuous fighting since December. Almost every pueblo had fallen to the rebels or risen in rebellion. The rebels attacked Puno in March, but were repelled. The next weeks saw open war in Chucuito; Juli was sacked by rebel troops, and on March 24, 1781, Indian nobles and Spaniards were massacred in Juli's San Pedro church.[57] After Tupac Amaru's execution, Diego Christobal Tupac Amaru moved southward, establishing his headquarters in the Choquehuanca house in Azángaro. His troops again laid siege to Puno, which the royalists abandoned in late May. Another cousin, Andres Tupac

53 For his account of the campaign, see AGI, Cuzco, Leg. 63.

54 Angles Vargas, *Historia del Cusco*, II, p. 1091–8.

55 Chayanta has often been the site of peasant uprisings. Serulnikov, "Disputed Images" and "Customs and Rules"; Penry, "Transformations"; Tristan Platt, "The Andean Experience of Bolivian Liberalism, 1825–1900: Roots of Rebellion in 19th-Century Chayanta (Potosí)," in *Resistance, Rebellion*, pp. 280–323; Eric Langer, "Andean Rituals of Revolt: The Chayanta Rebellion of 1927," *Ethnohistory* 37:3 (Summer 1990): 227–53.

56 Oscar Cornblit, *Power and Violence in the Colonial City: Oruro from the Mining Renaissance to the Rebellion of Tupac Amaru (1740–1782)* (Cambridge: Cambridge University Press, 1995), pp. 137–172.

57 "...la masacre de los caciques," as it was called by Mariano Ynojosa y Cutimbo. Among the dead were Doña Maria Ygnacia Chique Ynga Charaja of Pomata (wife of Ambrocio Quispe Cavana) and Doña Ysabel Ybaña Paca Nina Chambilla and Don Fermin Garcia Llaglla, one of Juli's cacical couples. ARC, RA, Ord., Legs. 30 (1798) and 33 (1799). Those killed were then defiled, especially Indian nobles. Two caciques had their hearts cut out, while the body of one cacique's wife had been drained of blood, reputedly drunk by the rebels. Szeminski, "Why Kill the Spaniard?," p. 171.

Amaru, led a campaign down the eastern shore of Titicaca. Sorata, where royalists from the eastern side of the lake had taken refuge, fell on August 4, 1781, and many of the region's creoles and Indian nobles were killed.[58] But the tide was turning against the rebels. Royalist reinforcements from Lima and Buenos Aires gradually reasserted authority. In December 1781, Diego Christobal entered into negotiations with del Valle, and Pedro Vilca Apasa surrendered at Sicuani in February 1782. Despite swearing allegiance to the king, Vilca Apasa sought to rekindle the rebellion; he was captured in March by del Valle and executed. The surviving Tupac Amarus were taken to Cusco. In March 1783 Quispicanchis' corregidor alleged discovery of a plot backed by them; on July 19 Diego Christobal, his mother, and others were executed and dismembered in Cusco. Their execution marks the end of the Great Rebellion, although with Diego Tupac Amaru's surrender in early 1782 it had largely run its course. Given the nature of the rebellion – in which the larger campaigns sparked, and were fueled by, countless pueblo *jacqueries* – pockets of rebellion remained into 1783, and tensions remained high until the next wave of unrest in the 1810s and 1820s.

The ultimate defeat of the rebellion owed much to the trajectory of the interrelated Catari rebellion and to the far greater military power and organization of the royalist forces. At two critical junctures, however, the internal politics and conflicts of Indian society struck crippling blows. First, the Incas blocked the rebellion to the north. Not only did rebel troops not seize Cusco, they did not circumvent it to move along the Lima road into the central highlands.[59] The failure to capture Cusco is generally attributed to the reluctance of its creole population – however angered by the Bourbon Reforms – to side with Tupac Amaru. While the *vecinos* of Cusco did, early on, consider treating with Tupac Amaru, its officials would not; and the refusal of the largest Spanish city in southern Peru to join a rural Indian rebellion is not very puzzling. However, not only creoles remained loyal to the crown: the surrounding Indian pueblos rejected Tupac Amaru's calls. In Paruro, along the Vilcanota north of Urcos, and on the Anta plain – that is, precisely the area under the rule of the Inca nobility – Indian tributaries as well as nobles refused to rebel and often joined the royalist forces.[60]

---

58 Including many Siñani of Carabuco and their son-in-law Blas Choquehuanca (ANB, EC, 1786–175); Blas's Spanish brother-in-law was also killed (ARC, NOT, Pedro Joaquin Gamarra, Leg. 79, 1off., January 15, 1808). Also Don Diego Viamonte of Conima and his son (ARC, RA, Ord., Leg 33, 1799); many Cornexo of Huancané (RREE, PSG, Exp. 256); a Chuquicallata (ibid., Exp. 115); and Ygnacio Mendoza Tatara of Moho (ARC, RA, Adm., Leg. 158, 1799).

59 Stern sees the inability of the rebellion to spread to the central highlands as crucial to its eventual failure, but locates this failure in the Spanish militarization of the central sierra after the Santos Atahuallpa insurgency, not in the actions of Cusco's Indian population. "Age of Andean Insurrection," pp. 63–76.

60 Mörner and Trelles, "A Test."

Second, in the Titicaca basin the rebellion quickly became a civil war. Caciques, the Indian elite, and Spaniards overwhelmingly sided with the crown, while many communities rose against them. To be sure, when Tupac Amaru's troops first came down the Ayavire valley in December 1780, many tributaries watched at a distance. A letter to Tupac Amaru from an Indian noblewoman in Cavanilla who supported his cause reported that she had "ordered all the Indians in this community that they appear before you, and those who have remained are en route; but the rest have removed themselves from this pueblo to a distance of three or four leagues."[61] Others joined their caciques in loyalist armies. However, as the rebellion dragged on for months, caciques lost hold over their tributaries. Diego Choquehuanca brought 2,000 people to the royalist forces in December 1780; in September 1782 he reported to the crown that he had had to abandon Carabuco in the summer of 1781. As "his laborious efforts and ardent zeal were incapable of . . . maintaining the Indians in his charge in the obedience of Your Majesty, and saddened to see himself without more recourse than that which heaven could provide him," he had fled to Arequipa.[62] His family took refuge in Sorata, and many were killed.

Thus, the Indian elites of the bishopric – the large Inca nobility around Cusco and the powerful cacical dynasties around Titicaca – served as a check to the rebellion. To attribute its failure only to this would be absurd, but the loyalty of the Indian nobility and the different patterns of conflict that the rebellion provoked raise two questions about the rebellion that shed considerable light on the social dynamics of late colonial society, and of the Indian republic. First, why did the Inca nobility around Cusco remain loyal to the crown, rather than join the self-proclaimed descendant of Tupac Amaru to reinstitute Inca rule? And, second, why did so many Indian tributaries of the Titicaca basin turn on the cacical elite when this clearly did not happen around Cusco?

The obvious explanation of the Indian nobility's loyalty is self-interest: as privileged members of a subject group, they accepted and supported colonial rule for the benefits that accrued to them. And, while the fiscal innovations of the Bourbon Reforms were disliked by the crown's increasingly taxed Andean subjects, not all suffered equally. The reparto rendered cacical office more threatening economically, but also potentially more rewarding. Anecdotally, resignations by caciques seem more common in the 1740s and 1750s than in the two decades before the rebellion.[63] The highland population increased in the half-century before the rebellion, presumably making the cacicazgo more lucrative. Certainly a number of Indian caciques were

61 Doña Juana Quispe Yupanqui, *CDBR*, III, p. 56.
62 AGI, Charcas, Leg. 537.
63 Appendix, for Ñuñoa; ANB, EC, 1793–11, 74v, for Chucuito.

prospering in the 1760s and 1770s.[64] Those dependent on the portage of goods from Cusco to Alto Peru were hard hit by the division of the viceroyalties, but (with exceptions, like Tupac Amaru) by then such trade was more the domain of creoles.

In addition, as O'Phelan has shown, fiscal measures were only a part of the Bourbon Reforms to affect the Indian nobility.[65] In the mid-1700s the crown began, slowly, to retreat from the ethnic division of colonial Andean society that had been the hallmark of Habsburg rule. Two modest innovations in particular affected the highland Indian elites. The first was the increasingly frequent appointment of Spaniards to vacant cacicazgos.[66] But in 1780 this had not yet eroded the cacical authority of the Incas around Cusco, nor of the major cacical dynasties of the Titicaca basin. More important to the upper reaches of the Indian nobility was the opening of the church to them.[67] With that, the Indian nobility gained access to the most powerful institution in the Andes, and its valuable offices. The decades before the rebellion saw the first Indian noble priests in the bishopric: in 1780 it appeared that the blurring of the boundary between the Indian nobility and its creole peers could result in a strengthening of the former, not their eclipse by the latter.

Ultimately, such material explanations of Indian noble loyalty are unsatisfying. First, they fail to account for Tupac Amaru's exceptionalism. More importantly, implicitly they reject that the loyalist Indian nobility acted on a set of political ideals: true political consciousness is reserved for Tupac Amaru and his followers. But just as the hanging of Arriaga and the storming of the Pomacanchis obraje were political actions by the tributary masses of the Vilcanota highlands, violent but articulate rejections of material and political relations in late colonial Peruvian society, so too the Inca nobility performed a political act when they marched to Sangarará to battle the rebels. Recent work has been more interested in recovering the political ideals and motivations of those choosing rebellion than of those rejecting it, and the Tupac Amaru rebellion is no exception. But two lengthy legal disputes of the 1770s provide considerable insight into the political ideology of the loyalist Inca nobility, and allow a comparison to the political goals articulated by Tupac Amaru and Bastidas.

The couple was captured five months after they seized Arriaga. In that time, they sent letters throughout the highlands and made proclamations

---

64 Chapter 7, pp. 239–240, for Mateo Pumacahua; AAC, XIII.3.59 for 1767–8 tithe contracts of the
   Succacahua of Umachire; ARC, NOT, Juan Bautista Gamarra, Leg. 146, 432ff., October 1, 1778,
   for Vicente Choquecahua's purchase of a hacienda for 2,070 pesos in cash (earned in the lamb trade).
65 O'Phelan Godoy, "Repensando."
66 O'Phelan Godoy, Kurakas, pp. 17–28.
67 See Chapter 4, pp. 142–145.

outlining their goals – most clearly in a letter from Tupac Amaru to the Cusco cabildo during the siege of the city.[68] Among his demands ("my desires") were the abolition of the office of corregidor and of the reparto (but not of tribute), and the replacement of each corregidor by "an Alcalde Mayor of the same Indian nation and other persons of good conscience, with no more jurisdiction than the administration of justice, the Christian education of the Indians and other individuals, assigning them a salary." He insisted on the creation of an *audiencia* in Cusco, to have its own viceroy, and the resumption of free commerce (and implicitly the removal of the land frontier between Lower and Upper Peru). Tupac Amaru had also been waging a decade-long battle to be recognized as the heir to Ñusta Beatriz, and he made explicit his claim to preeminence as an Inca royal, describing himself as the only person "that has remained of the royal blood of the Inca kings." At the same time, he expressly recognized the sovereignty of the King of Spain.

Other than its tone, Tupac Amaru's letter contained little that went beyond current political discourse. The abolition of the corregidor and the reparto was already under consideration and would shortly begin.[69] Central to the Bourbon Reforms was the division of unwieldy jurisdictions, and just seven years later Cusco received its own audiencia, albeit under the rule of the viceroy in Lima. The proposal to replace the corregidor with an Indian official was further from the mainstream of Peruvian political discourse, although strikingly the Inca nobility of Cusco had proposed something similar two years earlier.[70] And that the new provincial official would receive an adequate salary, and therefore not rely on extortion, forced sales, and so on, was a central (if unrealized) goal of the intendant regime soon to be implemented in Spanish America. Finally, the repeal of increases in the alcabala and of the internal duties was a basic demand of riots and conspiracies in Arequipa, Cusco, La Paz, and Cochabamba in the preceding decade.[71]

More problematic, for the Incas of Cusco and for the ideology of Spanish rule, was Tupac Amaru's assertion both of leadership among the Inca elite and that his self-proclaimed role as "Inca" established him as a legitimate authority in colonial society. To be sure, Tupac Amaru's ideal of political authority was monarchic and hierarchical; in its imperial vision, it was pro-Castilian. However, it was also anticolonial, rejecting the marginalization of Indian elites within the colonial order, asserting a larger sphere for Indian [Inca] authority within the Spanish empire, and reaffirming that

---

68 Quoted at length in Angles Vargas, *Historia del Cusco*, II, pp. 1039–41.
69 See Chapter 7, pp. 213–215, for the Intendant system and the *socorro*.
70 See below, p. 200.
71 O'Phelan Godoy, *Un siglo*, pp. 304–5.

Indian nobles were the appropriate rulers of the Indian commons. At the same time, he expressly courted the creoles of Cusco (and of the countryside), acknowledging them as countrymen and as fellow sufferers under the tyranny of the corregidores.

Why, then, did his peers not join him in this program that was consistent with soon-to-be-implemented royal reforms and the goals of Cusco's Incas? Events unfolded quickly between November 1780 and January 1781 and the actors left few explicit accounts of the beliefs and goals driving them. Nor were Indian nobles prolific writers: the few postrebellion accounts of their actions are formulaic assertions of loyalty.[72] Attempts to explore their political beliefs have focused on their performance during the rebellion, implicitly privileging as "political" actions taken in explicit defense or rejection of the colonial order. In fact, the Inca nobility of Cusco, and the rural Indian elites, were constantly involved in political battles – among themselves, with corregidores and priests, and with their communities. A central arena for these conflicts was the colonial courts, as participants articulated and sought to bring about their conceptions of the proper social order. Both the Inca nobility of Cusco and Tupac Amaru were involved in lengthy legal battles through the 1770s, which both reflected the political ideals of the participants and directly influenced the trajectory of the rebellion. The first was between the Inca nobility and the "alcalde mayor of the eight parishes" of Cusco, Don Bernardo Gongora; the second between Tupac Amaru and Don Diego Betancur Tupac Amaru over claims to be Ñusta Beatriz's heir. Both were *causes célèbres* in Cusco, huge lawsuits in which the power of Spanish officeholders, the extent of Inca privilege and exceptionalism, and the ancestral and ethnic claims of different sectors of the bishopric's elite were rehearsed and challenged before royal judges. If the Bourbon Reforms and Inca utopianism are the Andean context of the rebellion, these lawsuits are the local context.

From 1775 to 1778, Cusco's Inca nobility waged a legal war against Gongora, whose relation to the Indians of Cusco was like that of a rural corregidor to his subjects. Charged with collecting tribute from the city's caciques, he also introduced repartos and forced people to work on his properties, and he intervened in, and was drawn into, disputes within the Indian

---

72 The lengthiest indigenous account of the rebellion is Sahuaraura's *Estado del Perú*, in which he defends both bishop Moscoso and the Indian nobility. Other accounts are in ARC, RA, Ord., Leg. 11 (1792) (Mateo Pumacahua); ARC, COR, Prov., Civ., Leg. 76 (1780–4) (Diego Chuquicallata); ANB, EC, 1785–23 (Ambrocio Quispe Cavana). For other petitions for rewards: ARC, RA, Adm., Leg. 148 (1788–9) (Diego Choquehuanca); AGN-A, IX-31-4-6, Exp. 431, 1782 (Domingo Mango Turpa); RREE, PSG, Exp. 1769, 1796 (the Chuquicallata); ARC, RA, Adm., Leg. 149 (1789–90) and AGN, DI, Exp. 472, 1792 (Diego Cusiguaman); AGN, DI, Exp. 32–643, 1784 and Exp. 845, 1799 (the Sahuaraura).

republic. Gongora had served as *alcalde mayor* since the 1750s; from then until the 1780s, his main foe was Cayetano Tupa Guamanrimachi, the powerful "cacique principal" of San Sebastián. Their mutual lawsuits over land, water, and general abuses date to the mid-1750s.[73] Tupa Guamanrimachi himself was disliked by many in the Inca nobility, and Gongora forged an alliance with the anti-Cayetano faction in the 1760s.[74] In 1766 he joined the lawsuit by almost two dozen Inca nobles that denounced Tupa Guamanrimachi's abuse of office, and made the usual aspersions against his ancestry. In 1770 Gongora had Tupa Guamanrimachi jailed, but the cacique was soon released. The latter had the support of the corregidor and of another faction of the Inca nobility, and Gongora never won his removal from the cacicazgo.

The legal battles continued through the 1770s, and Tupa Guamanrimachi launched countersuits against Gongora. By the mid-decade the dynamics of intra-Inca politics had changed, and the focus of Inca animus shifted to Gongora. In May 1775 the *ayllu* caciques and *principales* of San Sebastián complained that Gongora had done a reparto of pigs in the parish.[75] At the time, seven other caciques from the parish joined Tupa Guamanrimachi in a complaint against the alcalde mayor; these included some of Tupa Guamanrimachi's staunchest foes. The complaints against Gongora grew rapidly: in June, the city's Protector of Indians accused Gongora of orchestrating the unlawful arrest of Tupa Guamanrimachi in 1770; of hitting Doña Catalina Tisoc Sayritupa – a cacical heiress in Santiago – and causing her to abort; and of conducting the illegal reparto, claiming that it was at the behest of the corregidor (who joined the complaint against Gongora).[76] Gongora's property was embargoed and an order was issued for his arrest. The case dragged on until 1778, and was joined by Inca nobles of other parishes.[77]

The goal of the Inca nobility was clearly Gongora's removal from office. To that end, in November 1777 two dozen Inca nobles complained about Gongora's abuses to the Royal Treasury in Cusco. They made an

---

73 See Tupa Guamanrimachi's two complaints against Gongora in 1754: ARC, CAB, Ped., Leg. 112 (1733–59); ARC, COR, Ped., Leg. 90 (1753–65).

74 See Chapter 3, pp. 90–91; and Garrett, "Descendants," pp. 596–606.

75 ARC, COR, Prov., Civ., Leg. 85 (1783–5).

76 ARC, CAB, Crim., Leg. 98 (1774–6). The accusation that an abusive official had caused a woman to abort was common in colonial litigation; in the 1777 additions to this complaint (see later), Gongora was also accused of causing the wives of Don Manuel Ramos Tito and Don Matias Arisa to abort. Further showing the complexity of the Inca nobility's politics, Catalina Tisoc Sayritupa and her husband were, at the time of the complaint, engaged in a separate suit over their cacicazgo against her sister and brother-in-law, Josef Manuel Tupa Guamanrimachi – Cayetano's son. In the later complaint against Gabriel Guamantica, ARC, INT, Gob., Leg. 13 (1787).

77 In the 1777 additions to the suit in ARC, CR, Leg. 8 (1777–81); also AGN, SG, Exp. 403 (1776).

extraordinary proposal: ". . . [S]ince in order to liberate us from the extortions that we suffer . . . it is necessary to appeal for remedy, we make present to Your Lordship for our alleviation, that we have at hand a subject of ability and fortune and distinction among those of our nation, Don Ambrocio Garces Chillitupa, former *alférez real* of the Yngas, such that he might administer the collection of tributes, if certainly with zeal and exactitude in favor of the Royal Estate, at the same time with love and compassion."[78]

It was an Inca response to the Bourbon Reforms. Under the Habsburgs the "alcalde mayor" had been an Inca noble; by the 1750s the office had passed to the city's creole elite.[79] In proposing Chillitupa – an Inca elector, former alférez real, and cacique in neighboring Oropesa – the Inca nobles sought to reassert one aspect of the earlier Habsburg ordering of the city. Initially, the attorney for the Royal Treasury in Cusco supported the removal of Gongora but opposed the appointment of Chillitupa, suggesting that the crown's officers were not sympathetic to a return to such Inca authority. But in the end the Royal Treasure rejected the attorney's suggestion, arguing that the charges against Gongora had not been proven, and he kept the office pending further investigation.

While the refusal of the treasury to remove Gongora might have been expected to lead the Incas to support the Silversmiths' Conspiracy early in 1780, the opposite was the case. The twenty-four electors of the Inca cabildo, along with caciques and parish principales, remained loyal to the crown; it was Pedro Sahauraura who detained Castillo when the conspiracy was revealed.[80] For the Incas' appeal had been rejected by officials in Cusco, not the crown court in Lima. The Indian nobility of the bishopric held its position of loyal vassalage to the crown in far higher regard than did the crown itself; nonetheless, they had faith that, brought to the attention of the king and viceroy, their loyalty would be rewarded.

Nor was this belief ill-founded. The survival of Inca noble privilege was the result of two centuries of intervention by the Lima audiencia against attempts by officials in Cusco to collect tribute from the Indian nobility, ignore the prerogatives of the Inca cabildo, and interfere in cacical succession.[81] Just as Gongora and Tupa Guamanrimachi began their lengthy fight, the Inca cabildo had given power of attorney to Don Juan Bustamente Carlos Ynga – one of the city's creole–Inca elite now resident in Madrid – to petition the king for rewards and recognition of their quality and services to the crown.[82] Bustamente Carlos Ynga also received such powers from

78 ARC, CR, Leg. 8 (1777–81), 3v.
79 Amado Gonzales, "El alférez real de los Incas," pp. 228–31.
80 Angles Vargas, *El Cacique Tamboguacso*, pp 169–70.
81 See Chapter 3, pp. 82–83.
82 ARC, NOT, Arias Lira, Leg. 32, [ ], December 16, 1756.

Cusco's creoles, equally eager to win some favor.[83] For the relatively poor provincial nobilities of Cusco – creole as well as Indian – this was a difficult task: appeals to Lima were expensive, and the chance to petition the royal court in Spain was rare indeed. Ferdinand VI's reception of Bustamente Carlos Ynga could only have strengthened the Incas' faith that Madrid's royalty was far more kindly disposed to them than the officials of Cusco. In an October 1781 letter to Diego and Mariano Tupac Amaru urging them to surrender, Bishop Moscoso specifically referred to what must have been common lore in the city: "You well know the recent example of Don Carlos Bustamente, who with the name of Carlos Ynca was treated in the splendid and magnificent court of the King with such distinction that not only was it the fulfillment of his claims, but greater than whatever he could have hoped, the Monarch making such a spectacle of him among the most outstanding people that it was the wonder of those who knew him in his earlier base fortune. . . . "[84] Few Inca nobles would have harbored hopes of meeting the king.[85] But the success of Bustamente Carlos Ynga in Madrid was simply the grandest reminder that appeals to Lima and Madrid had a good chance of being heard favorably.

The Inca nobility had another reason for not joining the Silversmiths: the conspiracy was quickly discovered. But the lawsuits of the 1770s underscore that the Inca nobility had its own mechanisms for challenging aspects of the colonial order that threatened them. Just as pueblo riots that targeted the corregidor functioned, and were generally understood to function, as complex negotiations between the communities involved and the government, so too did the lawsuits of the Inca nobility. These lawsuits often yielded beneficial results, particularly as they worked their way higher through the courts, where local officials (like Gongora) had less influence. As a result, integral to the Inca nobility's political consciousness was a belief that challenges to local authority and relations of power were best conducted through the royal courts.

Certainly not all Incas took this stance: Tamboguacso's role in the Silversmiths' Conspiracy, and that of the Cusipaucar in the Urubamba riots, is a reminder of the diversity of political ideals and actions even among the Inca nobility. Again, though, in both instances overwhelmingly the local elites implicated were creoles, not Incas. In general, the Inca nobility remained loyal to the crown in moments of open crisis, placing their faith

83 Including one by "Don Diego Betancur Tupa Amaro," to pursue his claim to Ñusta Beatriz's *mayorazgo* (ARC, NOT, Gonzalez Peñalosa, Leg. 190, [ ], December 10, 1753).

84 *CDBR*, II, p. 649. Bustamente Carlos Ynga won pensions for his own family: see the 1785 Royal Hacienda accounts, ARC, INT, RH, Leg. 167 (1785).

85 Joseph Joaquin Tamboguacso, son of Joseph Tamboguacso and Agustina Chacona of Taray, left Cusco for Spain in the 1750s or 1760s. ARC, NOT, Juan Bautista Gamarra, Leg. 133, 22, February 20, 1781.

in the royal courts rather than in the delicate negotiations of the local riot. This depended on their own privileged position in the colonial order; but it was precisely this privilege that informed their understanding of colonial politics. Spanish hegemony was neither unified nor coherent. In the particularities that constituted life in late colonial Cusco, the relations and order of Spanish colonial rule were open to constant challenge and negotiation, and the particular position of the Incas guided the form of their challenges. Thus, while many aspects of Tupac Amaru's program were widely accepted by the Inca nobility, and, indeed, were implicitly or explicitly advocated in their lawsuits against Gongora, the manner of his challenge contradicted their own political ideology.

Moreover, Tupac Amaru's letter to the Cusco cabildo came less than ten months after the Incas' strategy – of public loyalty and legal challenge – had met with resounding success. On May 19, 1780, their loyalty during the Silversmiths' Conspiracy reaped its reward: after years of frustrated appeals, Viceroy Guirior finally ruled in their favor in their case against Gongora, and ordered the corregidor of Cusco

> ... to call together the said electors and caciques and give them the due thanks for the faithfulness and zeal that they have shown in the current situation, making them see that very soon all this will be presented to the King Our Lord to procure the greatest relief for the Indian Nation ... [W]ith respect that [the caciques and Inca cabildo] complain of the tribute collector B[ernar]do Gongora, let it be arranged that, [Gongora] not having title of cacique conceded by this Royal Audiencia, or in propriety by this Superior Government, the Corregidor separate him from the office of Collector ... [and] inform me punctually about his conduct. ... "[86]

In appealing to the courts, and remaining loyal to the crown in the tense days of early 1780, the Incas worked within the logic of Spanish colonialism to assert their own position and contest certain relations of Bourbon Cusco; their acts were consummately political, and had been understood as such. So, too, in early November did the people of Tungasuca engage in political acts understood as such; but they were articulated in a vernacular foreign to that of the Inca nobility.

That the Inca nobility contested aspects of the colonial order through the courts rather than riot and rebellion was not the only reason they opposed Tupac Amaru. Their historic loyalty to the crown was reinforced by the suspicion with which they viewed him: Tupac Amaru's claim to be the sole survivor of the Inca royalty utterly alienated Cusco's Incas. Through the 1770s they had been interested bystanders in one of the more intriguing disputes of colonial Cusco: that between Jose Gabriel Tupac Amaru and

86 ARC, COR, Adm., Leg. 94 (1767–84).

Diego Betancur Tupac Amaru. In the 1760s, Jose Gabriel had discarded his paternal surname (Condorcanqui) and adopted that of the last monarch of Vilcabamba as part of his claim to the *mayorazgo* that Ñusta Beatriz had brought to the Marquises of Alcañices. That grandee family died out in 1744, leaving vacant the valuable mayorazgo – which included the *encomienda* of Maras, Guayllabamba, Urubamba, and Yucay.[87] According to Jose Gabriel, Tupac Amaru left an illegitimate daughter, the *coya* Juana Pilcohuaco; as Sayri Tupac's niece, she would have been Beatriz's cousin. Jose Gabriel alleged that Juana had married Don Diego Felipe Condorcanqui, a non-Inca cacique from the southern highlands. The couple ruled Surimana, on the border of Canas y Canchis and Quispicanchis, and left one child, Don Blas Tupac Amaru. He married Doña Francisca Torres; in 1687 their children presented this information to the corregidor of Canas y Canchis, who declared them the descendants of Tupac Amaru. One of Blas and Francisca's sons, Don Bartolome, succeeded to the office. After he died childless, his brother Don Sebastian became cacique of Surimana.[88] Sebastian married Doña Catalina del Camino; their son, Miguel, married Doña Rosa Noguera. Miguel died young, and Rosa's brother served as interim cacique until their son, Jose Gabriel Condorcanqui (born around 1738), was of age. Arguing that the mayorazgo should revert to the line of Juana Pilcohuaco as Beatriz's closest relative, Jose Gabriel launched a claim that would span the 1770s and bring him into conflict with the Inca and creole nobility of Cusco.

For he was not the only claimant. Opposing him was Don Diego Felipe Betancur Tupac Amaru of Cusco.[89] The product of an alliance between Cusco's creole and Inca elites, Diego Felipe had been born in the late seventeenth century. The Betancur claim argued that Felipe Tupac Amaru had left not a daughter but a son, Don Juan Tito Tupac Amaru. He had married Doña Leonora Yanqui Guallpa Rimachi; their son, Don Blas Tupac Amaro, had in turn married Doña Magdalena Ocllo. Their son Lucas Tupac Amaru had then married a creole woman, Doña Gabriela Arze; their daughter was Diego Betancur's mother (as Betancur rather grandly named her, Doña Manuela Tupac Amaru Arze y Ocllo Ñusta).[90] Diego, in turn, had married Doña Lucia de Bargas y Urbina, a Spaniard "of well-known nobility."[91] Based on this genealogy, Diego Betancur spent the three decades

---

87 See Chapter 1, pp. 29–30. The mayorazgo was declared vacant on October 16, 1744, cited by Diego Betancur in his will. ARC, NOT, Tomas Gamarra, Legajo 176, 497 ff., December 3, 1778.

88 Loayza, ed., *Genealogía de Tupac Amaru*.

89 See the thirteen-volume Colección Betancur in the ARC; Volume I for genealogical information. Also Betancur's will, ARC, NOT, Tomas Gamarra, Leg. 176, 497 ff., December 3, 1778.

90 Ibid.

91 ARC, BE, I, 117.

before his death trying to claim the mayorazgo for his family, and waging an endless battle against "an Indian from Pampamarca, Don Joseph Condorcanqui Noguera Balenzuela Camino y Torres, that he not call himself Tupac Amaru."[92]

Given the enormous importance of Jose Gabriel Tupac Amaru in Peruvian history, the merits of his claims and the Betancur's have excited academic interest.[93] More relevant to this work is the reaction of Cusco's nobility. That a highland cacique whose last (and questionable) link to the Incas was his great-great-grandmother would title himself the heir to Huayna Capac (and potentially the *encomendero* of some of the strongest Inca pueblos) was not well received in Cusco. Moreover, Tupac Amaru's wife, mother, and grandmother were provincial Spaniards, who, in Cusqueño eyes, ranked far behind both the Inca nobility and the "notoriously noble" creole families related to Betancur. In an extraordinary move, just before his death in 1778 Diego Betancur was appointed an elector of the Inca cabildo, in the house of Huayna Capac.[94]

For the Incas, Betancur's pretensions were preferable to those of Tupac Amaru. The Betancur were closely linked to Cusco's creole elite, with whom Inca nobles had strong ties and whom the Incas as a group needed as allies far more than the dominant family of a pueblo fifty miles to the south. Indeed, Betancur was much more the Inca nobility's peer than was the cacique of Surimana. For two centuries the Incas had lived and dealt with the conquistadores' descendants, and each group acknowledged the social standing of the other. In contrast, to acknowledge the claims of someone with almost no ties of kinship to the colonial Inca nobility as Beatriz's heir would undermine the basic premise of the colonial Incas: that it was their constant intermarrying that maintained Inca nobility, and that the bastardized Inca lines of the former empire had no role in Cusco's ceremonial and political life. At heart, the issue was whether the "Incas" had ceased to exist as a group in the sixteenth century, so that provincial elites with some Inca ancestry could claim to be "Inca" themselves, or whether the "Incas" were an ongoing ethnic nobility, zealously preserving their purity of blood (with allowances for judicious marriages to other Indian nobles and creoles of good family). And in that debate, the Incas of Cusco and Jose Gabriel Condorcanqui were necessarily on different sides.

92 ARC, NOT, Tomas Gamarra, Legajo 176, 497 ff., December 3, 1778.

93 John H. Rowe, "Genealogía y rebelión en el siglo XVIII: Algunos antecedentes de la sublevación de Jose Gabriel Thupa Amaro," *Histórica* [Lima] 6:1 (July 1982): 65–86; Carlos Daniel Valcárcel, "Documentos sobre las gestiones del cacique Túpac Amaru ante la Audiencia de Lima (1777)," *Letras* [Lima] 36:3 (1946): 452–466 and "La familia del cacique Túpac Amaru," *Letras* [Lima] 37:1 (1947): 44–89; and Lillian Estelle Fisher, *The Last Inca Revolt*, pp. 33–7.

94 The election took place on February 25, 1778. ARC, BE, I, 696–700.

The conflict over the mayorazgo paralleled, or perhaps had spilled over into, cacical politics in Tupac Amaru's own parish.[95] He had been confirmed as the cacique of Tungasuca, Pampamarca, and Surimana in 1766. Disputes with the corregidor of Tinta and other claimants led to his removal from 1769 to 1771; he was reinstated but the dispute smoldered on. As part of a renewed assault, early in 1780 a number of caciques and Indian nobles from the Pampamarca vicinity gave testimony about Tupac Amaru's ancestry. The allegations are the stuff of any succession battle and cannot be taken at face value. There had been no Doña Juana Pilcohuaco; or she was not the matriarch of the Condorcanquis; Jose Gabriel and his in-laws, the Nogueras, had stolen their documents from the true claimants; other papers were forged.[96] The most powerful cacique of the area, Doña Tomasa Tito Condemayta (later a supporter of the rebellion), testified that Tupac Amaru's father "...was always a poor, destitute [man], and without any right whatsoever to the name of Tupac Amaru and that the above mentioned took the name Tupac Amaru [just] as the Indians take that which seems [appealing] to them ... and the said Don Miguel was an ordinary Indian without any privileges."[97]

Witnesses also challenged the Condorcanqui claim to the cacicazgos of Pampamarca and Tungasuca.[98] In February 1780, Don Melchor Choquecondori y Sota of Pampamarca authorized a power of attorney in Cusco as part of his efforts to regain the cacicazgo.[99] In August, he appealed to the bishop to order the parish priest – whom he described as "a declared enemy [of mine], because he unjustly favors his *compadre*, who without being it calls himself Don Jose Tupa Amaru" – to provide a copy of his baptismal record.[100] Choquecondori had made no headway in his suit when the rebellion broke out; but that Tupac Amaru's claim to royal standing and exceptional authority within indigenous society were widely disputed is crucial to understanding the actions of the Incas of Cusco and other Indian nobles in the area of the rebellion.

These legal battles suggest two tenets of the Inca nobility's political ideology that put them at odds with Tupac Amaru. First, while Inca nobles actively challenged aspects of colonial rule that they opposed, they did so through petition to the crown and appeal to the court. Certainly in this they supported Spanish hegemony, but elements of that hegemony were open to challenge and revision through such sanctioned mechanisms. That the Inca

95 For the local and provincial politics surrounding Tupac Amaru, Stavig, "Eugenio Sinanyuca," and Glave, *Vida. símbolos*, pp. 117–78.
96 ARC, BE, II, 309–21.
97 Ibid., 321.
98 Ibid., 316–20, testimony of Don Bartolome Tupac Amaro.
99 ARC, NOT, Tomas Gamarra, Leg. 177, 401, February 8, 1780.
100 BNP, Man., C-2812, August 11, 1780; also Stavig, *The World of Túpac Amaru*, p. 249.

nobility, and the cacical elite to the south, asserted and lived up to their claims to be the "most loyal vassals" of the crown in no way required that they accept all aspects of the colonial order; but their form of rejection was distinct from that advanced by Tupac Amaru. Second, while they shared with Tupac Amaru a strong commitment to the recognition of colonial Inca authority, their definitions of that authority, and who should exercise it, differed radically. His claim to be the sole successor to Tupac Amaru resonated throughout the Vilcanota highlands, but it fell flat in Cusco. That a mestizo highlander descended (possibly) from an illegitimate child of Tupac Amaru and an Aymara cacique would claim precedence over the descendants of Paullu Ynga was unthinkable. Indeed, one of these descendants – Pedro Sahuaraura – led the Indian regiment at Sangarará. It is an ironic, and telling, indication of the complexity of colonial Andean society that Tupac Amaru himself adopted a very Spanish understanding of hereditary authority and succession, treating the Inca mantle as a mayorazgo.[101] To the Incas of Cusco it was a far more complex, and vibrant, elite identity, and, intentionally or not, Tupac Amaru's claims necessarily represented a threat to colonial Inca privilege as it was understood and constructed in Cusco.

Just as importantly, on the ground the rebellion developed in ways at odds with Tupac Amaru's own pronouncements, and both the actions of his followers and the constitution of the movement's leadership reinforced the ideological divide between Tupac Amaru and the Indian elite. Notwithstanding Tupac Amaru's pan-Andean rhetoric and his implicit insistence that Inca blood should translate into political authority in the Andes, the leadership of the rebellion from November 1780 to March 1781 was drawn from Tinta and southern Quispicanchis and came more from the rural Spanish population than from the Indian nobility.[102] On the one hand, that Tupac Amaru's principal officers and supporters were from his extended family and the area's elite is hardly surprising. By 1780, that elite was a mix of Inca and Aymara lineages and rural Spaniards, and the *arriero* profession, of which Tupac Amaru was part and which provided many of his allies, was dominated by the latter. However, that Tupac Amaru failed to recruit or win over the dominant Indian families north of Quiquijana or south of Sicuani underscores the narrow geographic boundaries of this provincial elite. In their own eyes, Cusco's Inca nobles were not tied to Tupac Amaru by

101 And that historians have concurred with Tupac Amaru's understanding of "just" succession; see n93 earlier. Equally telling, Diego Betancur and Jose Gabriel Tupac Amaru had almost identical ancestries, ethnically: both were 3/4 Spanish and 1/4 Indian noble. That Betancur is (and was) considered "creole" and Tupac Amaru is (and was) considered "Indian" says much about both the fluidity of ethnic classifications in the eighteenth-century Andes, and the politics of twentieth-century attributions.

102 Campbell, "Social Structure"; O'Phelan Godoy, *Un siglo*, pp. 308–17.

marriage, blood, or common cause; nor were the great dynasties of the Titicaca basin. The small area that supplied Tupac Amaru's leadership shows how kin solidarities formed limits to political consciousness in the late colonial highlands. While Tupac Amaru could articulate a political vision that rivaled (and paralleled) the viceroyalty in its scope, in the end he could not transcend the local and regional affiliations that structured the Indian elite. To the Incas of Cusco, Tupac Amaru was neither leader nor liberator, but rather an arrogant mestizo cacique from a small *puna* pueblo whose pretensions threatened their own understanding of colonial Inca authority.

In contrast, with its singular success in breaking past regional boundaries and mobilizing large swaths of the tributary population, the rebellion quickly moved beyond the limited, reformist ideology that Tupac Amaru had espoused. Perhaps he had always intended the radical turn that the rebellion took, offering a mild reformist program to the Cusco cabildo in the hopes of deceiving them into surrendering. Or perhaps Tupac Amaru was himself radicalized by Cusco's intransigence and the Indian nobility's rejection of his leadership.[103] Alternatively, the aggressive actions of the rebels may have reflected a peasant, anticolonial consciousness that took charge and placed the rebellion beyond Tupac Amaru's control. This unanswerable question remains a topic of debate.[104]

But that the rebellion radicalized as it progressed is beyond doubt.[105] It began with the violent, if routine, capture and execution of a corregidor by an enraged pueblo. For Cusco's Inca nobility, and its creoles, the action was comprehensible, and ultimately unthreatening. The exactions of corregidores violated the moral economy of the highlands, cutting across class and ethnic boundaries. The destruction of the obraje at Pomacanchis was a different anticolonial action and a challenge to urban Cusco. A fixture of the bishopric's landscape for more than a century, the obraje was a huge complex near the royal road with hundreds of workers.[106] To the surrounding pueblos, it symbolized the oppressive relations of colonial rule: a vast creole-owned property in which those who could not pay tribute, or had committed some crime, were confined to work, which competed with the pueblos for water and land and whose profits flowed to the city of Cusco. To Cusco's vecinos – Indian and creole – the obraje was instead a rural economic colony that produced some of the city's wealth (and was the foundation of the Count de Laguna's fortunes). While not even the richest caciques owned

103 That his pretensions were rebuffed by the Lima Audiencia as well as by Cusco's Inca nobility only strengthened his commitment to them: following the victory at Sangarará he and Micaela Bastidas commissioned portraits of themselves as Inca and Coya. Walker, *Smoldering Ashes*, p. 39.

104 Piel, "Cómo interpretar la rebelión," pp. 74–6; Walker, *Smoldering Ashes*, pp. 50–4.

105 Campbell, "Ideology and Factionalism"; O'Phelan Godoy, *La Gran Rebelión*, pp. 105–85.

106 Escandell-Tur, *Producción y comercio*, pp. 433–4.

anything approaching the obraje in scale, the popular strike against elite property raised concerns about the fate of their own small *chorrillos*, their private ranches, and their large houses filled with their families' movable wealth. Now the anticolonial actions of the rebels were directed not only against abusive, mid-ranking royal officials, but also against the structures of colonial society on which the fortunes of both rural elites and the city of Cusco depended.

The massacre at the church of Sangarará can only have exacerbated the opposition of Indian elites to the rebellion. The church was both the symbol of colonial rule in the rural pueblo and the symbol of the pueblo itself.[107] Andean elites were generally reasonably orthodox in their Catholic practice (if not their dogma), and accepted the basic Catholic pantheon of saints and the trinity. The symbolism of the massacre – and that at Juli – is striking: the Indian elites and the creoles of pueblos in rebellion sought refuge in their churches not only because they were the strongest buildings in town, but also because of the right of sanctuary. The assault on these temples, and their refugees, represented a profound rejection of the Church as a corrupt, colonial institution. Colonial elites criticized aspects of the colonial order, but they embraced colonial society: here the rebels rejected a fundamental institution and set of beliefs.

Finally, in the Titicaca basin the rebellion became an open assault on all aspects of colonial authority. Tributaries there expressed a strong resentment of the rural elite, as crowds assembled in pueblo plazas directed their wrath against Indian nobles and creoles alike. Indeed, such might have been the pattern even in the earliest stages of the rebellion: three of the caciques tried with Tupac Amaru – Tito Condemayta of Acos, Zamalloa of Sicuani, and Mamani of Tinta – all testified that they had been forced to join the rebellion by the mobs.[108] Such self-serving claims contain a grain of truth: in pueblos close to the epicenter of the rebellion, caciques had to make rapid decisions. To the south, whether provoked by their caciques' refusal to join the rebellion, or never giving them the chance, pueblos rose against the cacical elite. In Azángaro, the wife and daughters of the cacique of Urinsaya were hung in the main plaza by women from the pueblo; in Huancané, the hereditary cacique of Verenguelillo, Don Gregorio Ticona, suffered the same fate.[109]

107 The rebels killed almost no priests in the bishopric of Cusco. A "Relación de los sucesos desgraciados que han sufridos los curas" made clear that many had had their lives threatened and property destroyed, but only a Dominican friar in Pupuja had been killed. AGI, Cuzco, Leg. 63, Exp. 5.

108 O'Phelan Godoy, *Un siglo*, pp. 308–17.

109 For Azángaro, Salas Perea, *Monografía Sintética*, p. 22. For Verenguelillo, Ticona Sancho Larico's suit over the cacicazgo, ARC, INT, Prov., Ord., Leg. 99 (1802–3). For others, BNP, Man., C-1705; Rasnake, *Domination*, pp. 144–7.

That the rebellion became so much more radical in the Titicaca basin owed much to the social structure of the region. In the eighteenth century a handful of intermarried cacical lineages dominated the area's tributaries; these families amassed great wealth and formed a ruling class increasingly closed to and separated from others in the Indian republic. When the rebellion against colonial exactions and corrupt officials begun by Tupac Amaru spread from the remote pastoral and potato-growing pueblos of Tinta to the towns around the lake – separated by more than 100 miles and centuries of cultural and economic difference – its dynamics changed. The massacre of the caciques at Juli's San Pedro church was every bit as much an anticolonial rebellion as the hanging of Arriaga in Tungasuca. In the Titicaca basin the conjunctures of Andean history and the Spanish tributary-mining economy had produced the largest, richest, and most stratified Indian communities of colonial South America; and those who bore the burdens directed their destructive fury inward, toward the social order of the colonial pueblo.

The Tupac Amaru rebellion was a complex, contradictory social explosion; it spread so rapidly because it united, however briefly, the reformist demands of rural elites with the subaltern anticolonialism of highland pueblos. The interrelated divisions that constituted highland society determined the trajectory of the rebellion. It was above all a rising of the communities subject to the Potosí mita; its main success in spreading farther was to pueblos subject to the Huancavelica mita.[110] In turn, the mining mitas drew largely from the old Aymara *señorios*, and the rebellion spread only fleetingly to the traditionally Quechua areas surrounding these highlands, and failed absolutely to cross the Apurímac gorge into the Quechua societies of central Peru. The distinction was not strictly linguistic: the cradle of the rebellion was, by the 1700s, mainly Quechua-speaking. But economically and culturally the divide between the pastoral and potato-growing highlands, and the temperate, agricultural lands of the valleys, was as pronounced as under Inca rule. The initial surge of Tupac Amaru's forces down the Vilcanota was as much an invasion of the Inca agricultural pueblos by highland herders as it was an Indian rebellion against Spanish rule. Or so it must have seemed to the farmers whose fields were trampled, and the village notables who, despite their proud ancestry, saw themselves threatened by and subjected to Indian plebes from the south.

The rebellions were also rural uprisings. With the exception of Oruro, highland cities remained royalist. The creole elite fretted about the loyalties of the urban underclass, but city dwellers of both *repúblicas* rejected the rebels' call. Spanish rule favored the cities, and the rebels sought to lessen the extractions from the countryside on which the comfortable life of city-dwellers depended. Less than three decades later cities across Spanish South

---

110 For the Huancavelica *mita*, see the 1785 accounts in ARC, INT, RH, Leg. 168 (1785).

America led the rejection of European rule, using the invasion of Spain to assert their independence. Like those of 1780–3, these were anticolonial revolutions, but they reflected the interests of the cities and rejected the rule of audiencia, viceroyalty, and Council of Indies, not of corregidor, cacique, and private property.

Finally, the Indian elite remained overwhelmingly loyal to the crown. Their "colonial" consciousness proved as strong as the anticolonial consciousness of the rebels. Around Cusco, the tributary population joined in repulsing the rebels; in the Titicaca basin, it rose to attack the cacical elite. Ironically, while the Inca-dominated areas around Cusco were so aggressive in asserting a historical consciousness that treated the Spanish conquest as a defining moment of rupture, it was precisely in this area of heavy Spanish settlement, urbanization, strong regional markets, and colonial Inca privilege that the institutions and ideals of colonial rule had taken deepest root. For large segments of society in this area the sweeping anticolonial program of the rebels was far too self-destructive to gain support. In contrast, in the heavily burdened pueblos of the mita basin, the rejection of the corregidor, cacical power and wealth, and the demands of the colonial state proved enormously appealing. As a result, the Indian nobility of the Titicaca basin suffered greatly. The massacres at Juli and Sorata, and the death on the battlefield of many Indian nobles, threatened the physical survival of this small ruling class. In addition, the looting and burning of their houses, and even more the theft, slaughter, and dispersion of huge cacical flocks, wiped out cacical fortunes. Also lost in the destruction of their houses – indeed, a central target of the rebels' fury – were the documents that solidified their claims to office and to property. This loss proved catastrophic. For just as the rebellion evolved into a subaltern rejection of the colonial order, it spurred along an equally sweeping rejection of that order by the crown. Battered from their victory over the rebel forces, the loyalist Indian nobility would immediately face a royal administration committed to an assault on their privilege and power, an assault carried out in the courts rather than on the field.

7

The Breakdown of the Colonial Order

As much as the Great Rebellion was provoked by changes in the larger Andean political economy, it provoked a profound transformation in the local political economies of highland Indian communities. The segment of society that suffered most was the Indian nobility. The loss of life and property hit the great cacical houses of the Titicaca basin hard. The destruction of *obrajes* and flocks and the disruption of trade further severed the Cusqueño economy from the Altiplano, just when improvements in shipping made Buenos Aires a more attractive port-of-entry than Lima and royal policy began to encourage trade rather than limit it.[1] Cusco's textile and sugar industries, and portage across the Titicaca basin, thus declined further. Insofar as the cacical elite had drawn its wealth and power from their control over the contact between local economies and the regional market, they suffered proportionately.

Even more damaging for the Indian nobility of Cusco was the crown's rethinking of the organization of colonial rule. Throughout the Americas, Charles III and Charles IV sought to extend royal authority in a wave of state-building that paralleled and surpassed that of the Habsburgs in the sixteenth century. While the codification of Spanish rule in the late 1500s had imposed a colonial discipline on Andean society, the inability and reluctance to enforce royal justice had created great latitude for negotiation: "obedezco pero no cumplo" served as the unofficial motto of corregidores and caciques as well as of viceroys. From the mid-eighteenth century, the crown set out to reclaim control of royal government and of Indian tribute. In Upper Peru this had contributed to and combined with the erosion of cacical legitimacy that was itself a causal factor in the rebellions there.[2] In contrast, the Inca nobility of Cusco, and, to a large extent, the cacical dynasties of the northern Titicaca basin, had weathered the early Bourbon reforms successfully, profiting from the opening of church office to

---

1 Tulio Halperín Donghi, *Reforma y disolución de los imperios ibéricos, 1750–1850* (Madrid: Alianza Editorial, 1985), pp. 45–50.
2 Serulnikov, *Subverting Colonial Authority*; Thomson, *We Alone*.

Indian nobles, the opportunities of the *reparto*, and intermarriage with rural Spaniards. However, if in the Aymara societies of Upper Peru the rebellion reflected and produced the culmination of the rejection of indigenous elites by their communities, in Cusco the rebellion instead produced a paradoxical repudiation of the Indian nobility by the crown. In that, it was the crown's response to the rebellion, rather than the uprisings themselves, that proved devastating to the cacical elite. Despite the Indian nobility's demonstrated loyalty, the crown broke the Indian monopoly on tribute collection and began an aggressive campaign against Indian caciques. Across the highlands, Spaniards replaced those who could not prove hereditary claim or had not distinguished themselves as loyalists in the rebellion. The juncture between the pueblo and the viceregal network of tribute and trade moved into Spanish hands, greatly extending Spanish authority in the countryside. No longer willing to accept the fiscal, judicial, and social privileges of the impoverished Indian nobility around Cusco, after the rebellion the intendant, *audiencia*, and royal hacienda of Cusco also waged a twenty-five-year campaign against the Incas' tribute exemption.

Thus, following the rebellion the crown sought to dismantle the two bulwarks of colonial Indian privilege: the *cacicazgo* and blood nobility. But this was a lengthy project. The royal decrees and courts that had, over the centuries, disciplined the Indian nobility into a privileged yet subject stratum of colonial society now hindered the crown's efforts to abolish those privileges. Royal officers and courts were to some extent bound by earlier concessions, although they adopted more rigorous standards of review. The Indian nobility thus drew on the legacy of colonial rule as they negotiated the crown's reform of highland society. Also, the postrebellion erosion of boundaries between the upper ranks of the Indian nobility and creole Peru continued after the rebellion, and some Indian noblemen rose to unprecedented heights in the colonial order. Finally, even caciques who lost their offices did not necessarily lose local prominence, as erstwhile caciques became *alcaldes*, retained their private property, and generally remained leaders within their communities. The collapse of the Indian nobility was a lengthy process. No one failed to notice the sea change following the rebellion, but not until independence, and the abolition of cacicazgos and legal nobility, was the Indian nobility finally destroyed.

The Campaign against the Cacicazgo

The crown's response to the Great Rebellion was to pursue more aggressively the very reforms that had provoked the uprising, and following 1784 the bishoprics of Cusco and La Paz saw enormous fiscal and administrative changes. Cumulatively, they extended the crown's reach into rural pueblos and expanded its material demands on the Indian peasantry. Despite the loyalty of the Indian nobility, the crown's officers blamed Indian society, and the nobility at its head, for the rebellion. Therefore, the royal allies in these reforms were rural Spaniards, not the Indian nobility. Combined with the assault on Inca noble privilege, the replacement of Indian caciques in the 1780s would produce, by 1790, the most profound crisis that the Indian elite had confronted since the Spanish conquest.

In 1784 the intendant system was introduced into the highlands, establishing a clearer hierarchy of authority between provincial governors and the audiencia.[3] The corregidores were replaced by the very similar subdelegates, but they were now placed under the authority of an intendant in the main city of the region. The intendancy of Cusco included the entire bishopric except the three provinces south of the La Raya pass. These were joined to Huancané and Chucuito to form the intendancy of Puno, which straddled the bishoprics of La Paz and Cusco. And, in 1788, the crown established the Cusco Audiencia, with jurisdiction over the intendancies of Cusco and Puno.[4] Together, these reforms aimed to limit the power and abuses of provincial governors while rationalizing royal rule over the highlands and increasing royal revenues.

Cusco's first intendant, Benito Mata de Linares, ordered an aggressive enrollment of the Indian population. Tribute levels soared (Table 7.1): officials boasted that from 1784 to 1785 they climbed by half.[5] From 1786 until 1812 the Indians of the intendancy of Cusco paid between 250,000 and 300,000 pesos annually, quadruple the levels in the mid-1700s. The earlier figures had expenses deducted, while those from the 1780s and later are gross: not all tribute left Cusco. Tribute went to pay priests, subdelegates, and the intendant and to support Cusco's Indian Hospital. Following the rebellion, much of the crown's income in Cusco was spent on military expenses.[6] Still, in 1785 the largest item in the expenditure of tribute income was "remitida a Lima": 81,680 pesos. In the 1790s and 1800s, this figure surpassed 100,000, breaking 200,000 more than once.[7]

In addition, while the hated reparto was abolished, the *socorro* that replaced it was suspiciously similar. As Table 7.1 shows, the economic logic of colonial rule in Indian communities remained the same: a self-sufficient, tributary peasantry would sustain the larger, creole market economy. To ensure that the necessary labor flowed from the Indian republic, adult men had obligations of roughly ninety reales a year – or forty-five days of labor;

---

3 John R. Fisher, *Government and Society in Colonial Peru: The Intendant System, 1784–1814* (London: University of London, Athlone Press, 1970).

4 Lampa, Azángaro, and Caravaya were moved from the Audiencia of Charcas to Cusco's jurisdiction in 1788; Chucuito and Huancané remained under Charcas until 1795.

5 ARC, TAZ, Leg. 80 (1784).

6 The account book of the Royal Hacienda, ARC, INT, RH, Leg. 167 (1785).

7 TePaske and Klein, *The Royal Treasuries*, I, 204–23, passim.

Table 7.1. *Tributary Obligations, Intendancy of Cusco, 1786*

	Cusco	Abancay	Calca y Lares	Urubamba	Paucartambo	Quispicanchis	Paruro	Tinta	Aymaraes	Cotabambas	Chumbivilcas	Total
Tributary population	2490	3831	2321	2069	2104	4462	3183	7006	3118	3329	2820	36733
Annual tribute												
1784 (pesos)	5342	17784	5628	8739	8081	24358	15882	41725	20762	26490	12615	187406
1786 (pesos)	17138	28341	15421	17318	12544	35421	16697	52025	24973	38832	22652	281342
Socorro, 1785–90												
Bayeta de la Tierra (varas)	0	45000	16000	20000	11000	40000	23000	100000	17000	14000	35000	321000
Pañete (varas)	0	5000	2000	4000	0	0	2060	6600	17000	2000	4000	42660
Paño de Quito (varas)	0	0	0	410	200	0	0	1150	2000	0	640	4400
Iron (lb.)	0	25000	4750	8425	8000	10000	7000	23700	8200	8750	5050	108875
Steel (lb.)	0	500	0	525	0	0	0	500	2000	500	350	4375
Farm implements (pieces)	0	0	0	0	0	0	0	932	200	0	0	1132
Mining implements (pieces)	0	0	0	0	0	0	0	0	1674	60	0	1734
Knives	0	0	0	0	0	0	1350	6500	0	1200	1000	10050
Mules	0	1300	260	400	200	500	200	1130	1400	500	1160	7050
Donkeys	0	0	0	325	0	0	0	0	0	0	0	325
Est. annual cost of socorro (pesos)	0	23680	6266	11375	5120	13300	8002	34918	18080	8590	16736	146067
Est. burden per tributary (tribute + socorro), 1786 (pesos)	6.9	13.6	9.3	13.9	8.4	10.9	7.8	12.4	13.8	14.2	14.0	11.6

Note: For tribute ARC, TAZ, Leg. 80 (1784); for the socorro, ARC, INT, Ord., Leg. 1 (1784). All figures have been rounded to the peso, and thus the provincial figures do not add up to the "Total" figure. The farming implements are primarily hoes and other digging tools. The mining implements are metal sticks, hatchets, sieves, and lanterns. The quantities for the socorro are for five years, for the annual figures I have divided by five. Generally, quantities rather than value of goods are given; only the subdelegate of Chumbivilcas provided the prices at which goods were to be sold, and I have used them throughout. They were 33 pesos per mule, 1 peso per knife, and 1 peso per vara of bayeta and pañete de la tierra; iron and steel were 1 peso a pound. No prices were given for Quiteño cloth, for farming and mining tools, and for donkeys. I have calculated the donkeys at the cost of a mule, and I excluded the first three groups entirely; hence the annual burden should be read only as a gross estimate.

to raise the productivity of Indian society, these included the forced purchase of tools and mules. The abuses of the old repartos were acknowledged: Mata Linares declared of the socorro "that its prices, far from being so tyrannical and excessive as those of the corregidores, are not to surpass the cost of the goods."[8] Nonetheless, complaints suggest that tributaries and rural Spaniards did not see the difference so clearly as Mata Linares, and that subdelegates were reluctant to abandon the potential for profit.[9]

Subdelegates were personally responsible for tribute payments and had to provide guarantors. These *fianzas* clearly show the postrebellion power shift in rural areas, as few Indian nobles pledged surety. Indian guarantors appear most commonly in Tinta and Lampa: at the epicenter of the rebellion, loyalist Indian nobles retained their position in the provincial elite.[10] However, in the Inca provinces of Calca y Lares, Paucartambo, Quispicanchis, and Paruro no Indian nobles made such pledges; in urban Cusco a few did.[11] Instead, to obtain their offices, the subdelegates indebted themselves to provincial Spaniards, often of modest means and education. In 1804 the thirty-four Spanish *fiadores* for Caravaya's subdelegate included ten who could not sign their names; most pledged only 500 pesos.[12]

Even in the depressed decades following the rebellion, many Indian nobles could have made such a commitment. That they were not called upon to do so shows their changed relation to royal government. The cacical nobility between Cusco and La Paz had been among the most loyal sectors of society during the rebellion. A disproportionate number of those brought to trial for involvement were provincial creoles and mestizos, and in the dark days of December 1780 and January 1781 it had been caciques like Sahuaraura, Pumacahua, Choquecahua, Succacahua, Choquehuanca, and Quispe Cavana who had defended Cusco and resisted Tupac Amaru's march to Titicaca. Nonetheless, the crown saw the rebellion as an Inca uprising – ironically, accepting Tupac Amaru's claims that he was the true Inca heir rising against Spanish rule. In vain would Cusco's Inca nobility refer to him as "the traitor Jose Gabriel Condorcanqui, known as Tupac Amaru" in an attempt to disassociate themselves from the man whose kinship they had

---

8 ARC, INT, Ord., Leg. 1 (1784).

9 ARC, RA, Ord., Leg. 31 (1798) for the suit against Don Buenaventura de la Roca, subdelegate of Abancay.

10 In Tinta, Callo, Chuquitupa, Mamani, and Sinanyuca: ARC, INT: RH, Legs. 208 (1799) and 224 (1819–20); Gob., Leg. 141 (1789). In Lampa, Cama Condorsayna, Cava Apasa, Succacahua, Calisaya, Arevilca, and Ticona: ADP, INT, Exp. 41 (1800).

11 In Cusco Cercado, Mateo Pumacahua, Ysidro Bustinza y Uclucana, Joseph Santos Siccos, and Jose Ramos Tito Atauchi. ARC, INT, RH, Legs. 189 (1790), 201 (1795), and 211 (1801). Also, Pumacahua for Urubamba's subdelegate in 1789; ibid., Leg. 188 (1789).

12 BNP, Man., D-10033.

always rejected.[13] The crown made no such distinction: the decade following the rebellion witnessed a campaign against both the Indian nobility
and all that was Inca.

As early as 1781 the bishop of Cusco – Dr. Don Juan Manuel Moscoso –
had urged that the Incas' ceremonial dress be outlawed, along with the use
of "Ynga" by members of the Indian nobility.[14] Indian dances were banned,
and some effort made to educate pueblo leaders in Spanish.[15] As always
in the colonial Andes, execution fell far short of the intent and language
of the laws. Spanish dress did supplant ceremonial "Inca" garb: the nobles
marching to celebrate the audiencia's foundation wore "not their ancient
costume, but rather Spanish uniform on beautifully equipped horses."[16] But
despite efforts to curb the use of "Ynga," members of Cusco's Inca nobility
continued to use it in family names, and by the 1790s royal officials in Cusco
were again referring to the *cabildo* of "electores Yngas," not of "electores
indios."[17] Literacy and Spanish made inroads in rural society in the last
decades of the viceroyalty, but a serious assault on Quechua and Aymara
would have been utterly impossible, and dances and fiestas remained at
the core of pueblo life. In the end, the royal campaign against the Indian
nobility operated at the level of offices and noble privilege, not indigenous
culture.

The crown's abandonment of its commitment to Indian caciques hit
the Indian nobility hardest. By the 1750s Spanish and mestizo caciques,
appointed on an interim basis or ruling through their wives, were not
uncommon. But these did not reflect a rejection of Indian rule in the pueblo
so much as the reality of rural society. That changed after 1783. In response
to the rebellion the crown launched a campaign to wrest control of village
life from Indian elites: by 1790 the majority of the bishopric's pueblos
had Spanish caciques.[18] As the subdelegate of Caravaya observed in 1784
when he named a creole as cacique of Coasa, "the principal object . . . of our
Sacred Sovereign in the new system of government . . . is that of creating

13 ARC, NOT, Joseph Bernardo Gamarra, Leg. 121, 662 ff., November 11, 1796.
14 Although Moscoso was widely held to have sympathized with the rebellion. Sahuaraura, *Estado del Perú*, for his defense; Leon Campbell, "Rebel or Loyalist? Bishop Juan Manuel de Moscoso y Peralta and the Tupac Amaru Revolt in Peru, 1780–1784," *Revista de Historia de América* 88 (July–December 1978): 135–67.
15 Walker, *Smoldering Ashes*, pp. 53–4. ARC, RA, Adm., Leg. 171 (1815–16) for the 1782 decree calling for Spanish schools in Indian pueblos. For late colonial educational reforms in La Paz, Choque Canqui, *Sociedad*, pp. 87–93.
16 Castro, *Relación*, p. 81.
17 ARC, COR, Ord., Leg. 29, Exp. 620. Moscoso also called for portraits of Inca nobles to be destroyed; but in 1813 Martina Chiguantupa left "doze retratos de los Yngas de la Familia de Chiguantupa." ARC, NOT, Melendez Paez, Leg. 184, 529 ff., January 12, 1813.
18 Sala i Vila, *Y se armó*, pp. 268–72, for postrebellion Spanish caciques in the intendancy of Cusco.

Spanish caciques in each province and their respective pueblos."[19] In 1777, the cacicazgos of Caravaya had been almost entirely in Indian hands; after 1784, Indian caciques were rare.[20] Certainly rural Spaniards, whose efforts to expand their authority into the pueblo had long been checked by the Indian nobility, saw these reforms as the crown's concession of that authority to themselves.

Still, the assault was limited by a commitment to honoring hereditary cacicazgos and a desire to reward those who had defended the crown. This contradiction would drive the crown's policy toward the Indian nobility, and toward the structure of pueblo society, for the next three decades. A 1783 royal decree forbade viceroys and governors from naming new caciques, and confirmed the offices of those loyal in the rebellion.[21] The crown explicitly recognized the claims of hereditary caciques with clear royal confirmation of their rights. However, intendants and audiencia judges now adopted far more stringent criteria for assessing such claims, and decried innovations made by their predecessors over the past two centuries. A royal decree of May 9, 1790, "...ordered and commanded that the Audiencias of His Majesty in these dominions must be zealous...that the children of those who have been named [cacique] by the Lord Viceroys not become caciques nor succeed to such offices."[22]

So paraphrased the intendant of Cusco when he rejected Don Lucas Guampoco's efforts to win restitution of Santa Rosa's cacicazgo, held by his family since they founded the pueblo a century before.[23] By denying that cacical appointments made by the viceroys were hereditary, the royal decree placed postconquest political reorganizations of Indian society outside the realm of indigenous customary law. The royal decree of 1790 represented a radical departure from the status quo of the 1614 royal decree that defined cacicazgos as hereditary, revoking the presumption of hereditary authority that it had enshrined as Andean custom 180 years earlier.

But while the crown abandoned Indian caciques, it retained those aspects of the colonial economy that made caciques necessary: tribute and the *mita*. With many cacicazgos left vacant by the rebellion, and tribute levels soon to increase enormously, this policy created a vacuum in local administration. The solution was the "recaudador," or tribute collector.[24] Ideally, the recaudador was a person of property and good conduct appointed to

---

19 Don Manuel Herencia. In the cacical documents in RREE, PSG, Exp. 158.

20 In 1777 all nine caciques filing a complaint against the corregidor had indigenous names; only the Guaman Sullca of Crusero and Cotacallapa of Usicayos appear regularly as caciques after the rebellion. AGI, Charcas, Leg. 523; ARC, RA, Ord., Leg. 4 (1789).

21 Sala i Vila, *Y se armó*, pp. 68–76.

22 ARC, RA, Ord., Leg. 8 (1791), 27.

23 See Chapter 2, p. 70.

24 Sala i Vila, *Y se armó*, pp. 77–97 for *recaudadores* in the intendancies of Puno and Cusco.

collect tribute, guaranteeing payment with a pledge of personal property. The recaudador was to enjoy none of the ill-defined cacical privileges. As a judge of the Cusco Audiencia declared in 1801, "... [the recaudador is] without the titles, concept, or authority of the cacique, nor does he have any other superiority over the Indians, nor enjoy the services, plots, nor lands for his job, nor does he receive any other reward than the one percent [of tributes]...."[25]

The recaudador marked an enormous shift in the organization of the pueblo. With the Indian cacique, the Habsburgs had placed the frontier of the two republics outside the pueblo. In practice, Spaniards had long had authority in Indian pueblos, and even served as caciques. But as late as the 1750s the Audiencia of Charcas had criticized Lampa's corregidor for appointing a Spanish cacique in Pucará; after the rebellion such a criticism would have flown in the face of royal policy.[26] For centuries, the Indian nobility had depended on the imperfect, but nonetheless real, support of the crown to prevent just such a Spanish expansion into pueblo politics, and uphold the ideal that Indian pueblos enter the political and economic networks of colonial rule through the Indian nobility. Following the rebellion, the crown detected in this system a dangerous threat of Indian defiance of Spanish rule, and instead promoted a tribute-collecting bureaucracy that drew its ranks from the upper strata of provincial society – loyalist Indian nobles, but especially Spaniards. The recaudador was to be more professional than the cacique: a well-paid official who collected tribute but otherwise did not interfere in the pueblo. This office would be the culmination of the Toledan Reforms of the 1570s, only with these provincial officials drawn from the Spanish colonial society that had emerged in the past two centuries, rather than from the Indian elite.

Although widespread, this innovation occurred unevenly throughout the southern highlands. Caciques who had led troops to the crown's defense generally retained their offices. But where cacical families had been wiped out, or had lost their wealth and documents, the office often passed to creoles. Equally important, the nature of proprietary claims influenced whether caciques were replaced. The interplay of these factors produced a complex political geography in the Audiencia of Cusco during its thirty-seven-year existence, although three broad geographic patterns, and three trends, emerge. Around the Titicaca basin, the great loyalist cacical houses often retained their offices, at least until the end of the century, although they faced constant challenges from Spanish and Indian alike. In contrast, in the Vilcanota highlands that had formed the epicenter of the rebellion, Spanish caciques became the norm. The Incas of Cusco, despite their loyalty and

25 ARC, INT, Gob., Leg. 150 (1800–2) [Catca].
26 ANB, EC, 1775–176, 13r.

ancestry, also suffered the widespread alienation of their cacicazgos. Across these geographical variations, the bishopric as a whole witnessed the breaking of hereditary succession, a shift of cacical power from Indian nobles to rural Spaniards, and the growing importance of other Indian institutions and offices within the pueblo – above all, the cabildo and the alcalde.

The dispossession of Indian caciques was pronounced in the Vilcanota highlands, particularly in southern Quispicanchis and northern Canas y Canchis, the epicenter of the rebellion. The cacical elite from this area had been singularly supportive of the rebellion, and by 1790 almost no prerebellion caciques remained in office from Andaguaylillas to Tinta.[27] In southern Tinta, where Tupac Amaru had made little headway with the caciques, the battered remnants of the Indian elite were more successful in holding onto their offices. Several loyalist caciques fared very well. In Sicuani, Simon Callo remained a powerful force in this huge pueblo into the nineteenth century.[28] In Coporaque, Eugenio Sinanyuca received rewards from a grateful crown and ruled unchallenged until his death in 1804.[29] Strikingly, some caciques who supported Tupac Amaru early in the rebellion but then switched sides remained in office as well: Don Andres Chuquitupa of Tinta, Don Francisco Guambotupa of Yauri, and Doña Catalina Pachacutic y Salas of Yanaoca.[30]

South of the La Raya pass, the cacical elite had remained overwhelmingly loyal to the crown. As a result, in Cupi, Macarí, Umachire, Juliaca, Cavanilla, Caminaca, Juli, Chucuito, Azángaro, Saman, and San Taraco loyalist Indian caciques retained their authority through the eighteenth century.[31] Indeed, immediately following the rebellion loyalist caciques were named as interim caciques in pueblos whose caciques had joined the rebels or been killed. In 1782 the Mango Turpa of Azángaro Urinsaya were granted the cacicazgos of Asillo Anansaya and Urinsaya.[32] In 1783 Don Andres Calisaya, cacique of Tiquillaca, was appointed "interim [cacique] of Puno, Coata, and Capachica . . . in remuneration of the services provided to the King and to the country, with the total loss of his houses, furnishings and

---

27 Tomasa Tito Condemayta's son-in-law, Don Evaristo Delgado – who was loyal in the rebellion – remained cacique of Papres until 1797. ARC, RA, Ord., Leg. 25 (1797). Other families remained locally prominent: in 1797 Don Marcos Solis Quivimasa Ynga was again an ayllu cacique in Quiquijana. ARC, INT, RH, Leg. 204 (1797). For the area's caciques generally, Garrett, "Descendants," pp. 644–59.

28 ARC: INT, Gob., Legs. 138 and 139 (1786); RA, Ord., Legs. 27 and 28 (1798).

29 ARC, NOT, Vargas, Leg. 236, 357 ff., November 27, 1804.

30 *CDBR*, IV, p. 326; ARC, INT, RH, Leg. 216 (1805); *CDBR*, IV, p. 326, and ARC, INT, RH, Leg. 193 (1791); *CDBR*, IV, pp. 20 and 25; ARC, NOT, Zamora, Leg. 292, 402–13, October 21, 1785; ARC, NOT, Rodriguez Ledezma, Leg. 248, 153 ff., July 4, 1796.

31 Garrett, "Descendants," pp. 663–6, 672–88, and 692–700.

32 AGN-A, IX-31-4-6, Exp. 431.

livestock."[33] The crown's initial response to the rebellion around Titicaca was to create cacical fiefdoms, ceding much of the Azángaro valley to the Mango Turpas and the pueblos around Puno to Calisaya.

Nonetheless, the principle of Indian cacical rule was broken here as well. The rebellion had been especially destructive and long-lived in this region, and many caciques had been killed or had lost their property and papers. While the crown did recognize the claims of proprietary caciques, many established families could not meet the more rigorous standards of proof, and after 1784 the clear preference was to appoint Spaniards.[34] The most comprehensive information comes from Lampa. In 1794 the acting intendant of Puno, Don Leandro Piñaso y Dolz, deposed many caciques in Lampa, Chucuito, and Huancané and appointed his allies (many paying him more than 100 pesos). The caciques of Lampa then complained to the Cusco Audiencia.[35] Usually hostile to Indian cacical claims, the Audiencia was more troubled by Piñaso y Dolz's actions and quickly removed him for this serious abuse of office. The deposed caciques' complaints provide an unusually comprehensive list of caciques in Lampa. Roughly half the pueblos remained under the rule of Indian nobles, although Spanish caciques had made great inroads. Along the royal road, Santa Rosa, Ayavire, Pucará, and Nicacio came under Spanish rule, as did Orurillo and Ñuñoa to the north. Pueblos to the south and west – Macarí, Cupi, Umachire – remained under Indian cacical families.[36] Along the Cavana river, Cavanilla, Cavana, Juliaca, and Hatuncolla retained their cacical dynasties.[37] The caciques of Lampa and Calapuja were Spaniards married to cacical heiresses.[38]

In Azángaro and Chucuito, cacical dynasties also fared relatively well. While the Guaguacondori of Asillo – implicated in the rebellion – were deposed, the Mango Turpa, Choquehuanca, and Chuquicallata retained their cacicazgos. In the face of local riots, the Mango Turpa lost control of Asillo within a decade, and a cadet line challenged their hold on Azángaro Urinsaya in the 1790s. Nonetheless, until independence and beyond, these

---

33 RREE, PRA, Exp. 263.

34 The Guampoco of Santa Rosa, the Tapara of Ñuñoa, the Pachari of Nicacio, and the mixed-ancestry cacical families of eastern Paucarcolla all lost appeals to the court to retain or regain their offices. Garrett, "Descendants," pp. 666–8, 670–1, 689–92.

35 RREE, PRA, Exp. 268; ARC, RA: Ord., Leg. 28 (1798) and Adm., Leg. 153 (1794–5).

36 Cama Condorsayna, Guacoto Puma Caxia, and Succacahua, respectively. See n35; also ARC, RA, Ord., Leg. 14; Joseph Bernardo Gamarra, Leg. 124, 233 ff. (1799).

37 Castillo men governed Cavana for the length of the eighteenth century; ARC, COR, Civ., Leg. 43, Exp. 912; ADP, INT, Exp. 38 (1798). After Quispe Cavana's death, the cacicazgo principal of Cavanilla passed to the Arevilca, hereditary caciques of several ayllus in the pueblo: RREE, PRA, Exps. 189 (1793), 268 (1795–7). In 1798 the Cava Apasa retained their cacicazgo in Juliaca, as did the Chura in Hatuncolla; ARC, RA, Ord., Leg. 28 (1798).

38 Both Pacoricona: ADP, INT, Exp. 35 (August 1797); ARC, RA, Ord., Leg. 33 (1799); RREE, PRH, Exp. 184.

families remained local powers.[39] Chucuito, Acora, Juli, and Yunguyo also remained under their cacical families in the 1790s.[40] But Indian caciques were replaced by Spaniards almost completely in Caravaya, while in eastern Huancané the Spanish–Indian cacical families lost their proprietary claims, although some retained their office.[41]

Finally, the Inca caciques around Cusco were hard hit, as Spaniards replaced most Inca caciques between 1780 and 1795. By 1790 Coya, Lamay, Guayllabamba, Maras, Guarocondo, and Pacarectambo had interim Spanish caciques. In Pisac and Taray, Sebastian Unzueta ruled in the name of his wife, Rita Tamboguacso, and in Anta, Ramon Riquelme ruled through his wife, the daughter of Nicolas Rosas and Maria Quispeguaman.[42] The extent of Inca dispossession is striking in light of the Inca nobility's loyalty in the rebellion and of the well-established tradition of Inca rule in these pueblos. Several factors contributed. First was the widespread distrust of all things Inca after the rebellion. Second, Inca cacicazgos often meandered from brother to cousin to son-in-law, all Inca nobles but considered interim caciques by royal officers, with no proprietary rights. Last, the provinces near Cusco had large creole populations, so there was no shortage of Spanish subjects of property and standing to assume control of tribute collection. Dispossession was not universal. Pumacahua remained cacique in Chinchero and Choquecahua in Andaguaylillas. Both Inca dynasties in Oropesa had been at the front of the royalist defenses, and so Marcos Chillitupa held onto his cacicazgo and the Sahuaraura children had their claim recognized.[43] In San Sebastián, the bastion of colonial Inca privilege, creole rule made almost no inroads until the very end of the colonial period. The continuation of Inca *ayllu* caciques in San Sebastián suggests that the fractured pueblo and ayllu organization of the Incas protected ayllu autonomy. Local creoles became recaudadores, but many ayllus remained under Inca control, operating below the level of the latest reforms.[44] However, this rural nobility had lost control over the pueblo's principal office.

39 For the Asillo riots, Sala i Vila, *Y se armó*, pp. 118–28; AGN-A, IX-7-4-3 (1790); ARC, RA: Crim., Leg. 103 (1790) and Ord., Legs. 7 (1791) and 14 (1794); RREE, PRA, Exp. 212 (1794) and Exp. 242 (1795); for the cacicazgos after the rebellion, Garrett, "Descendants," pp. 675–88.

40 Ibid., pp. 692–701.

41 Ibid., pp. 668–70 and 689–92.

42 Ibid., pp. 611–42.

43 Also Don Matias Quispe Tupa Guambo, of San Salvador; ARC, CAB, Ped., Leg. 115 (1787–99) for his 1794 complaint against Hacienda Vicho.

44 In Pucyura the Uscamayta, Corimanya, and Ñancay continued to hold office; Garrett, "Descendants," pp. 615–16. In Yucay ayllus remained under Inca rule into the 1800s; see the Sanchez Machuca – Pilcotupa dispute, ARC, RA, Ord., Leg. 76 (1812). In Paruro, in 1792 Don Juan Cusipaucar y Leon remained cacique of two ayllus in Araypalpa. Don Gregorio Pumahuallpa Quehuaracha remained cacique of Corca through the 1790s; in 1801 his two sons (Eugenio and Cayetano) were, respectively, alcalde mayor and recaudador. Garrett, "Descendants," pp. 642–3.

Thus, regional factors influenced the speed and thoroughness of the cacical elite's dispossession. But local histories unfolded in a regional political
climate that had changed dramatically with the rebellion. The campaign
against hereditary cacical rule and the introduction of the recaudador were
radical innovations in royal policy toward Andean communities. The presumption that Indian authority within the pueblo would be hereditary
was abolished: in certain exceptional and well-documented cases the crown
recognized hereditary rule, but overall the crown now insisted that the cacicazgo was an office utterly within its gift. This shift in royal policy was a
response to the rebellion, but it also reflected the attempts of a rationalizing,
enlightened monarchy to dissolve what it saw as the outdated, and illegitimate, hereditary possession of office and to replace it with royal control.
One pillar of the colonial Indian elites' hereditary authority thus collapsed
as the Bourbons sought to modernize their Habsburg empire.

Officials viewed Spanish recaudadores as improvements over Indian
caciques for two reasons. First, the recaudador was to have a higher salary
and fewer powers than the cacique, and therefore was to be less abusive. Second, the general superiority of Spaniards over Indians moved to the center
of colonial ideology after the rebellion, and as its assertions became more
categorical they elided the ideological space occupied by the Indian nobility. Opposing Lucas Guampoco's efforts to reclaim Santa Rosa's cacicazgo,
the subdelegate of Lampa well expressed this view. He claimed that the
instigation came from Casimiro Condori, the pueblo's alcalde, who sought
Guampoco's appointment, "that being how they manage to live in their
liberty without subjection to their superiors."[45] The office of recaudador
was a fiscal innovation; it was also the mechanism by which Spanish officials, and Spanish Peruvians, undertook a new colonization of indigenous
society, at the level of the pueblo's economy and government.

Spanish assumption of pueblo authority was the true innovation of the
1780s. The idealistic goals justifying the new recaudador regime went
unrealized. As Sala i Vila has observed, like so many royal reforms this
one foundered on the lack of money: in the end recaudadores were no better paid than caciques, and their exposure to risk even greater as tribute
burdens climbed.[46] Thus, the distinction between recaudador and cacique
went largely unnoticed in the pueblo: the two terms were used inter-
changeably, or merged into "cacique recaudador." The burdens of office
were as considerable as the opportunities for enrichment, and recaudadores
assumed the role that caciques had held in the pueblo economy. They also
inflicted corporal punishment (always an integral part of tribute collection),
and as there was no clear boundary between production for tribute and

45 ARC, RA, Ord., Leg. 8 (1791), 33.
46 Sala i Vila, *Y se armó*, p. 77.

other aspects of village life, they usurped many of the cacique's traditional powers.

These tribute collectors were widely seen as more abusive than their predecessors. The appointment of recaudadores fell within the purview of the subdelegate, and pueblos complained that subdelegates were selling the offices to local Spaniards.[47] Subdelegates governed for five years, so recaudadores had a short time to extract as much as possible from their tributaries. Abusive as they could be, caciques who had often ruled for decades had been able to take a longer view, subsidizing tribute short-fall in one year and making large profits in another. Also, cacical couples in general had had strong ties to their pueblos. In the 1780s and 1790s, Spaniards from other pueblos might serve as tribute collectors, with no interest in establishing long-term relations with communities under their rule.[48] To be sure, a number of creole families with long histories in their pueblos assumed the new office, and some Spanish recaudadores were well liked.[49] But overall, the reform introduced an outsider into a position of considerable power, with a goal of maximizing extraction from the community.

These innovations provoked angry responses from the pueblos. The two decades after the rebellion saw many court cases launched by communities and cacical claimants against these cacique–cobradores.[50] The case of Lamay parallels others throughout the region in its broad contours, though the specifics are of course rooted in local events.[51] In 1780 Don Manuel Prado Sunatupa was cacique; his wife, Doña Bernarda Paucarpuña Corimanya, had ancestral claim to the cacicazgo. Their daughter, Doña Melchora, married Don Miguel Guaypartupa y Pomayalli, an Inca noble who served as a captain in the regiment of Indian nobles during the rebel-lion. For a year Guaypartupa battled "the traitors Joseph Gabriel and Diego Christobal Condorcanqui, known as Tupac Amaru."[52] The rebels burned his house, but with Guaypartupa's loyalty having established his author-ity in Lamay, his father-in-law renounced the cacicazgo in his favor. Prado Sunatupa sent to Lima for approval, but the audiencia did not reply. In the meantime, Guaypartupa had a falling out with the corregidor (Don Pedro

---

47 See Lamay (discussed below); also Pacarectambo, ARC, INT, Gob., Leg. 142 (1790).

48 Tresierra in Guayllabamba and Caycay, ARC, INT, Ord., Legs. 14 (1787) and 3 (1785); Don José Herrera y Talavera of Ñuñoa, ARC, RA, Ord., Leg. 34 (1799).

49 ARC, INT, Ord., Leg. 61 (1806), Guanoquite; ARC, RA, Adm., Leg. 153 (1794-5), Ayavire; and RREE, PRA, Exp. 329 (1797), Santiago [Azángaro].

50 Sala i Vila, *Y se armó*, pp. 651-62. For a particular case, that against Don Agustin Nuñez de la Torre of Maras. ARC, INT: Ord., Legs. 31 (1793) and 34 (1794); Gob., Leg. 143 (1790-1); RH, Leg. 199 (1794). For others, Garrett, "Descendants," p. 468, n74.

51 Unless specified, all information from ARC, RA, Ord., Leg. 18 (1795).

52 Ibid., 15v.

de Zentero), who deposed him in 1782 and appointed Don Martin Reyes, who (in Guaypartupa's words) "in all the time of the rebellion [did nothing but] preserve his property."[53] Lamay's priest testified that Guaypartupa had saved his life in the rebellion, and was an upstanding leader of the pueblo. An extraordinary array of witnesses testified to his loyalty, ability, and nobility: among them were Mateo Pumacahua and the Mariscal del Valle.[54] However, Zentero replied that Guaypartupa had never been appointed cacique, and that Prado Sunatupa had simply been an interim cacique, with no right to choose his successor.

Zentero was an unpopular corregidor – not least with the Spaniards he appointed as recaudadores, from whom he demanded 100 pesos a year.[55] Reyes's hold on the office did not survive Zentero's term, but Guaypartupa did not regain the cacicazgo. Instead, it went to Don Ildefonso Unzueta, whose brother Sebastian was cacique of neighboring Pisac and Taray.[56] Ildefonso held the cacicazgo until 1788, when it went to Don Ambrocio Vargas. In 1795 Guaypartupa launched a concerted effort to regain the office, organizing numerous complaints against Vargas and presenting more than twenty-five witnesses in support of his own claims. They accused Vargas of a catalog of cacical abuses: he forced Indians to plow cacical fields, paying them only in coca and *chicha* and requiring those who did not own oxen to rent animals for the occasion. He had imposed a contribution of 200 adobes per household to reconstruct the church, and then used them for his own house, where he also had many *mitanis* working. Vargas demanded lambs from the tributaries during the annual division of the communal land and forced some to work on his coca plantation in Lares.[57] Antonio Alvarado, a seventy-year-old Spanish *vecino*, testified that all charges were true; that those who testified against Guaypartupa were servants of Vargas; and that Guaypartupa had been loyal during the rebellion and lost his house, while "Don Ambrosio Vargas was not seen in any expedition, and . . . the rebels did no damage to his hacienda in Lares."[58] Vargas disputed very few of these facts (although he denied charges that he had killed Guaypartupa's mother-in-law and torn down his house). These were, he argued, the customary privileges of the cacique and were necessary to collect tribute. He only sent those who would not pay tribute to his hacienda; the adobes had gone for the church (but the Indians had not wanted to provide them); he had many

53 Ibid., 20r.
54 Also the priests of Coya and Lamay and Calca's justicia mayor. Ibid., 9–14.
55 ARC, INT: Ord. Leg. 2 (1784); Gob., Legs. 130 (1784) and 133 (1785); RH, Leg. 162 (1784) for complaints against him.
56 ARC, INT, Gob., Leg. 131 (1784–5); for Sebastian Unzueta, see Chapter 3, pp. 94–96.
57 ARC, RA, Ord., Leg. 18 (1795), 1–3 and 46–104.
58 Ibid., 51.

mitanis weaving in his house, but these were widows and spinsters whom the village sent to him to support.[59]

Vargas' assumption of the mechanisms through which caciques manipulated and controlled the pueblo economy was the source of widespread anger. Almost certainly Vargas increased the burdens placed on the community: the crown's demands had grown dramatically, and to the people of Lamay the doubling in tribute was an abuse by the cacique, not the king. In the end, the support of the subdelegate and of Lamay's new priest proved decisive. Despite the many witnesses who supported Guaypartupa's claims, and the clear evidence of his loyalty, the audiencia preferred to retain a disliked *hacendado* who used his office to supply labor to his coca plantation in Lares. Guaypartupa and his wife did not resign themselves to the loss: in her 1799 will Melchora Prado Sunatupa Paucarpuña insisted that she was the successor to the cacicazgo, and that it should go to her husband and then her sons.[60] (And, in a reminder of how complicated pueblo politics could be, she dictated her will to the notary whom Guaypartupa had denounced as biased in favor of Vargas; and as her executor she named the former interim cacique, Ildefonso Unzueta.) However, it does not appear that her sons regained the cacicazgo. Rather, the Vargas emerged as a dominant family in Calca y Lares. From 1789 on Vargas was also cacique of the coca-growing pueblo of Lares, where he had his plantation.[61] In 1819 Don Francisco Vargas was cacique of Lamay, appearing in court to answer charges against him by various tributaries for the same abuses his father had allegedly committed.[62]

Lamay well illustrates postrebellion changes in rural society. Most obvious is the loss of cacical authority by Indian nobles and its assumption by creoles. Lamay had a hereditary cacicazgo, albeit not one recognized by the crown. For at least four generations the cacicazgo had passed from mother to daughter among the descendants of Micaela Paucarpuña. The rejection of the family's cacical claim, coupled with the preference for Spaniards in the reformed cacicazgos, left the most lucrative post in the local economy in the hands of a creole hacendado. Similar appointments gave power to rural Spaniards as a class, who already dominated private property and market transactions. From the 1780s to independence, families like the Vargas and Unzueta displaced the Tamboguacso, Chiguantupa, and other Inca noble lineages that had long dominated pueblo economies.

The rebellion, and the crown's response to it, changed the rural order in other ways as well. The social conflicts unleashed in 1780–2 remained

---

59 Ibid., 113–20.
60 ARC, NOT, Tomas Santos Gamarra, Leg. 181, [ ], July 17, 1799.
61 ARC, INT, Ord., Leg. 19 (1789).
62 ARC, INT, RH, Leg. 220 (1818–19).

long after royal authority was restored, and continued to play themselves out, occasionally in rebellion – most notably in Asillo, which rose against the Mango Turpa in 1790 – but more often through legal battles.[63] The rebellion had left the highlands exhausted and divided. The appointment of loyalists as caciques of rebel strongholds did little to dissipate the rancor of the rebellion; and the victors – like the Mango Turpa – had little interest in fair and compassionate rule. The dislocations produced by the postrebellion reforms added to the tensions, as in Lamay. As a result, the 1780s and 1790s were the most litigious decades of the colonial period for Indian communities. The growth of litigation owed much to the new bureaucratic apparatus: the intendancy system and the Cusco Audiencia extended the crown's reach into provincial life, and rural subjects' ability to contest the decisions of their governors increased dramatically. Until the 1780s, those wanting to appeal a governor's ruling had to turn to Lima or Chuquisaca; now, courts of appeal were in Cusco and Puno. The reforms thus provided recourse to those injured or disaffected by the expansion of the Spanish republic, but simultaneously strengthened royal authority. The semiautonomy of the pueblo that had held sway under the *corregimiento* system (from both a positive commitment by the crown and the lack of a royal administrative infrastructure that reached into the pueblo) was curtailed as Spanish justice and administration examined pueblo life more closely.

At the same time, as the power of cacical elites declined the cabildo and alcalde began to flourish.[64] Mentions of pueblo cabildos in prerebellion Cusco are rare. Caciques' role in the economy concentrated local power in cacical households, and left the alcalde and cabildo of secondary importance – an eclipse furthered by the recognition of the cacicazgo as hereditary. The postrebellion period saw a dramatic shift in this balance of power. The crown's preference for aristocratic authority in the Indian pueblos gave way to support for the more democratic ideal of the cabildo and alcalde, which subdelegates sought to strengthen. Election records exist for almost every province in the 1780s, as subdelegates went from village to village to oversee and record the annual appointment of pueblo officials.[65] These were divided by republic, with an "alcalde mayor de españoles" and "alcalde ordinario de indios." The different titles show the assertion of Spanish superiority in the countryside, although the Indian republic was

63 Sala i Vila, *Y se armó*, pp 118–28; AGN-A, IX-7-4-3 (1790); ARC, RA, Crim., Leg. 103 (1790); ARC, RA, Ord., Legs. 7 (1791) and 14 (1794); RREE, PRA, Exps. 212 (1794) and 242 (1795).
64 O'Phelan Godoy, *Kurakas sin Sucesiones*, pp. 53–66, and Thomson, *We Alone*, pp. 232–68.
65 RREE, PC, Leg. 438, for Puno. ARC, INT, Gob.: Legs. 138 (1786) and 141 (1789) (Urubamba); 131 (1784–5) (Paruro); 141 (1790) (Tinta); 138 (1786) (Quispicanchis); 134 (1786) (Cotabambas).

still far larger, and the elections include up to half a dozen Indian alcaldes, *fiscales*, and *regidores* to the one Spaniard invariably elected.

Some dispossessed caciques – including Guaypartupa of Lamay – appeared as alcaldes ordinarios; some were even elected alcalde mayor de españoles.[66] In the 1790s Don Jacinto Cama Condorsayna of Macarí – son of the late cacique Gabriel – served as both recaudador and alcalde de españoles.[67] The local standing of cacical families allowed many individuals to retain their authority. But cacique and alcalde were fundamentally different offices. The cacique's tenure was indefinite and often lifelong, and successful caciques often passed their office to their children. In contrast, alcaldes were elected and served short terms, and while more prominent families in a community were undoubtedly overrepresented, village government was no longer ideally in the hands of one individual or family for long stretches at a time. This change emphasized a more corporate rule within the pueblo, continued in the republican period.[68]

The goal of strengthening the cabildo was not to institute popular rule: following the rebellion, Spaniards added open fear to the general contempt in which they held the Indian commons. In 1790 the subdelegate of Lampa supervised the election in Pucará " ... [s]o that election of alcaldes ... be made from the Indian residents of this pueblo who are competent in the Castilian language, and of good conduct, for the good rule and government therein, and likewise four regidores be named from the *principales*, who possess the same qualities and circumstances, so that the elections are made by these from among the said subjects."[69] The acting "cacique" – referred to as such, not as "recaudador" – was the Spanish alcalde mayor, and the current officeholders (an alcalde from each of the pueblo's four ayllus, and four regidores) gathered in his house to choose their successors. All the alcaldes merited "Don": these were the parish's "principales" organizing its rule among themselves. As the subdelegate of Huancané put it in 1792, "let those Indians who are most distinguished in agriculture and [the ability] to speak Spanish ...... be preferred for these offices."[70] What is striking is the shift in the crown's strategy, from its earlier preference for rule by individual Indian nobles and for the hereditary passage of that rule; to an active support for rule by elective alcaldes and cabildos.

66 ARC, RA, Ord., Leg. 18 (1795), 26. BNP, Man., C-581; RREE, PRA, Exp. 154. Also Cusihuaman's nobility claim, ARC, INT, RH, Leg. 218 (1807), 2r, for Orcoguaranca in Guasac.
67 RREE, PRA, Exp. 110.
68 Jacobsen, *Mirages*, pp. 121–48 and 259–288; Walker, *Smoldering Ashes*, pp. 186–221; Víctor Peralta Ruíz, *En Pos del Tributo en el Cusco rural. 1826–54* (Cusco: Centro Bartolomé de Las Casas, 1991).
69 RREE, PC, Exp. 6.
70 RREE, PC, Exp. 12; Exp. 2, for the Huancané elections of 1787.

The Campaign against Indian Nobility

The assault on the cacical elite was mirrored by an aggressive campaign against the privileges of Indian nobility. In Spain, too, the Bourbons challenged the innate "nobility" – and fiscal privileges – of their many subjects who enjoyed that status.[71] But this campaign had a different meaning in Cusco: the focus on Indian nobility made this campaign not just a fiscal reform, but a broader assertion of Spanish (and creole) authority. Moreover, the repudiation of Inca privilege was a repudiation of the colonial order that the Incas had rallied to defend against Tupac Amaru and his forces. To be sure, Inca nobility had been challenged in the decades before the rebellion: in the 1760s, the Inca nobles of Cusco had successfully defended their privileges from the corregidor Diego Manrique y Lara. But that success had depended on the support of the Lima Audiencia, and after 1780 this support evaporated, replaced by thinly veiled hostility.

Spurred by the distrust of anything "Inca" following the rebellion, in April 1785 the last corregidor of Cusco (Don Mathias Baulen) forbade the election of the *alférez real*. For the Incas, it was a stunning blow: far from being rewarded for their loyal service in the rebellion, they were to lose the ceremony that for two centuries had marked their position of privilege. Thirteen electors immediately petitioned the newly appointed intendant (Mata Linares), informing him of their historic right to elect "an Alférez in every year so that he carry the Royal standard in the procession... of the Apostle Santiago... and for this also they have preserved the title of the 24 electors." To eliminate that privilege "would be scandalous, the supplicants having distinguished themselves in the defense of the religion, of the King their lord, and [of] the country against the rebellion of the infamous Tupa Amaru."[72] Mata Linares requested information from Baulen, who justified his action in a terse articulation of the changed attitude toward the Inca nobility.

First, Baulen insisted that "being that we are, Spaniards and Indians, vassals of one monarch, it seems out of conformity with all politics to permit two banners to signify his sovereignty in the same population." The ideological underpinning of the colonial system – that Spaniard and Indian shared a lord and a territory, but were part of two separate societies – was neatly erased, replaced with an assertion of Spanish and Indian as co-subjects. But to Baulen, Indians nursed a deep-rooted hatred for Spaniards: "... [W]ith such a bad disposition... they remember with great vividness their past and the liberty of which they falsely suppose themselves deprived, ... [and]

---

71 One in eight Spaniards was noble in 1700; one in twenty-five in 1797. Bush, *Rich Noble*, pp. 7–8. Paradoxically, Peru's aristocracy expanded rapidly as rich creoles bought titles. Unanue, *Guía*, pp. 156–78.

72 ARC, INT, Gob., Leg. 133 (1785) [unless noted, following quotes are from this suit].

not only style themselves nobles, but also descendants of the Yngas their kings. . . . I well know that in all nations of the world there is nobility, and by it is distinguished a proportion of the subjects. But . . . it is not the same to be noble and to be a descendant of royal blood, which circumstances introduce a right of sovereignty, a preoccupation of this class extended too far in favor of the traitor Jose Gabriel Condorcanqui."

To Baulen, the pretensions of Cusco's Incas were a repudiation of Spanish rule and an assertion of Inca sovereignty, not an attempt to position themselves in colonial society through claims of royal ancestry. Baulen's model of colonial society transformed the boundary between Indian and Spaniard, from the separated inequality of the republics to a unified hierarchy with Spaniard above Indian. This order had been emerging in the eighteenth century, but royal officials had largely refrained from articulating it; now it was left to the Incas to defend an order that had already been passed. Mata Linares referred the matter to the viceroy, who in June replied in support of Baulen. Mata Linares then informed the cabildo that the election of an alférez was suspended.

The Incas responded immediately, citing custom and royal decrees in their favor, not least one from May 7, 1781 – after the capture of Tupac Amaru – which ordered "that from that date forward the corregidor of Cusco not contrive that the Mascapaycha be given to any Indian who had not qualified and proved his nobility." Their point was that they had so proven their nobility and qualifications. They were particularly offended by Baulen's (incorrect) suggestion that the Inca cabildo had been sympathetic to " . . . Jose Gabriel Condorcanqui y Noguera, feigned Tupac Amaro, and supposed cacique of pueblos who was not nor could be, because all know . . . that the vile subversive was not [one] who commanded such a title, nor had the origin which he falsely appropriated, but rather was a poor muleteer of vile and unknown extraction . . . , and his mother a vilest Indian subject to the contribution of tribute, and other personal services, which are proper for their birth and origin." Baulen's assault on the cabildo's privileges was, to the Incas, proof that he did not respect the lines along which Andean society stratified. The Incas whose loyalty was displayed annually in the procession of Santiago, and had been performed during the rebellion, were to lose the marks that set them apart from the Andean masses.

The assault against Inca privilege intensified the following year, when tribute exemptions came under attack. When Mata Linares compiled Cusco's tribute lists in early 1786, he reduced the Inca nobility to tributary status, reflecting the shift in the government's understanding of the demarcations in Andean society, as Indians generically became tributaries and peasants, and the distinction between mestizo and Indian became more important than that between noble and tributary. The ministers of the

Royal Hacienda supported this move; like Baulen, they did not deny the existence of a tribute exemption for Inca nobles, but they argued that this applied to " . . . those who appear to be legitimate descendants of [the Incas] by the male line, and it appearing that at present there is not a single one, Your Lordship can order that they do not enjoy this liberty, by which Your Lordship can maintain Justice."[73]

The Incas responded, presenting bundles of faded documents to support their claims. Those of the Quispe Ynga brothers, descendants of Huayna Capac, included Lima's 1772 ruling acknowledging the nobility and exemption of sixty-three Inca nobles in Cusco.[74] These documents forced the intendant to reconsider the crackdown on Inca nobility. As Mata Linares wrote to the viceroy on February 12,

> . . . the solicitudes of the Indians, that they be exempted from paying tribute, are endless, and particularly on account of the title of Nobility, . . . which is certain, but as the number of those who call themselves nobles is quite extensive, and some of them have no documents [and] others present snippets . . . , I find myself perplexed, because regulation 7 Title 6 Book 2 [of the *Recopilación*] . . . is very clear in not conceding tribute exemption for nobility alone . . . [but] only [to] proprietary caciques and their eldest sons. . . . [But], after I saw [the Quispe Ynga papers], I know that many are correct but not which of them . . . , nor whether all their families and descendants should have it, as they claim, in this manner the number exempted being very large. . . .[75]

With that, he again referred the problem to Lima. At heart was the question of Inca, and Cusqueño, particularity. As the Bourbons sought to rationalize their realms, the distinction between the Incas and Indians became an inconvenient anachronism and an expense to the treasury. But Bourbon rule remained legalistic, and Inca privilege had been confirmed repeatedly over the centuries. And so while Lima deliberated, Mata Linares took pledges from Cusco's creoles in lieu of collecting tribute from the Inca nobility. The sums were small: the compromise suggests the unwillingness of the Incas to pay in the interim lest this establish the custom. And the pledges well show the bonds between Inca and creole, as men like Don Gaspar Arias (master fringer) and Don Gregorio Valas ("person of known worth") joined San Sebastián's parish priest in pledging payment for their neighbors, fellow guildsmen, and parishioners.[76]

The campaign against noble privilege was not limited to Cusco. Incas on the Anta plain, in Paruro, and along the Vilcanota were enrolled as

73 In the response to the Tisoc petition. ARC, INT, RH, Leg. 179 (1786), 72.
74 In the notes on tribute; ARC, INT, RH, Leg. 173 (1785), 43–4 and 59–61.
75 Ibid., 62.
76 ARC, INT, RH, Leg. 177 (1786), for a collection of fianzas.

tributaries in the mid-1780s.[77] Nor were the Incas the only targets: in 1785 the Spanish cacique of Mollepata – "ignorant of the exemptions that I should enjoy" – matriculated Don Pedro Nolasco Aronis as a tributary.[78] Son of Don Diego Aronis and Doña Petrona Ayquipa Arcos Guachaca, Pedro came from families that had dominated Collana Aymara in Aymaraes since before the conquest; he had married an Inca noblewoman and settled on his sugar hacienda. His appeal carries the hallmarks of the high Indian nobility: he had studied at San Borja in Cusco; his brother was alférez of Aymaraes' infantry regiment; and Pedro signed his petition with a perfect hand and attached to it a bundle of documents dating to the 1500s. Such a display swayed even the ministers of the Royal Hacienda, who declared him exempt from tribute. However, Mata Linares overruled them, arguing that Pedro Nolasco had not proven that his father was a proprietary cacique (which would exempt him as the son).

Such equivocation and contradictions were the norm. Just weeks before, on June 28, the viceroy had decided not to address the issue directly: Indians in possession of nobility should continue to enjoy it, while no new petitions would be heard. But Mata Linares did not announce the decision. Still, the Inca nobility in Cusco would not pay tribute: in 1788 another batch of fianzas were recorded.[79] In December 1788 the General Accountant for Tribute argued against the noble exemption, "since by simply taking the family names and borrowing, selling, or pawning the papers – which method is common among the Indians – they succeed in defrauding Your Majesty." In 1789 Lima ruled that as a group Cusco's Inca nobles would lose their privileges, but those able to prove individual claims could do so.[80] As with the cacical elite, the courts would recognize well-documented claims of particular families. However, an innate nobility was no longer understood as a necessary and integral part of the Indian republic, just as the Indian cacique was no longer necessary to the pueblo.

Superficial Reprieve

And yet, from the late 1780s until independence, the Inca nobility of Cusco underwent a corporate revival. Three years after Baulen suspended the election of the alférez real, the electoral book resumed, and on July 12,

---

77 The Tito brothers of Yaurisque (ARC, INT, RH: Leg. 179, 1786); Tacuri Cusipillaca of Paruro (Leg. 176, 1786); the Pumahuallpa Quehuaracha of Corca (Leg. 212, 1801); the Cusipaucar y Leon of Araypalpa (ARC, INT, Gob., Leg. 145, 1792–3); the Alferez Poma Orcosupa of Pucyura (AGN, DI, Exp. 413, 1785).

78 ARC, INT, RH, Leg. 203 (1796).

79 Diego Cusiguaman's 1792 petition, in the Cusihuaman nobility claim, ARC, INT, RH, Leg. 218 (1807), 11–15. For the 1788 fianzas, ibid., Leg. 186 (1788).

80 ARC, INT, RH, Leg. 186 (1788), 35–8.

1788, "all the nobles of the eight parishes of this city gathered together to elect the alférez real."[81] In September 1789, the various electors presented their titles and documents of office. The royal officer in charge reported that only one of them had a title of elector specifically granted by Lima; nonetheless, he had continued with the process, and the electors chose new members to fill the vacant positions. From then until 1820 – with a three-year hiatus in 1813, 1814, and 1815 – the cabildo met annually to elect their standard-bearer.

They also met for exceptional circumstances. In March 1805, the commissary of the regiment of Indian nobles (Diego Cusiguaman) called together the cabildo to elect an ambassador to meet the newly appointed Audiencia president. In informing the intendant of their choice, Cusiguaman made clear that this fell within the purview of the cabildo. The electors met again that year, as Cusiguaman was sent into exile for his alleged involvement in an anti-crown conspiracy; on July 23 they elected Mateo Pumacahua to replace him as commissary. The Incas dutifully assembled on September 17, 1808, to elect an alférez real for the procession in which Cusco swore loyalty to Ferdinand VII. A few months later, on April 21, 1809, the electors publicly swore allegiance to the Junta Central of Cádiz.[82] And in June 1824, Don Luis Ramos Tito Atauchi presented the petition from the cabildo to the viceregal court for permission to elect an alférez "in memory of the triumph of our invincible catholic arms."[83] Over two hundred and fifty years, the catholic arms were transformed from theirs to ours, as the Incas saw their imperial power replaced with the privileges of a noble vassalage performed to the end for a king whose Andean realms had been sorely reduced.

The revival of the cabildo paralleled a tacit restoration of noble privilege. After Mata Linares's term as intendant had ended, Don Diego Cusiguaman began pressing the issue again. On May 16, 1791, Cusco's Indian nobles and electors had given power of attorney to Cusiguaman to pursue any case in defense of their noble privileges.[84] He in turn had authorized a power of attorney to a lawyer in Lima to bring to the viceroy's attention both this case and Mata Linares's failure to announce the earlier ruling.[85] And so, in September 1792 Lima confirmed the earlier decision, that no innovations be made in the collection of tribute from those who already possessed noble exemptions. In 1801 Cusiguaman again presented the 1786 ruling and the 1792 confirmation to the Royal Hacienda of Cusco, successfully rebutting

81 ARC, COR, Civ., Leg. 29, Exp. 620.
82 ARC, INT, Ord., Leg. 66 (1808).
83 ARC, INT, Vir., Leg. 160 (1823–24).
84 ARC, NOT, Joseph Bernardo Gamarra, Leg. 116, 147, May 16, 1791.
85 ARC, NOT, Joseph Bernardo Gamarra, Leg. 118, 403, February 10, 1792.

yet another attempt to enroll the Inca nobility in the tributary class.[86] At
no point did officials recognize the Incas' claims; they simply declined to
innovate. Thus, only tangential evidence shows the preservation of Inca
privileges. A 1796 list signed by an Audiencia judge names thirty-one Inca
nobles.[87] This list addressed the nobility of individuals: most Inca nobles
enjoyed their status as members of ayllus in San Sebastián and San Gerónimo.
The best evidence that these retained their legal privileges is their absence
from the tributary rolls.[88] And in November 1801 Don Antonio Suta of
Ayllu Sucso appeared before the intendant to cancel the fianza for his tribute
pledged a decade before by Don Agustin de Vera, as it was no longer
needed.[89]

The revival of the Incas in the 1790s was part of what appeared, superfi-
cially, to be an ebbing of the crown's assault on Indian elites. Spanish rule
remained legalistic, and many Indians had documents confirming nobility
or possession of cacicazgos. In the sixteenth century royal officers had used
recognition of indigenous elites to both co-opt and discipline them. Two
centuries later, the legacy of this recognition imposed a less stringent discipline on the crown as it sought to dismantle that earlier order. The retreat
from the anti-Indian-elite stance of the 1780s had less to do with a commitment to indigenous nobility than with acting in the limits of legality.
A mid-1790s decree made clear that the principal being upheld was legal
precedent, not Inca and Indian noble privilege. In 1797 Don Blas Quispe
Uscamayta of Pucyura requested that the Royal Hacienda in Cusco receive
information about his "nobility and descent from the lord kings of Peru," as
a descendant "of the Uscamaytas, cacique-governors of the parish of Belén,
and of the Incas Huayna Capac and Mayta Capac."[90] The attorney refused,
arguing that " ... by law 119 it is ordered that the Royal Audiencias of the
Indies only preserve the decrees of *hidalguía* for those who had it, and also
the privileges of exemption, without involving themselves in knowing the
reasons for these hidalguías. ... " The recognition of Indian nobility was
no longer adherence to an ideology of social stratification rooted in natural
law, but rather acknowledgment of a colonial, legal artifact.

In addition, the many petitions by loyalist Indian nobles, detailing their
losses and suffering in defense of the crown, apparently produced recognition

---

86 In the Cusihuaman nobility claim, ARC, INT, RH, Leg. 214 (1807), 11–15.

87 ARC, INT, RH, Leg. 202 (1796).

88 The 1785–6 rolls of San Sebastián had listed as noble the entire ayllus of Sucso, Pumamarca,
   Ayarmaca, and Sahuaraura; and twenty-two of Chimapanaca's sixty-five adult men. Sucso, Pumamarca, and Sahuaraura are not included in the 1796 lists, and Chima had but thirty-two tributaries;
   nor did other ayllus grow to include the nobles listed in 1786. ARC, INT, RH, Legs. 203 (1796)
   and 173 (1785).

89 ARC, INT, RH, Leg. 212 (1801).

90 ARC, RA, Adm., Leg. 156 (1797), 48–9.

of the patent injustice of stripping these loyal subjects of their privileges and offices. Thus, the same 1790 decree that insisted that viceregal appointments to cacicazgos were not hereditary stressed that proprietary claims of loyalist caciques had not been abrogated.[91] A 1795 decree further ordered audiencias to hear claims for the restitution of such cacicazgos. Word of this spread quickly among cacical families – witness Guaypartupa's effort to regain the cacicazgo of Lamay. In December 1796, Doña Felipa Campos Alacca appealed to the Audiencia of Charcas to reinstate her as *cacica* of Laxa, since "it has arrived at my notice that it has served ... Your Highness to order ... that the legitimate caciques who have remained by descent be reinstated to their offices."[92] The cacicazgo had passed through the family of her father to her and her husband (Don Rafael Ramirez). They had ruled until the rebellion, when Ramirez was killed by rebels; she had then been deposed by the corregidor. In March 1797, the Audiencia reinstated her as cacica.

But Campos Alacca's success was exceptional. Overall, the call for the restitution of hereditary Indian caciques had little effect, and cacicazgos that had passed into Spanish hands rarely reverted to Indian nobles. A number of Guaypartupa's Inca peers sought restitution after 1795, but none appears to have been successful.[93] Working against Inca cacical claims were Spanish suspicion of all things "Inca" as threats to Spanish rule, the absence of clear familial claims to many cacicazgos, and the sizable Spanish colonies in the Inca pueblos. But even around Titicaca, with its ancient, powerful cacical dynasties, the 1795 decree did not revitalize the Indian nobility. Many pueblos did not have such dynasties: cacical lines had died out, or moved to cadet branches, frequently throughout the colonial period. What had preserved the cacical elite was the need for them: where death or poverty created a cacical vacuum, other Indian nobles soon filled it. After the rebellion, those vacuums were filled by Spaniards, and the decree allowing restitution did not alter this basic change: where cacical families collapsed, they were not to be replaced.

Moreover, the crown's rejection of the cacical elite was apparent to all. While Indian communities opposed the appointment of Spanish caciques, they were also aware that unpopular Indian caciques were now vulnerable to lawsuits. Around Cusco, the surviving Inca caciques did not face widespread opposition (although some parish priests sought their removal).[94] But to

91 Sala i Vila, *Y se armó*, pp. 73–4; Díaz Rementería, *El cacique*, pp. 192–3.
92 ANB, EC, 1796–97, 1; for a summary of the decree, 14.
93 ARC: RA, Adm., Leg. 157 (1797–8), for Don Sebastian Tupa Orcoguaranca of Guayllabamba; RA, Ord., Leg. 27 (1798), for Don Mauricio Uscamayta of Maras; INT, Gob., Leg. 152 (1806–9), for competing claims to Caycay.
94 Quispe Uscamayta and Corimanya (ARC, INT: RH, Leg. 211, 1801); Copa Cusicondor of Guarocondo (Gob., Leg. 133, 1785); Riquelme of Anta (RH, Leg. 204, 1797).

the south the antagoni·ms unleashed during the rebellion remained in play. Indian caciques faced legal challenges in Sicuani and Pitumarca; in Copacabana tributaries pursued a massive suit against Chuquimia.[95] Their opponents made traditional claims of illegitimacy: that Chuquimia had usurped the old Tito Atauchi cacicazgo and that the Aymitumas in Sicuani were interim appointments and abusive. Strikingly, communities around Titicaca also challenged established cacical dynasties. In addition to their rejection by Asillo, the Mango Turpa saw their hold on Azángaro Urinsaya successfully challenged by the community — unthinkable twenty years earlier.[96]

In Saman and San Taraco, centuries of Chuquicallata authority came under assault, as an 1802 letter from Doña Isabel Mango (the widow of Don Martin Chuquicallata) to the intendant of Puno shows. Describing herself as "of a house of the Royal Chain, and Coat of Arms, cacica of . . . Taraco," she complained that

> . . . it being the custom to propose stalwart subjects of good conduct for the alcaldes that govern the Indians under my rule, . . . it succeeded that they laughingly cast aside my proposal, appointing Pablo Quispe . . . in spite of the prevalence in this individual of a disobedient spirit, perturbing with it the tranquility of these people. It thus being necessary to repair that . . . Quispe is authorized with the Royal Insignia, I put at the attention of Your Excellency . . . , that Quipse [ought] not have authority over the Indians, since he conspired in the late rebellion . . . against the patria, state, and monarchy.[97]

Isabel and her son (Don Cipriano Chuquicallata) had been in conflict with Quispe for more than a decade. A "principal of Taraco," he was a focal point of opposition to the cacical house.[98] That a pueblo the size of Taraco was divided into factions was nothing new; nor were tense relations between alcalde and cacique. However, that in electing an alcalde according to the newly established procedure the community chose someone hostile to the cacica, and that she had no recourse, marked a shift in pueblo politics. Indian cacical authority was no longer inevitable in Spanish eyes; it was also no longer inevitable in those of the pueblo.

Not only caciques suffered a loss of authority. The assault on legal nobility is clearest in Cusco, where the Incas' nobility was well documented and came primarily from the crown. But the large pueblos around Titicaca also had

95 For Chuquimia, ANB, Ruck, Exp. 217 (1801–7); the Aymituma, ARC, INT, Gob., Leg. 133 (1785); Colquehuanca, ARC, RA, Crim., Leg. 130 (1804).
96 ARC, INT, Ord., Leg. 34 (1794); ARC, RA, Ord., Legs. 6 (1790) and 14 (1794); RREE, PRA, Exps. 236, 331, 342, 537.
97 RREE, PRA, Exp. 320.
98 RREE, PRA, Exps. 139 (1792) and 320 (1796–1802); and RREE, PRH, Exp. 207 (1796).

pronounced internal hierarchies rooted in ancestry. Another complaint from
San Taraco, from a cadet branch of the Chuquicallata, suggests that such
hierarchies began to break down after the rebellion.[99] In 1802 Don Lucas
Cutisaca y Chuquicallata complained that he was being called on to perform
communal obligations. He insisted that his parents were " . . . noble persons
and servants of the sovereign, just as my ancestors were, their services
in the late rebellion well known. . . . And even though I . . . ought to be
exempt from mechanical services and others that correspond to Indians
of low station, the alcaldes, without considering the privileges that they
should award me, [moved] by a spirit of vengeance want to burden me
with them."[100] Based on this, the subdelegate ordered the community
not to burden him. But four years later Lucas returned, claiming that once
again pueblo officials were requiring him to perform community labor. This
appeal reached the intendant of Puno, who ordered the Indian Protector to
provide more information; ominously for Lucas, the intendant observed that
"there is no law that exempts [Indians] from personal service."[101]

Other Indian nobles of the Titicaca basin suffered the same fate, as
Spanish caciques and subdelegates enrolled the men of old cacical families as
tributaries, and their communities assigned "base" community obligations
to them.[102] Lucas's complaints were not about tribute exemption, the core
of the conflict between royal officials and the Incas. In Cusco, the crown led
the campaign against Indian noble privilege to increase royal tribute. In
the Titicaca basin, where the community dominated the economy and the
heaviest burdens were the mita and communal obligations, the main privilege of nobility had been the exemption from such "servicios mecánicos."
Following the rebellion, nobles saw these privileges challenged by their
communities. To be sure, authority often remained personal. Whether communities continued to respect the authority and privileges of their nobles
and cacical families after the rebellion even in the absence of royal support –
for example, by electing them as alcaldes – or whether they turned against
the erstwhile elite and sought to reduce them to ordinary membership in
the community varied by pueblo. Nonetheless, taken as a group the cacical elite and pueblo nobility suffered an irrecoverable loss of authority and
privilege.

Cacical families did not passively witness their own demise. The lesser
pueblo nobility was probably impotent to combat its loss of standing.
However, for the upper reaches of the Indian elite, another alternative presented itself: cacical families abandoned the Indian republic. The rebellion

99 Also BNP, Man., C-1705 (1791–1803) for complaints by Tico Chipana of Zepita.
100 RREE, PRA, Exp. 482.
101 Ibid. No outcome is given.
102 RREE, PRA, Exp. 295 (1796); ARC, RA, Adm., Leg. 161 (1801–2) for Andres Cruz of Acora.

devastated the cacical aristocracy of Lampa, Azángaro, Chucuito, Huancané, and Omasuyos. Almost all lost relatives at Sorata and Juli; many had seen family members humiliated and executed in their own plazas. As a result, the complex web of intermarried noble families was largely destroyed, and many pueblos were left with orphaned, impoverished cacical heiresses. A few sought to reproduce the marriage alliances between cacical dynasties.[103] But the marriage of cacical heiresses to creoles became the norm: royal policy now favored Spanish caciques, and many postrebellion cacical claims were launched by the Spanish husbands of the daughters of late caciques.[104] The Pacoricona heiresses of Lampa married Spaniards, and the Spanish cacique of Ayavire married Succacahua's illegitimate daughter.[105] In Coporaque, after Eugenio Sinanyuca's death in 1804, claim to the cacicazgo fell to his granddaughter Petrona. She was the product of an impressive alliance: Asencio Sinanyuca and Tomasa Cama Condorsayna (daughter of Gabriel of Macarí).[106] Tellingly, they had married before the rebellion. Their daughter made a different sort of alliance, marrying Don Sebastian Obando, a creole who had settled in Coporaque: the daughter of two of the most prominent cacical lines along the Lampa–Tinta border was wed to a Spanish fortune-hunter.[107] In Cusco, too, Inca cacical families with proprietary control of their offices married Spaniards.[108]

Cacical families had long sought alliances with provincial creoles. But until the rebellion their dynastic strategies showed a preference for ties

---

103 In the early 1780s Don Pedro Mango Turpa of Azángaro Urinsaya married Doña Ana Maria Choquehuanca y Siñani, daughter of the late Don Blas Choquehuanca and Doña Marta Siñani, and through her sought the cacicazgo of Carabuco. RREE: PSG, Exp. 149 (1790); PRA, Exps. 290, 389, 392, and 398. ANB, EC: 1789–80, 1807–11, and 1805–19. Don Mariano Quispe Cavana, son and heir of Ambrocio Quispe Cavana, married the orphaned daughter of another cacical line from Juli, Doña Maria del Rosario Llaglla Garcia Paca. Mariano died within the decade, leaving two children to his father's care. RREE, PRA, Exp. 186.

104 Doña Bernarda Mango Turpa, daughter of Pedro Mango Turpa and Ana Maria Choquehuanca, married a Spaniard from La Paz; ANB, EC, 1805–19 and 1807–11. Doña Maria Cicilia Chiqui y Cachicatari, an heiress in Juli, married a Spaniard from Juli; ARC, RA, Ord., Leg. 30 (1798), 109v. Indian noblemen also married Spanish women: Don Fernando Tapara y Soria and Doña Polonia Bellota (Santa Rosa); ARC, RA, Adm., Leg. 167 (1809); and Don Francisco Arevilca and Doña Gabriela Madarriega (Cavanilla), ADP, INT, Exp. 170.

105 ARC, RA, Ord., Leg. 33 (1799) and ADP, INT, Exp. 35 (1797). For Diego Sanchez and Eulalia Succacahua, ARC, INT, Ord., Leg. 63 (1807).

106 See the Cama Condorsayna dispute, ARC, CSJ, Leg. 18 (1829).

107 The marriage was a disaster: Sebastian was abusive and lost the office for drunkenness. In 1809 Petrona fled to Cusco with their children and sought a divorce. AAC, LXIV.4.62.

108 In 1789 the sixteen-year-old Doña Maria Ynga Paucar eloped with Don Hermengildo Unzueta; they then successfully pursued the cacicazgo of Coya. ARC, RA, Ord., Legs. 6 (1790) and 9 (1791). Pedro Sahuaraura's children Eulalia and Pedro married Don Francisco Alvarez and Doña Petronila Merino Ybarra. ARC, INT, Gob., Leg. 150 (1800–2) for Eulalia and Francisco's claim to Ayllu Cachona; ARC, JC, Leg. 20 (1831) for a lawsuit over a Merino *capellanía*.

within the Indian nobility, conforming themselves to Spanish policies that preferred Indian nobles as caciques. As a result, cacical families succeeded for several generations in straddling the two republics and creating an elite that, if of mixed ancestry, self-consciously styled itself an Indian nobility. After the rebellion, the logic of familial power changed dramatically. The reformed cacicazgo was a bureaucratic post, not a family possession, and it was awarded through the networks of Spanish Peru. While much of the daily authority in Indian communities remained in the hands of lineages that had long dominated life, and produced the alcaldes, *segundas*, and sacristans, the most valuable position in the pueblo economy passed to the Spanish republic.

The collapse of the cacical elite and the Indian nobility took a generation. Some with proprietary claims held onto their offices, or were reinstated after the wave of anti-cacical sentiment passed. However, by 1800 it was clear that the Indian nobility was an anachronism that resolutely asserted its privileges. The crown's earlier, half-hearted support of the Indian nobility's privileges was replaced by a whole-hearted hostility, albeit checked to some extent by legal precedent and earlier royal concessions. Provincial governors allied themselves with rural Spaniards, creating the late colonial phenomenon of the Spanish cacique. While cacical families and communities protested through riot and the courts, all recognized the change.[109] In many pueblos the authority and privileges of noble families were challenged from within, and nobles aggressively sought out Spanish spouses to replace their lost privileges with those attached to the Spanish republic. Families like the Sahuaraura, Choquehuanca, and Cutimbo often retained local authority well into the republican period; but usually the last Indian–Indian alliance had happened in the 1780s or before, and notwithstanding familial pride in their distinctive ancestry, they formed a part of the provincial, creole and mestizo elite.

Individual Successes

The Indian nobility as a class survived only as a shell from 1784 to 1825. But these years saw a few Indian noblemen reach unprecedented heights in colonial administration, and play a far greater role in regional politics than at any point since the Toledan reforms. For while the crown refused to recognize the loyalty of the Indian nobility as a group, it rewarded individuals for their service during the rebellion. In the 1780s and 1790s the cacical empires of the Mango Turpa and Calisaya left them with authority

109 See n39 for Asillo and Azángaro; also ALP, EC, Leg. 122, Exps. 4, 8, and 25 for unrest in Jesús de Machaca.

at the provincial level unheard of before the rebellion. In an unprecedented gesture, Indian nobles actually received money from the royal treasury: the Sahuaraura children won royal pensions, and Vicente Choquecahua, the Chuquicallata, Eugenio Sinanyuca, and Diego Cusiguaman received commissioned posts in provincial militias.[110] In 1789, in recognition of the late Don Pablo Soria Condorpusa's services, the new Cusco Audiencia took the extraordinary step of appointing his son, Gregorio, as its chaplain.[111] Other Indian nobles found success in the church, the literate professions, and the bureaucracy as royal policy was now to treat the uppermost ranks of the Indian republic more or less as Spaniards in the awarding of lesser offices.[112] Loyalist Indian nobles were also awarded the royal medal in mark of the crown's appreciation.[113]

Moreover, despite the region's economic difficulties following the rebellion, prominent caciques again acquired wealth. By the 1790s, the fortunes of Ambrocio Quispe Cavana, Diego Choquehuanca, and Bernardo Succacahua had recoverd (and even exceeded) their prerebellion dimensions: in 1795 Succacahua purchased the tithe contract for the entire province of Lampa for 12,000 pesos.[114] Manuel Antonio Chuquimia of Copacabana, who had assumed the cacicazgo in 1778 and had been at the forefront of the royalist forces during the rebellion, amassed a fortune of tens of thousands of pesos.[115] Perhaps two dozen Indian caciques in the bishopric survived the rebellion and the legal assault of the 1780s with appreciable fortunes, the result of their traditional position in the colonial economy and the crown's gratitude to them individually.

But one rose far above the rest. Mateo Pumacahua was widely credited with having defeated Tupac Amaru's Cusqueño campaign. On May 1, 1781, while Tupac Amaru was being tried in Cusco and the rebellion still raged, Pumacahua received a commissioned captaincy, with a salary of eighty pesos a month. For the next thirty-four years he was without question the most powerful Indian noble in the bishopric – indeed, the viceroyalty – and one of its most important men. Born in the 1740s and reared to assume Chinchero's cacicazgo, he studied at San Borja, and well before the rebellion

---

110 RREE, PSG, Exp. 115 (1795–6); ARC, NOT, Vargas, Leg. 236, 357 ff., November 27, 1804; ARC, RA, Adm., Leg. 150 (1790–1) and AGN, DI: Exps. 472 (1792) and 643 (1784).

111 ARC, RA, Adm., Leg. 149 (1789–90).

112 Chapter 4, p. 142. Also ANB, EC: 1795–112, 2r (Mariano Quispe Cavana) and 1785–4, 1r (Petrona Peres Catacora and Felipe Hernani).

113 Domingo Mango Turpa repeatedly referred to this award in documents. Also ARC, JC, Leg. 15 (1830) for Don Juan Guallpa.

114 RREE, PRA, Exp. 186 and ANB, EC, 1785–23, 6v; RREE, PRA, Exp. 413; ARC, NOT: Joseph Bernardo Gamarra, Leg. 124, 233 ff. [1799] and Valencia, Leg. 272, 96ff. [1795].

115 AGN-A, IX, 30-1-3, Exp. 17; ANB, Ruck, Exp. 217, 12r.

had begun building his fortune.[116] Following the rebellion, Pumacahua greatly expanded his presence in the region's agricultural economy. By 1790 he had rented three haciendas, each valued at 8,000–12,000 pesos.[117] In the following decades, he continued to acquire properties, usually through rental.[118] In 1799 he bought the Hacienda Guaypu in Chinchero from Cusco's Mercederian community, and the following year paid 8,000 pesos to purchase a hacienda in neighboring Guayllabamba.[119] Pumacahua extended his holdings in the city, buying numerous properties and a seigniorial house on Calle Sapi.[120] In all, he controlled property worth tens of thousands of pesos, making him the peer of Cusco's dilapidated creole aristocracy – and far more dynamic.

Like all who were successful in colonial Peru, Pumacahua used his wealth to assert his position in society and aggressively perform his allegiance to the crown. In 1792, when Cusco celebrated the ascension of Charles IV to the throne, "... Colonel Don Mateo Pumacagua celebrated with applause and jubilee ... with a running of the bulls ... and with fireworks at the end of the afternoon; and ... he gave refreshment that evening to all the ladies, lords, officials and gentlemen of distinction of this city."[121] So stated a Spanish vecino in a secret report to Lima. Pumacahua had requested the rank of colonel of the Indian regiment, and the Audiencia was gathering information.[122] The witnesses were unanimous in their praise for Pumacahua, who provided large numbers of tributaries to build roads and an aqueduct for the city. To Cusco's creoles, Pumacahua was the perfect cacique: utterly hispanicized, he had defended the city from Tupac Amaru, provided tributary labor for public works, and took on more than his share of Cusco's ceremonial burdens. The Audiencia concurred, and forwarded his request to Lima with a favorable recommendation. But in an indication that the bureaucratic elite did not quite know where Pumacahua fit in the changing colonial order, they observed that "in the fiestas celebrated in this city for the coronation of His Majesty this Indian has been one of

---

116 ARC, NOT: Villavisencio, Leg. 287, [ ], March 13, 1777; Acuña, Legs. 11, 33 ff., March 1, 1775, and 12, 115 ff., May 22, 1776.

117 In Andaguaylillas, Chonta, and Guayllabamba. ARC, NOT: Zamora, Leg. 292, 162 ff., April 26, 1787; Rodriguez Ledezma, Leg. 243, 484 ff., October 4, 1788; Villagarcia, Leg. 278, 220 ff., September 26, 1786.

118 ARC, NOT, Joseph Bernardo Gamarra, Leg. 117: 114 ff., July 7, 1792; and 354 ff., December 15, 1792.

119 ARC, NOT: Vargas, Leg. 275, 39 ff., February 6, 1799; Joseph Bernardo Gamarra, Leg. 124, 395 ff., July 28, 1800.

120 The notary books from the period contain roughly a dozen urban property transactions by Pumacahua. For example, ARC, NOT: Rodriguez Ledezma, Leg. 246, 297 ff., March 12, 1793; and Cuevo, Leg. 70, 348 ff., May 27, 1793.

121 Dr. Don Pedro Joseph Lastero. ARC, RA, Ord., Leg. 11 (1792), 5.

122 AGS, Secretaria de Guerra, Leg. 7092, Exp. 77; Leg. 7096, Exp. 62; Leg. 7100, Exp. 40.

those who most proclaimed [his allegiance]," and then crossed out "this Indian."[123]

Lima's reply showed a similar confusion. On April 13, 1793, his request was rejected. A royal decree following the Silversmiths' Conspiracy had ordered that the Indian militias of Peru be disbanded gradually. Despite their crucial role in defending the crown during Tupac Amaru's uprising, the rebellion had strengthened royal determination "that things be arranged such that the Indians have no armed offices whatsoever."[124] But viceregal authorities did not want to alienate so important a vassal. Therefore, on a separate sheet marked "reservado" they instructed the authorities in Cusco to return Pumacahua's papers to him, "explaining to him that the confirmation of this Superior Government is not at all necessary"; whether Pumacahua ever learned that his rank of colonel had not been approved is unclear.[125]

Others also viewed Pumacahua's success with unease. From his appointment as commissary of Indian nobles in 1790 until his exile in 1805, Diego Cusiguaman was an ardent defender of Inca privilege and the primacy of the descendants of Manco Capac.[126] Like most Inca nobles, he was also impoverished. As a master tailor, the interim cacique of an ayllu in San Gerónimo, and the recipient of a small royal salary, he was prosperous by the woeful standards of the Inca nobility; but his few hundred pesos a year paled next to Pumacahua's wealth, and this descendant of Capac Yupanqui was decidedly eclipsed by the cacique of Chinchero.[127] In 1802, Cusiguaman took the highly unusual step of objecting to Pumacahua's election as alférez real, suggesting resentment of Pumacahua's ascendancy over the "capac" Incas of the cabildo.[128] And Pumacahua did seek familial ties with the royal Incas. His two daughters (Polonia and Ignacia) married two brothers, Fermin and Thomas Borja Quispe Carlos Ynga, descendants of Huayna Capac.[129] Pumacahua also added "Ynga" to his name sporadically from the 1770s on; however, he was never an elector of the cabildo, a privilege reserved for the "capac" Incas.

For some, then, years of unprecedented prosperity and authority followed the rebellion. During the nineteenth century, the frontier between Indian and Spanish society was not so much erased as moved, leaving all but the

123 ARC, RA, Ord., Leg. 11 (1792).

124 Cited in Lima's decision on Pumacahua's request; BNP, Man., C-1384.

125 Ibid.

126 In 1797 he petitioned the Audiencia to restore San Borja (ARC, RA, Ord., Leg. 26); and in 1802 he successfully asserted the Inca cabildo's claim to the "cacicazgo" of the Cathedral's sacristans (BNP, Man., D-6047).

127 For Andamachay, ARC, INT, Crim., Leg. 112 (1797–9). For his salary, ARC, RA, Adm., Leg. 150 (1790) and AGN, DI, Exp. 472 (1792).

128 ARC, COR, Civ., Leg. 29, Exp. 620.

129 ARC, NOT, Mar y Tapia, Leg. 165, 137v, July 10, 1826.

most local positions of authority in Spanish hands (or, rather, defining as non-Indian those who held them). However, in the 1790s, for a number of Indian nobles the barrier to offices of provincial importance, in the church and in secular institutions, was crumbling. In a way this interlude between the colonial order and the republican mirrored the half-century between the conquest and the Toledan reforms. Then the upper ranks of the Inca elite – Beatriz and Melchor – had been absorbed into Spanish society. They could have done little else: born of imperial stock, they married into the new imperial elite while their Inca relatives were reduced to a provincial nobility. But Toledo's legislation had created a space – and a need – for this Indian nobility. The imperial network now firmly in Spanish hands, local authority in the pueblos remained (less absolutely) in Indian hands. Two hundred years later, the upper ranks of that nobility were again absorbed into Spanish society. The alliance of Rita Tamboguacso and Sebastian Unzueta was a pale reflection of Beatriz's marriage to Martin Garcia Loyola: the eighteenth-century descendant of Huayna Capac married a local hacendado, not the corregidor of Cusco. Just as the Spanish had conquered the Inca empire in the 1500s, in the 1780s and 1790s they conquered the Inca villages – along with those of the Aymara, and the countless pueblos that were the offspring of Andean society and Spanish colonialism. In the process, the space of the Indian nobility was destroyed.

The End of Spanish Rule

The defeat of the rebellions restored the southern highlands to a precarious peace, but did not address the grievances that had provoked the mass uprisings. The reform of pueblo governance, and the dramatic increase in tribute, brought a torrent of resistance in the endless stream of court cases and the occasional riot. In the cities, too, disaffection grew. Cusco had rallied to defend the status quo against Tupac Amaru's army, but the city suffered considerably from the Bourbon reforms. These expanded trade between Spain and America, stimulating the parts of the Spanish American economy well situated to engage in maritime trade.[130] Cusco fared poorly: overland trade from Lima to Potosí declined, along with the Upper Peruvian market for Cusco's products.[131] The expansion of royal government also brought

---

130 John R. Fisher, *Commercial Relations between Spain and Spanish America in the Era of Free Trade, 1778–1796* (Liverpool: University of Liverpool, 1985).

131 For the decline of Abancay's sugar-growing areas, compare *Cuzco 1689*, pp. 178–215, to the tribute rolls in ARC, INT, RH, Leg. 194 (1792). Cusco also lost its coca markets to La Paz; Herbert S. Klein, "Coca Production in the Bolivia Yungas in the Colonial and Early National Periods," in *Coca and Cocaine: Effects on People and Policy in Latin America*, eds. D. Pacine and C. Franquemont (Boston: Cultural Survival, 1986), pp. 53–64. *Obrajes* suffered similarly: Cusco's annual production fell by almost 80% between 1780 and 1803. Escandell-Tur, *Producción*, pp. 412–4; Jacobsen, *Mirages*, pp. 40–51.

far greater involvement by the crown's officers in the day-to-day life of Cusco. Mata Linares meddled with Cusco's Spanish cabildo as well as its Inca one – a serious assault on the local autonomy to which Cusco's creoles were accustomed.[132] He sought the removal of Cusco's creole bishop, Don Juan Manuel Moscoso y Peralta, who had excommunicated Tupac Amaru but was viewed by royal officials as having been sympathetic to the rebel cause.[133] Generally, peninsular officials viewed Cusco's creoles with as much suspicion as they did its Incas. As an official of the Royal Hacienda wrote when asking the viceroy not to appoint creole officers to the Soria battalion, "I do not like their mode of thinking, and I am informed of some conversations that indicate little affection for the Nation, because in the end their heart is American, and this can never be Ours."[134]

To say that Cusco was a focal point of anticolonial sentiment would be too strong. In the years following the rebellion, Cusco was a proud and ancient city in decline, unhappy with perceived slights and excessive demands by the crown. And, far to the edge of the European world, Cusco's people were well aware of political changes taking place with stunning speed. But the crown had militarized Cusco with a standing army.[135] Until the early years of the nineteenth century, Cusqueño discontent manifested itself principally in an occasional flier attached to a public building.[136] Although they never faced the frontal assault suffered by the Indian nobility, Cusco's "gente decente" languished in the decades following the rebellion, as the long-established domination of the bishopric by Indian caciques who ruled the pueblos and the urban creole elite who lived on rents and church incomes collapsed. While a new class of rural Spaniards fared quite well, the creoles of urban Cusco saw the demands made on them by the crown grow as the value of their properties, and their income from trade, declined.[137]

The most serious manifestation of this unrest came in July 1805, with the exposure of a conspiracy against the crown.[138] Led by Don Gabriel Aguilar (a creole from Huánuco who claimed descent from Huascar), members of Cusco's middle and upper strata planned to seize the jail, expel Spanish officials, and proclaim an Inca monarchy.[139] In many ways the conspiracy resembled that of the Silversmiths twenty-five years before, only

---

132 Luis Durand Flórez, *El Proceso de Independencia en el Sur Andino: Cuzco y La Paz*, 1805 (Lima: Universidad de Lima, 1993), pp. 139–53.

133 In 1783 Moscoso was sent to Spain. Durand Flórez, *El Proceso*, pp. 129–38.

134 "Expediente relativo a . . . [la] batallon de Soria," ARC, INT, Gob., Leg. 131 (1784–5).

135 Also ARC, INT, RH, Leg. 193 (1791) for construction of a gunpowder store.

136 Durand Flórez, *El Proceso*, pp. 150–1.

137 For the late-eighteenth-century decline generally, Burns, *Colonial Habits*, pp. 177–85.

138 Durand Flórez, *El Proceso*, pp. 225–395; Flores Galindo, *Buscando un Inca*, pp. 175–242.

139 Their "Inca" was Don Manuel Valverde Ampuero de las Infantas, a *hacendado* from Yucay who descended from Huayna Capac's daughter Iñes and Francisco Pizarro. Durand Flórez, *El Proceso*, p. 252.

now it was the literate professions, not the artisan elite, who were plotting against Spanish rule. In the end, Aguilar's conspiracy achieved no more than the Silversmiths', and in December he was hung in Cusco's main plaza. But the conspiracy shows the disaffection with the reformed order among Cusco's traditional colonial elites, and, in the millenarian visions of Aguilar, suggests the ideological responses to it. The conspiracy was the mirror image of Tupac Amaru's rebellion: this time put forward by urban creoles, it sought to reassert the social order of the mid-eighteenth-century highlands, and to do so in the name of the Inca. Now, however, the con- spirators sought to reclaim Peru for the Spanish population of the highland cities, not for the caciques and tributaries of the Indian pueblos. This mes- sage did not resonate with the masses; the one Indian implicated was Diego Cusiguaman, whose grievances as an urban Inca noble closely mirrored the conspirators'.[140]

In the end it would be Napoleon who toppled the Spanish monarchy. In March 1808, after letting French troops cross Spain to invade Portugal, Charles IV abdicated in favor of his son Ferdinand. Napoleon instead placed his own brother Joseph on the Spanish throne, provoking rebellion and five years of civil and international war on the peninsula. By the end of 1808, only Cádiz remained free; there, a junta sought to rule whatever it could of Spain's possessions in the name of Ferdinand VII (now imprisoned in France), and it was to this Junta Central that the Incas of Cusco swore allegiance on April 21, 1809. In Upper Peru the rule of Cádiz was less readily accepted. Chuquisaca rejected the Audiencia president's authority in May 1809; a more aggressive rejection of the Junta Central occurred in July in La Paz, and for the next four months an independent junta of the city's creole citizenry ruled in the name of Ferdinand.[141] They were crushed by armies from Cusco and Buenos Aires at the end of 1809; Buenos Aires then rose in early 1810, creating a new, creole-dominated viceregal government that professed loyalty to Ferdinand VII but not to Cádiz. Forces of this new government marched north to free the now-resubjugated Upper Peru. Late in 1810 troops from Cusco and Lima marched south to reestablish peninsular rule; leading them was Mateo Pumacahua with 3,500 Indian troops.[142] Don Jose Domingo Choquehuanca of Azángaro joined with another 1,200 troops: once again the Indian nobility of Cusco and the Collao sided with the defenders of Spanish rule, not its opponents.[143] In 1811 the combined forces reestablished Lima's jurisdiction in Upper Peru after defeating the

---

140 Flores Galindo, *Buscando un Inca*, p. 191; Durand Flórez, *El Proceso*, pp. 507–9.
141 La Paz was also site of an unsuccessful conspiracy in 1805; Durand Flórez, *El Proceso*, pp. 397–433.
142 Walker, *Smoldering Ashes*, p. 90. According to caciques' lists, 307 tributaries from the Cercado went on the campaign to Alto Peru. ARC, INT, RH, Leg. 220 (1811–4).
143 Altuve Carrillo, *Choquehuanca*, pp. 93–4.

Porteño army on the southern shore of Titicaca, although fighting continued between the rival viceroyalties.

Meanwhile, in Cádiz in 1810 the Spanish Cortes had been called to legislate in the absence of Ferdinand VII.[144] They promulgated a series of liberal decrees, including the abolition of Indian tribute (in May 1810 for Mexico, in March 1811 for the rest of the Indies) and the establishment of legal equality of Indian and Spaniard.[145] In 1812, the Cortes enacted a liberal constitution. Shortly thereafter, Spanish and English troops succeeded in driving out Napoleon's forces from Spain; in 1814 Ferdinand returned, and far from rewarding the Cortes he suppressed the constitution, aggressively persecuted its liberal supporters, and sought to reestablish Bourbon absolutism in Spain and its American possessions. In March 1815 Lima forwarded to Cusco a ruling that repealed all the decrees, laws, and honors of the Cortes, along with the 1812 Constitution.[146]

The reorganizations of 1810–15 exacerbated the political and economic chaos in southern Peru. The repeal of Indian tribute threatened the viceroyalty's economy, which, given the near collapse of long-distance trade, depended desperately on tribute.[147] It also undermined the logic of the highland economy, in which the flow of labor from Indian villages to Spanish properties depended on tributaries' need for pesos. Nor did it meet with support from highland elites – not least the clergy, whose salaries were paid from tribute. In December 1812 Don Dionicio Ynca Yupanqui, an Inca noble and Peruvian deputy to Cádiz, wrote to Arequipa's bishop explaining the repercussions for clerical livings.[148] But by then the viceroy had addressed the fiscal crisis by instituting a voluntary–obligatory "contribución provisional," to tribute what the socorro had been to the reparto.[149]

There was no one response to the political and economic turmoil of these five years. In July 1812 the tributaries of Oropesa, under the loyalist Inca Don Marcos Chillitupa, "their spirits inflamed with the noblest sentiments of loyalty and love, [and] without other stimulus or persuasion than these virtuous and faithful impulses, asked and requested that they be allowed to continue the payment of [tribute]." The viceroy readily accepted. In return, the tributaries of Oropesa would retain their traditional benefits (especially exemption from the *alcabala*, which had been extended to the Indians as part of their new status), but they would still share in the new-found and "perfect equality with the rest of the vassals [and] citizens that make up the heroic

---

144 Jaime E. Rodríguez O., *The Independence of Spanish America* (Cambridge: Cambridge University Press, 1998), pp. 75–106 and 192–205.
145 Sala i Vila, *Y se armó*, pp. 165–70.
146 ARC, RA, Adm., Leg. 172 (1815–16).
147 ARC, INT, RH, Legs. 220 (1811–14) and 222 (1816) for the Guaro obraje.
148 BNP, Man., D-11711.
149 Sala i Vila, *Y se armó*, pp. 170–90.

Spanish nation."[150] The loyalty and largesse of Chillitupa and his community were not selfless. For this pueblo fifteen miles from Cusco's markets, the alcabala on animals, produce, and cloth could amount to more than their tribute, the pesos for which were readily earned on nearby Spanish haciendas or in the urban markets. For Chillitupa, the abolition of tribute threatened his control over the pueblo economy. Unlike Pumacahua, Chillitupa had not managed to propel himself into the bishopric's landowning elite after the rebellion. As a loyalist Inca cacique, he had, however, been confirmed in his office, and he depended on the traditional tributary system to maintain his local authority.

At roughly the same time, Don Manuel Choquehuanca – a loyalist colonel – was instigating the tributaries of Azángaro not to pay the personal contribution.[151] In March 1813 Puno's intendant complained to Lima that Choquehuanca had told the Indians that the new contribution was voluntary. Lima replied, condemning Choquehuanca's actions but confirming that tribute was no longer obligatory; if the pueblo preferred, the Indians could pay the taxes levied on Spaniards.[152] Here in the Titicaca basin the political and economic logic of reform was different. The pueblos of Azángaro had always been largely self-sufficient, selling to the distant urban markets (on very poor terms) to pay tribute – for them, trading tribute for the alcabala was a boon indeed. For Choquehuanca, the end of tribute in Azángaro would weaken the control of the subdelegate and his faction.

In its reply, Lima specifically reprimanded Azángaro's subdelegate – Don Ramon Escovedo – for his references to "recaudadores."[153] The post had now been abandoned: alcaldes were to collect the personal contribution and turn it over to the subdelegate. In addition to abolishing tribute, the Cádiz government had instituted sweeping reforms of pueblo government. With the distinction between Spaniard and Indian removed, a new system of *ayuntamientos* – local councils that represented and ruled all in the pueblo – was to be established.[154] This was a dramatic change from the late Bourbon efforts to extend royal authority in the countryside by increasing the power of the subdelegate. Now, the pueblo's renovated cabildo was to assume responsibility for ordering the local economy and polity, and it was

---

150 BNP, Man., D-11670.

151 Manuel had renounced the cacicazgo in 1799, but successfully sought reinstatement in 1808. RREE, PSG, Exp. 179; ARC, RA, Adm., Leg. 166 (1808).

152 AGN, DI, Exp. 848.

153 Ibid.

154 The impact of the *ayuntamiento* on the Andean pueblo has received little attention. For its impact on Mexican pueblos, Michael T. Ducey, "Village, Nation, and Constitution: Insurgent Politics in Papantla, Veracruz, 1810–1821," *Hispanic American Historical Review* 79:3 (Summer 1999): 463–93; and Peter Guardino, *Peasants, Politics and the Formation of Mexico's National State, Guerrero, 1800–1857* (Stanford: Stanford University Press, 1996), pp. 85–94.

to be chosen from within the pueblo, not appointed by the subdelegate. Indeed, Escovedo's complaint against Choquehuanca was part of a larger conflict between the elite of Azángaro and the subdelegate. At the same time the intendant of Puno wrote to Lima, the "vecinos de Azángaro" sent their own complaint directly to the viceroy, bypassing the intendant whom they considered an ally of Escovedo.[155] Escovedo's son had found an anti-crown flier posted in the plaza; the subdelegate had then sent it to Puno, accusing the Azangareños of treason. They denied this and accused Escovedo of numerous abuses.

The newly formed ayuntamiento had met in February 1813 and had agreed to implement a decision by Cusco's Royal Hacienda, published in 1809 but unenforced, that a sale of communal land by the previous intendant had been illegal; that land was occupied by Don Mariano Escovedo, a relative of the subdelegate. In response, they claimed,

> ... Escovedo has excited his ill-will against the ayuntamiento, because this new cabildo installed so recently is composed in large part of loyal Indians who have grown old serving the sovereign and of few Spaniards ... accustomed to the abuse, the humiliation, the insult, the degradation, and the games of the subdelegates, and all being made servants at their own doors for the most vile services[.] [But] today they compose a new hierarchy, established of regidores to maintain the public order, to investigate the properties and rents of the parish of which the subdelegates alone were the absolute arbiters, to defend the just rights of the landless Indian forever oppressed[.] [W]itnessing the unforeseen transformation [Escovedo] has raised his voice in slander, because in this manner he believes he can dissolve the ayuntamiento that was formed by 17 parish electors.[156]

In Azángaro, the constitutional reforms promised greater freedom from the provincial governor – aspirations that could unite even this pueblo's fractious elite: signing the letter were Domingo and Fermin Mango, who had battled over Urinsaya's cacicazgo for more than a decade; Mariano Deza, from the creole family who held the interim cacicazgo of Asillo in the mid-1790s until they renounced because of Domingo Mango's instigation against them; four other *indios principales*; and two other creoles.[157]

In theory, the reforms of the early 1810s were far more sweeping than those of the 1780s. The latter had simply removed the pueblo juncture of the two republics from the Indian nobility, and given it to rural Spaniards, while increasing tributary demands on Peru's Indians. The reforms of the Cortes, in contrast, sought a reformulation of the relationship between

155 BNP, Man., D-656.
156 Ibid.
157 Also ARC, RA, Ord., Leg. 78 (1813), for Don Mauricio Quispe Uscamayta y Uscapaucar, "indio noble y sindico procurador del Ayuntamiento Constitucional de la Villa de Maras."

Indian and Spanish that had been in force for nearly three centuries. They also sought to return much of the authority over the rural political economy assumed by subdelegates to the pueblos themselves, but these pueblos were now conceived of as mixed communities of Indian and Spanish. The Cortes' actions thus broke with the underlying philosophy of the Toledan reforms. However, the post-Tupac Amaru reforms had been accompanied by administrative action unparalleled since the time of Toledo; no such effort accompanied the Cortes' decisions.

Between the French occupation of the peninsula and the ongoing war with the viceroyalty of La Plata, royal officials had little ability to enforce such decrees. That is not to say they had no effect: the liberal provisions of 1810–13 broadened the political discourse of the highlands and legitimated competing visions of society. They also brought confusion. With competing governments, and competing views of the rural order, the numerous fault lines that divided Andean society again came to the fore. And, once again, they were complex, often visible only at the local level. In Azángaro, it was the established Indian and Spanish families of the pueblo against a grasping subdelegate. Forty-five miles away in the neighboring capital of Lampa, with its far larger Spanish population, the divide was between the Spanish elite and the Indian masses, as three dozen vecinas wrote to Lima complaining that the pueblo's Indians (with "their arrogant and seditious character") were threatening rebellion over " . . . the new voluntary contribution which the Señor General in Chief recommends to this Illustrious Ayuntamiento for the subsistence of the Royal army under his command, [the Indians] claiming that the said exaction is for no other end than for the allies of the Intendant, the Subdelegate, and the Ayuntamiento."[158] Province by province and pueblo by pueblo the divisions varied, as those living together splintered by republic or class, or united against an abusive official.

Around Cusco, the gradual elimination, from 1808 to 1815, of legal distinctions between Indian and Spaniard allowed the leaders of the Inca nobility to play a greater role in political life. By far the greatest beneficiary – on a scale unique in the Americas – was Pumacahua, who in 1812 and 1813 served as the interim president of the Audiencia. When he signed a power of attorney to Dionicio Ynca Yupanqui on September 25, 1812 (to seek further rewards from the Cortes in Cádiz), Pumacahua was "brigadier of the Royal Armies, Colonel of the Infantry Regiment of the Noble Militias, cacique *gobernador* by right of blood of the pueblo of Chincheros, distinguished with the Royal Bust and the Red Banner, interim president of the Royal Audiencia, Intendant Governor [and] Vice Patron of its Province,

158 BNP, Man., D-6075. Among those signing was Doña Ignacia Calbo y Pacoricona, a descendant of the town's cacical family.

commander General of the Arms, Subdelegate of the mails."[159] Others followed in his wake (albeit far behind); in 1813, two cabildo members signing the appointment of a Judge of Police (forwarded to them by Pumacahua) were Incas: Juan Guallpa Ynga, an Inca elector and longtime cacique of two ayllus in Belén, and Jose Santos Sicos Guallparimachi, also an Inca elector.[160] The military campaigns of 1810–11 also created a demand for soldiers and officers, and once again the city's Inca noblemen marched and rode in the city's Indian regiment, and again won commissioned offices.

But in the end the commitment to equality proved hollow. In 1813 Pumacahua was removed as president of the Audiencia.[161] Less dramatically, in June 1813 two Tito Quecaño brothers from San Gerónimo appealed their matriculation as tributaries in the latest tribute rolls. They argued that as Inca nobles, and as soldiers, they were exempt from tribute. They also wanted to be declared Spanish, "... to enjoy, in accordance with the new constitution of our Spanish Monarchy, the privileges of Spanish Citizens in all, conforming ourselves also to the [position] recently resolved by the extraordinary Junta Superior of Lima, such that we might freely choose either the provisional contribution, or to pay the taxes of a Spaniard, choosing for ourselves the latter."[162] It was an extraordinary gesture, and captures the awkward position of the Indian nobility: to continue to distinguish themselves from Indian tributaries, the Tito Quecaño wanted to be termed Spanish, effectively turning away from the Indian republic in which their ancestors had held privileged positions for centuries. The response was telling: despite their claims of nobility, and the constitution that clearly spelled out their right to elect to pay Spanish duties, the Royal Hacienda rejected their request.

For Pumacahua and the Tito Quecaño, 1813 made clear the unwillingness of royal officials to implement the new policy at the heart of the reforms: the equality of Indian and Spaniard. At the same time, in creole Cusco the disaffection that had prompted the Aguilar conspiracy had grown over the decade. Cusco had remained loyal to the viceregal government in Lima when La Paz led Upper Peru into rebellion in 1809. However, the burden of that loyalty had fallen disproportionately on Cusco: its trade and markets lost, and its impoverished pueblos increasingly called upon to support the viceregal government with tribute and to supply soldiers for the military campaigns.[163] That loyalty went largely unrewarded: Pumacahua's brief

159 ARC, NOT, Chacon y Becerra, Leg. 65, 458, September 25, 1812.
160 BNP, Man., D-12017 (February 1813).
161 Walker, *Smoldering Ashes*, p. 97.
162 ARC, INT, RH, Leg. 220 (1811–14).
163 See the efforts by Sgt. Major Fermin Borja Quispe Carlos Ynga to get pay for his troops. ARC, INT, Gob., Leg. 153 (1809–15).

tenure as the president of the Audiencia notwithstanding, royal officials continued to be drawn from outside Cusco's citizenry. By 1813 relations were extremely tense.[164] On November 5, after the Audiencia arrested a number of Cusqueños (alleging a plot to seize the barracks), soldiers fired on protesters and killed two. This provoked bitter dispute between Cusco's cabildo and Audiencia, culminating in the arrest of cabildo members in early 1814. In August a mutiny set them free, and the Audiencia's peninsular members were jailed. The second rebellion to sweep southern Peru in just thirty-five years had begun.

The rebellion of 1814–15 – referred to at the time as the Angulo rebellion, for the two creole brothers at its head, although now generally named for the cacique of Chinchero – covered much the same region as that of Tupac Amaru, although it had its origins in a different sector of society.[165] It started as an urban creole rebellion against peninsular rule, and proved more successful in drawing Inca allies than had Tupac Amaru. The most faithful defender of Limeño and peninsular rule in the south Andes for forty years, Pumacahua joined the rebels, and in November captured Arequipa; Marcos Chillitupa of Oropesa also rebelled and led 200 Indian troops into battle.[166] In 1780, the loyalist creoles and Incas of Cusco had blocked the rebel's march to Chinchaysuyo; now, launched from Cusco the rebellion swept across the Apurímac and through the bishopric of Huamanga. To the south, Puno joined and La Paz was again besieged.[167] In Cusco, the rebels had complete control and organized a new government; Pumacahua's son-in-law Fermin Quispe Carlos Ynga became subdelegate.[168] The rebels proclaimed Juan Angulo "captain general" of Cusco, creating a new jurisdiction outside the Peruvian viceroyalty but in conformity with the political configurations of colonial Spanish America.[169] The countryside was overwhelmed with the same chaotic violence that had broken out thirty-five years before, as pueblos rose against those who had enforced and profited from the crushing demands of the intendant system. Once again royalist forces from Lima and from the south (now Upper Peru, recently reconquered by Cusqueño forces) crushed the uprising. In March 1815 the final battles took place in the highland pueblos of Tinta and Lampa where the earlier

---

164 Walker, *Smoldering Ashes*, pp. 97–8.
165 Jorge Cornejo Bouroncle, *Pumacahua: La revolución del Cuzco de 1814* (Cuzco: H. G. Rozas, 1956); David Cahill and Scarlett O'Phelan, "Forging Their Own History: Indian Insurgency in the Southern Peruvian Sierra, 1815," *Bulletin of Latin American Research* 11:2 (April 1992): 125–67; Walker, *Smoldering Ashes*, pp. 97–105; Sala i Vila, *Y se armó*, pp. 227–46.
166 ARC, INT, Ord., Leg. 74 (1814–15).
167 Walker, *Smoldering Ashes*, 97–101.
168 ARC, INT, Ord., Leg. 74 (1814–15) for Don Nicolas Peres Alferes' house sale.
169 For Angulo as Captain General, see the Chillitupa treason sentence, ARC, INT, Ord., Leg. 74 (1814–15).

rebellion had begun, culminating at Umachire. Pumacahua was captured and executed at Sicuani, and the Angulo brothers and Chillitupa hung in Cusco's plaza.[170]

Beyond its leaders, the extent of Indian noble support for the rebellion is hard to gauge. Pumacahua's sons-in-law supported him, and died as a result; after Pumacahua's defeat in March a mob sacked the Cusco house of his newly widowed daughter Ignacia.[171] So too did Don Gregorio Sihua, hereditary cacique of Santiago's small Ayllu Collagua and former alférez real; his house was also sacked by anti-Angulo mobs after the defeat of the rebellion.[172] Don Manuel Guamansullca y Cotacallapa, the cacique of Usicayos and scion of its noble families, sent troops to aid Angulo at Umachire; he received a pardon in 1818.[173] Justo Sahuaraura, now the priest of Soraya, was accused of seizing 8,000 pesos in tribute and sending it to Cusco at Angulo's orders. This was not denied, but in the end Sahuaraura was absolved of any responsibility.[174] But despite the Inca nobles at the head of the rebellion, most of Cusco's Inca nobility appear to have remained either neutral or loyal to the existing government. The Inca cabildo held no elections in 1813, 1814, or 1815, but when it met in 1816, twelve of the sixteen who had voted in 1812 were again present. The cabildo limped along, and the vacant seats were only filled in 1824, when the viceroy renewed the cabildo for its annual procession (although in 1817 Diego Cusiguaman returned from his ten-year exile in Lima and resumed his electorship).[175] But that the majority retained their seats suggests that they played only minor parts in the rebellion, if any at all. In any case, the viceregal forces were in no position to mount the systematic assault on Indian (and now creole) Cusqueños that they had in the 1780s. Gregorio Sihua retained his cacicazgo in Santiago, and the royal government in Cusco respected the property claims of Pumacahua's children. For the last decade of Spanish rule Cusco's Indian nobility simply joined the rest of the city in its slow decline.

The failure of the rebellion left the Peruvian highlands pacified, although local tumults were frequent in these turbulent years.[176] The timing of the 1814–15 rebellion proved atrocious. Had Cusco risen in 1809 with the cities of Alto Peru, the collapse of Spanish rule in the Andes might have been quite different. However, when Ferdinand reclaimed the throne he launched an aggressive campaign to regain Spanish America: Cusco rebelled just as

170 Ibid.; Walker, *Smoldering Ashes*, p. 100.
171 ARC, INT, Gob., Leg. 153 (1809–15).
172 RREE, CSJ, Exp. 65.
173 BNP, Man., D-8733 (1818).
174 ARC, INT, Ord., Leg. 75 (1815–16); ARC, CE, Leg. 19 (1817–24).
175 For the renovation of the cabildo, ARC, INT, Vir., Leg. 160 (1823–4).
176 Walker, *Smoldering Ashes*, pp. 105–20; Sala i Vila, *Y se armó*, pp. 252–9.

royal authority was gathering the strength to reassert itself. Not until the early 1820s did the forces of Bolívar take Nueva Granada and move south to Peru, while those of San Martín moved north from Chile. From 1821 to 1824 Peru's battle for independence was fought along the coast, not in the highlands. In 1823 Viceroy de la Serna retreated to Cusco, which became the capital of Peru; in 1824 he led an army against the Bolivarian forces marching up from Lima, and on December 6 the royalists were utterly defeated at Ayacucho, effectively ending Spanish rule in Peru.

Independence ushered in a new order, in which both ideology and self-interest supported the expansion of creole power. Occasional interest in establishing an Inca monarchy notwithstanding, the new nation of Peru rose on the uneasy foundation of two ideologies: republican fraternity and European superiority. Neither had space for an Indian nobility. In the early 1820s Bolívar had abolished tribute and ordered a sweeping land reform; these extended to Cusco in 1825. The land reform distributed communal land to tributaries as private, alienable property; the threat of massive Indian dispossession led to a decree in July 1825 preventing Indians who had acquired this communal land from selling it. While recognizing the land claims of hereditary caciques, Bolívar also abolished the cacicazgo.[177] Noble privilege was also ended – here an assault on the titled aristocracy, but extending to Indian peasant-nobles – so that independence swept away the two pillars of the colonial Indian elite. The national governments then sought a restructuring of Indian society as sweeping as Toledo's 250 years before. The introduction of private property was to end the pueblo's existence as a landowning corporation, and Indians were to enter the body politic not through their pueblos but as free citizens of the republic. The Indian nobility thus lost their role as the mediator between the market and tribute economies of Spanish Peru and the Indian village.

These republican dreams foundered on the hard realities of the post-colonial Andes. The republican government in Lima proved as dependent on Indian pesos as its predecessor, and in 1826 tribute was reintroduced, to continue until the guano boom of the 1850s.[178] While the office of recaudador was abolished along with that of cacique, repeated proclamations to that effect show the endurance of the office: like the Bourbons, the republican government proved unable to both maintain tribute and abolish the enormous local power of the tribute collector.[179] The government in Lima had great difficulty exerting authority in the southern highlands; indeed, in the late 1830s the area from Cusco to Titicaca came under the rule of Bolivia's president, Andres Santa Cruz, in the short-lived

---

177 Jacobsen, *Mirages*, pp. 122–4.
178 Peralta Ruíz, *En pos del tributo*.
179 RREE, CJD, Exp. 36.

Peru–Bolivia Confederation. And highland society generally suffered wrenching upheaval. Urban elites, dependent on church office and rural property, were ruined by the collapse of the economy and rural unrest; while civil war, between different *caudillos* and between those with different ideals for the Peruvian nation, was endemic.[180] The rural economic order that gradually emerged, particularly after the abolition of tribute in 1854, was dominated by the hacienda.[181] The mechanisms by which Indian produce and labor were appropriated by Spanish Peru became direct ownership of land, and Spanish middlemen became the nexus between the Indian household and the market.

As a result, as a group the Indian nobility collapsed. As families and individuals, those who made the transition from Indian noble to provincial elite in the last decades of colonial rule fared as well (or poorly) as their creole neighbors. The Pumacahua were once again heroes. Ignacia and Polonia, who had defended their property rights in the late 1810s by lamenting their late father's madness in rebelling, now appeared as the "wives and widows of patriots who died in the year 1814 for the cause of independence."[182] Their brother, Jose Mariano, served as a deputy to the Peruvian congress, as did Francisco Alvarez (Eulalia Sahuaraura's husband) and Jose Domingo Choquehuanca.[183]

These were as exceptional in the early republic as in the colonial era. However, as they had after the Tupac Amaru rebellion, a number of Indian nobles received rewards for their loyalty (now to the rebellion, not the crown) during the wars of independence. In 1829 Cusco's agricultural commission awarded Diego Cusiguaman six topos of land, observing " ... that it is most unusual that the aged Patriot ... has not been rewarded in any form, notwithstanding the common knowledge of his services made for the cause of Independence."[184] In the same year Sihua, proclaiming his allegiance to the 1814 rebellion, received confirmation of some cacical–familial land.[185] And throughout the highlands as communal lands were distributed, cacical and noble families managed to claim larger shares than tributaries. In all provinces some nobles joined the ranks of leading republican citizens. Among those who met to elect Urubamba's Deputy to the Peruvian Congress in 1829 were Valentin and Mariano Tupayachi,

180 Walker, *Smoldering Ashes*, pp. 121–230; Peralta Ruíz, *En pos del tributo*; Burns, *Colonial Habits*, pp. 186–221; Jacobsen, *Mirages*, pp. 31–77 and 107–48.
181 Jacobsen, *Mirages*, pp. 198–258; Gavin Smith, *Livelihood and Resistance: Peasants and the Politics of Land in Peru* (Berkeley: University of California Press, 1989), pp. 59–95.
182 In their suit for the Hacienda Sala i Vieja. ARC, JC, Leg. 5 (1826).
183 For Pumacahua, ARC, JC, Leg. 9 (1827); for Choquehuanca, Altuve Carrillo, *Choquehuanca*, pp. 235–337; for Alvarez, *Correo de Encomiendas* 9 (November 7, 1832), pp. 3–4.
184 RREE, CJD, Exp. 45.
185 RREE, CJD, Exp. 65.

Ambrosio Uscapaucar, Francisco Ataupaucar, and a half-dozen other Indian nobles.[186] In 1828 when the electors of Chucuito met in Juli to elect their Deputy, many of the electors came from the old cacical families.[187] In Pucyura, the old cacical lines continued to control the mill and serve as alcalde.[188] In Chinchaypucyo the descendants of the Guachaca remained prominent, repeatedly buying the parish's tithe contracts from the 1820s through the 1850s.[189]

The changes implemented by republican rule could not immediately change reality on the ground. By the late colonial period, Cusco's Indian elite was composed of families who were prominent, and privileged, in their communities. They made up the small group of Indian property owners at independence, and the republican government, with its strong liberal prejudices, recognized such property. In Cusco's Inca parishes and the agricultural villages surrounding the city, descendants of those families continued to wage legal battles among themselves over the right to dilapidated houses, a few topos of land, and the other wealth of the pueblo elite. But property and wealth had never been bulwarks of the colonial Indian elite. Members of the families continued to occupy local offices, but the Indian nobility's monopoly on them and the particular power of the cacique were gone, and rural Spaniards grew increasingly dominant. Property and wealth also became the prerequisites of authority and political voice in the Republic of Peru. In the early 1830s a new constitution brought restrictions on the franchise: electors were to be married men with an income of 1,000 pesos a year. In Lima, such a policy restricted the vote to the more prosperous *burguesía*; in Cusco, only 110 people qualified.[190] Of the thirty-five electors from the Cathedral parish in 1833, only one was Indian.[191] In 1835, none of the eight electors of San Blas – historically the core of Inca Hanansaya – was Indian, and in Santa Ana, Don Luis Ramos Tito Atauchi was the lone Inca among six electors.[192]

Indians continued to play a central role in the Cusqueño economy and prospered as butchers, traders, and other artisans. But now bourgeois Cusco was defined as Spanish, and those Indians who entered this nineteenth-century middle class were identified as such. In 1852 Don Mariano Ramos

186 ARC, NOT, Grajeda, Leg. s/n 488 ff., [ ]. Also Lucas Uscamayta y Uscapaucar, "vecino y indígena principal," versus Benacio Galdos (ARC, CSJ, Leg. 10, 1852).

187 BNP, Man., D-12932.

188 ARC, CC, Leg. 9, Cuaderno 37 for Don Lucas Uscamayta (Blas's son); also the 1841 dispute between Lucas and his brother-in-law, ARC, JC, Leg. 47.

189 ARC, DZ, Legs. 64 (1826–8), 65 (1828–9), 73 (1843–4), 78 (1853–4). Other descendants of the Indian nobility numbered among the region's tithe-farmers. ARC, DZ, Legs. 63–80, passim.

190 *El Correo de Encomiendas* 8 (August 18, 1832) and 9 (October 11, 1832).

191 Don Sebastian Yanquirimachi, *El Correo de Encomiendas* 13 (February 1833).

192 *Cusco Libre* 25 (November 8, 1834) for San Blas; ibid., 33 (January 10, 1835) for Santa Ana.

sought confirmation as a notary public. The son of Luis Ramos Tito Atauchi, Mariano was clearly part of Cusco's "gente decente": he had studied Latin grammar at the convent of San Francisco and was certified by the University as a reader of philosophy, logic, metaphysics, physics, and ethics; he had also studied the theory and practice of the notary.[193] But it is striking that this descendant of Huayna Capac and Paullu Ynga, whose family had been the most visible presence of the urban Inca nobility through the eighteenth century, had now dropped the Inca family name, retaining only its one, non-descript, Spanish component.

The abolition of the cacicazgo and of legal nobility culminated a process that had begun forty years earlier – or rather, several processes. The assault on the Indian nobility began as part of the expansion of a rationalizing absolutist state, eager to reassert and reinvigorate its empire by tackling the privileges of groups no longer necessary to royal authority, and not strong enough to offer effective resistance. In the Spanish world, this expansion of the monarchic state accompanied a general assertion of European superiority in a colonial, racialized hierarchy. One product of this would be the alienation of urban creoles, who saw Peninsular Spaniards preferred to themselves. But in the rural Andes the result was the seizure of political and economic authority by Peruvian Spaniards. Indeed, the crown's decision to place rural authority in the hands of these provincial Spaniards was an exemplary colonial "misreading," in which the crown repudiated the loyalist Indian nobility not because of their actions, but because of the crown's miscomprehension of the rebellion and of Indian (especially Inca) noble claims of privilege. Finally, the crisis of Spanish colonial rule, provoked by the invasion of Spain and irreparably exacerbated by Ferdinand's restoration of absolutism, led to the diffusion in the Andes of a liberal, republican political ideology that stressed Spanish superiority. Its victory in 1825 marked the definitive end of the cacicazgo and Indian nobility.

The destruction of the Indian nobility was the result of two enormous changes in highland society. The first lay in the political economy: however poorly it performed the new ideal, the republican government was a liberal institution, committed to the preservation of private property and the political freedom of the individual. The corporatist ideology of the Spanish monarchs had created a space for the Indian nobility in the constricted world of the communal economy, now aggressively destructured by the national government. Also ascendant in Peru was an ideology that equated authority and prosperity with Spanish society. The intermarriage between Spanish and Indian continued apace, and while a wave of European immigration helped the upper ranks of provincial society to "whiten" their

193 ARC, CSJ, Leg. 107.

pedigrees, the genealogies of rural families continued to be the complex mix of Spanish, Quechua, and Aymara that they had become during centuries of imperial expansion and rule. But the possibility of amassing hereditary wealth and power within the pueblo – the foundation of the colonial Indian nobility – had been eliminated with the abolition of hereditary cacicazgos and nobility. Conversely, the possibility of moving into the "Spanish" elite increased greatly with the republican reforms, as property and wealth came to define social (and "ethnic") rank. To be Indian was to be poor and lack social standing: after three centuries of colonial rule, Indian and noble had become contradictory terms.

Conclusion

For two and a half centuries, three fundamental aspects of Spanish rule in the Andes created and preserved a social space for an Indian elite. The establishment of the *república de indios* as a legal space placed the great majority of the indigenous population outside the domain of private Spaniards, and created the "pueblo de indios" as the physical manifestation of the Indian republic. Second, the co-option and reordering of Inca tribute as the basic material relationship between the crown and its Indian vassals, and the insistence that tribute be monetized, created a need for middlemen to negotiate the collection of tribute in labor and kind, and its conversion into specie. Finally, guided by a largely unchallenged belief in innate nobility and the natural justice of social hierarchy, the crown and its officials preserved and reworked the hierarchies of the Inca empire to produce a colonial Indian elite that oversaw both the local aspects of the tributary economy and the political life of the pueblo.

If the colonial order established in the late sixteenth century defined the relations and institutions of the Indian republic for two centuries, the indigenous societies of the Andes did not go unchanged during that period. Demographic collapse and internal migration variously destroyed, created, and reworked particular communities. The imposition of monogamy transformed the structure of kinship and household, especially among historically polygamous elites; it also reworked the relations between these elites and their communities. The introduction of private, alienable property also altered relations within the community: while differential control of resources had long marked the hierarchies of Andean society, private property and the emergence of a monetized market produced and perpetuated novel relations. Finally, the growth of an Andean Spanish population and a Spanish-dominated market economy, and the alienation of land from indigenous communities, transformed the larger society of which the Indian republic was part. The interaction of the legal ordering imposed in the sixteenth century, the structural changes provoked in indigenous society by Spanish rule, and the expansion of the Spanish population and economy, all these constituted the eighteenth-century Indian republic.

Crucial to the organization of that republic was an Indian nobility: indigenous communities, and particularly the substantial pueblos of a thousand or more people, were often deeply and hereditarily stratified. At the top were the caciques; but Indian society more broadly contained a complex, if fluid, elite of office and blood, the marks of which were generally status and authority, rather than great material wealth. At the same time, the colonial economy, the royal courts, and the everyday politics of the pueblo provided considerable room for the negotiation and contestation of authority and rank within Indian communities, although these challenges of particular relations generally accepted and reproduced the larger parameters of the colonial order.

The colonial pueblo and its hierarchies were neither stagnant remnants of preconquest society nor simple by-products of the expansion of the world market and European colonialism. Far more than a transitional stage between the archaic political economy of the Inca empire and the capitalist, neofeudal political economy of republican Peru, for two centuries the corporate ideal of Andean society, defined by the pueblo, its internal hierarchies, and the ethnic division of Peru, was aggressively propagated both by the crown and its officials and by the indigenous peoples of the Andes.[1] This order produced its own structural and ideological contradictions, as well as mechanisms that promoted the reproduction of that order. Foremost among the contradictions were those between Spanish and Indian, between the subsistence economy of the pueblo and the colonial market, between *ayllu* and pueblo, between competing elite lineages, and between the (masculinist) democratic ideal of the *cabildo* and the aristocratic ideal of the *cacicazgo*. Promoting the reproduction of the colonial pueblo order were the courts' commitment to upholding this order formalized by colonial law, the structural necessity of the cacique in the colonial economy, and the active performance of patriarchal benevolence and noble superiority.

The broader relations between Spanish and Indian, and the hierarchies within the Indian republic, became naturalized into indigenous society. By 1750, the Indian communities of the Andes were products of two centuries of "Hispanicization," just as those of 1530 were the products of a century of aggressive "Incafication." The Indian elites of Cusco were simultaneously the most hispanicized sector of indigenous society, and the axiomatic representation of that society. The detailed study of the bishopric's Indian elites in the decades before the Tupac Amaru rebellion allows a number of specific conclusions about the reproduction of authority in Indian communities, and the conflicts that it produced and negotiated. Three areas of

---

1 For the problem of "transitional" economies, see Robert DuPlessis and Martha Howell, "Reconsidering the Early Modern Urban Economy: The Cases of Leiden and Lille," *Past and Present* 94 (February 1982): 49–84.

potential conflict emerge as determinant: between the elite and the community, between competing elites, and between Indian and Spanish. Implicitly, I have argued that the first two figured more prominently in the politics of Indian society in the decades before the rebellion; while after the rebellion competition between Indian and Spaniard moved to the fore.

The eighteenth-century Indian elites of the bishopric of Cusco were a diverse group. In and around the city of Cusco, a self-identified Inca nobility continued to dominate pueblo life until the end of the eighteenth century. The colonial Incas' imperial history, and the concession of hereditary privileges in the sixteenth century, made them unique among the colonial Indian elite. The thousand or so Inca nobles around Cusco formed a ruling caste that had a near monopoly on cacical office and reproduced itself through marriage. Nonetheless, the size of this Inca nobility created great competition for positions of authority within it. How cacical authority was negotiated varied from pueblo to pueblo. In a number of communities, cacicazgos were, by the eighteenth century, clearly the possession of particular families. In others, cacical office often moved between lineages, passing through cacical heiresses to their husbands. Colonial rule preserved Inca privilege and political authority in their historic heartland, but fractured them, so that they were repeatedly contested and redefined.

To the south, the Vilcanota highlands had no such larger, interprovincial elite, and cacical authority was determined more by the complex, inter-ayllu politics of the pueblo. While most caciques in the area on the eve of the rebellion belonged to elite lineages, cacicazgos appear to have moved more fluidly between them, and often families retained possession of the office for just one or two generations. In contrast, in the Aymara societies of the Titicaca basin, a number of families that descended from hybrid Aymara–Inca lineages had, by the mid-1700s, established hereditary control of major cacicazgos. In the decades before the Tupac Amaru rebellion, these cacical dynasties married among themselves, and with Spaniards, to form an ill-defined but powerful network of cacical dynasties that dominated the Indian republic around the lake. Thus, while cacical authority was at the heart of the Indian pueblo, its possession was the object of widespread competition among elites, and how that competition was resolved varied dramatically by region, a product of the historical organization of the societies and the effects of the colonial economy.

The cacique played a central role in that economy. As the nexus between communal production and viceregal tribute and markets, the cacique also controlled much local production through the ownership of the means of production, as well as by customary enjoyment of communal land and labor. As a result, the cacical household was invariably the richest in the community, producing its own contradiction in the pueblo economy, as the competing logics of pueblo autonomy and familial authority required that caciques both protect and exploit their communities. Here as in the organization of cacical authority, regional varieties were pronounced. In the bishopric's southern half, the relative absence of Spanish settlement and properties, the size of Indian communities, and their position in the vicere-gal economy produced some of colonial Peru's richest Indian families. In contrast, the wealth of Inca noble families tended to be modest, a factor of Spanish competition, the smaller scale of pueblo economies around Cusco, and the more fluid cacical succession. Indeed, the richest Inca nobles gen-erally owed their fortunes to the urban economy of Cusco. As a result, the economies of Inca cacical households were not so large as to remove them from the pueblo; while in the Titicaca basin the richest cacical dynasties formed a distinct aristocratic class.

Considerable attention has been focused on whether these cacical dynas-ties formed a class of agrarian capitalists, and based on the information from the bishopric of Cusco this work argues that they did not, for several reasons. First, evidence from the seventeenth century suggests that already caciques were acquiring personal and familial wealth as substantial as that held in the eighteenth century.[2] However, by and large the eighteenth century witnessed no real expansion of this wealth. That is, while private wealth took deep root among the Indian elite, a capitalist logic that privileged the use of that wealth for the expansion of capital did not. This was due to the limits of the Andean market and to the legal structures of colonial society. Entailed property was not adopted in the Indian republic; the divi-sion of parental wealth equally among children, as required by Spanish law, repeatedly fractured the holdings of the cacical households. To be sure, the substantial wealth of cacical families imposed on them particular dynastic strategies, one of which – intermarriage with provincial Spaniards – drained wealth from pueblo economies to the agrarian capitalism of Spanish Peru. However, the principal asset of cacical houses was almost invariably cacical office itself. As a result, the organization of colonial Indian society retarded the separation of the household economies of the rural Indian elite from those of their pueblos. In the mid-eighteenth-century highlands, private, cacical wealth was deployed above all in maintaining possession of cacical office, and thereby followed the dictates of the legal structure of colonial society.

Because cacical office remained the principal mechanism for acquiring wealth and authority in Indian society, its possession was at the heart of social conflict in Indian communities. This conflict generally affirmed the office of cacique, challenging only its possession by particular individuals. The importance of cacicazgos led to the mapping of other social conflicts onto legal battles for their possession, particularly between Spanish and

2 Stern, *Peru's Indian Peoples*, pp. 158–83; Rivera, "El Mallku."

Indian; over the limits of cacical wealth and authority; over the definition of community; and between rival elite families. Precisely because control of the cacicazgo was both valuable and contested, its occupants tried to legitimate their possession. By establishing private networks of obligation within their pueblos through loans and communal debts, caciques positioned themselves at the heart of the material and symbolic economies of the Indian pueblo. They used their wealth and their education to defend the rights of their communities in court, and to defend their own claims to office. Finally, the Indian nobility aggressively performed their superiority, both by emphasizing their illustrious lineage and by engaging in conspicuous displays of wealth. Far from being rejected by Indian society generally, the stratification and hierarchies of the colonial pueblo were essential to its organization and repeatedly asserted to affirm their legitimacy.

While the mature colonial order required and reproduced an Indian elite, that order's internal contradictions and the effects of changes in larger systems of which it was a part provoked its collapse in the late eighteenth century. The material and political inequalities enshrined in the pueblo by colonial legislation and the colonial economy necessarily produced internal antagonisms. At the same time, the expansion of Spanish Peru threatened the power of Indian elites and the autonomy of the pueblo, and transformed the meaning and effects of the traditional mechanism for negotiating the competition between rural Spaniards and Indian elites – intermarriage. Finally, the Spanish crown and its officials actively sought to reform the imperial order that had been established in the sixteenth century and survived, both through the strength of its own legitimacy and through the inertia and weakness of the crown, for two centuries.

There is suggestive evidence that the distance between the Indian commons and the cacical elite was growing in the eighteenth century, especially in the Titicaca basin. Innovations like the entry of Indian noblemen into the church drew elite families away from the Indian republic, and it appears that the great cacical houses were less interested in marrying into their pueblos than in forging alliances with peers in other communities. The growth of the Spanish population exacerbated this, as common interest and marriage alliances drew together the cacical elite and provincial Spaniards. But the social tensions in the bishopric of Cusco were not as pronounced as those along the Altiplano, nor was anti-cacical agitation, and violence, nearly as common. Anti-cacical lawsuits in the decades before the rebellion suggest incipient class tension – particularly complaints about the alienation of communal property and forced labor – but they were not a widespread phenomenon. And while the 1770s saw an appreciable increase in rural unrest in the bishopric, this was directed primarily at royal officials. Class antagonisms within the pueblo were not strong enough on their own to provoke the downfall of the local colonial order. Similarly, the occasional

appointment of Spanish, interim caciques, and the succession of Spanish
husbands to cacicazgos in the name of their Indian noble wives, produced
a shift of power to rural Spaniards, and further removed cacical dynasties
from their communities. Again, however, this shift would be most dramatic
after the rebellion.

Ultimately, in Cusco the collapse of the colonial order of the pueblo was
provoked by external factors. The Bourbon effort to redefine the colonial
political economy undermined the long-established order of the rural highlands. The legalization of the *reparto* in 1756 increased the material burden
on Indian communities and produced widespread discontent; it also showed
the crown's determination to make the Andes more profitable. This commitment led to the division of the viceroyalty in 1776 and the institution
of internal customs between La Paz and Cusco. More than any other single
factor, this was the structural precipitant of the rebellion in Cusco.[3]

If the rebellion began as an attempt by Indian communities of the
Vilcanota highlands to force back the Bourbon reforms, it soon grew to much
more: Tupac Amaru's violent challenge to the Bourbon order unleashed the
latent conflict in the rural highlands. The rebellion reveals the complex
geography of the Indian republic. In the Inca-ruled pueblos around Cusco,
the rebellion made no headway. That the Inca nobility remained loyal to the
crown is not surprising: the Indian nobility generally rose in defense of the
colonial order. That the tributaries of the valleys near Cusco did not respond
to Tupac Amaru's calls says much about the historical division between these
pueblos and the pastoral highlands. Class differentiation within Indian society was less pronounced in the Inca-ruled pueblos: deeply stratified, their
hierarchies were nonetheless defined more by privilege, status, and authority
than by wealth. To the south, in the Titicaca basin, the reformist rebellion
of Tupac Amaru quickly transformed into a class war, in which much of
the tributary population rose against the Spanish and Indian noble elite.
For the Indian nobility around Titicaca, the results were catastrophic. Their
families were massacred, their wealth destroyed, and their papers burned;
as a group they bore the brunt of the rebellion.

Violent and destructive of the nobility though it was, the rebellion did
not itself cause the collapse of the Indian nobility. Rather, that collapse was
caused by the crown's repudiation of that elite in the decade following the
rebellion, when the crown's officers waged a campaign against Indian nobles'
privileges and against their control of Indian pueblos. Opting instead to
place control of pueblo economies with rural Spaniards, the crown destroyed
two of the bulwarks of Indian noble privilege: the recognition of hereditary
elites and the insistence that the cacicazgo be an Indian office. With the
removal of the crown's defense of their privilege, the Indian nobility lost

---

3 O'Phelan Godoy, *Un siglo de rebeliones*.

much of their authority within the pueblo. To be sure, the collapse of the Indian elite was a drawn-out process, lasting a generation. The most prominent loyalist caciques generally retained control of their office, and in the 1790s the crown relented in its assault. Even deposed caciques, transformed into *alcaldes*, often retained power within the community. But the newly invigorated offices of alcalde and *cabildo* also allowed factions in the pueblo to wage campaigns against surviving cacical families. In any case, the crown's relenting in the 1790s simply recognized that some cacical families had strong legal claim to their office – it did not return to the earlier policy of insisting that pueblos have Indian caciques. Finally, the turmoil of the Peninsular Wars and the liberal constitution of the Spanish junta further undermined the hierarchical, corporate ideal of society that had required and preserved an indigenous elite, and cleared the way for the formal removal, with the creation of the Republic of Peru, of the two bulwarks of Indian elite privilege: legal nobility and the cacicazgo.

Appendix

The Election of Don Antonio Tapara as Cacique of Urinsaya, Ñuñoa, Lampa, August 5, 1759 [ARC, RA, Adm., Leg. 167 (1808–9)]

Don Antonio Joseph de Pro[]l, corregidor and *justicia mayor* [appointed] by his Majesty of the Province of Lampa, Cavana, Cavanilla and part of Canas:

I say that because Don Ramon Basques, interim cacique of the partiality of Urinsaya of the *repartimiento* of this pueblo, renounced the *cacicazgo* because finding himself very poor he could not deposit with the punctuality that he ought the Royal Tributes under his charge, and it being certain that in the *tercios* that have passed during my [tenure] he has been very remiss in said deposits, and [the] said partiality needing to ensure [the election] of [a] cacique so that he not fall behind in the collection of the tributes for the tercio of San Juan of this present year and [he] be able to make the deposit to the Royal Treasury at the time that his Majesty has disposed and ordered, I went to this Pueblo and ordered to assemble all the Indian *Principales* and plebeians of the said partiality, who found themselves in this Pueblo, in the larger part, because it is the day in which they should hear mass and attend church, [and] I ordered to be said in the general language by Don Diego Lazarte who served in the office of Interpreter, [that] they propose to me three subjects of the said partiality in whom there were the qualities that are required and necessary to obtain said office, to elect from them [the one] who seemed most convenient[.] [T]hey proposed only two, who were Don Ramon Basques who is the said cacique who renounced, and Don Antonio Tapara, saying that there were no others in the said moiety of sufficient [wealth;] in the said [comments] they concurred asking at the same time that for no reason should I name a cacique who was not Indian, because those who have had mestizos have received many wrongs, and if such were to occur in order not to experience [the wrongs] they would see themselves compelled to abandon their houses and the Pueblo of their origin; on account of which and attending to the justified reasons which they alleged, in the name of his Majesty and in virtue of the royal authority that [He] has confided in me, I elect and name as interim cacique of said moiety of Urinsaya of the repartimiento of this Pueblo, Don Antonio Tapara, *indio principal* and descendent of the legitimate caciques who have been. . . . [A]nd at the same time I order the *alcaldes, alguaciles*, principal Indians and commoners,

Spanish residents and transients of this jurisdiction, that they have as their interim cacique Don Antonio Tapara, that they obey [him], maintaining his privileges and exemptions while at the same time providing him with the services and assistance that he ought to enjoy as cacique, as Your Majesty has disposed and ordered in Your Royal Ordinances, and [that] the said Don Antonio Tapara will perform the greatest efficiency in the collection of the Royal Tributes under his charge in order to make the payments at their required times, and at the same time he will take care, as his obligation, that the Indians attend church and mass the days on which they should, so that they can be instructed in the mysteries of Our Sainted Faith; he is charged to take particular care in maintaining them in peace and good conduct, treating them with love, and equity, and avoiding that harm is done to their persons or possessions, and very particularly he is charged not to tolerate scandals, adulteries, dances, nor drunkenness, from which result offenses to God. . . .

Glossary

q: Quechua   s: Spanish

alcalde (s)	The highest ranking office in Spanish local government; awkwardly translated as "mayor." The main elected figure in the indigenous pueblo from the reforms of the late 1500s on, the alcalde stood in counterpoint to the cacique, although alcaldes were generally eclipsed by powerful caciques. Following the Great Rebellion, the office appears to have expanded in authority with the eclipse of the cacicazgo.
alférez (s)	Standard-bearer; a municipal office.
Altiplano (s)	The highland plain that extends from Lake Titicaca south to Argentina, at an altitude of 13,000 feet.
anexo (s)	An Indian pueblo with its own church but contained within the parish boundaries of another pueblo.
Antisuyo (q)	The northeastern quadrant of the Inca empire, including the Paucartambo valley, and the Yungas of southern Peru and Bolivia.
audiencia (s)	A Spanish royal court of justice. The region studied was under the jurisdiction of the audiencias of Lima and Charcas; an audiencia was established in Cusco in the 1780s.
ayllu (q)	A grouping of people for productive and reproductive purposes; a village, settlement, clan, extended family. The basic unit of Andean society, almost always bound together by kinship, real or fictive. Often distributed across several settlements.
cabildo (s)	Town council. In theory, cabildos were established in Indian pueblos, although documentary evidence suggests that this aspect of Castilian municipal government did not take firm root until the end of the colonial era; more important was the alcalde, and all forms

	of elected municipal office were often overshadowed in indigenous communities by the cacique.
cacicazgo (s)	The office of the cacique.
cacique	The Indian authority within an ayllu or group of ayllus; a chieftain or lord. The term is Carib, and was applied to Andean rulers by the Spanish.
capitán de mita (s)	The Indian official responsible for delivering a community's contingent of mitayos to Potosí, and supervising them while there.
carga (s)	A unit of volume used to measure crops; a basket- or sackful; approximately half a fanega.
cercado (s)	The immediate environs of a city that fall under its legal jurisdiction; generally includes outlying suburban parishes.
chambi (q)	An Andean battle hammer.
chichería (s)	A tavern serving chicha, a fermented corn drink.
Chinchaysuyo (q)	The northwestern quadrant of the Inca empire, including central and northern Peru, and Ecuador.
chorrillo (s)	A small factory for producing and finishing inexpensive woolen cloth, generally water-powered and located along a stream.
chuño (q)	Potatoes freeze-dried by being soaked in water and then exposed to the cold air.
Collasuyo (q)	The southeastern quadrant of the Inca empire, including the southern Vilcanota valley, the Titicaca basin, and the Bolivian Altiplano.
composición (s)	The sale by the crown of "vacant" Indian communal land to private individuals (Indian and Spanish).
Condesuyo (q)	The southwestern quadrant of the Inca empire, including the Apurímac highlands; encompassing Arequipa and its Pacific coast.
corregidor (s)	Spanish governor of a province, responsible for the execution of justice and the collection of tribute, generally appointed for five-year terms, although this was by no means absolute. Invariably Spanish.
corregimiento (s)	A province in the Spanish empire; those in the eighteenth-century Andes had populations of 5,000–40,000. Many followed the boundaries of preexisting ethnic polities and Inca provinces.
coya (q)	An Inca woman of royal blood; according to Inca Garcilaso, a "queen."
creole	[s: criollo] An American-born person of Spanish blood.

curaca (q)	Chieftain or lord; the prevalent term in the early colonial period, largely replaced by "cacique" in the eighteenth century.
encomendero (s)	The holder of an encomienda grant.
encomienda (s)	An "entrusting" of a group of Indians by the Spanish crown to a Christian (usually to a Spaniard, though in instances to an Inca royal), to supervise their Christianization. It brought the right to exact "traditional" tribute.
estancia (s)	A ranch. In the bishopric of Cusco, the term referred both to privately owned ranches (generally for sheep) and to small, pastoral Indian settlements scattered throughout the highlands.
fanega (s)	A Spanish bushel (1.58 English bushels).
fanegada (s)	The amount of land that can be sown with a fanega; approx. 1.58 acres.
forastero (s)	An Indian immigrant to an established community, who did not have access to communal lands, paid a reduced tribute to the crown, and did not perform the mita.
fuero (s)	A legal code or legal privilege, whose customary use by a certain group was recognized by the Spanish crown.
hacienda (s)	A privately owned agricultural estate. Larger haciendas often consisted of several properties that were not contiguous, but fell within the same (or adjacent) parishes.
hidalgo (s)	Literally "hijo d'algo," or "son-of-something [-one]." A gentleman. The basic rank of Spanish nobility, it brought legal privileges and exemption from certain taxes. Indian nobles enjoyed privileges of hidalguía.
intendencia (s)	A colonial province, created in the 1780s by the Bourbon reforms as a grouping of subdelegados; the intendancy of Cusco roughly followed the bishopric, with the Titicaca basin provinces attached to the intendancy of Puno.
jilakata (q)	Ayllu or pueblo official in charge of keeping records.
ladino (s)	An hispanicized Indian, generally competent or fluent in Spanish.
lliclla (q)	A rectangular piece of cloth, worn over the shoulders; a standard piece of women's clothing in Andean society.
mascapaycha (q)	A scarlett cloth fringe worn by the Inca emperors across their foreheads; the mark of Inca authority.
mayorazgo (s)	An entailed estate.

mestizo (s)	A person of mixed Indian and Spanish ancestry.
mita (q)	Compulsory, paid labor service to which originarios were subject. Mitas provided labor for colonial cities, haciendas, obrajes, but especially silver and mercury mines. In theory, originarios in the mining areas were to work for six months of every forty-two in the mines.
mitayo (q)	A tributary serving his mita term.
ñusta (q)	An Inca woman of royal blood; according to Inca Garcilaso, a "princess."
obraje (s)	A workhouse; usually applied to rural textile factories, with mixed work forces of wage-laborers, convicts, and Indian peons.
orejón (s)	Literally, "big ear": a term for the Incas at the time of the conquest (a reference to their use of large earplugs); in the eighteenth century, the term was applied occasionally to the preconquest Incas.
originario (s)	An adult male Indian tributary enrolled as a native of his community, who had access to communal lands and was responsible for full tribute (ranging from five to ten pesos a year) and personal service, including the mita.
panaca (q)	An Inca royal ayllu.
peninsular (s)	A person born in Spain.
principal (s)	An Indian village or ayllu prominent.
pueblo (s)	A rural community established under Spanish rule as a basic unit of rural Indian society; a village or town.
reparto (s)	The forced sale of goods by corregidores and other officials to those under their rule.
reservado (s)	An Indian man over fifty years of age, no longer responsible for paying tribute.
segunda (s)	An assistant to a cacique, often responsible for collecting tribute from ayllus and households.
señorio (s)	Lordship; kingdom. Used widely by the Spanish, and later scholars, to describe the smaller polities (with populations in the tens of thousands) of the preconquest Andes.
subdelegado (s)	A local province, replaced the corregimiento during the Bourbon Reforms. Also, the official in charge of the province.
Tawantinsuyu (q)	"The Four Quarters": the Inca empire, composed of its four quadrants with Cusco at the heart.
topo (q)	(1) Ideally, the amount of land that will maintain a couple for a year; its measure was not standardized. Cobo put it at one-third of a hectare, or a bit less than

one acre; Inca Garcilaso as three times as much.[1] (2) A large pin or brooch used by women.

trajinante (s)   An Indian muleteer or llamateer.

vecino (s)   ["Neighbor"]. A resident or citizen of a Spanish city. Roughly analogous to "burgher."

---

1 D'Altroy, *The Incas*, p. 247; Glave and Remy, *Estructura Agraria*, p. 524.

Bibliography

Archival Sources

AAC: Archivo del Arzobispado del Cusco [Cusco, Peru]
ADP: Archivo Deparmental de Puno [Puno, Peru]
      INT: Intendencia
      JPI: Juzgado de Primer Instancia
      NOT: Notariales
AGI: Archivo General de las Indias [Seville, Spain]
      Charcas
      Cuzco
      Escribanía
AGN: Archivo General de la Nación [Lima, Peru]
      DI   Derechos Indígenas
      SG   Superior Gobierno
AGN-A: Archivo General de la Nación [Buenos Aires, Argentina]
      Sala IX
AGS: Archivo General de Simancas [Simancas, Spain]
      Secretaria de Guerra
ALP: Archivo de La Paz [La Paz, Bolivia]
      EC: Expedientes Coloniales
ANB: Archivo Nacional de Bolivia [Sucre, Bolivia]
      Ruck: Colección Ruck
      EC: Expedientes Coloniales
ARC: Archivo Regional del Cusco [Cusco, Peru]

CAB:	Cabildo		INT:	Intendencia
	Civ.:	Causas Civiles		Crim.:	Causas Criminales
	Ped.:	Pedimentos		Gob.:	Gobierno
CR:	Cajas Reales			Ord.:	Causas Ordinarias
CE:	Causas Eclesiásticas			Prov.:	Provincias
BE:	Colección Betancur			Ord.:	Causas Ordinarias
CC:	Colegio de Ciencias			RH:	Real Hazienda
COR:	Corregimiento			Vir.:	Virreynato
	Adm.:	Administrativos		JC:	Judiciales Civiles
	Civ.:	Causas Civiles		JT:	Junta de Temporalidades
	Ped.:	Pedimentos		NOT:	Notariales
	Prov.:	Provincias		RA:	Real Audiencia
		Civ.:	Causas Civiles		Adm.:	Administrativo
		Crim.:	Causas Criminales		Crim.:	Causas Criminales

CSJ: Corte Superior de Justicia   Ord.:   Causas Ordinarias
DZ: Diezmos   Ped.:   Pedimentos
                                                         SC: Santa Cruzada
                                                         TAZ: Tazmías
BNP: Biblioteca Nacional [Lima, Peru]
          Man.:   Manuscritos, Siglos XVIII and XIX
JCB   John Carter Brown Library [Providence, Rhode Island, USA]
RREE: Archivo del Ministerio de Relaciones Exteriores [Lima, Peru]
          CC: Cusco, Cabildo   PC: Puno, Cabildo
          CJD: Cusco, Justicia Departmental PE: Puno, Eclesiástico
          CN: Cusco, Notariales   PM: Puno, Minería
          CRA: Cusco, Real Audiencia   PN: Puno, Notariales
          CRH: Cusco, Real Hazienda   PRA: Puno, Real Audiencia
          CSG: Cusco, Superior Gobierno   PRH: Puno, Real Hazienda
                                               PSG   Puno, Superior Gobierno

Abbreviations

CDBR: *Colección Documental del Bicentenario de la Revolución Emancipadora de Túpac Amaru.*

Primary Sources

Arriaga, Pablo José de. *The Extirpation of Idolatry in Peru*, translated by L. Clark Keating (Lexington: University of Kentucky Press, 1968).

Ballesteros, Thomas de. *Tomo primero de las ordenanzas del Perú* (Lima: Francisco Sobrino y Bados, 1752).

Betanzos, Juan de. *Narrative of the Incas*, translated by Roland Hamilton and Dana Buchman (Austin: University of Texas Press, 1996).

Bueno, Cosme. *El conocimiento de los tiempos. Efeméride del año de 1768* (Lima, 1767).

"Carta de los Comisarios . . . sobre la perpetuidad y otras cosas." In *Nueva colección de documentos inéditos para la historia de España y sus Indios*, ed. Francisco de Zabálburu, Vol. VI (Madrid: M. G. Hernández, 1892–6), pp. 41–105.

Castro, Ignacio de. *Relación del Cuzco*, ed. Carlos Daniel Valcárcel (Lima: Universidad Nacional de San Marcos, 1978).

Cobo, Bernabé. *History of the Inca Empire*, translated by Roland Hamilton (Austin: University of Texas Press, 1979).

Cobo, Bernabé. *Inca Religion and Customs*, translated by Roland Hamilton (Austin: University of Texas Press, 1990).

Colección Documental del Bicentenario de la Revolución Emancipadora de Túpac Amaru, ed. Luis Durand Flórez. 5 vols. (Lima: Comisión Nacional del Bicentenario de la Rebelión Emancipadora de Túpac Amaru, 1980).

El Correo de Encomiendas, Cusco. Nos. 8, 9, 13 [1832–3].

Cusco Libre, Cusco. Nos. 25 and 33 [1834–5].

Cuzco 1689, Documentos: Economía y sociedad en el sur andino, edited with Introduction by Horacio Villanueva Urteaga (Cusco: Centro Bartolomé de Las Casas, 1982).

Esquivel y Navia, Diego de. *Noticias cronológicas de la gran ciudad del Cusco*, ed. Félix Denegri Luna. 2 vols. (Lima: Banco Wiese, 1980).

Garcilaso de la Vega, Inca. *Royal Commentaries of the Incas and General History of Peru*, translated by Harold V. Livermore (Austin: University of Texas Press, 1994).

Genealogía de Tupac Amaru por José Gabriel Tupac Amaru (documentos inéditos del año 1777), ed. Francisco A. Loayza (Lima, 1946).

Guaman Poma de Ayala, Felipe. *El primer nueva corónica y buen gobierno*, ed. Juan V. Murra and Rolena Adorno. 3 vols. (Mexico City: Siglo Veintiuno, 1980).

The Huarochirí Manuscript: A Testament of Ancient and Colonial Andean Religion, translated by Frank Salomon and George L. Urioste (Austin: University of Texas Press, 1991).

"Indios de sangre real," *Revista del Archivo Histórico del Cusco*, 1:1 (1950), pp. 204–30.

Las Casas, Bartolomé de. *Brevísima relación de la destrucción de las Indias* (Madrid: Sarpe, 1985).

Matienzo, Juan de. *El gobierno del Perú*, edited with Prologue by Guillermo Lohmann Villena (Lima-Paris: L'Institut Français d'Études Andines, 1967).

El Observador. Cusco. No. 3 (1833).

Recopilación de Leyes de los Reynos de Las Indias, mandadas imprimir y publicar por la Magestad Católica del Rey Don Carlos II. 4th ed. (Madrid: Ibarra, 1791).

Sahuaraura Ramos Tito Atauchi, José Rafael. *Estado del Perú*, ed. Francisco A. Loayza (Lima: D. Miranda, 1944).

Sahuaraura, Justo. *Recuerdos de la Monarquia Peruana, o Bosquejo de la historia de los Incas* (Paris: Rosa, Bouret, 1850).

TePaske, John J. and Herbert S. Klein. *The Royal Treasuries of the Spanish Empire in America* (Durham: Duke University Press, 1982).

Túpac Amaru, Juan Bautista. *Cuarenta años de cautiverio*, ed. Francisco A. Loayza (Lima: D. Miranda, 1941).

Unanue, Hipólito. *Guía política, eclesiástica y militar del virreinato del Perú*, ed. José Durand (Lima: COFIDE, 1985).

Vega, Fray Bartolomé de la. "Memorial al Real Consejo de Indias sobre los agravios que reciben los Indios del Perú," in *Nueva colección de documentos inéditos para la historia de España y sus Indios*, ed. Francisco de Zabálburu, Vol. VI (Madrid, 1896), pp. 106–31.

Xérez, Francisco de. *Verdadera relación de la conquista del Perú* (Madrid: Historia 16, 1985).

Secondary Sources

Abercrombie, Thomas. *Pathways of Memory and Power: Ethnography and History among an Andean People* (Madison: University of Wisconsin Press, 1998).

Alaperrine-Bouyer, Monique. "Saber y poder: la cuestión de la educación de las elites indígenas," in *Incas e indios cristianos: elites indígenas cristianas en los Andes coloniales*, ed. Jean-Jacques Decoster (Cusco: Centro Bartolomé de las Casas, 2002), pp. 145–67.

Alberti, Giorgio and Enrique Mayer, eds. *Reciprocidad e intercambio en los Andes peruanos* (Lima: Instituto de Estudios Peruanos, 1974).

Alberti Manzanares, Pilar. "La influencia económica y política de las acllacuna en el incanato," *Revista de Indias*, 45:176 (1985), pp. 557–85.

Albó, Xavier. "Jesuitas y culturas indígenas. Perú, 1568–1806. Su actitud, métodos y criterios de aculturación," *América Indígena*, 26:3 (July 1966), pp. 249–308 and 26:4 (October 1966), pp. 395–446.

Altman, Ida. *Emigrants and Society: Extremadura and America in the Sixteenth Century* (Berkeley: University of California Press, 1989).

Altuve Carrillo, Leonardo. *Choquehuanca y su Arenga a Bolívar* (Buenos Aires: Planeta, 1991).

Amado Gonzales, Donato. "El alférez real de los Incas: resistencia, cambios y continuidad de la identidad indígena," in *Incas e indios cristianos: elites indígenas e identidades cristianas en los Andes coloniales*, ed. Jean-Jacques Decoster (Cusco: Centro Bartolomé de las Casas, 2002), pp. 221–50.

Amado Gonzales, Donato. "Establecimiento y consolidación de la hacienda en el Valle de Chinchaypucyo (1600–1700)," *Revista Andina*, 16:1 (July 1998), pp. 67–98.

Anderson, Benedict. *Imagined Communities: Reflections on the Origin and Spread of Nationalism*. 2nd ed. (London: Verso, 1991).

Andrien, Kenneth. *Andean Worlds: Indigenous History, Culture, and Consciousness under Spanish rule, 1532–1825* (Albuquerque: University of New Mexico Press, 2001).

Andrien, Kenneth. *Crisis and Decline: The Viceroyalty of Peru in the Seventeenth Century* (Albuquerque: University of New Mexico Press, 1985).

Angles Vargas, Víctor. *El Cacique Tambohuacso: Historia de un proyectado levantamiento contra la dominación española* (Lima: Industrial Gráfica, 1975).

Angles Vargas, Víctor. *Historia del Cusco (Cusco colonial)*. 2 vols. (Cusco, 1983).

Bakewell, Peter. *Miners of the Red Mountain: Indian Labor in Potosí, 1545–1650* (Albuquerque: University of New Mexico Press, 1984).

Baskes, Jeremy. *Indians, Merchants and Markets: A Reinterpretation of the Repartimiento and Spanish Indian Economic Relations in Colonial Oaxaca 1750–1821* (Stanford: Stanford University Press, 2000).

Bauer, Brian S. *The Development of the Inca State* (Austin: University of Texas Press, 1992).

Borah, Woodrow. *Justice by Insurance: The General Indian Court of Colonial Mexico and the Legal Aides of the Half-Real* (Berkeley: University of California Press, 1983).

Bourdieu, Pierre. *Outline of a Theory of Practice*, translated by Richard Nice (Cambridge: Cambridge University Press, 1977).

Brading, David. *The First America: The Spanish Monarchy, Creole Patriots and the Liberal State* (Cambridge: Cambridge University Press, 1991).

Burga, Manuel. *De la encomienda a la hacienda capitalista: el valle del Jequetepeque del siglo XVI al XX* (Lima: Instituto de Estudios Peruanos, 1976).

Burga, Manuel. "El Corpus Christi y la nobleza inca colonial: memoria e identidad," in *Los conquistados: 1492 y la población indígena de las Américas*, ed. Heraclio Bonilla (Bogotá: FLACSO, 1992), pp. 317–28.

Burga, Manuel. *Nacimiento de una utopía: Muerte y resurrección de los incas* (Lima: Instituto de Apoyo Agrario, 1988).

Burns, Kathryn J. *Colonial Habits: Convents and the Spiritual Economy of Cuzco, Peru* (Durham: Duke University Press, 1999).

Bush, M. L. *Rich Noble, Poor Noble* (Manchester: Manchester University Press, 1983).

Cahill, David. "Curas and Social Conflict in the Doctrinas of Cuzco, 1780–1814," *Journal of Latin American Studies*, 16:2 (November 1984), pp. 241–76.

Cahill, David. "The Inca and Inca Symbolism in Popular Festive Culture: The Religious Processions of Seventeenth-Century Cuzco," in *Habsburg Peru: Images, Imagination and Memory*, ed. Peter T. Bradley and David Cahill (Liverpool: Liverpool University Press, 2000).

Cahill, David. "Popular Religion and Appropriation: The Example of Corpus Christi in Eighteenth-Century Peru," *Latin American Research Review*, 31:2 (1996), pp. 67–110.

Cahill, David and Scarlett O'Phelan Godoy. "Forging Their Own History: Indian Insurgency in the Southern Peruvian Sierra, 1815," *Bulletin of Latin American Research*, 11:2 (May 1992), pp. 125–67.

Campbell, Leon G. "Ideology and Factionalism during the Great Rebellion, 1780–1782," in *Resistance, Rebellion and Consciousness in the Andean Peasant World, 18th to 20th Centuries*, ed. Steve J. Stern (Madison: University of Wisconsin Press, 1987), pp. 110–139.

Campbell, Leon G. *The Military and Society in Colonial Peru, 1750–1810* (Philadelphia: American Philosophical Society, 1978).

Campbell, Leon G. "Rebel or Royalist? Bishop Juan Manuel de Moscoso y Peralta and the Tupac Amaru Revolt in Peru, 1780–1784," *Revista de Historia de América*, 88 (July–December 1978), pp. 135–67.

Campbell, Leon G. "Social Structure of the Túpac Amaru Army in Cuzco, 1780–81," *Hispanic American Historical Review*, 61:4 (November 1981), pp. 673–93.

Campbell, Leon G. "Women and the Great Rebellion in Peru, 1780–83," *The Americas*, 42:2 (1985), pp. 163–96.

Carcelén Reluz, Carlos. "Las doctrinas de Chaclla – Huarochirí en los siglos XVI y XVII," *Revista Andina*, 31 (July 1998), pp. 99–118.

Cardoso, Fernando Henrique and Enzo Faletto. *Dependency and Development in Latin America*, translated by Marjory Mattingly Urquidi (Berkeley: University of California Press, 1979).

Chamberlain, Robert S. "The Concept of the *Señor Natural* as Revealed by Castilian Law and Administrative Documents," *Hispanic American Historical Review*, 19:2 (May 1939), pp. 129–37.

Chance, John K. and William B. Taylor. "Cofradías and Cargos: An Historical Perspective on the Mesoamerican Civil-Religious Hierarchy," *American Ethnologist*, 12 (1985), pp. 1–26.

Choque Canqui, Roberto. "Los caciques frente a la rebelión de Túpak Katari en La Paz," *Historia y Cultura*, 19 (1991), pp. 83–93.

Choque Canqui, Roberto. *Sociedad y economía colonial en el sur andino* (La Paz: Hisbol, 1993).

Choque Canqui, Roberto. "Una iglesia de los Guarachi en Jesús de Machaca (Pacajes-La Paz)," in *La venida del reino: Religión evangelización y cultura en América, Siglos XVI–XX*, ed. Gabriela Ramos (Cusco: Centro Bartolomé de Las Casas, 1994), pp. 135–49.

Christian, William A. *Local Religion in 16th-Century Spain* (Princeton: Princeton University Press, 1981).

Coatsworth, John H. "Patterns of Rural Rebellion in Latin America: Mexico in Comparative Perspective," in *Riot, Rebellion and Revolution: Rural Conflict in Mexico*, ed. Friedrich Katz (Princeton: Princeton University Press, 1988), pp. 21–62.

Cole, Jeffrey A. *The Potosí Mita: Compulsory Indian Labor in the Andes* (Stanford: Stanford University Press, 1985).

Collier, George A., Renato I. Rosaldo, and John D. Wirth, eds. *The Inca and Aztec States, 1400–1800: Anthropology and History* (New York: Academic Press, 1982).

Cook, Noble David. *Born to Die: Disease and New World Conquest, 1492–1650* (Cambridge: Cambridge University Press, 1998).

Cook, Noble David. *Demographic Collapse: Indian Peru, 1520–1620* (Cambridge: Cambridge University Press, 1981).

Cornblit, Oscar. *Power and Violence in the Colonial City: Oruro from the Mining Renaissance to the Rebellion of Tupac Amaru (1740–1782)* (Cambridge: Cambridge University Press, 1995).

Cornblit, Oscar. "Society and Mass Rebellion in 18th-Century Peru and Bolivia," in *Latin American Affairs* (St. Anthony's Papers 22), ed. Raymond Carr (Oxford: Oxford University Press, 1970), pp. 9–44.

Cornejo Bouroncle, Jorge. *Pumacahua: La revolución del Cuzco de 1814* (Cuzco: H. G. Rozas, 1956).

Cornejo Bouroncle, Jorge. *Túpac Amaru, la revolución precursora de la emancipación continental* (Cusco: Universidad Nacional San Antonio Abad, 1947).

Covarrubias Pozo, Jesús. *Cusco colonial y su arte* (Cuzco: Editorial Rozas, 1958).

Crespo Rodas, Alberto, Mariano Baptista Gamucio, and José de Mesa. *La Ciudad de La Paz: Su historia, su cultura* (La Paz: Alcaldía Municipal, 1989).

D'Altroy, Terence. *The Incas* (Oxford: Blackwell, 2002).

D'Altroy, Terence. *Provincial Power in the Inka Empire* (Washington, D.C.: Smithsonian Institution Press, 1992).

Davies, Keith. *Landowners in Peru* (Austin: University of Texas Press, 1984).

Dean, Carolyn. "Ethnic Conflict and Corpus Christi in Colonial Cuzco," *Colonial Latin American Review*, 2 (1993), pp. 93–120.

Dean, Carolyn. *Inka Bodies and the Body of Christ: Corpus Christi in Colonial Cuzco, Peru* (Durham: Duke University Press, 1999).

Dean, Carolyn. "The Renewal of Old World Images and the Creation of Colonial Peruvian Visual Culture," in *Converging Cultures: Art and Identity in Spanish America*, ed. Diana Fane (New York: Harry N. Abrams, 1996), pp. 171–82.

Decoster, Jean-Jacques, ed. *Incas e indios cristianos: elites indígenas e identidades cristianas en los Andes coloniales* (Cusco: Centro Bartolomé de las Casas, 2002).

Díaz Rementería, Carlos J. *El cacique en el virreinato del Perú: estudio histórico-jurídico* (Seville: Universidad de Sevilla, 1977).

Diez, Alejandro. *Pueblos y cacicazgos de Piura, siglos XVI y XVII* (Piura: Biblioteca Regional, 1988).

Domínguez Ortiz, Antonio. *La sociedad española en el siglo XVIII* (Madrid: Instituto Balmes de Sociología, 1955).

Ducey, Michael T. "Village, Nation, and Constitution: Insurgent Politics in Papantla, Veracruz, 1810–1821," *Hispanic American Historical Review*, 79:3 (Summer 1999), pp. 463–93.

DuPlessis, Robert and Martha Howell. "Reconsidering the Early Modern Urban Economy: The Cases of Leiden and Lille," *Past and Present*, 94 (February 1982), pp. 49–84.

Durand Flórez, Luis. *El Proceso de Independencia en el Sur Andino: Cuzco y La Paz, 1805* (Lima: Universidad de Lima, 1993).

Durand Flórez, Luis. *Independencia e integración en el plan político de Túpac Amaru* (Lima: Editorial P.L.V., 1974).

Duviols, Pierre. *La destrucción de las religiones andinas (conquista y colonia)*, translated from French by Albor Maruenda (Mexico: Universidad Nacional Autónoma de México, 1977).

Duviols, Pierre. "La dinastía de los Incas: Monarquía o diarquía?" *Journal de la Société des Américanistes*, 66 (1979), pp. 67–83.

Escandell-Tur, Neus. *Producción y comercio de tejidos coloniales: los obrajes y chorrillos del Cusco, 1750–1820* (Cusco: Centro Bartolomé de las Casas, 1997).

Escobari de Querejazu, Laura. *Producción y comercio en el espacio sur andino en el siglo XVII: Cuzco-Potosí, 1650–1700* (La Paz: Embajada de España, 1985).

Espinoza Soriano, Waldemar. "El alcalde mayor indígena en el virreinato del Perú," *Anuario de Estudios Americanos*, 17 (1960), pp. 183–300.

Espinoza Soriano, Waldemar. *Lurinhuaila de Huacjra: un ayllu y un curacazgo huanca* (Huancayo, Peru: Casa de la Cultura de Junín, 1969).

Fane, Diana, ed. *Converging Cultures: Art and Identity in Spanish America* (New York: Harry N. Abrams, 1996).

Farriss, Nancy. *Maya Society under Colonial Rule: The Collective Enterprise of Survival* (Princeton: Princeton University Press, 1984).

Fisher, John R. *Commercial Relations between Spain and Spanish America in the Era of Free Trade, 1778–1796* (Liverpool: University of Liverpool, 1985).

Fisher, John R. *Government and Society in Colonial Peru: The Intendant System, 1784–1814* (London: University of London, Athlone Press, 1970).

Fisher, John R. "La rebelión de Túpac Amaru y el programa imperial de Carlos III," in *Túpac Amaru II – 1780: sociedad colonial y sublevaciones populares*, ed. Alberto Flores Galindo (Lima: Retablo de Papel, 1976), pp. 109–28.

Fisher, John R. *Silver Mines and Silver Miners in Colonial Peru, 1776–1824* (Liverpool: University of Liverpool, 1977).

Fisher, Lillian Estelle. *The Last Inca Revolt, 1780–1783* (Norman: University of Oklahoma Press, 1966).

Flores Galindo, Alberto. *Arequipa y el sur andino: ensayo de historia regional (siglos XVIII–XX)* (Lima: Editorial Horizonte, 1977).

Flores Galindo, Alberto. *Buscando un inca: identidad y utopia en los Andes.* 3rd ed. (Lima: Editorial Horizonte, 1988).

Florescano, Enrique. *Memory, Myth, and Time in Mexico: From Aztecs to Independence*, translated by Albert G. and Kathryn Bork (Austin: University of Texas Press, 1994).

Forster, Robert and Jack Greene, eds. *Preconditions of Revolution in Early Modern Europe* (Baltimore: Johns Hopkins University Press, 1970).

Frank, André Gunder. *Capitalism and Underdevelopment in Latin America: Historical Studies of Chile and Brazil*, revised edition (London: Monthly Review Press, 1969).

Fraser, Valerie. *The Architecture of Conquest: Building in the Viceroyalty of Peru, 1535–1635* (Cambridge: Cambridge University Press, 1990).

Gagliano, Joseph A. *Coca Prohibition in Peru: The Historical Debates* (Tucson: University of Arizona Press, 1994).

Galdo Gutiérrez, Virgilio. *Educación de los curacas: una forma de dominación colonial* (Ayacucho: Ediciones Waman Puma, 1970).

Garcia, J. Uriel. "El alferazgo real de indios," *Revista Universitaria*, 26 (1937), pp. 193–208.

Garrett, David T. "Descendants of the Natural Lords Who Were: The Indian Nobility of Cusco and the Collao under the Bourbons" (Ph.D. diss., Columbia University, 2002).

Garrett, David T. "'His Majesty's Most Loyal Vassals': The Indian Nobility and Túpac Amaru," *Hispanic American Historical Review*, 84:4 (November 2004), pp. 575–617.

Garrett, David T. "La Iglesia y el poder social de la nobleza indígena cuzqueña, siglo XVIII," in *Incas e indios cristianos: elites indígenas cristianas en los Andes coloniales*, ed. Jean-Jacques Decoster (Cusco: Centro Bartolomé de las Casas, 2002), pp. 295–310.

Garrett, David T. "Los Incas borbónicos: la elite indígena cusqueña en vísperas de Túpac Amaru," *Revista Andina*, 36 (Spring 2003), pp. 9–63.

Gibbs, Donald. "Cuzco, 1680–1710: An Andean City Seen through Its Economic Activities" (Ph.D. diss., University of Texas-Austin, 1979).

Gibson, Charles. "The Aztec Aristocracy in Colonial Mexico," *Comparative Studies in Society and History*, 2 (1959), pp. 169–96.

Gibson, Charles. *The Aztecs under Spanish Rule: A History of the Indians of the Valley of Mexico, 1519–1810* (Stanford: Stanford University Press, 1964).

Gibson, Charles. *The Inca Concept of Sovereignty and the Spanish Administration in Peru* (Austin: University of Texas Press, 1948).

Gibson, Charles. *Tlaxcala in the Sixteenth Century* (New Haven: Yale University Press, 1952).

Glave, Luis Miguel. *De Rosa y espinas: Economía, sociedad y mentalidades andinas, siglo XVII* (Lima: Instituto de Estudios Peruanos, 1998).

Glave, Luis Miguel. *Trajinantes: Caminos indígenas en la sociedad colonial, siglos XVI y XVII* (Lima: Instituto de Apoyo Agrario, 1989).

Glave, Luis Miguel. *Vida, símbolos y batallas: Creación y recreación de la comunidad indígena. Cusco, siglos XVI–XX* (Lima: Fondo de Cultura Económica, 1993).

Glave, Luis Miguel and Isabel Remy. *Estructura agraria y vida rural en una región Andina: Ollantaytambo entre los siglos XVI y XIX* (Cusco: Centro Bartolomé de Las Casas, 1983).

Goldwert, Marvin. "La lucha por la perpetuidad de las encomiendas en el Perú virreinal (1550–1600)," *Revista Histórica* [Lima], 22 (1955–6), pp. 350–60, and 23 (1957–8), pp. 207–20.

Golte, Jürgen. *Repartos y rebeliones: Túpac Amaru y las contradicciones de la economía colonial* (Lima: Instituto de Estudios Peruanos, 1980).

Gruzinski, Serge. *The Conquest of Mexico: The Incorporation of Indian Societies into the Western World, 16th–18th Centuries*, translated by Eileen Corrigan (Cambridge: Polity Press, 1993).

Guardino, Peter. *Peasants, Politics and the Formation of Mexico's National State, Guerrero, 1800–1857* (Stanford: Stanford University Press, 1996).

Guevara Gil, Jorge Armando. *Propiedad agraria y derecho colonial: los documentos de la Hacienda Santotis, Cuzco (1543–1822)* (Lima: Pontificia Universidad Católica del Perú, 1993).

Guillén Guillén, Edmundo. *La guerra de reconquista inka: historia épica de como los incas lucharon en defensa de la soberanía del Perú o Tawantinsuyo entre 1536 y 1572* (Lima: R. A. Ediciones, 1994).

Gutiérrez, Ramón. "Notas sobre la organización artesanal en el Cusco durante la colonia," *Histórica* [Lima] 3:1 (July 1979), pp. 1–15.

Gutiérrez, Ramón, Carlos Pernaut, Graciela Viñuales, Hernán Rodríguez Villegas, Rodolfo Vallin Magaña, Bertha Estela Benavides, Elizabeth Kuon Arce, and Jesús Lamberti. *Arquitectura del altiplano peruano* (Buenos Aires: Libros de Hispánoamerica, 1986).

Halperín Donghi, Tulio. *Reforma y disolución de los imperios Ibéricos, 1750–1850* (Madrid: Alianza Editorial, 1985).

Hanke, Lewis. *All Mankind Is One: A Study of the Disputation between Bartolomé de Las Casas y Juan Ginés de Sepúlveda in 1550 on the Intellectual and Religious Capacity of the American Indians* (DeKalb: Northern Illinois University Press, 1974).

Hanke, Lewis. *Bartolomé de las Casas: An Interpretation of his Life and Writings* (The Hague: M. Nijhoff, 1951).

Hanke, Lewis. *The Spanish Struggle for Justice in America* (Boston: Little Brown, 1965).

Harris, Olivia. "From Asymmetry to Triangle: Symbolic Transformations in Northern Potosí," in *Anthropological History of Andean Polities*, ed. John V. Murra, Nathan Wachtel, and Jacques Revel (Cambridge: Cambridge University Press, 1986), pp. 260–79.

Harris, Olivia, Brooke Larson, and Enrique Tandeter, eds. *La participación indígena en los mercados surandinos: estrategias y reproducción social, siglos XVI a XX* (La Paz: CERES, 1987).

Haskett, Robert S. *Indigenous Rulers: An Ethnohistory of Town Government in Colonial Cuernavaca* (Albuquerque: University of New Mexico Press, 1991).

Hidalgo Lehuede, Jorge. "Amarus y cataris: aspectos mesiánicos de la rebelión indígena de 1781 en Cusco, Chayanta, La Paz y Arica," *Chungará*, 10 (March 1983), pp. 117–38.

Hidalgo Lehuede, Jorge. "Indian Society in Arica, Tarapaca, and Atacama, 1750–1793, and Its Response to the Rebellion of Túpac Amaru" (Ph.D. diss., University of London, 1986).

Hughes, Nada B. "Poder y abuso: el cacicazgo de Lamay, siglo XVII," *Revista del Archivo Departmental del Cusco*, 14 (November 1999), pp. 61–76.

Hyslop, John. *Inka Settlement Planning* (Austin: University of Texas Press, 1990).

Instituto Nacional de Planificación. *Atlas histórico, geográfico, y de paisajes peruanos* (Lima, 1970).

Iriarte, Isabel. "Las túnicas incas en la pintura colonial," in *Mito y simbolismo en los Andes: la figura y la palabra*, ed. Henrique Urbano (Cusco: Centro Bartolomé de Las Casas, 1993), pp. 53–86.

Jacobsen, Nils. *Mirages of Transition: The Peruvian Altiplano, 1780–1930* (Berkeley: University of California Press, 1993).

Julien, Catherine J. *Condesuyo: The Political Division of Territory under Inca and Spanish Rule* (Bonn: Seminar für Völkerkunde, Universität Bonn, 1991).

Julien, Catherine J. *Hatunqolla: A View of Inca Rule from the Lake Titicaca Region* (Berkeley: University of California Press, 1983).

Julien, Catherine J. "Inca Decimal Administration in the Lake Titicaca Region," in *The Inca and Aztec States, 1400–1800: Anthropology and History*, ed. George A. Collier, Renato I. Rosaldo, and John D. Wirth (New York: Academic Press, 1982), pp. 119–51.

Julien, Catherine J. "La organización parroquial del Cuzco y la ciudad incaica," *Tawantinsuyu*, 5 (1988), pp. 82–96.

Julien, Catherine J. *Reading Inca History* (Iowa City: University of Iowa Press, 2000).

Katz, Friedrich. "Rural Uprisings in Preconquest and Colonial Mexico," in *Riot, Rebellion and Revolution: Rural Conflict in Mexico*, ed. Friedrich Katz (Princeton: Princeton University Press, 1988), pp. 65–94.

Kellogg, Susan. "From Parallel and Equivalent to Separate but Unequal: Tenochca Mexica Women, 1500–1700," in *Indian Women of Early Mexico*, ed. Susan Schroeder, Stephanie Wood, and Robert Haskett (Norman: University of Oklahoma, 1997), pp. 123–44.

Klein, Herbert S. *The American Finances of the Spanish Empire: Royal Income and Expenditures in Colonial Mexico, Peru, and Bolivia, 1680–1809* (Albuquerque: University of New Mexico Press, 1998).

Klein, Herbert S. "Coca Production in the Bolivia Yungas in the Colonial and Early National Periods," in *Coca and Cocaine: Effects on People and Policy in Latin America*, ed. D. Pacine and C. Franquemont (Boston: Cultural Survival, 1986), pp. 53–64.

Klein, Herbert S. *Haciendas and ayllus: rural society in the Bolivian Andes in the eighteenth and nineteenth centuries* (Stanford: Stanford University Press, 1993).

La Barre, Weston. *The Aymara Indians of the Lake Titicaca Plateau, Bolivia*, Memoir Series of the American Anthropological Association, No. 68 (Kenosha, WI: American Anthropological Association, 1948).

Langer, Eric. "Andean Rituals of Revolt: The Chayanta Rebellion of 1927," *Ethnohistory*, 37:3 (1990), pp. 227–53.

Larson, Brooke. *Cochabamba, 1550–1900: Colonialism and Agrarian Transformation in Bolivia*. 2nd ed. (Durham: Duke University Press, 1998).

Lavallé, Bernard. *El Mercader y el Marqués: las luchas de poder en el Cusco, 1700–1730* (Lima: Banco Central de la Reserva, 1988).

Levillier, Roberto. *Francisco de Toledo, supremo organizador del Perú: su vida, su obra (1515–1582)*. 3 vols. (Buenos Aires, 1935–42).

Lewin, Boleslao. *Túpac Amaru el rebelde: su época, sus luchas y su influencia en el continente* (Buenos Aires: Editorial Claridad, 1943).

Loayza, Francisco A., ed. *Juan Santos, el invencible* (Lima: [Editorial Miranda], 1942).

Lockhart, James. *The Nahuas after the Conquest: A Social and Cultural History of the Indians of Central Mexico, Sixteenth through Eighteenth Centuries* (Stanford: Stanford University Press, 1992).

Lockhart, James. *Nahuas and Spaniards: Postconquest Central Mexican History and Philology* (Stanford: Stanford University Press, 1991).

Lockhart, James. *Spanish Peru, 1532–60: A Colonial Society* (Madison: University of Wisconsin Press, 1968).

Lohmann Villena, Guillermo. *El Corregidor de Indios en el Perú bajo los Austrias* (Madrid: Ediciones Cultural Hispánica, 1957).

Lohmann Villena, Guillermo. *Las ideas jurídico-políticas en la rebelión de Gonzalo Pizarro: La tramoya doctrinal del levantamiento contra las Leyes Nuevas en el Perú* (Valladolid: Casa-Museo del Colón y Seminario Americanista, Universidad de Valladolid, 1977).

Lounsbury, Floyd G. "Some Aspects of the Inka Kinship System," in *Anthropological History of Andean Polities*, ed. John V. Murra, Nathan Wachtel, and Jacques Revel (Cambridge: Cambridge University Press, 1986), pp. 121–36.

MacCormack, Sabine. *Religion in the Andes: Vision and Imagination in Early Colonial Peru* (Princeton: Princeton University Press, 1991).

Malaga Medina, Alejandro. "Las reducciones en el Perú (1532–1600)," *Historia y Cultura* [Lima], 8 (1974), pp. 141–72.

Mallon, Florencia E. *The Defense of Community in Peru's Central Highlands: Peasant Struggle and Capitalist Transition, 1860–1940* (Princeton: Princeton University Press, 1983).

Mannheim, Bruce. *The Language of the Inka since the European Invasion* (Austin: University of Texas Press, 1991).

Meiklejohn, Norman. *La Iglesia y Los Lupaqas durante la Colonia* (Cusco: Centro Bartolomé de las Casas, 1988).

Mesa, José de and Teresa Gisbert. *Historia de la pintura cusqueña*. 2nd ed. (Lima: Fundación Banco Wiese, 1982).

Mills, Kenneth. *Idolatry and Its Enemies: Colonial Andean Religion and Extirpation, 1640–1750* (Princeton: Princeton University Press, 1997).

Miró Quesada, Aurelio. *El Inca Garcilaso* (Lima: Pontificia Universidad Católica del Perú, 1994).

Moore, Sally Falk. *Power and Property in Inca Peru* (New York: Columbia University Press, 1958).

Moreno Cebrián, Alfredo. *El Corregidor de Indios y la Economía Peruana del siglo XVIII: Los Repartos Forzosos de Mercancias* (Madrid: Instituto G. Fernández de Oviedo, 1977).

Moreno Cebrián, Alfredo. "La 'Descripción de Perú' de Joaquin Bonet," *Revista de Indias*, 149–50 (1977), pp. 753–63.

Mörner, Magnus. *Perfil de la sociedad rural del Cuzco a fines de la colonia* (Lima: Universidad del Pacífico, 1978).

Mörner, Magnus and Efraín Trelles. "The Test of Causal Interpretations of the Túpac Amaru Rebellion," in *Resistance, Rebellion and Consciousness in the Andean Peasant World, 18th to 20th Centuries*, ed. Steve J. Stern (Madison: University of Wisconsin Press, 1987), pp. 94–109.

Mujica Pinilla, Ramón. *Angeles apócrifos en la América virreinal* (Lima: Fondo de Cultura Económica, 1992).

Mujica Pinilla, Ramón. *Rosa limensis: Mística, política e iconografía en torno a la patrona de América* (Lima: IFEA-FCE-BCRP, 2002).

Muro Orejón, Antonio. "La igualdad entre indios y españoles: la real cédula de 1697," in *Estudios sobre la política indigenista española en América*, Terceras Jornadas Americanistas de la Universidad de Valladolid Vol. I (Valladolid: Universidad de Valladolid, 1975), pp. 365–86.

Murra, John V. "Aymara Lords and Their European Agents at Potosí," *Nova Americana*, 1 (1978), pp. 231–43.

Murra, John V. *The Economic Organization of the Inka State* (Greenwich, CT: JAI Press, 1980).

Murra, John V. *Formaciones económicas y políticas del mundo andino* (Lima: Instituto de Estudios Peruanos, 1975).

Murra, John V., Nathan Wachtel, and Jacques Revel, eds. *Anthropological History of Andean Polities* (Cambridge: Cambridge University Press, 1986).

Nader, Helen. *Liberty in Absolutist Spain: The Habsburg Sale of Towns, 1516–1700* (Baltimore: Johns Hopkins University Press, 1990).

Niles, Susan A. *Callachaca: Style and Status in an Inca Community* (Iowa City: University of Iowa Press, 1987).

O'Phelan Godoy, Scarlett. *Kurakas sin sucesiones: Del cacique al alcalde de indios, Perú y Bolivia 1750–1835* (Cusco: Centro Bartolomé de Las Casas, 1997).

O'Phelan Godoy, Scarlett. *La Gran Rebelión en los Andes: De Túpac Amaru a Túpac Catari* (Cusco: Centro Bartolomé de Las Casas, 1995).

O'Phelan Godoy, Scarlett. "Repensando el Movimiento Nacional Inca del siglo XVIII," in *El Perú en el siglo XVIII: la era borbónica*, ed. Scarlett O'Phelan Godoy (Lima: Pontificia Universidad Católica del Perú, 1999), pp. 263–78.

O'Phelan Godoy, Scarlett. *Un siglo de rebeliones anticoloniales: Perú y Bolivia, 1700–83* (Cusco: Centro Bartolomé de Las Casas, 1988).

Pagden, Anthony. *The Fall of Natural Man: The American Indian and the Origins of Comparative Ethnology* (Cambridge: Cambridge University Press, 1986).

Pagden, Anthony. *Spanish Imperialism and the Political Imagination. Studies in European and Spanish–American Social and Political Theory, 1513–1830* (New Haven: Yale University Press, 1990).

Pardo, Luis A. *El imperio de Vilcabamba: el reinado de los cuatro últimos Incas* (Cusco: Editorial Garcilaso, 1972).

Patch, Robert W. *Maya and Spaniard in Yucatan, 1648–1812* (Stanford: Stanford University Press, 1994).

Pease, Franklin. *Curacas, reciprocidad y riqueza* (Lima: Pontificia Universidad Católica del Perú, 1992).

Pease, Franklin. "The Formation of Tawantinsuyu: Mechanisms of Colonization and Relationship with Ethnic Groups," in *The Inca and Aztec States, 1400–1800: Anthropology and History*, ed. George A. Collier, Renato I. Rosaldo, and John D. Wirth (New York: Academic Press, 1982), pp. 173–98.

Penry, S. Elizabeth. "Transformations in Indigenous Authority and Identity in Resettlement Towns of Colonial Charcas (Alto Perú)" (Ph.D. diss., University of Miami, 1996).

Peralta Ruíz, Víctor. *En Pos del Tributo en el Cusco rural, 1826–54* (Cusco: Centro Bartolomé de Las Casas, 1991).

Phelan, John. *The Kingdom of Quito in the Seventeenth Century* (Madison: University of Wisconsin Press, 1967).

Piel, Jean. *Capitalismo agrario en el Perú* (Lima/Salta: IFEA/Universidad Nacional de Salta, 1995).

Piel, Jean. "Cómo interpretar la rebelión panandina de 1780–1783," in *Tres Levantamientos Populares: Pugachóv, Túpac Amaru, Hildago*, ed. Jean Meyer (Mexico: CEMCA, 1992), pp. 71–80.

Platt, Tristan. "The Andean Experience of Bolivian Liberalism, 1825–1900: Roots of Rebellion in 19th-Century Chayanta (Potosí)," in *Resistance, Rebellion and Consciousness in the Andean Peasant World, 18th to 20th Centuries*, ed. Steve J. Stern (Madison: University of Wisconsin Press, 1987), pp. 280–323.

Platt, Tristan. *Estado boliviano y ayllu andino: tierra y tributo en el norte de Potosí* (Lima: Instituto de Estudios Peruanos, 1982).

Platt, Tristan. "Mirrors and Maize: The Concept of *Yanantin* among the Macha of Bolivia," in *Anthropological History of Andean Polities*, ed. John V. Murra, Nathan Wachtel, and Jacques Revel (Cambridge: Cambridge University Press, 1986), pp. 228–59.

Powers, Karen Vieira. *Andean Journeys: Migration, Ethnogenesis and the State in Colonial Quito* (Albuquerque: University of New Mexico Press, 1995).

Puente Brunke, José de la. *Encomienda y encomenderos en el Perú: estudio social y político de una institución colonial* (Seville: Diputación Provincial, 1992).

Pulgar Vidal, Javier. *Geografía del Perú: las ocho regiones naturales del Perú* (Lima: Textos Universitarios, 1972).

Ramirez, Susan E. "The 'Dueño de Indios': Thoughts on the Consequences of the Shifting Bases of Power of the 'Curacas Viejos Antiguos' under the Spanish in Sixteenth Century Peru," *Hispanic American Historical Review*, 64:4 (November 1987), pp. 575–610.

Ramos, D., ed. *La ética en la conquista de América: Francisco de Vitoria y la escuela de Salamanca* (Madrid: Consejo Superior de Investigaciones Científicas, 1984).

Rasnake, Roger Neil. *Domination and Cultural Resistance: Authority and Power among an Andean People* (Durham: Duke University Press, 1988).

Redondo Redondo, María Lourdes. *Utopia vitoriana y realidad indiana* (Madrid: Fundación Universitaria Española, 1992).

Restall, Matthew. *The Maya World: Yucatec Culture and Society, 1550–1850* (Stanford: Stanford University Press, 1997).

Ringrose, David. *Madrid and the Spanish Economy, 1560–1850* (Berkeley: University of California Press, 1983).

Rivera, Silvia. "El Mallku y la sociedad colonial en el siglo XVII: el caso de Jesús de Machaca," *Avances* [La Paz], 1 (1978), pp. 7–27.

Rodríguez O, Jaime E. *The Independence of Spanish America* (Cambridge: Cambridge University Press, 1998).

Romero, Carlos Alberto. "Idolatrías de los indios Huachos y Yauyos," *Revista Histórica* [Lima], 6 (1981), pp. 180–97.

Romero, Emilio. *Monografía del Departamento de Puno* (Lima: Imp. Torres Aguirre, 1928).

Rostworowski de Diez Canseco, María. *Curacas y Sucesiones, costa norte* (Lima: Imprenta Minerva, 1961).

Rostworowski de Diez Canseco, María. *History of the Inca Realm*, translated by Harry B. Iceland (Cambridge: Cambridge University Press, 1999).

Rostworowski de Diez Canseco, María. "Los Ayarmaca," *Revista del Museo Nacional* [Lima], 36 (1969–70), pp. 58–101.

Rostworowski de Diez Canseco, María. *Señorios indígenas de Lima y Canta* (Lima: Instituto de Estudios Peruanos, 1978).

Rowe, John H. "Absolute Chronology in the Andean Area," *American Antiquity*, 10:3 (1945), pp. 265–84.

Rowe, John H. "Colonial Portraits of Inca Nobles," in *The Civilization of Ancient America. Selected Papers of the XXIX International Congress of Americanists*, ed. Sol Tax (Chicago: University of Chicago Press, 1951), pp. 258–68.

Rowe, John H. "El movimiento nacional Inca del siglo XVIII," *Revista Universitaria* [Cusco], 7 (1954), pp. 17–47.

Rowe, John H. "Genealogía y rebelión en el siglo XVIII: Algunos antecedentes de la sublevación de José Gabriel Thupa Amaro," *Histórica* [Lima], 6:1 (July 1982), pp. 65–86.

Rowe, John H. "Inca Culture at the Time of the Spanish Conquest," in *The Handbook of South American Indians*, ed. Julian Steward, vol. II (Washington, DC: General Printing Office, 1946), pp. 185–330.

Rowe, John H. *An Introduction to the Archaeology of Cuzco*, Papers of the Peabody Museum 27:2 (Cambridge, MA: The Museum, 1944).

Rowe, John H. *Quechua Nationalism in the Eighteenth Century* (Berkeley: University of California Press, 1959).

Rowe, John H. "What Kind of a Settlement was Inca Cusco?" *Ñawpa Pacha*, 5 (1967), pp. 59–76.

Saignes, Thierry. "Ayllus, mercado y coacción colonial: el reto de las migraciones internas en Charcas (siglo XVII)," in *La participación indígena en los mercados surandinos: estrategias y reproducción social, siglos XVI a XX*, ed. Olivia Harris, Brooke Larson, and Enrique Tandeter (La Paz: CERES, 1987), pp. 111–58.

Saignes, Thierry. *Caciques, Tribute and Migration in the Southern Andes: Indian Society and the Seventeenth Century Colonial Order* (London: University of London, 1985).

Saignes, Thierry. "De la borrachera al retrato: Los curacas andinos entre dos legitimidades," *Revista Andina*, 5:1 (1987), pp. 139–70.

Saignes, Thierry and Thérèse Bouysse-Cassagne. "Dos confundidas identidades: mestizos y criollos del siglo XVII," in *500 Años de Mestizaje en los Andes*, eds. Hiroyasu Tomoeda and Luis Millones (Lima: Museo Etnológico de Japón [Osaka] and Biblioteca Peruana de Psicoanálisis, 1992), pp. 29–44.

Sala i Vila, Nuria. *Y se armó el tole tole: tributo indígena y movimientos sociales en el virreinato del Perú, 1784–1814* (Huamanga: Instituto de estudios regionales José María Arguedas, 1996).

Salas Perea, Gilberto. *Monografía Sintética de Azángaro* (Puno: Editorial Los Andes, 1966).

Salomon, Frank. "Ancestor Cults and Resistance to the State in Arequipa, ca. 1748–1754," in *Resistance, Rebellion and Consciousness in the Andean Peasant World, 18th to 20th Centuries*, ed. Steve J. Stern (Madison: University of Wisconsin Press, 1987), pp. 148–65.

Salomon, Frank. *Native Lords of Quito in the Age of the Inca: The Political Economy of North Andean Chieftains* (Cambridge: Cambridge University Press, 1986).

Sánchez-Albornoz, Nicolás. *Indios y tributos en el Alto Perú* (Lima: Instituto de Estudios Peruanos, 1978).

Sánchez-Albornoz, Nicolás. "The Population of Colonial Spanish America," in *The Cambridge History of Latin America*, ed. Leslie Bethell, vol. II (Cambridge: Cambridge University Press, 1984), pp. 16–35.

Sempat Assadourian, Carlos. *El sistema de la economía colonial: el mercado interior, regiones, y espacio económico* (Mexico: Nueva Imagen, 1983).

Sempat Assadourian, Carlos. *Transiciones hacia el Sistema Colonial Andino* (Lima: Instituto de Estudios Peruanos, 1994).

Serulnikov, Sergio. "Customs and Rules: Bourbon Rationalizing Projects and Social Conflicts in Northern Potosí during the 1770s," *Colonial Latin American Review*, 8:2 (December 1999), pp. 245–74.

Serulnikov, Sergio. "Disputed Images of Colonialism: Spanish Rule and Indian Subversion in Northern Potosí, 1777–1780," *Hispanic American Historical Review*, 76:2 (May 1996), pp. 189–226.

Serulnikov, Sergio. *Subverting Colonial Authority: Challenges to Spanish Rule in Eighteenth-Century Southern Andes* (Durham: Duke University Press, 2003).

Silverblatt, Irene. *Moon, Sun, and Witches: Gender Ideologies and Class in Inca and Colonial Peru* (Princeton: Princeton University Press, 1987).

Smith, Gavin. *Livelihood and Resistance: Peasants and the Politics of Land in Peru* (Berkeley: University of California Press, 1989).

Spalding, Karen. *De Indio a Campesino: Cambios en la estructura social del Perú colonial* (Lima: Instituto de Estudios Peruanos, 1974).

Spalding, Karen. *Huarochirí: An Andean Society under Inca and Spanish Rule* (Stanford: Stanford University Press, 1984).

Spalding, Karen. "Kurakas and Commerce: A Chapter in the Evolution of Andean Society," *Hispanic American Historical Review*, 54:4 (November 1973), pp. 581–99.

Spalding, Karen. "La otra cara de la reciprocidad," in *Incas e indios cristianos: elites indígenas cristianas en los Andes coloniales*, ed. Jean-Jacques Decoster (Cusco: Centro Bartolomé de las Casas, 2002), pp. 61–78.

Spalding, Karen. "Social Climbers: Changing Patterns of Mobility among the Indians of Colonial Peru," *Hispanic American Historical Review*, 50:4 (November 1970), pp. 645–64.

Spier, Fred. *Religious Regimes in Peru: Religion and State Development in a Long-Term Perspective and the Effects in the Andean Village of Zurite* (Amsterdam: Amsterdam University Press, 1994).

Stavig, Ward. "Ethnic Conflict, Moral Economy, and Population in Rural Cuzco on the Eve of the Thupa Amaro II Rebellion," *Hispanic American Historical Review*, 68:4 (November 1988), pp. 737–70.

Stavig, Ward. "Eugenio Sinanyuca: Militant, Nonrevolutionary *Kuraka*, and Community Defender," in *The Human Tradition in Colonial Latin America*, ed. Kenneth J. Andrien (Wilmington: Scholarly Resources, 2002), pp. 241–58.

Stavig, Ward. *The World of Túpac Amaru: Conflict, Community and Identity in Colonial Peru* (Lincoln: University of Nebraska Press, 1999).

Stern, Steve J. "The Age of Andean Insurrection: A Reappraisal," in *Resistance, Rebellion and Consciousness in the Andean Peasant World, 18th to 20th Centuries*, ed. Steve J. Stern (Madison: University of Wisconsin Press, 1987), pp. 34–93.

Stern, Steve J. "Feudalism, Capitalism, and the World-System in the Perspective of Latin America and the Caribbean," *American Historical Review*, 93:4 (October 1988), pp. 829–72.

Stern, Steve J. *Peru's Indian Peoples and the Challenge of Spanish Conquest: Huamanga to 1640* (Madison: University of Wisconsin Press, 1982).

Stern, Steve J., ed. *Resistance, Rebellion, and Consciousness in the Andean Peasant World, 18th to 20th Centuries* (Madison: University of Wisconsin Press, 1987).

Stern, Steve J. "The Rise and Fall of Indian–White Alliances: A Regional View of 'Conquest' History," *Hispanic American Historical Review*, 61:3 (August 1981), pp. 46–91.

Stern, Steve J. *The Secret History of Gender: Women, Men, and Power in Late Colonial Mexico* (Chapel Hill: University of North Carolina Press, 1995).

Szeminski, Jan. *La Utopia Tupamarista* (Lima: Pontificia Universidad Católica del Perú, 1993).

Szeminski, Jan. "Why Kill the Spaniard? New Perspectives on Andean Insurrectionary Ideology in the 18th Century," in *Resistance, Rebellion and Consciousness in the Andean Peasant World, 18th to 20th Centuries*, ed. Steve J. Stern (Madison: University of Wisconsin Press, 1987), pp. 166–92.

Tandeter, Enrique. *Coacción y Mercado: La minería de la plata en el Potosí colonial, 1692–1826* (Cusco: Centro Bartolomé de Las Casas, 1992).

Taylor, William B. *Drinking, Homicide, and Rebellion in Colonial Mexican Villages* (Stanford: Stanford University Press, 1979).

Taylor, William B. *Landlord and Peasant in Colonial Oaxaca* (Stanford: Stanford University Press, 1972).

Temple Dunbar, Ella. "Don Carlos Inca," *Revista Histórica* [Lima], 17 (1948), pp. 135–79.

Temple Dunbar, Ella. "Un linaje incaico durante la dominación española: Los Sahuaraura," *Revista Histórica* [Lima], 18 (1949), pp. 45–77.

Terraciano, Kevin. *The Mixtecs of Colonial Oaxaca: Ñudzahui History, Sixteenth through Eighteenth Centuries* (Stanford: Stanford University Press, 2001).

Thompson, E. P. "The Moral Economy of the English Crowd in the Eighteenth Century," *Past and Present*, 50 (February 1971), pp. 76–136.

Thomson, Sinclair. *We Alone Will Rule: Native Andean Politics in the Age of Insurgency* (Madison: University of Wisconsin Press, 2002).

Tord Nicolini, Javier. "El corregidor de indios del Perú: comercio y tributos," *Historia y Cultura* [Lima], 8 (1974), pp. 173–210.

Tutino, John. *From Insurrection to Revolution in Mexico: Social Bases of Agrarian Violence, 1750–1940* (Princeton: Princeton University Press, 1986).

Urteaga, Horacio H. *Relación del sitio del Cusco y principio de las guerras civiles del Perú hasta la muerte de Diego de Almagro, 1535–9* (Lima: Librería Gil, 1934).

Urton, Gary. *The History of a Myth: Pacariqtambo and the Origin of the Inkas* (Austin: University of Texas Press, 1990).

Valcárcel, Carlos Daniel. "Documentos sobre las gestiones del cacique Túpac Amaru ante la Audiencia de Lima (1777)," *Letras* [Lima], 36 (1946), pp. 452–66.

Valcárcel, Carlos Daniel. "La familia del cacique Túpac Amaru," *Letras* [Lima], 37 (1947), pp. 44–89.

Valcárcel, Carlos Daniel. *La Rebelión de Túpac Amaru* (Mexico: Fondo de Cultura Económica, 1947).

Valcárcel, Carlos Daniel. *Túpac Amaru, precursor de la Independencia* (Lima: Universidad Nacional de San Marcos, 1977).

Valencia Vega, Alipio. *Julián Túpaj Katari* (La Paz: Juventud, 1977).

Valle de Siles, María Eugenia del. *Historia de la rebelión de Túpac Catari, 1781–2* (La Paz: Editorial Don Bosco, 1990).

Varón Gabai, Rafael. *Curacas y encomenderos: acomodamiento nativo en Huaraz, siglos XVI y XVII* (Lima: P. L. Villanueva, 1980).

Wachtel, Nathan. "The *Mitimas* of the Cochabamba Valley: The Colonization Policy of Huayna Capac," in *The Inca and Aztec States, 1400–1800: Anthropology and History*, ed. George A. Collier, Renato I. Rosaldo, and John D. Wirth (New York: Academic Press, 1982), pp. 199–235.

Wachtel, Nathan. *Le Retour des Ancêtres: Les Indiens Urus de Bolivie XXeme-XVIeme siècle: Essai d'Histoire Régressive* (Paris: Gallimard, 1990).

Wachtel, Nathan. *The Vision of the Vanquished: The Spanish Conquest of Peru through Indian Eyes, 1530–1570*, translated by Ben and Siân Reynolds (New York: Harper and Row, 1977).

Walker, Charles F. *Smoldering Ashes: Cuzco and the Creation of Republican Peru, 1780–1840* (Durham: Duke University Press, 1999).

Wightman, Ann. *Indigenous Migration and Social Change: The Forasteros of Cuzco, 1520–1720* (Durham: Duke University Press, 1990).

Zamora, Margarita. *Language, Authority, and Indigenous History in the Comentarios Reales de los Incas* (Cambridge: Cambridge University Press, 1988).

Zavala, Silvio. *El servicio personal de los indios en el Perú, extractos del siglo xvi*. 3 vols. (Mexico: Colegio de México, 1978).

Zimmerman, Arthur F. *Francisco de Toledo, Fifth Viceroy of Peru, 1569–81* (Caldwell, ID: The Caxton Printers, 1938).

Zuidema, R. Tom. *The Ceque System of Cusco: The Social Organization of the Capital of the Inca* (Leyden: E. J. Brill, 1964).

Zuidema, R. Tom. "'Descendencia paralela' en una familia indígena noble del Cuzco (documentos del siglo XVI hasta el siglo XVIII)," *Fénix*, 17 (1967), pp. 39–62.

Zuidema, R. Tom. *Inca Civilization in Cusco*, translated by Jean-Jacques Decoster (Austin: University of Texas Press, 1990).

Zulawski, Ann. "Migration and Labor in Seventeenth Century Alto Peru" (Ph.D. diss., Columbia University, 1985).

Index

CPSIA information can be obtained at www.ICGtesting.com
Printed in the USA
LVOW11s2130090116

469917LV00013B/630/P